Praises For

Leadership-in-Community

In our experience, actual people rarely match up to the way they are perceived by others. However, Lee Carter defies what is typical. *Leadership in community* beautifully describes the lessons he has taught and modeled for us to follow. This book is grounded in Scripture and perfectly describes the benefit of the ethics and missiology of community leadership. Each chapter provides memorable lessons we are attempting to model to this day in Latin American churches, just as he has done for us in Bible League International.

— Dr. Rafael Serrano, M.Div, Ph.D
Author, Senior editor, the *Palabra de Dios para Todos* (Bible League International) and *Nueva Traduccion Viviente* (Tyndale Publishers)

***

In *Leadership-in-Community* Lee Carter plugs a hole that has been gaping for too long. In missional circles there has existed a void of material relevant to boots-on-the-ground team leadership that eschews hierarchical authoritarianism and instead adapts the servant posture modeled by Jesus. Drawing on scripture and best global mission practice, Carter provides a clear and practical road map for orienting a team around a biblical framework for understanding leadership. This tool will serve this generation and future generations in providing a much-needed alternative to the majority of leadership pipeline tools that focus on faulty models of leadership.

—Peyton Jones
Evangelist, Author of *Church Zero: Raising 1st Century Churches Out of the Ashes of the 21st Century Church*, *Reaching the Unreached: Becoming Raiders of the Lost Art*, and *Church Plantology: The Art and Science of Planting Churches*

***

Dr. Carter has developed a spiritual formation curriculum, *Leadership-in-Community: The Missiology, Community & Ethics of Missional Leadership*, that will not only help one grow closer to Jesus but will expand one's understanding of the missional nature of God. The power of the curriculum is walking through the eight movements of reflection and study. It will be a powerful study to walk through in a small group setting or with church staff.

— Dr. W. David Winner

Adjunct professor, *Business and Leadership at Regent University*, USA.

***

Lee Carter understands the struggles encountered by leaders in their deep desire to lead effectively and wisely. Leaders silently go through struggles on their own without much help and with questions unanswered. Common statements I have always heard about leadership are, *"Leadership is a very lonely place"* and secondly, *"The higher you go the cooler it becomes."* Is it cooler? In what way? And can it ever be cooler?

Leadership-in-Community rallies leaders and those who desire to sit in positions of leadership to look at leading as never in isolation of people and within an environment. Using different biblical incidences and contexts, he has formed an in-depth study for leaders. It contains questions and hypothesis, tested on different leaders within diverse contexts. It will help every committed leader, to lead in perspective.

— Lillian Mutambi

National Director, *Bible League International*, Kenya. East-Africa.

***

This book will help form your heart for long term leadership through the disciplines of *lectio missio*. Many leadership authors will say that personal growth is key for development as leaders. At the heart of Christian leadership is a necessary process of values clarification. Lee Carter provides a Bible-based curriculum for personal growth to be used by small groups of leaders. If you go through the process outlined in this book, the community God has called you to lead will deeply thank you.

— Dr. Yancy Smith

Author of *The Mystery of Anointing: Hippolytus' Commentary on the Song of Songs in Social and Critical Contexts*, Senior Director of *Translation Services for Bible League International*

Leadership-in-Community

The Missiology, Community & Ethics of Missional Leadership

A Spiritual Formation Curriculum for Missional Leaders

Lee A. Carter

Published by KHARIS PUBLISHING, imprint of KHARIS MEDIA LLC.

Copyright © 2021 Lee A. Carter

ISBN-13: 978-1-63746-082-5

ISBN-10: 1-63746-082-1

Library of Congress Control Number: 2021950008

Unless otherwise noted, all Scripture references are from the Holy Bible: Easy-to-Read Version (ERV) ©1987, 2004 Bible League International. Used by permission.

Oratio prayers are adapted from *The Prayer Wheel: A Daily Guide to Renewing Your Faith with a Rediscovered Spiritual Practice* ©2018 by Patton Dodd, Jana Riess, and David Van Biema and *Celtic Daily Prayer: Prayers and Readings from the Northumbria Community* ©2002 by The Northumbria Community Trust Ltd.

All KHARIS PUBLISHING products are available at special quantity discounts for bulk purchase for sales promotions, premiums, fund-raising, and educational needs. For details, contact:

Kharis Media LLC
Tel: 1-479-599-8657
support@kharispublishing.com
www.kharispublishing.com

KHARIS
PUBLISHING

Table of Contents

Table of Figures

Introduction:

Leadership-in-Community

In the summer of 2001, I served with a staff team on a Global Project to Kenya with InterVarsity Christian Fellowship. For seven weeks, we accompanied over 40 American university students to experience a taste of God's global mission. We were hosted by Kenyan university students who shared their country and their lives with us for one unforgettable summer. During our time in Kenya, we savored a variety of cross-cultural and missional experiences. We served with a church that was caring for the spiritual and physical needs of residents in Nairobi's Methare Valley slum. We attended a debate between Christian and Muslim apologists at a university campus. We visited Hindu temples guided by a missionary whose ministry focused on evangelism among Hindu people. We met church planters and Bible translators who toiled long and hard years to bring the Scriptures to the remotest corners of the earth. These experiences expanded our worldviews and galvanized our commitments to global Christian witness. Every day was like a new discovery of Jesus' call: "You will be my witnesses. You will tell people everywhere about me…in every part of the world" (Acts 1:8).

The highpoint of the Global Project was our three-week ministry assignments. All participants were placed in small teams and were sent throughout the country to serve in various ways. My team of three traveled west of Nairobi to a small Maasai village outside of Narok. We lived with a pastor and his family in his small three-room mud hut, and we served him in any way he asked. I especially enjoyed our daily visits to the local children's home where we would sing with the kids and share with them the Word of God. But my fondest memories were of our hosts. For three weeks, these beautiful people welcomed three strangers, with their strange ways and strange tongue, into their family to share life, worship, and ministry with them. This was, for me, a truly phenomenal and formative experience.

That summer opened up for me the global horizon of God's Kingdom. But it also stretched my beliefs about mission and leadership. I thought leadership was about having the power, knowledge, and self-confidence to get things done and move things forward. I assumed that my position of leadership guaranteed that others should just go where I pointed. But that presumption failed me when I found myself in a world I did not understand. I encountered behaviors and beliefs that were strange to me. And somehow, I was supposed to lead through that so that our students would have a great cross-cultural experience! Quickly, I ran out of my pat answers (they did not work anyway) and I felt completely powerless.

But I also found the mercy of the Lord in that powerlessness. A simple, almost unnoticeable incident proved to be a defining moment for my summer – and my development as a leader. One morning, we planned to hand-wash our clothes in a small pool of water that diverged from the stream flowing past the village. This place was the "community laundromat" and a group of local women had already gathered that morning to wash clothes for their families. I wanted to take a picture to remember this unique experience. But as I pulled out my camera, I was told that the women did not want me to take their picture. As inoffensive and harmless as their request may seem now, it was just the spark my simmering frustration and disequilibrium needed to vent into a full burn. *I was angry!* I threw the camera in my bag, grabbed a basin, and stormed off to a spot away from everyone where I attacked my clothes with rage. I did not understand these people! Everything I said or did was wrong! I was completely lost.

As I stewed there in my anger and self-pity, one of the village women waded quietly over toward me. She grabbed some of my clothes and began to wash them for me. I guess she thought this American stranger clearly did not know what he was doing. This woman, who just a moment before was an object of my anger and contempt, offered me a hand of friendship that broke through my hostility and bridged our strangeness to one another. Her kindness completely took the steam out of my anger, and I was overcome by a wave of humility, gratitude, grace, and a little embarrassment. We did not speak the same language, so I could not express my sincere thanks. She simply served me because, at that moment, I was part of her community and I was in desperate need. She led me with grace and humility and, consequently, restored me to the blessing God had for me that summer. She may never know the impact of her kindness. But it was for me a model of leadership that has influenced me ever since.

Today's complex world renders the most influential and "common sense" leadership theories or models inadequate for Christian mission. The diversity of cultures, perspectives, practices, and worldviews amid dramatically shifting environments tend to push us further into strangeness from one another. How can we develop and prepare leaders for the mission of God that brings people together and moves them forward? As the Maasai woman demonstrated to me, leadership in the mission of God is more about relationship, service, and humility that makes friends out of strangers. This is leadership that develops through spiritual formation.

This Shifting Landscape of Global Christianity

The Spirit of God continues to move in Christian missions even in post-Christian or non-Christian environments. A 2020 Barna research study commissioned by the International Mission Board of the Southern Baptist Convention found that North American Christians who are actively engaged in their faith believe that missionary work is very valuable.[1] The majority of these Christians take personal responsibility for the Great Commission.[2] It fuels their commitment to share the Gospel, give financially to missions, pray for missionaries, and learn about other cultures.[3]

However, within this group of engaged Christians, Barna found a subgroup that it labels "supportive skeptics" who financially support missions work or have been on at least one overseas missions trip but still express reservations about the *how* and *why* of missions.[4] The largest group of supportive skeptics are Millennials and Gen Z (26%), but adults age 35 and older also make up a significant portion (19%) of those who are concerned that historically Christian mission has been tainted by its association with colonialism and domination over other cultures.[5] According to Barna, supportive skeptics are deeply concerned about a prevalent view of Christian mission that has "taken hold in the North American cultural imagination of a 'white savior' evangelist who exports their narrow, Western-centric version of faith with more passion than cultural competence."[6] While supportive skeptics wholeheartedly agree that legitimate missionary work involves showing other people God's love (88%), helping Christians understand their faith better (76%), and sharing the Gospel with non-Christians (76%), they believe that missionary work can lead to unhealthy local dependencies on charity (66%) and that Christianity should "fix its reputation before doing more missions" (63%).[7]

Indeed, when we stop to look around, we discover that the landscape of global Christianity has changed significantly in the last 100 years. A 2011

---

[1] The research reports that 72% of U. S. young adults ages 18 to 34 and 74% of older adults age 35 and older believe that missionary work is valuable. Barna Group, *The Future of Missions: 10 Questions About Global Ministry the Church Must Answer with the Next Generation* (Ventura: Barna, 2020), p. 18.

[2] Ibid. p. 39-41.

[3] Ibid.

[4] Ibid. p. 19.

[5] Ibid. p. 19, 23-25.

[6] Ibid. p. 17-18.

[7] Ibid. p. 28-29.

Pew Research Center report on global Christianity reported that the majority of Christians, about 61% (around 1.3 billion), live in Africa, Asia, and Latin America compared to 39% (about 860 million) who live in North America, Europe, Australia, Japan, and New Zealand (called the "Global North").[8] This represents a significant shift since 1910 when two-thirds of Christians were located in Europe.[9] Furthermore, the trend indicates that the number of Christians in the Global North will continue to decline while those in Africa, Asia, and Latin America will grow.[10] Historian Philip Jenkins concludes:

> We are currently living through one of the transforming moments in the history of religion worldwide. Over the past five centuries, the story of Christianity has been inextricably bound up with that of Europe and European-derived civilizations overseas, above all in North America. Until recently, the overwhelming majority of Christians have lived in white nations.... Over the last century, however, the center of gravity in the Christian world has shifted inexorably away from Europe, southward, to Africa and Latin America, and eastward, toward Asia. Today, the largest Christian communities on the planet are to be found in those regions.[11]

Many of these Christian communities are churches and student movements in such places as Nigeria, Korea, the Philippines, Brazil, Colombia, and Hong Kong that have been ignited by the Holy Spirit with a zeal for missionary activity.[12] They are sending their own missionaries throughout the world, even to post-Christian Europe and North America, to share the Gospel and plant churches.[13] Therefore, the caution of our supportive skeptics emerges primarily from the shifting reality of global Christianity rather than from what may seem to be the influence of our increasingly skeptical age.[14] They are, indeed, a gift to the church. Their concerns are a prophetic voice calling us to new paradigms of leadership,

---

[8] Pew Research Center, "Global Christianity: A Report on the Size and Distribution of the World's Christian Population," December 19, 2011, accessed August 29, 2020. https://www.pewforum.org/2011/12/19/global-christianity-exec/

[9] Barna, *The Future of* Missions, p. 19.

[10] Graham Hill, *GlobalChurch: Reshaping Our Conversations, Renewing Our Mission, Revitalizing Our Churches* (Downers Grove: InterVarsity Press, 2016), p. 14.

[11] Philip Jenkins, *The Next Christendom: The Coming of Global Christianity*, 3rd ed. (Oxford: Oxford University Press, 2011), p. 1.

[12] Samuel Escobar, *The New Global Mission: The Gospel from Everywhere to Everyone* (Downers Grove: InterVarsity Press, 2003), p. 52.

[13] Ibid.

[14] Ibid. p. 19.

partnership, and practice in Christian mission as we endeavor to faithfully obey the Lord's call to make followers of all people in the world (Matt. 28:19).

Because the missionary movement is no longer the domain of Western Christianity, leadership development for global mission will become increasingly inclusive and collaborative with a focus on learning. True mission rejects "professional" paradigms of leadership reinforced and sustained by centralized power structures, including church or political institutions, that prioritize hierarchy, control, high power distance, and status.[15] Barna Group's research, in fact, points to the "deleterious effects on missionaries' character and spiritual life" when they are epitomized or even idolized.[16] One participant in the research, a child of former missionary parents, commented:

> Putting human beings in a context where they are always 'special' and celebrated, at home and in the field, is spiritually destructive to self and others. It breeds narcissism and can have far-reaching effects. Obviously not everyone falls into this trap but those who aren't self-aware and vigilant inevitably do.[17]

Leadership paradigms that venerate the professional leader tend to exclude others and their diverse perspectives, insights, and experiences that are, after all, *necessary* for the kind of learning that leads to effective mission. They are lauded as the unquestioned experts, teachers, managers, strategists, healers, or even priests. To challenge them almost seems like blasphemy! Unfortunately, these leadership paradigms have left a trail of destruction in the lives of people (both of leaders and their followers) and for the reputation of God in whose name we are on mission. The honor of our King Jesus and his great mission to redeem the world deserves much better! We need a paradigm of leadership that welcomes and celebrates the diverse perspectives, callings, and giftings of Christian brothers and sisters in our own neighborhoods and around the world.

A New Missional Leadership: Leadership-in-Community

Ecuadorian theologian C. René Padilla describes the missionary movement of the 19th and 20th centuries, labeled by missiologists as the

---

[15] Kirk J. Franklin, *Towards Global Missional Leadership: A Journey Through Leadership Paradigm Shift in the Mission of God* (Oxford: Regnum Books International, 2017), p. 37-39, 71.
[16] Barna, *The Future of Missions*, p. 26.
[17] Ibid. p. 26-27.

"modern missionary movement," as the Christian West crossing geographic frontiers to take the Gospel to the non-Christian world.[18] This model has inspired generations of missionaries who left their homelands to share the Gospel in the far reaches of the earth.[19] Due to their courageous commitment of faith, they spread the good news of Jesus Christ across the entire world! Much of the success of the church in Africa, Latin America, and Asia is a legacy of their faith.

Yet, despite the modern missionary movement's significant contribution to the growth of global Christianity, Padilla acknowledges that it entrenched four harmful dichotomies into missional leadership thinking and practice:

1. It distinguishes between churches that *send* missionaries and those that *receive* missionaries,

2. It distinguishes between the missionary's *home* and his or her mission *field*,

3. It distinguishes between *missionaries* who have a special call from God and *common Christians* who are somehow exempt from God's mission in the world, and

4. It distinguishes between the *life of a church* from the *mission of the church* so that mission lies overseas and not within the church's own community.[20]

Sadly, this fractured mindset has dismissed the calling and responsibility of *all* followers of Jesus, without exception, to participate in his great mission.

We need new models of Christian mission that prioritize and mobilize all followers of Christ to cross what Padilla describes as the frontiers of faith.[21] The mission of God sends all of us beyond the borders of faith to the places of "no faith" which may, in fact, not involve crossing geographic boundaries. It may not even involve leaving our neighborhoods, workplaces, or homes! The historic movements of Christianity demonstrates that it is a faith that makes its home with the people it encounters wherever it goes, and

---

[18] C. René Padilla, "What is Integral Mission?" *Del Camino Network for Integral Mission in Latin America*, n. d., accessed September 7, 2020.
http://www.dmr.org/images/pdf%20dokumenter/C._Ren%C3%A9_Padilla_-_What_is_integral_mission.pdf.

[19] Ibid.

[20] Ibid.

[21] Ibid.

it transforms them from within.[22] Christian mission that crosses the frontiers of faith to no faith is identified by its peculiar hospitality. It welcomes strangers and foreigners,[23] even enemies,[24] as friends with a common need for the grace and mercy of *God our Savior* (*El yeshu'atenu* in Hebrew from which the name Jesus derives). We see this hospitality at work when Jesus stayed at the home of the traitorous Zacchaeus (Luke 19:1-10) or when he had to go through the despised country of Samaria to offer a woman living water (John 4:1-42). Christian mission, as it originates not from human enterprise but from the sending heart of God, is the gospel witness encultured in the lives of men and women, empowered by the Holy Spirit, who translate the presence and reign of God into the "foreign fields" of no faith.[25]

A new paradigm of missional leadership begins with this hospitality principle. Missional leadership is not a professional paradigm of leadership. Rather, missional leadership is a paradigm of *participation*.[26] Missional leadership still invests in the development of the expertise and skills of people, but it does this so that they can share their resources with others to advance the mission rather than protect or control those resources to advance themselves. In contrast to the fragmented mindset of the modern missionary movement, participatory leadership affirms that:

1. All churches send and all churches receive – every church has something to teach and something to learn from other churches,

2. The whole world is a mission field in which every follower of Christ is called to demonstrate, in both word and deed, the reality of the Kingdom of God,

3. Every follower of Jesus is called to commit to the mission of God and to use his or her God-given gifts to serve, and

4. Christian life and mission are integrated so that mission is a whole-life dynamic that demonstrates the recovery of "God's original purpose for the relationship of the human person with his Creator, with his neighbor, and with all of creation."[27]

---

[22] Escobar, *The New Global Mission*, p. 36.

[23] See Deut. 10:19, Lev. 19:34, and Ezek. 47:22.

[24] See Matt. 5:43-44 and Matt. 25:35-40.

[25] Andrew F. Walls, *The Missionary Movement in Christian History: Studies in the Transmission of Faith* (Maryknoll: Orbis Books, 1996), p. 27.

[26] Franklin, *Towards Global Missional Leadership*, p. 39.

[27] Padilla, "What is Integral Mission?"

Participatory leadership prepares *all* followers of Jesus to find their identity and the purpose of their lives in the mission of God. We are all invited and called to participate together with God in an amazing adventure as he redeems the world and expands his glorious Kingdom to the cosmos! Participatory leadership is *leadership-in-community*: a community that includes our King Jesus, others, and ourselves. This community is identified by the mercy of God and it is animated by a vision of *shalôm*, of the entire cosmos put to rights by the good reign of God. It is a community empowered by the Holy Spirit to live in unity with and service to one another so that this vision becomes real in the places of "no faith" where God sends it out on mission.

Getting the Physics Right: Missional Leadership in a Complex World

Leadership-in-community challenges modernist leadership theories that have defined organizational leadership development for the past century. These theories focus on individual leaders: the traits, skills, behaviors, attitudes, and interactions that they adapt to influence others. Leadership scholar Peter G. Northouse defines leadership as "a process whereby an individual influences a group of individuals to achieve a common goal."[28] In his survey of leadership theories since 1900, he highlights several iterations that emerged from the basic commitments of his definition.[29] Whether a trait, skills, behavioral, or situational approach, modernist leadership theory is based on three distinct entities: leaders, followers, and their shared goals.[30] We have assumed that these are indispensable to leadership – an essential tripod upon which the leadership apparatus stands securely.

The modernist leadership tripod presumes a world of linear cause and effect, predictability, and certainty.[31] It deals with reality as only the physical and visible phenomena it can observe, measure, and manipulate.[32] Newtonian physics, having influenced the modernist worldview for three centuries, reduced organizations to their component parts management engineers to

---

[28] Peter G. Northouse, *Leadership: Theory and Practice*, 7th ed. (Thousand Oaks: SAGE Publications, Inc., 2016), p. 6.

[29] Ibid. p. 6-7.

[30] Wilfred H. Drath, Cynthia D. McCauley, Charles J. Palus, Ellen Van Velsor, Patricia M. G. O'Connor, & John B. McGuire, "Direction, Alignment, Commitment: Toward a More Integrative Ontology of Leadership," *The Leadership Quarterly* 19 (2008): p. 635.

[31] Michael J. Marquardt, *Building the Learning Organization: Achieving Strategic Advantage through a Commitment to Learning*, 3rd ed. (Boston: Nicholas Brealey Publishing, 2011), p. 17.

[32] Ibid.

function together as an efficient machine.[33] The modernist world places a heavy burden on leaders because of their responsibility to arrange the machine's components and ensure they run well. Failure to lead well results in inefficient production and the failure to achieve the planned outcomes of that production. So, we look for the latest and greatest leadership theories, models, and practices that we believe we can simply insert into our leadership development, like universal principles, to raise the level of our leaders and get the best out of our organizational machines.[34]

But the world of contemporary missions is not predictable, certain, or linear. The global expansion of technology, economics, politics, culture, media, and the marketplace has exponentially increased the interconnectedness of people and communities around the world.[35] Small tremors in remote parts of the world set off ripple effects with random and significant consequences for communities on the other side of the world.[36] The intensification of social and market exchanges along with the free flow of information, currency, and trade facilitated by rapidly advancing technology has heightened the pace of change to a fever pitch.[37]

Nor does the mission of God traffic exclusively in physical and visible phenomena. We recognize that spiritual, psychological, cultural, and social forces at play exert significant influence on our team members, organizations, and the environments around us. The world in which Jesus calls us to be his witnesses is volatile, uncertain, chaotic, and ambiguous (VUCA). It overturns any modernist leadership theories, models, and best practices as proper parlance for Christian mission.

Quantum physics arose in the 20th century because of a late 19th century crisis around the Newtonian commitment to absolute time and space – the belief that time and space remain immovable and independent of any point of reference.[38] Quantum physics, with its undergirding theory of relativity, argued that reality is not determined by concrete objects – such as leaders, followers, and shared goals – and the absolute laws that govern

---

[33] Sam Wells & Josie McLean, "*One Way Forward* to Beat the Newtonian Habit with a Complexity Perspective on Organisational Change," *Systems* 1 (2013): p. 68.

[34] Ibid.

[35] Franklin, *Towards Global Missional Leadership*, p. 46.

[36] Ibid.

[37] Ibid.

[38] Thomas S. Kuhn, *The Structure of Scientific Revolutions: 50th Anniversary Edition* (Chicago: The University of Chicago Press, 2012), p. 72.

them.[39] Rather, reality is composed of the intricate patterns, relationships, and movements between people and objects.[40] Therefore, reality is as uncertain in quantum physics as it is certain in Newtonian physics.[41] It is filled with as much possibility for creativity and innovation as the infinite number of possible interactions between people and the world around them.

Leadership-in-community can respond to the emerging themes, issues, and priorities undreamt of by earlier generations.[42] As the global church embraces its mission to "bring Christ to the big issues which are closest to men's hearts," as missiologist Andrew Walls describes,[43] leadership-in-community embraces a new physics of relationship and interconnectedness – between people and the world they inhabit – as the orientation of new missional leadership. Leadership-in-community celebrates Christian mission as exploration into the creative possibilities in the Kingdom of God. Its heart is kindled with the desire to see that Kingdom become reality in and through their relationships and interactions.

The Quantum Leap: Relationship and Dialogue

The quantum leap in missional leadership development shifts focus away from the traditional leadership tripod of leaders, followers, and shared goals and toward the relationships and interactions between these entities. Those relationships energize creative enterprise. Missional leadership is a relational dynamic embodied within real contexts (organizational, cultural, political-social, economic, and spiritual). It is shaped through the interactions between people and the world in which they live. And consequently, it is increasingly peer-like and collaborative through both shared power and humble servanthood.

Relationship and dialogue are the primary means of leadership-in-community for the mission of God in a complex world. The global church is a community of communities. It is bound together by a common identity whose mission is enriched in meaning and creativity through its diversity and differences. It is energized by friendship. It is characterized by the intimacy that first existed within the triune God and is now released by the Spirit's

---

[39] Marquardt, *Building the Learning Organization*, p. 18.
[40] Ibid.
[41] Wells & McLean, "*One Way Forward…*," p. 68.
[42] Andrew F. Walls, "Culture and Coherence in Christian History," *Evangelical Review of Theology* 9, no. 3 (1985): p. 223.
[43] Ibid.

power into human friendships.[44] And it is recognized by unity, self-sacrificing love, listening, and servanthood.[45] Missional leadership, then, is not about how to be a better leader. It is about how to have better relationships.

Relational dialogue is the *modus operandi* of leadership-in-community. In fact, within complex environments, leadership is constructed through relational processes.[46] Wilfred H. Drath, senior fellow at the Center for Creative Leadership, asks, "When there is shared work among people who make sense of that work and the world from differing worldviews, how can those people accomplish the leadership task while holding their differing worldviews as equally worthy and warrantable?"[47] Traditional leadership theories that promote either personal dominance or interpersonal influence necessarily exclude, in some respect, the worldviews and perspectives of others to accomplish the leadership task. But relational dialogue functions on the belief that reality is constructed through relationship. This is the essence of leadership-in-community. Drath continues:

> It is highly practical and useful for the development of a third leadership principle to understand that people construct *a* (not *the*) reality when they explain things to one another, tell each other stories, create models and theories…, and write about all this in books; when they offer intuitions to others for consideration, form judgments and test them with others in word and action, and evaluate outcomes and work with others to improve outcomes according to set criteria; and generally when they interact through thought, word, and action to bring into being what is important, worthy, real, and actual. In other words, people live from day to day in continuous interaction with and knowledge of others, and it is a day-to-day practical reality that is so usefully understood as a relational construction.[48]

The traditional leadership tripod of leaders, followers, and shared goals impose debilitating limitations for missional leadership and practice in a VUCA world. But the relationships between them have the creative power to unleash new horizons for mission in a world that is increasingly complex.

---

[44] Franklin, *Towards Global Missional Leadership*, p. 78.

[45] Ibid.

[46] Wilfred H. Drath, *The Deep Blue Sea: Rethinking the Source of Leadership* (San Francisco: Jossey-Bass, 2001), "People Make Sense of Reality Through Relational Processes," para. 1. Kindle.

[47] Ibid. Chapter 5 "Relational Dialogue," para. 1.

[48] Drath, *The Deep Blue Sea*, "People Make Sense of Reality Through Relational Processes," para. 2.

Spiritual Formation as Leadership Development: *Lectio Missio*

The development of leadership-in-community is not something that can be taught in classrooms, workshops, textbooks, or even on-the-job training. At its heart, missional leadership emerges from the spiritual formation of people who have received mercy and a new identity in Christ, and who are called by Christ to extend that same mercy to others.[49] For this reason, the purpose of this curriculum is to equip emerging as well as seasoned leaders with an experience of spiritual formation in community with others on mission in this crazy, complex, VUCA world.

The primary method of spiritual formation this curriculum uses is called *lectio missio*. *Lectio missio* is a spiritual practice that combines Scripture readings, prayer, contemplation, and small group interaction to help a missional team listen to the voice of Jesus as the Holy Spirit calls their vision and leadership to life. It also provides an experiential learning approach that includes inductive Bible study, theological and devotional readings, and mission experiences that help the team connect significant missional themes in Scripture with their day-to-day calling to participate in God's great mission.[50] *Lectio missio* is comprised of eight movements:

- **Movement 1: *Adspecto*** (gaze) – An introductory Scripture reading and reflection that encourages the participants to listen carefully to the Lord as he speaks through his Word.

- **Movement 2: *Lectio*** (read) – An inductive Bible study for both personal and small group reflection along with a devotional reading that helps the participants dive more deeply into the Scripture text.

- **Movement 3: *Meditatio*** (meditate) – A meditation that allows the participants to consider important missiological, community, and ethical themes of leadership-in-community prompted by the Scripture reading and reflection.

- **Movement 4: *Oratio*** (prayer) – A responsive prayer.

- **Movement 5: *Imitatio*** (imitate) – An exercise of personal and group reflection upon emerging missional insights and applications.

---

[49] Sherwood G. Lingenfelter, *Leading Cross-Culturally: Covenant Relationships for Effective Christian Leadership* (Grand Rapids: Baker Academic, 2008), p. 75.

[50] Craig S. Keener, *Spirit Hermeneutics: Reading Scripture in Light of Pentecost* (Grand Rapids: William B. Eerdmans Publishing Company), p. 24-25, 40-43.

- **Movement 6:** *Missio* (witness) – An exercise of personal commitment to practice mission.

- **Movement 7:** *Communio* (fellowship) – A group participation in a service or mission project along with an after-action reflection upon the experience in a small group.

- **Movement 8:** *Contemplatio* (contemplate) – A small group exercise of celebration, prayer, worship, and thanksgiving to God for the ways he has revealed himself to the group through the study.[51]

How to Use this Curriculum

This study is designed to be a journey of exploration, adventure, and discovery. As you traverse through these movements in both personal and small group study, your hearts, minds, and spirits will be engaged in the great mission of God! You will survey the breathtaking vision of God's good reign that is putting all things to rights and restoring wholeness, peace, justice, and uninterrupted joy in God's presence throughout the entire cosmos. Philosopher James K. A. Smith captures the motivation behind true leadership-in-community:

> To be human is to be on a quest. To live is to be embarked on a kind of unconscious journey toward a destination of your dreams…. The place we unconsciously strive toward is what ancient philosophers of habit called our *telos* – our goal, our end. But the *telos* we live toward is not something that we primarily know or believe or think about; rather, our *telos* is what we *want*, what we long for, what we crave. It is less an ideal that we have ideas about and more a vision of "the good life" that we desire. It is a picture of flourishing that we *imagine* in a visceral, often-unarticulated way – a vague yet attractive sense of where we think true happiness is found…. To be human, we could say, is to desire the kingdom – *some* kingdom… That's why there's something *ultimate* about this vision: to be oriented toward some sense of the good life is to pursue some vision of how the world *ought* to be.[52]

This study's primary purpose is not to provide you with set of leadership skills, best practices, theories, or models (although hopefully you will find many interesting insights about leadership herein). Its primary aim is

---

[51] Hill, *GlobalChurch*, p. 438-441.
[52] James K. A. Smith, *You Are What You Love: The Spiritual Power of Habit* (Grand Rapids: Brazos Press, 2016), p. 10-11.

that you will be captured by the wonderful story of God's love, expressed through Jesus Christ, for a lost world that he intends to save. The best way to use this study is to let it immerse you in that story so that it fills your affections, imagination, priorities, and life! For, indeed, it is those whose real treasure is Jesus that God calls to participate in his great mission (Matt. 13:44).

The Architecture of the Study

The curriculum is organized in three major sections that form the overall structure of the study. Each section builds upon the previous one so that, by the end of the study, you will have a strong framework for your participation in missional leadership. The three sections include the *missiology*, *community*, and *ethics* of leadership-in-community. The following diagram illustrates that missiology is the essential core of leadership-in-community that will shape our community relationships and our ethics. All three form and move together as a comprehensive architecture that supports our leadership-in-community for the mission of God.

The Architecture of Leadership-in-Community

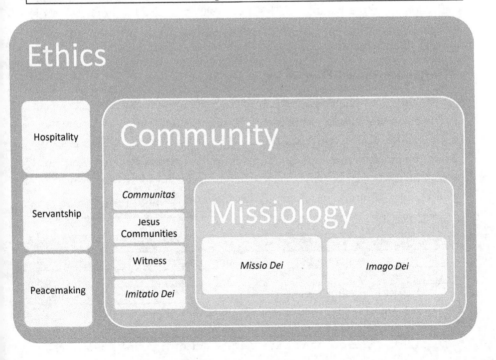

Section 1: The Missiology of Leadership-in-Community. The study begins with the missiology of our leadership-in-community. The mission in which God invites us to participate is his mission – the *missio Dei* – from start to finish. It originates from the sending heart of our Triune God and extends outward from him to his image-bearers – the *imago Dei* – as he calls them to be fruitful and multiply, to create cultures through loving and self-sacrificing relationships that expand his good reign to the cosmos. This is God's mission to redeem the world!

Section 2: The Community of Leadership-in-Community. Just as the mission of God originates from within the loving community of our triune God who eternally exists as Father, Son, and Holy Spirit, so too the nature of our leadership in mission must reflect the same loving community in our diversity. As we serve one another in love and self-sacrifice, our worship and work together images our God whose presence lives among us in the real-life contexts we inhabit. In those places, our leadership-in-community witnesses to the greatness of God's mercy and welcomes others to belong to him.

Section 3: The Ethics of Leadership-in-Community. Finally, the study explores the implications of our leadership-in-community for mission. It asks the question of how, then, do we live out the values of our King Jesus? With reflection on three parables of Jesus, we will consider the importance of hospitality, servantship, and peacemaking within the community of God's people.

The Recommended Progression of the Movements

The recommended approach to the study outlined below guides you and your small group as you progress through the *lectio missio* movements for each chapter over a two-week period. The study involves a high level of commitment for you and your small group members. However, this recommended outline ensures that you have the best experience of leadership-in-community as you walk together on this journey.

Week 1			
Individual Study			
	Instruction	Movement	Time
Day 1			
1.	Read the introduction		10 minutes
2.	Open with prayer from the selected Psalm	Movement 1: *Adspecto*	1 minute
3.	Read the Scripture text	Movement 1: *Adspecto*	5 minutes

16

4.	Reflect on the Scripture text	Movement 1: *Adspecto*	10 minutes
		Total time	**26 minutes**
Day 2			
1.	Open with prayer for guidance		1 minute
2.	Read the Scripture text	Movement 2: *Lectio*	5 minutes
3.	Respond to the Scripture study questions	Movement 2: *Lectio*	15 minutes
		Total time	**21 minutes**
Day 3			
1.	Open with prayer for illumination		1 minute
2.	Read the reading	Movement 2: *Lectio*	15 minutes
3.	Close with the *Oratio* prayer	Movement 4: *Oratio*	1 minute
		Total time	**17 minutes**
Group Study			
1.	Open with prayer from the selected Psalm	Movement 1: *Adspecto*	1 minute
2.	Read the Scripture text together	Movement 1: *Adspecto*	5 minutes
3.	Reflect on the Scripture text	Movement 1: *Adspecto*	10 minutes
4.	Respond to the Scripture study questions	Movement 2: *Lectio*	40 minutes
5.	Close with the *Oratio* prayer	Movement 4: *Oratio*	1 minute
		Total time	**57 minutes**
Week 2			
Individual Study			
Day 1			
1.	Open with prayer from the selected Psalm	Movement 1: *Adspecto*	1 minute
2.	Read the Scripture text	Movement 1: *Adspecto*	5 minutes

3.	Reflect on the Scripture text	Movement 1: *Adspecto*	10 minutes
		Total time	**16 minutes**
Day 2			
1.	Open with prayer for illumination		1 minute
2.	Read the *Meditatio*	Movement 3: *Meditatio*	15 minutes
3.	Close with the *Oratio* prayer	Movement 4: *Oratio*	1 minute
		Total time	**17 minutes**
Day 3			
1.	Open with the *Oratio* prayer	Movement 4: *Oratio*	1 minute
2.	Reflect on the individual reflection questions	Movement 5: *Imitatio*	15 minutes
3.	Reflect on your personal commitment to mission	Movement 6: *Missio*	5 minutes
4.	Close with a prayer of thanksgiving	Movement 8: *Contemplatio*	1 minute
		Total time	**22 minutes**
Group Study			
1.	Open with the *Oratio prayer*	Movement 4: *Oratio*	1 minute
2.	Read the Scripture text together	Movement 1: *Adspecto*	5 minutes
3.	Reflect on the Scripture text	Movement 1: *Adspecto*	10 minutes
4.	Discuss the following: "What ideas or insights from the *Meditatio* were significant for you?"	Movement 3: *Meditatio*	20 minutes
5.	Respond to the group reflection	Movement 5: *Imitatio*	10 minutes
6.	Close with celebration, thanksgiving, and praise!	Movement 8: *Contemplatio*	10 minutes
		Total time	**56 minutes**

18

Learning from Mission Experience

Mission experience is a critical aspect of learning that will contribute greatly to your spiritual formation into leadership-in-community. For this reason, this study highly recommends that you and your small group embrace three levels of mission experience throughout the course of this study:

Movement 6: Missio. The first two levels of mission experience are found in Movement 6: *Missio.* Level 1 Awareness encourages you to begin each day with a prayer asking the Lord to send you into his mission that day and to end each day with a reflection on how you saw God on the move that day. As you practice Level 1 Awareness, you will begin to see that God is active in your life and will discover how he calls you to participate in all he is doing in the world around you.

Level 2 Personal Commitment encourages you to commit to serve on mission in whatever way you sense God may be directing you. Perhaps he calls you to serve in some capacity in your local church. Or perhaps he calls you to volunteer for a service organization in your local community. Ask the Lord to open your heart and mind to where he wants to use your gifts and experiences to bless others.

Movement 7: Communio. The most impactful learning you will have during this study is through experiencing a mission or service project together with your small group. In Movement 7: *Communio,* your small group is highly encouraged to find a mission or service project that you can do together. These small group mission experiences will enhance, reinforce, and enlighten your small group study with amazing new insights about God's great mission. While performing a small group mission or service project is not required to continue through this study, you will find that your commitment to serve together will bless your small group relationships and what you learn from one another.

The Leadership Declaration

The final capstone project of this study is the Leadership Declaration, described in the Conclusion. The Leadership Declaration is a personal exercise in which you will draft a life-long vision for your leadership based on significant guiding principles of leadership-in-community that you may have embraced during this study. Your Leadership Declaration will be a manifesto challenging you to continually grow in the direction of leadership that God has called you.

Opening Blessing

As you begin this journey, let the following prayer of blessing send you and your small group on your way:

> *May the peace of the Lord Christ go with you,*
> *   wherever He may send you.*
> *May He guide you through the wilderness,*
> *   protect you through the storm.*
> *May He bring you home rejoicing*
> *   at the wonders He has shown you.*
> *May He bring you home rejoicing*
> *   once again into our doors.*
>
> *In the name of the Father, and of the Son, and of the Holy Spirit.*
> *Amen.*[53]

---

[53] The Northumbria Community, *Celtic Daily Prayer: Prayers and Readings from the Northumbria Community* (New York: HarperCollins, 2002), p. 19.

Section 1:

The Missiology of Leadership-in-Community

Chapter 1

Missio Dei

At the time of this writing, the world is caught in a global pandemic. The COVID-19 virus has infected millions and killed thousands across the planet. Government leaders are looking for the right measures to control its spread and many have quarantined their citizens to their homes. Economies have slowed. Many people have lost their jobs. Social distancing has kept people away from families, friends, churches, and communities. Anxiety and fear have gripped our hearts and we have begun to wonder if things will ever return to normal. At the same time, racial tensions, social unrest, political controversies, and natural disasters – an endless stream of bad news – leaves us in a state of helpless despair.

The struggles we experience make us feel that this world is not as it should be. The Bible's opening chapter tells about the Creator God who spoke into a formless and empty earth and created an ordered space that was very good (Gen. 1:2; 31, NIV).[1] The "formless and empty" (Hebrew *tohu wabohu*) described a desert wasteland, an emptiness, or an exile that opposed the order of creation and threatened it with desolation.[2] In contrast to the creation stories of other ancient Near Eastern cultures that were filled with conflict and chaos between warring gods, the Bible portrays the Spirit of God moving freely over the surface of the earth. And with the ease of his creative word, God transforms it into various forms – day and night, sky, land, and seas – and filled these forms with life.[3] Author Andy Crouch explains that "the writer of Genesis looks at the world, from stars to starfish, and sees a purposeful, engaged, creative intelligence at work."[4] In his creation, God established an inhabitable world suitable for human flourishing and ongoing creativity.[5]

Yet, something went very wrong. Since the disobedience of the man and the woman against God (Gen. 3), the formless and empty have made a resurgence into this world. We were created for joyful intimacy with God, our Creator, and the satisfying fulfillment of his seventh-day rest (Gen. 2:1). But this broken world, and our broken hearts, make that an elusive dream we long for but can never quite reach. James K. A. Smith describes this state of

---

[1] Andy Crouch, *Culture Making: Recovering Our Creative Calling* (Downers Grove: InterVarsity Press, 2009), p. 20.

[2] See Deut. 32:10: Job 6:18, 12:24; Is. 24:10, 34:11, 40:23, 45:18; Jer. 4:23. Robin Routledge, "Did God Create Chaos? Unresolved Tension in Genesis 1:1-2," *Tyndale Bulletin* 61, no. 1 (2010), p. 73-74.

[3] Ibid. p. 72-75.

[4] Crouch, *Culture Making*, p. 21.

[5] Ibid.

longing as a refugee spirituality. He says, "The alienation is real. The sense of frustration, futility, of never arriving, never feeling settled with ourselves – these are not figments of the imagination to be papered over with pious assertions of homecoming."[6] We are fractured and fragmented.[7]

In C. S. Lewis' classic tale, *The Lion, the Witch and the Wardrobe*, the land of Narnia is overtaken by the evil White Witch who has placed it under an eternal winter. She has imprisoned many of its inhabitants for their treasonous hope that the human Sons of Adam and Daughters of Eve will once again sit on the throne in Cair Paravel. In fact, she turned the faun, Mr. Tumnus, into stone for helping Lucy escape from her grasp. But a whisper begins to circulate that Aslan, the great Lion and true ruler of Narnia, is on the move:

> "Who is Aslan?" asked Susan.

> "Aslan?" said Mr. Beaver. "Why, don't you know? He's the King. He's the Lord of the whole wood, but not often here, you understand. Never in my time or my father's time. But the word has reached us that he has come back. He is in Narnia at this moment. He'll settle the White Queen all right. It is he, not you, that will save Mr. Tumnus."

> "She won't turn him into stone too?" said Edmund.

> "Lord love you, Son of Adam, what a simple thing to say!" answered Mr. Beaver with a great laugh. "Turn *him* into stone? If she can stand on her two feet and look him in the face it'll be the most she can do and more than I expect of her. No, no. He'll put all to rights as it says in an old rhyme in these parts:

>> *Wrong will be right, when Aslan comes in sight,*
>> *At the sound of his roar, sorrows will be no more,*
>> *When he bares his teeth, winter meets its death,*
>> *And when he shakes his mane, we shall have spring again.*[8]

The hope of the whole Kingdom of Narnia rests in the return of the great King Aslan who, by his sacrifice on the Stone Table for the wayward Edmund, redeems the Son of Adam and redeems Narnia to his rightful rule.

---

[6] James K. A. Smith, *On the Road with Saint Augustine: A Real-World Spirituality for Restless Hearts* (Grand Rapids: BrazosPress, 2019), p. 40.

[7] Ibid.

[8] C. S. Lewis, *The Lion, the Witch and the Wardrobe* (New York: HarperTrophy, 1950), p. 85.

This children's tale is a poignant allegory of the great redemption story in which all followers of Jesus Christ are immersed. God is on the move! His mission is the redemption of this world made desolate by the sorrow and evil of the invading formless and empty. We dream of a renewed world where God welcomes us into his promised rest, that sacred space where life once again flourishes under his good reign. Theologian N. T Wright explains:

> ...the reason we have these dreams...is that there is someone speaking to us...someone who cares very much about this present world and our present selves, and who has made us and the world for a purpose which will indeed involve justice, things being put to rights, *ourselves* being put to rights, the world being rescued at last.[9]

This is the *missio Dei* – the great mission of God.[10]

Christianity is, by nature, a faith of great hope. Its source is our missionary God who, in his unending love, sent his Son to redeem the world through his death and resurrection.[11] Our victorious King, Jesus Christ, now sits at God's right hand (Mark 16:19) and sends the Holy Spirit to us to continue his work of redemption that extends his glorious reign over the cosmos.[12] The apostle Paul expressed this vision with stunning magnificence:

> But God is rich in mercy, and he loved us very much. We were spiritually dead because of all we had done against him. But he gave us new life together with Christ. (You have been saved by God's grace.) Yes, it is because we are a part of Christ Jesus that God raised us from death and seated us together with him in the heavenly paces. God did this so that his kindness to us who belong to Christ Jesus would clearly show for all time to come the amazing richness of his grace. (Eph. 2:4-7)

We are called to participate in his great mission because we are a part of Christ Jesus! Theologian Samuel Escobar explains, "Missions exists because God is a missionary God who sends his people to be a blessing to all of

---

[9] N. T. Wright, *Simply Christian: Why Christianity Makes Sense* (New York: HarperCollins, 2006), p. 8-9.
[10] Douglas McConnell, *Cultural Insights for Christian Leaders: New Directions for Organizations Serving God's Mission* (Grand Rapids: Baker Academic, 2018), p. 2.
[11] Ibid. p. 2-3.
[12] Ibid. p. 3.

humankind."[13] In this chapter, we will discover the missionary heart of God and his invitation to us to participate in his great mission.

Movement 1: Adspecto

Prayer

✦ Pray for the Holy Spirit to speak to you through the Scripture. Use the following words of Psalm 63:1 as a prayer:

> *God, you are my God.*
> *I am searching so hard to find you.*
> *Body and soul, I thirst for you*
> *In this dry and weary land without water.*

Scripture Reading

✦ **Read John 4:1-42.** Listen for words or phrases from the passage that stand out to you.

---

[1]Jesus learned that the Pharisees had heard the report that he was making and baptizing more followers than John. [2](But really, Jesus himself did not baptize anyone; his followers baptized people for him.) [3]So he left Judea and went back to Galilee. [4]On the way to Galilee, he had to go through the country of Samaria.

[5]In Samaria Jesus came to the town called Sychar, which is near the field that Jacob gave to his son Joseph. [6]Jacob's well was there. Jesus was tired from his long trip, so he sat down beside the well. It was about noon. [7]A Samaritan woman came to the well to get some water, and Jesus said to her, "Please give me a drink." [8]This happened while his followers were in town buying some food.

[9]The woman answered, "I am surprised that you ask me for a drink! You are a Jew and I am a Samaritan woman!" (Jews have nothing to do with Samaritans.)

---

[13] Escobar, *The New Global Mission*, p. 94.

¹⁰Jesus answered, "You don't know what God can give you. And you don't know who I am, the one who asked you for a drink. If you knew, you would have asked me, and I would have given you living water."

¹¹The woman said, "Sir, where will you get that living water? The well is very deep, and you have nothing to get water with. ¹²Are you greater than our ancestor Jacob? He is the one who gave us this well. He drank from it himself, and his sons and all his animals drank from it too."

¹³Jesus answered, "Everyone who drinks this water will be thirsty again. ¹⁴But anyone who drinks the water I give will never be thirsty again. The water I give people will be like a spring flowing inside them. It will bring them eternal life."

¹⁵The woman said to Jesus, "Sir, give me this water. Then I will never be thirsty again and won't have to come back here to get more water."

¹⁶Jesus told her, "Go get your husband and come back."

¹⁷The woman answered, "But I have no husband."

Jesus said to her, "You are right to say you have no husband. ¹⁸That's because, although you have had five husbands, the man you live with now is not your husband. That much was the truth."

¹⁹The woman said, "Sir, I can see that you are a prophet. ²⁰Our fathers worshiped on this mountain. But you Jews say that Jerusalem is the place where people must worship."

²¹Jesus said, "Believe me, woman! The time is coming when you will not have to be in Jerusalem or on this mountain to worship the Father. ²²You Samaritans worship something you don't understand. We Jews understand what we worship, since salvation comes from the Jews. ²³But the time is coming when the true worshipers will worship the Father in spirit and truth. In fact, that time is now here. And these are the kind of people the Father wants to be his worshipers. ²⁴God is spirit. So the people who worship him must worship in spirit and truth."

²⁵The woman said, "I know that the Messiah is coming." (He is the one called Christ.) "When he comes, he will explain everything to us."

²⁶Then Jesus said, "He is talking to you now—I am the Messiah."

[27]Just then Jesus' followers came back from town. They were surprised because they saw Jesus talking with a woman. But none of them asked, "What do you want?" or "Why are you talking with her?"

[28]Then the woman left her water jar and went back to town. She told the people there, [29]"A man told me everything I have ever done. Come see him. Maybe he is the Messiah." [30]So the people left the town and went to see Jesus.

[31]While the woman was in town, Jesus' followers were begging him, "Teacher, eat something!"

[32]But Jesus answered, "I have food to eat that you know nothing about."

[33]So the followers asked themselves, "Did someone already bring him some food?"

[34]Jesus said, "My food is to do what the one who sent me wants me to do. My food is to finish the work that he gave me to do. [35]When you plant, you always say, 'Four more months to wait before we gather the grain.' But I tell you, open your eyes, and look at the fields. They are ready for harvesting now. [36]Even now, the people who harvest the crop are being paid. They are gathering crops for eternal life. So now the people who plant can be happy together with those who harvest. [37]It is true when we say, 'One person plants, but another person harvests the crop.' [38]I sent you to harvest a crop that you did not work for. Others did the work, and you get the profit from their work."

[39]Many of the Samaritan people in that town believed in Jesus. They believed because of what the woman had told them about him. She had told them, "He told me everything I have ever done." [40]The Samaritans went to Jesus. They begged him to stay with them. So he stayed there two days. [41]Many more people became believers because of the things he said.

[42]The people said to the woman, "First we believed in Jesus because of what you told us. But now we believe because we heard him ourselves. We know now that he really is the one who will save the world."

Reflection

✛ When you have finished reading, remain silent for one or two minutes.

➕ Read the entire passage again. If you have an audio Bible, listen through the passage.

- o *Personal Reflection*: Journal your thoughts on the following questions:
  - What words or phrases from the passage stand out to you?
  - How do these words or phrases connect with your life right now?
  - How is God inviting you to respond to this passage?

Movement 2: Lectio

Scripture Study

➕ Read or listen to **John 4:1-42.**

➕ Answer the following study questions:

1. What do you observe about how Jesus interacts with the Samaritan woman?

2. How does he lead her through the conversation to discover who he is?

3. What does the woman learn about Jesus through the conversation? How can you tell that she learns this?

4. What do you think Jesus meant by "living water" (vs. 10, 13-14)?

5. The conversation moves from living water to the woman's marital situation and finally to worship. How do you think these relate to each other?

6. What kind of worshippers does the Father want (vs. 23)?

7. What does it mean to worship the Father in spirit and in truth (vs. 23-24)?

8. Where do you see the Trinity involved in this encounter?

9. What does Jesus say is his food (vs. 34)?

10. What does that mean for his followers, including us (vs. 38)?

Reading
The Context of John

The Gospel of John was written so that its readers may reflect deeply upon the identity and significance of Jesus.[14] The author, who was the apostle John according to tradition, presented his purpose in writing the Gospel:

> Jesus did many other miraculous signs that his followers saw, which are not written in this book. But these are written so that you can believe that Jesus is the Messiah, the Son of God. Then, by believing, you can have life through his name. (John 20:30-31)

At the time the Gospel was written, both Jewish and Gentile Christians faced rejection and opposition because of their faith in Jesus. Jewish Christians had once belonged to a faith community with a rich identity as God's chosen people reinforced by the stories of God's redemptive acts on their behalf, the Sinai covenant and the Mosaic Law, and their religious festivals and traditions.[15] But by the time that John wrote, the Jewish communities were scattered throughout the Roman Empire, alienated from their homeland and eager to preserve the traditions that distinguished them from the nations around them.[16] Those who believed in Jesus as their long-awaited Messiah were labeled apostates and expelled from these communities.[17] Jewish Christians began establishing a new kinship group, one that worshiped Jesus as Lord, and that equally welcomed Gentiles as God's people! This was perhaps even more contemptible to their Jewish kin.

At the same time, Gentile Christians faced exclusion from their former communities as well. We may not fully grasp the impact of that exclusion. So much of a person's identity and welfare – their social status, political power, and economic opportunities – were dependent upon the recognized prestige of the groups to whom they belonged.[18] The "Jesus communities" were often publicly disgraced because of their ridiculous claims of the incarnation and

---

[14] David A. deSilva, *An Introduction to the New Testament: Contexts, Methods & Ministry Formation* (Downers Grove: InterVarsity Press, 2004), p. 417.

[15] N. T. Wright & Michael F. Bird, *The New Testament in its World: An Introduction to the History, Literature, and Theology of the First Christians* (Grand Rapids: Zondervan Academic, 2019), p. 662-663.

[16] DeSilva, *An Introduction to the New Testament*, p. 402-403.

[17] Ibid. p. 403.

[18] Bruce J. Malina, *The New Testament World: Insights from Cultural Anthropology* 3rd Ed. (Louisville: Westminster John Knox Press, 2001), p. 30-32.

suffering of Christ.[19] In ancient Greco-Roman thought, gods simply could not suffer physically or be otherwise affected by the material world.[20] But the Christians not only worshipped a crucified man, they also refused to worship the Roman emperor.[21] While the Roman Empire could be quite accommodating to local deities, the public cult of the emperor was non-negotiable for all Roman districts because it united the empire despite its cultural and religious pluralism.[22] The Christians' courageous profession of Jesus as Lord was an affront to the empire that decreed its emperor as divine and lord.[23] They worshiped Jesus as the only Lord to whom the whole world owed allegiance.[24]

In the honor-shame cultures of the first-century Mediterranean world, people were not free to choose their beliefs, lifestyles, or worship according to their individual preferences. As in many parts of the world today, kinship was the primary principle around which Roman society was constituted.[25] *Belonging* was the foremost concern of people! An individual's membership in specific groups, such as their family, defined their identity and prescribed acceptable behavior according to the group's rules of order, conduct, and relationships.[26] Such behavior honored their family's name and any deviance was not tolerated.[27] Honor was "the value of a person in his or her own eyes (that is, one's claim to worth) *plus* that person's value in the eyes of his or her social group."[28] When people acted within the boundaries of their kinship group's social map, they expected society to acknowledge their honor.[29] But when they acted outside those boundaries, they could have expected to be regarded as profane, unclean, and excluded.[30]

The men and women that worshipped Jesus as their Messiah fell outside those boundaries. They did not reproduce the values and norms of

---

19 Ibid. p. 401.
20 DeSilva, *An Introduction to the New Testament*, p. 401.
21 Ibid.
22 Vinoth Ramachandra, *The Recovery of Mission: Beyond the Pluralist Paradigm* (Grand Rapids: William B. Eerdmans Publishing Company, 1996), p. 226.
23 Ibid.
24 Ibid.
25 Malina, *The New Testament World*, p. 29.
26 Ibid.
27 Ibid.
28 Ibid. p. 30.
29 Ibid. p. 31.
30 Ibid. p. 28.

their former kinship groups.[31] Consequently, they experienced tremendous pressure to reject this "ridiculous" Jesus, who was publicly shamed on a Roman cross, and return to the kinship groups they had spurned. John's intent, then, was to rezone the boundaries of kinship for these newly constituted Jesus communities.[32] Now, they *belonged* to Jesus and they must reflect his values in their lives.[33] John invited his readers to contemplate the "significance and richness of the treasure they have received in Jesus, and to encourage them to keep their hold on this treasure."[34] He affirmed their identity in Christ Jesus even as the world excluded them. Theologian Vinoth Ramachandra explains, "The gospel constituted a new category of human being, a new way of being human. Their primary identity was found in a new familial community whose social inclusiveness was unparalleled."[35] These Jesus communities were identified by love, servanthood, and unity even with their diverse makeup of cultural, ethnic, and class backgrounds.[36]

The advent of Jesus Christ was so significant, in fact, that the entire narrative of God's chosen people is utterly recast in him! N. T. Wright and Michael F. Bird argue that the Gospel of John is a new Genesis, Exodus, and Pentecost narrative.[37]

Genesis. Wright and Bird believe John's opening phrase, "In the beginning..." (John 1:1), pointed back to the creation story and announced to its readers that the Creator has come to remake this dark world.[38] They point out that the resurrection account reads like a new creation story that begins on the first day of the week (John 20).[39] Furthermore, they compare the creation of the humans in God's image (Gen. 1:26) with the climax of John's prologue in which the "Word became a man and lived among us" (John 1:14).[40] This Word-man *imaged* God: "We saw his divine greatness – the greatness that belongs to the only Son of the Father" (John 1:14).

Exodus. Wright and Bird explain that the Word who became man and "lived among us" (John 1:14) points back to the tabernacle in the Exodus

---

[31] Ibid. p. 31.
[32] DeSilva, *An Introduction to the New Testament,* p. 436.
[33] Ibid.
[34] Ibid. p. 403.
[35] Ramachandra, *The Recovery of Mission,* p. 226.
[36] Ibid. p. 403.
[37] Wright & Bird, *The New Testament in Its World,* p. 650.
[38] Ibid. p. 650.
[39] Ibid.
[40] Ibid.

story, which was eventually replaced by the temple in Jerusalem.[41] This was the place where God lived with his people.[42] John's Gospel drew from temple imagery to express God living with and in his people through his Spirit (e. g. John 14:15-17).[43]

Pentecost. Finally, Wright and Bird believe that John indicated a new Pentecost celebration whereby the Spirit of God was poured upon a new multiethnic people like streams of living water (John 4:10-14) .[44] Pentecost was the traditional harvest festival of ancient Israel commemorated with joyous thanksgiving to their God who delivered them from Egypt, removed their sin, and blessed them with a fruitful harvest.[45] In John, Jesus foreshadowed the new Pentecost – a harvest of people who worship the Father in Spirit and truth (John 4:21-24, 34-38).

Through this retelling of Israel's history, the Gospel of John re-centers the identity of God's people in Jesus Christ.[46] Jesus fulfills the story of Israel and extends it to the whole world![47] He is the King who restores the honor of his people through his death, resurrection, and ascension to God's right hand. He demonstrates the values of his Kingdom by washing their feet (John 13:12-17). Wright and Bird conclude, "This is the story of Jesus *told as* the true and redeeming story of Israel, *told as* the true and redeeming story of the creator and the cosmos."[48]

The Woman at the Well

In Jewish tradition, wisdom was frequently personified as a companion and coworker of God.[49] The book of Proverbs, for example, describes wisdom as a master craftsman at God's side enjoying, even "laughing and playing in," the world God made (Proverbs 8:30-31). Those who find wisdom find life and God's favor, while those who do not find wisdom, or even hate it, "put their lives in danger" (Proverbs 8:35-36).

---

[41] Ibid.

[42] Ibid.

[43] Ibid.

[44] Ibid. p. 651.

[45] "Pentecost, Feast of," In *New Bible Dictionary* 2nd ed., Eds. J. D. Douglas, F. F. Bruce, J. I. Packer, N. Hillyer, D. Guthrie, A. R. Millard, & D. J. Wiseman (Downers Grove: InterVarsity Press, 1982), p. 909.

[46] Scot McKnight, *The King Jesus Gospel: The Original Good News Revisited* (Grand Rapids: Zondervan, 2016), p. 50.

[47] Ibid.

[48] Wright & Bird, *The New Testament in Its World*, p. 665.

[49] DeSilva, *An Introduction to the New Testament*, p. 418.

The wisdom literature was a rich source for reflection in the early church on the life and mission of Jesus Christ.[50] The Gospel of John also drew from this tradition as it identifies Jesus Christ as the Word of God who was with God in the beginning, through whom everything was made, and is, in fact, God (John 1:1-3). In the Old Testament, the "word of God" is often used to indicate God's action in creation, revelation, and deliverance.[51] Just like Aslan of Narnia, Jesus, the Word of God, is God on the move! John includes many stories of people who, upon encountering Jesus, come to life-changing faith in him.[52] As with wisdom, those who found Jesus found life (John 1:4).[53] They found "grace and truth" and received "one blessing after another" (John 1:16).

John introduced us to a Samaritan woman who encountered Jesus and found "living water" (John 4:1-42). In the story, Jesus was traveling from Judea to Galilee and, on his way, he *had* to go through the country of Samaria (John 4:4, italics added). Already, we can sense that Jesus was on a mission! He had a purpose for going through Samaria. As he rested alone beside Jacob's well in Sychar, he asked the Samaritan woman for a drink of water. But the interaction that would follow would reveal to the woman that Jesus was the Messiah (John 4:29). In this encounter, Jesus stepped right into the middle of historical and cultural tensions – tensions that had left a "formless and empty" landscape – so that he could redeem true worship for his Father! He brought "living water" to this barren context. Let's look at these tensions.

Jews and Samaritans. The text states matter-of-factly that "Jews have nothing to do with Samaritans" (John 4:9). A centuries-old schism existed between Jews and Samaritans, beginning with a split between Israel's northern and southern kingdoms in 930 BCE. When the Assyrians overran the northern kingdom in 722 BCE, they exiled its leadership in order to destabilize the nation politically.[54] The Assyrians also relocated foreign people into the region of the northern kingdom to intermarry with the locals and create a mixed race that would be unlikely to unify and revolt against their

---

[50] Ibid.

[51] David J. MacLeod, "The Eternality and Deity of the Word: John 1:1-2," *Bibliotheca Sacra* 160, no. 637 (January-March 2003), p. 55-56.

[52] Ibid. p. 402.

[53] DeSilva, *An Introduction to the New Testament*, p. 419.

[54] Lawrence H. Schiffman, "The Samaritan Schism," Biblical Archaeology Society, last modified August 11, 2014, https://www.biblicalarchaeology.org/daily/ancient-cultures/daily-life-and-practice/the-samaritan-schism/

Assyrian rulers.[55] Ever since, the Jews considered the Samaritans an unclean, mixed race. Furthermore, when then Judeans returned from their Babylonian exile in 520 BCE, the Samaritans offered to help them rebuild the Jerusalem temple.[56] However, the Jews refused their offer out of disdain for their mixed heritage and syncretistic worship.[57]

Having been slighted by this insult, the Samaritans established their own center of worship on Mt. Gerizim near Shechem.[58] They did not believe in any of the prophets after Moses.[59] Instead, their hope was set upon a "future restorer" who would be like Moses, which was why the woman's acknowledgement of Jesus as a prophet is significant (John 4:19).[60] The Samaritans were antagonistic toward the traditions of the Pharisees and their strict adherence to the law.[61] In return, the Jewish people considered the Samaritans apostates from the true faith.[62] The increasing religious and political tensions culminated in the Jewish destruction of the Samaritan temple on Mt. Gerizim during the Hasmonean period.[63]

Generally, Jewish travelers went the long way around Samaria to avoid any contact with Samaritans, even though the shortest route between Judea and Galilee was through Samaria.[64] But the missionary heart of Jesus prompted him to walk right into the heart of Samaria! Gail R. O'Day explains, "Jesus' vocation compelled him to make the gift of God available to those whom Jewish religious orthodoxy deemed unworthy."[65] He was on mission to restore true worship where religious divides had reigned for so long.

Men and Women. As the disciples returned from the town, they were "surprised because they saw Jesus talking with a woman" (John 4:27). We sense from this that it was unorthodox for a man and a woman to converse publicly in the same manner as Jesus and the Samaritan woman. According

---

[55] Ibid.

[56] Ibid.

[57] Ibid.

[58] Ibid.

[59] Keener, *Spirit Hermeneutics*, p. 71.

[60] Ibid.

[61] Paul Hertig, "The Powerful and Vulnerable Intercultural Encounters with Jesus," *Mission Studies* 32 (2015), p. 307.

[62] Sherri Brown, "Water Imagery and the Power and Presence of God in the Gospel of John," *Theology Today* 72, no. 3 (2015), p. 294.

[63] Keener, *Spirit Hermeneutics*, p. 72.

[64] Yousaf Sadiq, "Jesus' Encounter with a Woman at the Well: A South Asian Perspective," *Missiology: An International Review* 46, no. 4 (2018), p. 367.

[65] Gail R. O'Day, *The Word Disclosed: Preaching the Gospel of John* (St. Louis: Chalice Press, 2002), p. 35.

to Josephus, a Jewish historian contemporary to the time that John's Gospel was written, speaking to a woman in public was considered an indiscretion for a rabbi.[66] It roused public suspicion, and so, it was often controlled through consequences in regard to the social honor of both the man and the woman.[67]

Women were, unfortunately, given an inferior place within the society of Jesus' time.[68] They were generally excluded from public spaces, such as religious rites or festivals.[69] Bruce Malina notes that a woman's honor was thought to be found in her discretion, shyness, restraint, and timidity.[70] Her behavior reflected directly upon the honor of the men in her life, so she would be careful to maintain her integrity by guarding it against any, even slight, advances by other men into her private space.[71]

But Jesus, weary from his journey and alone, engaged with this Samaritan woman, and in so doing, regarded her as worthy dialogue partner (John 4:6).[72] In his weariness and vulnerability as a stranger and sojourner, he defied social convention to ask her for a drink (John 4:7). The encounter occurred at midday which was an unusual time for people to draw water from the well.[73] She was there at a time when people in the ancient Mediterranean world usually stopped work and rested in the shade.[74] Some scholars believe that she came at a time when she knew she would be there alone because she was not welcome among the other women who usually came in the morning or evening to draw water for cooking.[75] The ensuing dialogue with Jesus may have suggested what was the central source of her exclusion – the men in her life! She previously had five different husbands and the man she currently lived with was not her husband (John 4:18). The reality of her social context was that social position and welfare of women was often tied to their fathers, husbands, and sons whose responsibility was to protect the honor of their

---

[66] Ibid.
[67] Hertig, "The Powerful and Vulnerable," p. 306.
[68] Ibid.
[69] Ibid.
[70] Malina, *The New Testament World*, p. 47.
[71] Ibid.
[72] Peter C. Phan, "An Interfaith Encounter at Jacob's Well: A Missiological Interpretation of John 4:4-42," *Mission Studies* 27 (2010), p. 164.
[73] Ibid. p. 307.
[74] Keener, *Spirit Hermeneutics*, p. 71.
[75] Ibid. p. 71.

families.[76] It was the duty of responsible men to protect and defend the honor of their women which reflected directly upon their own honor.[77]

The focus in the narrative is not the woman's presumed sinfulness or lack of virtue. Rather, the focus was the failure of the men in her life.[78] She had been disappointed, dishonored, and abandoned (whether widowed or divorced)[79] by these men who should have secured and defended her social identity and welfare. Instead, she was marginalized and excluded. But again, Jesus stepped into the barrenness of her situation and invited her to draw living water from him.

Holy and Unclean. The story's backdrop of ethnic, religious, political, and gender conflicts led to the ultimate question of who is worthy to worship God – who belongs to his people. Twice in the text, Jesus' actions provoked surprise (John 4:9, 27) as he crossed impenetrable divides to invite this Samaritan woman to be a true worshipper of the Father (John 4:21-24). For the first-century Jew, true worship of God required a clear distinction between the holy and the profane.[80] Because of the foregoing tensions, Samaritan women were considered pejoratively as unclean from birth.[81] Any association with the unclean would endanger one's purity and worthiness to worship. So, Jesus' actions in the story put him at risk of severe social disgrace. Purity regulations demanded that a person of Jesus' station should rigorously avoid anyone or anything with an inferior and unclean status.[82] Jesus is on very shaky ground in this story! Engaging with this woman, accepting water from her hand, could have endangered his purity.[83]

Their dialogue about worship may seem like an odd change of subject. However, the overarching concern of the narrative is about who belongs to the people of God. Paul Hertig comments that "Jesus' unconcern for the purity system of Judaism opens a radical new way of communication that leads to personal and social transformation."[84] Jesus' engagement with this

---

[76] Jacobus Kok, "Why (Suffering) Women Matter for the Heart of Transformative Missional Theology Perspectives on Empowered Women and Mission in the New Testament and Early Christianity," *HTS Teologiese Studies/Theological Studies* 72, no. 4 (2016), p. 2.

[77] Malina, *The New Testament World*, p. 47.

[78] Hertig, "The Powerful and Vulnerable," p. 308.

[79] Murray D. Gow, "Jesus and the Samaritan Woman," *Stimulus* 6, no. 1 (February 1998), p. 30.

[80] Kok, "Why (Suffering) Women Matter," p. 3.

[81] Ibid.

[82] Sadiq, "Jesus' Encounter with a Woman at a Well," p. 366.

[83] Ibid.

[84] Hertig, "The Powerful and Vulnerable," p. 306.

woman overcame centuries-old religious and cultural taboos[85] so that she may find the Messiah who redeems her as a worshipper of the Father in spirit and truth. Hertig continues:

> Jesus not only communicated across cultural boundaries, but he has also transported her across cultural boundaries into a new social location that sets her free. Jesus welcomes her into the domain of fictive-kinship and thus bestows upon her new honor and inclusiveness."[86]

Once excluded, she is now included! Jesus reversed the hardened "formless and empty" social and cultural divides that excluded the unclean and untouchable from the people of God.[87] The people of God will now be identified by the Messiah whose living water made the unclean accepted and welcome.[88] They become the new temple where God is present and worshipped in spirit and truth.

Movement 3: *Meditatio*

Mission is God's initiative from start to finish. It is not reserved for those who have a special calling or vocation.[89] God's people must be on mission because we are all called to serve, obey, and image our missionary God.[90] Samuel Escobar agrees, "Mission exists because God is a missionary God who sends his people to be a blessing to all of humankind... But mission begins in the heart of God, and it is his initiative to which we humans respond."[91] The *missio Dei* is God's unwavering intention to redeem the world.[92] The entire Bible, in fact, is a mission narrative – the story of God's redemptive actions throughout history, from creation to the fulfillment of his Kingdom in the end.[93]

---

[85] Kok, "Why (Suffering) Women Matter," p. 3.
[86] Hertig, "The Powerful and Vulnerable," p. 311.
[87] Sadiq, "Jesus' Encounter with a Woman at the Well," p. 366.
[88] Ibid.
[89] Padilla, "What is Integral Mission?"
[90] Hill, *GlobalChurch*, p. 31.
[91] Escobar, *The New Global Mission*, p. 94.
[92] Scott W. Sunquist, *Understanding Christian Mission: Participation in Suffering and Glory* (Grand Rapids: Baker Academic, 2013), p. 7.
[93] McConnell, *Cultural Insights for Christian Leaders*, p. 3.

Missiological Themes

The story of Jesus' encounter with the Samaritan woman at the well highlights five missiological themes that will shape our leadership-in-community: our Triune God, living water, temple, harvest, and transformation.

Our Triune God. First, we find that our Triune God – Father, Son, and Holy Spirit – is involved from start to finish in the woman's encounter with Jesus. This important truth reveals that the *missio Dei* begins with "the sending heart of the Triune God."[94] Throughout the Gospel of John, Jesus asserted that he was sent by the Father and that his words and actions follow from his Father.[95] He also promised that the Father and the Son will send the Holy Spirit to live in his followers, remind them of what he taught, and help them produce fruit.[96] The trinitarian nature of the *missio Dei* has profound implications for the ethos of our leadership-in-community. Missional leadership forges on in the context of loving relationships, first with God, and then with one another in mutuality, interdependence, and unity that reflects the glory of God in the world.[97] Escobar, reflecting on Luke 10:21-22, describes it this way:

> In these words of Jesus we see how a profound sense of mission is grounded in the assurance of a relationship with God as loving Father, and that such assurance comes with joy from the Holy Spirt. This is one of those passages of the Gospels that has both a missionary as well as a trinitarian thrust, because the biblical foundation of mission is trinitarian, which explains why great moments of missionary advance are born in the cradle of spiritual revival. When, by a special visitation of the Holy Spirit, Christians have a renewed sense of the majesty, power and love of God, the grace and compassion of Jesus Christ, and the renewing fire of the Holy Spirit, the outcome is the renewal of missionary vocation.[98]

As followers of Jesus Christ, we are members of a global community whose proclamation and demonstration of Jesus as Lord springs from the profoundly relational depth of a trinitarian *missio Dei.*

---

[94] Ibid. p. 2.
[95] See John 5:19-20, 30; 8:28, 12:49-50; 14:10. Phan, "An Interfaith Encounter," p. 165.
[96] See John 14:15-17, 25-26; 16:5-15. Ibid. p. 165-166.
[97] Scot McKnight, *The Blue Parakeet* 2nd ed. (Grand Rapids: Zondervan, 2018), p. 76-77.
[98] Escobar, *The New Global Mission*, p. 95.

Jesus told the Samaritan woman, "*I am* the Messiah" (John 4:26, italics added). With these words, Jesus resonated with the God who revealed himself in the Exodus: the "I am who I am" (Exodus 3:14) that delivered his people from slavery in Egypt, whose Presence stayed with them through the desert, and who led them on to the promised land. This same God crossed ethnic, cultural, political, and religious wastelands (the "formless and empty," the *tohu wabohu*) to welcome this woman into his Kingdom. And because we are citizens of that Kingdom, the mission of our Triune God also describes our identity and purpose.[99] To follow Jesus is to be on mission. Our mission is to embody the values of the Kingdom of God as witnesses to the grace and truth of Jesus Christ, the Word of God (John 1:16-18). He has empowered us by his Spirit to worship him in the desert wastelands of "no faith" in the hope that the "formless and empty" will be transformed into springs of living water under the good reign of God.[100]

Living Water. In the text, Jesus' mission was to offer living water to the woman so that she would become a true worshipper of the Father. Throughout the Scripture, water is a symbol of life, purification, abundance, and immortality.[101] The Psalms often used physical thirst as the picture of a spiritual longing for God's presence.[102] Jesus, in his vulnerability and need, asked the woman for a drink (John 4:7). In doing so, he rejected the religious and cultural social map that determined who was "in" or "out" from the blessings of God.[103] He had living water to offer her: "You don't know what God can give you. And you don't know who I am, the one who asked you for a drink. If you knew, you would have asked me, and I would have given you living water" (John 4:10).

The conversation that followed highlighted two places of deep spiritual thirst in the narrative: the personal life of the woman and the public worship of the people of God. These areas needed to be refreshed by God's presence. Jesus promised that this refreshment was coming:

> But the time is coming when the true worshippers will worship the Father in spirit and truth. In fact, that time is now here. And these are the kind of people the Father wants to be his worshipers. God is spirit.

---

[99] Hill, *GlobalChurch*, p. 31.
[100] Padilla, "What is Integral Mission?"
[101] Hertig, "The Powerful and Vulnerable," p. 307.
[102] See Ps. 42:2; 63:1; 143:6. Brown, "Water Imagery," p. 292.
[103] Ibid. p. 294.

So the people who worship him must worship in spirit and truth. (John 4:23-24)

This living water is the Holy Spirit living within his people and satisfying them with God's presence.[104] The prophet Amos had warned of a time of famine when people would not be thirsty for water but for the words of the Lord (Amos 8:11). But in his prologue, John signaled the reversal of this famine in the advent of the Word of God who John introduced as the "gift of God" that restored covenant relationship with God (John 1:12-18).[105] Jesus offers living water, not only to the woman, but to anyone who would ask him! He brings a new relationship with God through his Spirit living in us and transforming our spiritual thirst into true worship.

Temple. The place of appropriate worship weighs prominently in the conversation between Jesus and the Samaritan woman. The temple represented the place where God's presence lived with his people.[106] It was the place "where God meets God's people, where sacrifices for sin are offered, where forgiveness is obtained, and where God will hear the prayers of God's people."[107] The temple, along with Torah, was central to the Israel's identity and religious devotion.[108] N. T. Wright remarks that the Jerusalem temple was designed as a microcosm of the greater world which God intends to fill with his presence and glory.[109] However, it became a place of national pride and a symbol of God's exclusive favor upon Israel.

Even the temple's design reflected the distance between God and the Gentiles. They were only allowed into the Court of the Gentiles outside of the inner courts.[110] By the time of Jesus, the Court of the Gentiles was so empty of meaning that it was used for the convenience of moneychangers and vendors (Mark 11:15-17).[111] This place that was supposed to flourish as a "house of prayer for all the nations" was barren and fruitless – as fruitless as the fig tree Jesus cursed before he entered the temple and drove out the vendors (Mark 11:12-14).[112]

---

[104] DeSilva, *An Introduction to the New Testament*, p. 430.

[105] Brown, "Water Imagery," p. 294.

[106] N. T. Wright, *After You Believe: Why Christian Character Matters* (New York: HarperCollins Publishers, 2010), p. 83.

[107] DeSilva, *An Introduction to the New Testament*, p. 216.

[108] Ibid.

[109] Wright, *After You Believe*, p. 83.

[110] DeSilva, *An Introduction to the New Testament*, p. 216

[111] Ibid.

[112] Ibid.

In John's Gospel, Jesus represents himself as the new temple: "...Believe me when I say that you will all see heaven open. You will see 'angels of God going up and coming down' on the Son of Man'" (John 1:51). In this text, Jesus alluded to Jacob's dream of the angels ascending and descending on Bethel (which is Hebrew for "the house of God") and God's promise that Jacob would have many descendants by which "all the families on earth will be blessed..." (Gen. 28:10-14). Upon awakening, Jacob recognized that God was present in the place where he slept. He exclaimed that it is a "very great place. This is the house of God. This is the gate to heaven" (Gen. 28:16-17). In John, Jesus declared that he is that place! Jesus' mission is that all families on earth will be blessed. The temple was a sign of what God intended to do with the whole creation.[113] Now, that will be accomplished through Jesus.

In his conversation with the Samaritan woman, Jesus disarmed the longstanding feud between Jerusalem and Mt. Gerizim.[114] The conflict was now moot because only Jesus gives living water that wells up to eternal life (John 4:13-14). He explained the radical implications of this: the place of worship is wherever people worship God in spirit and truth (John 4:23-24)! Because God is Spirit, he cannot be confined to any place. Where God's Spirit lives is the place of God's presence. In the Last Supper Discourse, Jesus comforts his disciples with this promise:

> If you love me, you will do what I command. I will ask the Father, and he will give you another Helper to be with you forever. The Helper is the Spirit of truth. The people of the world cannot accept him, because they don't see him or know him. But you know him. He lives with you, and he will be in you. I will not leave you all alone like orphans. I will come back to you.
>
> In a very short time the people in the world will not see me anymore. But you will see me. You will live because I live. On that day you will know that I am in the Father. You will know that you are in me and I am in you. Those who really love me are the ones who not only know my commands but also obey them. My Father will love such people, and I will love them. I will make myself known to them. (John 14:15-21)

---

[113] Wright, *After You Believe*, p. 84.
[114] DeSilva, *An Introduction to the New Testament*, p. 421.

The Psalmist asked, "Where can I go from your Spirit? Where can I flee from your presence?" (Psalm 139:7, NIV). Jesus' unequivocal answer is nowhere! Wherever God's Spirit lives *in his people*, that is the holy place – the place of deep encounter with God.[115]

Harvest. After his disciples returned to him, Jesus reflected upon his conversation with the woman by referencing two proverbs about harvest (John 4:34-38). Harvest is a significant missiological theme. Most likely, Jesus was referring to the Jewish harvest festival, *Shavuot*, which foreshadowed the outpouring of God's spirit at Pentecost (Acts 2). At *Shavuot*, two wheat loaves were brought into the temple and waved before God as a sign that the firstfruits of the wheat harvest belonged to God.[116] The firstfruits were presented as two baked loaves with leaven.[117] According to Mike Moore, baked loaves with leaven were a picture of the incorporation of both Jews and Gentile believers into the people of God through Christ.[118]

The harvest signaled the hope of the fuller harvest – the ingathering of people from all over the world into God's Kingdom.[119] In that light, Jesus made an extraordinary claim: the fields were ready for harvest (John 4:35)! The time had come when the "true worshippers will worship the Father in spirit and truth" (John 4:23)! Even many Samaritans in the town believed in Jesus because of the Samaritan woman's testimony (John 4:39).

The *missio Dei* heralds that the Spirit of God is already at work in the world, across the desert wastelands, planting and sowing the seeds of faith.[120] Even before we set foot out the door, the Father is *actively* seeking people to worship him in spirit and truth (John 4:23, NIV). The followers of Jesus on mission will reap where God's Spirit has already sown.[121] And this is cause for both celebration and confidence to go as he sends us. Graham Hill explains that Christianity is a religion of hope:

> God compels the church to work toward the final reconciliation and restoration of all things. The eschatological kingdom shapes our theology, social ethics, mission, community, reconciliation, and justice. It forms our desire for the new humanity in Christ, and our efforts

[115] Ibid.
[116] Mike Moore, "Pentecost and the Plan of God," *The Reformed Theological Review* 72, no. 3 (December 2013), p. 182.
[117] Ibid.
[118] Ibid.
[119] Ibid. p. 183.
[120] Phan, "An Interfaith Encounter," p. 170
[121] Ibid. p. 171.

toward peace and reconciliation. We need to root our theology in practices of compassion, forgiveness, grace, and love, *as a response to eschatological hope*. We need to relinquish self-centeredness and embrace generosity, compassion, and forgiveness. We do this to show the inaugurated, but not yet consummated, kingdom of God.[122]

The *missio Dei* leads us, as followers of King Jesus in whom his Spirit lives, across the boundaries from faith into the places of "no faith" where the "formless and empty" exists. And as we go, we go in the hope that the harvest is ready (John 4:35).

Transformation. The ultimate hope, or *telos*, of the *missio Dei* is a new creation in which we participate in the "glorious rule and reign of Christ, as he restores all creation, makes all things new through and according to his glory."[123] The Good News of Jesus is not only about our personal salvation as God deals with our sin and pain.[124] It moves us beyond conversion and into a glorious life adventure of the *missio Dei!* Our King Jesus calls us to participate in God's cosmic work of reconciliation that restores the entire creation under the good reign of God.[125]

Jesus told the Samaritan woman, "I am the Messiah" (John 4:26). He is the giver of living water, the fulfillment of the Jerusalem temple, and the hope of the final harvest. Through his reign as Messiah, God restores the wholeness and fruitfulness, or in Hebrew, the *shalôm* of the world he created. Cornelius Plantinga expresses so beautifully what *shalôm* means for our mission:

> The webbing together of God, humans, and all creation in justice, fulfillment, and delight is what the Hebrew prophets call *shalom*. We call it peace, but it means far more than mere peace of mind or a cease-fire between enemies. In the Bible, *shalom* means *universal flourishing, wholeness and delight* – a rich state of affairs in which natural needs are satisfied and natural gifts fruitfully employed, a state of affairs that inspires joyful wonder as its Creator and Savior opens doors and

---

[122] Graham Hill, *Salt, Light, and a City: Ecclesiology for the Global Missional Community, Volume 1: Western Voices* 2nd ed. (Eugene: Cascade Books, 2017), p. 7-8.

[123] Graham Hill, *Salt, Light, and a City: Conformation – Ecclesiology for the Global Missional Community, Volume 2: Majority World Voices* 2nd ed. (Eugene: Cascade Books, 2020), p. 164.

[124] Ibid. p. 164.

[125] Ibid.

welcomes the creatures in whom he delights. Shalom, in other words, is the way things ought to be.[126]

Transformation is the goal of God's mission! We want the living water of God to spring up into eternal life and true worship in the barren wastelands of our broken world. We long for the *shalôm* of restored fellowship between God, people, and the creation.[127] And we hope for the renewal of God's image – the *imago Dei* – through whom that transformation happens. We will explore that theme in the next chapter.

Movement 4: *Oratio*

Heavenly Father,

> Create in me each day a clean heart and renew my attitudes and priorities.

> Keep me in your presence and preserve my soul with your Holy Spirit.

> Restore in me a daily gratitude for new life in God, and that moment when I first understood that I belonged to you.

> That's what the Psalmist prayed many centuries ago (Psalm 51), and it's the cry of my heart today.

> It's also the cry of all who follow you, and I join my prayer to theirs.

> We are yours, Lord. Shape our affections and loyalties to reflect and honor our higher calling in the world.

> On this road of repentance, make us true disciples and heralds of the good news of your kingdom.

> Thank you that I can come to you in full assurance of faith.

> Thank you for hearing and answering the cry of my heart.[128]

---

126 Cornelius Plantinga, *Not the Way It's Supposed to Be: A Breviary of Sin* (Grand Rapids: William B. Eerdmans Publishing Company, 1996), p. 160.

127 Hill, *Salt, Light, and a City: Volume 2*, p. 5.

128 Prayer adapted from the ancient spiritual practice of the Prayer Wheel. Patton Dodd, Jana Riess, & David Van Biema, *The Prayer Wheel: A Daily Guide to Renewing Your Faith with a Rediscovered Spiritual Practice* (New York: Convergent Books. 2018), p. 41.

In Jesus' name, Amen.

Movement 5: *Imitatio*

- Individual Reflection
  - Journal your responses to the following questions:
    - What key points of the *missio Dei* is God leading you to embrace and grow into?
    - How can you live this out in your life and leadership?
    - How can your missional leadership group pray for you in living this out?

- Group Reflection
  - In your missional leadership group, share your individual reflections with each other.
  - Pray for one another.

Movement 6: *Missio*

- Experiencing Mission
  - Level 1 *Awareness*
    - Pray each day that the Lord sends you into his mission that day.
    - At the end of each day, reflect on or journal about one experience you had that day where you witnessed the *missio Dei* personally. Describe what happened. What was significant about that experience for you?

  - Level 2 *Personal Commitment*
    - Ask the Lord where he may be sending you to be his witness on a regular basis.
    - Make a commitment to serve in that way.

Movement 7: *Communio*

- Experiencing Mission
  - Level 3 *Group Experience*

- If possible, the small group may consider performing a mission or service project together to experience mission as a community.

✛ Group Reflection

- o Where did you see the *missio Dei* in action this past week?

- o What were the most significant or surprising observations you made about your experience?

- o What did you learn about God from that experience? What did you learn about yourself from that experience?

- o What difference does that make in your leadership? How will you apply what you have learned?

Movement 8: *Contemplatio*

Each week in your small group, spend time celebrating how your group has seen "God on the move" in the past week.

✛ Spend some time in prayer or singing in thanksgiving and praise to our missionary God.

Chapter 2

Imago Dei

In the 1999 Academy Award-winning film, *The Matrix*,[1] a programmer named Thomas Anderson, alias "Neo," is a computer hacker who suspects that the world in which he lives is an illusion. He meets a mysterious person named Morpheus who offers him the truth. But the choice is Neo's: he can take the red pill which reveals the truth, or he can take the blue pill and return to life as he knows it. Neo chooses the red pill and awakens to find himself attached to a machine as his reality dissolves into a dystopian world. This world is controlled by intelligent machines who use human bioelectricity as their energy source. The machines pacify their human captives with a simulated reality called the Matrix. Morpheus' freedom fighters rescue Neo from the machine and Neo joins their resistance. Their mission is to save others from the Matrix and recruit them into battle. But they are in constant danger from the Sentinels – powerful programs sent to destroy any threat to the system. The resistance risks everything to free enslaved people from the Matrix and bring them to the city of Zion, the last refuge of free humans.

As the story unfolds, we discover that Neo is "the One" who was prophesied to finally free humanity and end the war. In the climax of the movie, Neo enters the Matrix to save Morpheus who has been betrayed and captured by the Sentinels. However, Neo is ambushed and killed by Agent Smith, his main antagonist in the film. But Neo is "resurrected" by Trinity who declares her love for him and kisses him. He arises with new power to overcome the Matrix. He defeats Agent Smith and disables the Sentinels. In the final scene, Neo makes a call from within the Matrix to the machines vowing that he will "show their prisoners a world where anything is possible." He hangs up and flies into the sky.

When we read the opening chapter of Genesis, we find the Spirit of God moving like a storm over the unformed world as we anticipate the creative drama about to unfold (Gen. 1:2). Then, with such intimacy, the Creator speaks and the world that was "without life and not yet useful for anything" (Gen. 1:2) becomes a habitable place where life can develop and grow (Gen. 1:3-31).[2] Contrary to other ancient Near Eastern creation myths, the story in Genesis 1 depicts no conflict between warring deities in the creation of the world.[3] Rather, we find that the Creator lovingly, and almost effortlessly, speaks over the "formless and empty" earth (Gen. 1:2, NIV) and

---

[1] *The Matrix*. Written & Directed by The Wachowskis. Burbank: Warner Bros. Pictures, 1999.
[2] Andreas Schuele, "Uniquely Human: The Ethics of the *Imago Dei* in Genesis 1-11," *Toronto Journal of Theology* 27, no 1. (2011), p. 13.
[3] Crouch, *Culture Making*, p. 21.

creates an ordered and purposeful creation.[4] As we learned in the last chapter, the "formless and empty" (Hebrew *tohu wabohu*) denotes chaos, futility, and a trackless wasteland.[5] But as God's creative word is spoken, the formless and empty comes to life! Andy Crouch states, "The first chapter of Genesis records a series of divisions – order from chaos, light from darkness, heaven from earth, sea from land – each of which makes the world more amenable for the flourishing of creativity."[6] The world as it should be is a world of remarkable possibilities.

Genesis presents God as both the Creator and Ruler of the well-ordered cosmos he created.[7] He made new things out of nothing and assigned everything he made its value, place, and meaning.[8] But on the sixth day, he created the humans "in his own image" (Gen. 1:27, NIV) and instructed them to rule over the earth and all that live in it (Gen. 1:28). Volumes have been written about the meaning of "in his own image." But, in the light of God's creative activity, the phrase suggests that the vocation of the humans is to continue to shape the world God made with creativity.[9] They are regents of the Creator God who commissioned them to expand his good rule over the cosmos.[10] N. T. Wright describes it this way:

> Creation, it seems, was not a tableau, a static scene. It was designed as a *project*, created in order to go somewhere. The creator has a future in mind for it; and Human – this strange creature, full of mystery and glory – is the means by which the creator is going to take his project forward. The garden, and all the living creatures, plants and animals, within it, are designed to become what they were meant to be through the work of God's image-bearing creature in their midst. The point of the project is that the garden be extended, colonizing the rest of creation; and Human is the creature put in charge of that plan. Human is thus a kind of midway creature: reflecting God into the world, and reflecting the world back to God. That is the basis for the "truly human" vocation.[11]

---

[4] Ibid. p. 21.
[5] Derek Kidner, *Genesis: An Introduction and Commentary* (Downers Grove: IVP Academic, 1967), p. 48. Kindle.
[6] Ibid.
[7] Ibid.
[8] Ibid. p. 51.
[9] Crouch, *Culture Making*, p. 21-22.
[10] Ibid.
[11] Wright, *After You Believe*, p. 74-75.

What Wright describes as the human vocation is a *priestly* role: reflecting God into the world by ruling and cultivating and reflecting the world back to God in worship.[12] It is as if the cosmos is a temple in which God draws near and makes himself known to his creation. And the humans are God's priests in that temple. They interface between him and his creation, advancing his wise and generous rule in the world while also articulating the creation's grateful praise back to its Creator.[13] Through the spread of human life, the entire cosmos will become increasingly a place of stability, order, and amazing possibilities.[14]

But something went wrong! In Genesis 3, we read that the humans disobeyed the God whose image they were meant to reflect in their ruling and creating. Now, the creation rebels against them (Gen 3:17-20).[15] The tragedy of their disobedience was their attempt to be self-made, to know about "good and evil" and become "like God" (Gen. 3:4).[16] Hereafter, they would *take* their knowledge, satisfaction, and values from the world rather than *receive* them graciously from God.[17] They were designed to draw the nutrients of their lives from God, but now they would seek them from the "limited space of the world, and so succumb to greed and passion and wrath..."[18] The primordial "formless and empty" still lurks in this world with the potential to threaten the flourishing life God intended for his creation.[19] This darkness creeps in to veil the existence and the good reign of God over the cosmos meant to be filled with purpose and meaning.

The image of God, the *imago Dei*, is the primary means by which God advances his *missio Dei*. Through the priestly rule of humans, renewed in the image of Christ, the cosmos can once again display the glory of its good Creator and King.

---

[12] Ibid. p. 78.

[13] Ibid. p. 80-81.

[14] Schuele, "Uniquely Human," p. 14.

[15] David H. Johnson, "The Image of God in Colossians," *Didaskalia (Otterburne, Man.)* 3, no. 2 (1992), p. 10.

[16] Kidner, *Genesis*, p. 68.

[17] Ibid.

[18] Casey Thornburgh Sigmon, "Homiletical Possibilities and Challenges in Colossians," *Review and Expositor* 116, no. 4 (2019), p. 459.

[19] Schuele, "Uniquely Human," p. 13.

Movement 1: *Adspecto*

Prayer

✦ Pray for the Holy Spirit to speak to you through the Scripture. Use the following words of Psalm 84 as a prayer:

> *LORD All-Powerful, the place where you live is so beautiful!*
> *LORD, I cannot wait to enter your Temple.*
> *I am so excited!*
> *Every part of me cries out to be with the Living God.*
> *LORD All-Powerful, my King, my God, even the birds have found a home in your Temple.*
>
> *They make their nests near your altar, and there they have their babies.*
> *Great blessings belong to those who live at your Temple!*
> *They continue to praise you.*
>   *Selah*
>
> *Great blessings belong to those who depend on you for strength!*
> *Their heart's desire is to make the trip to your Temple.*
> *They travel through the Baca Valley,[20] which God has made into a place of springs.*
>
> *Autumn rains form pools of water there.*
> *The people travel from town to town on their way to Zion, where they will meet with God.*
>
> *LORD God All-Powerful, listen to my prayer.*
> *God of Jacob, listen to me.*
>   *Selah*
>
> *God, watch over the king, our protector.*
> *Be kind to him, the one you have chosen.*
> *One day in your Temple is better than a thousand days anywhere else.*
> *Serving as a guard at the gate of my God's house is better than living in the homes of the wicked.*

---

[20] The Baca Valley was a place near Jerusalem that may have been lined with tombs and was traditionally rendered as a "valley of weeping." It was a dry place. "Baca, Valley Of," In *New Bible Dictionary* 2nd ed., Eds. J. D. Douglas, F. F. Bruce, J. I. Packer, N. Hillyer, D. Guthrie, A. R. Millard, & D. J. Wiseman (Downers Grove, InterVarsity Press, 1962), p. 119.

The LORD God is our protector and glorious king.
He blesses us with kindness and honor.
The LORD freely gives every good thing to those who do what is right.
LORD All-Powerful, great blessings belong to those who trust in you!

Scripture Reading

✦ **Read Colossians 3:1-17.** Listen for words or phrases from the passage that stand out to you.

Your New Life

¹You were raised from death with Christ. So live for what is in heaven, where Christ is sitting at the right hand of God. ²Think only about what is up there, not what is here on earth. ³Your old self has died, and your new life is kept with Christ in God. ⁴Yes, Christ is now your life, and when he comes again, you will share in his glory.

⁵So put everything evil out of your life: sexual sin, doing anything immoral, letting sinful thoughts control you, and wanting things that are wrong. And don't keep wanting more and more for yourself, which is the same as worshiping a false god. ⁶God will show his anger against those who don't obey him, because they do these evil things. ⁷You also did these things in the past, when you lived like them.

⁸But now put these things out of your life: anger, losing your temper, doing or saying things to hurt others, and saying shameful things. ⁹Don't lie to each other. You have taken off those old clothes—the person you once were and the bad things you did then. ¹⁰Now you are wearing a new life, a life that is new every day. You are growing in your understanding of the one who made you. You are becoming more and more like him. ¹¹In this new life it doesn't matter if you are a Greek or a Jew, circumcised or not. It doesn't matter if you speak a different language or even if you are a Scythian. It doesn't matter if you are a slave or free. Christ is all that matters, and he is in all of you.

Your New Life With Each Other

¹²God has chosen you and made you his holy people. He loves you. So your new life should be like this: Show mercy to others. Be kind, humble, gentle, and patient. ¹³Don't be angry with each other, but forgive each other. If you feel someone has wronged you, forgive them. Forgive others because the

Lord forgave you. ¹⁴Together with these things, the most important part of your new life is to love each other. Love is what holds everything together in perfect unity. ¹⁵Let the peace that Christ gives control your thinking. It is for peace that you were chosen to be together in one body. And always be thankful.

¹⁶Let the teaching of Christ live inside you richly. Use all wisdom to teach and counsel each other. Sing psalms, hymns, and spiritual songs with thankfulness in your hearts to God. ¹⁷Everything you say and everything you do should be done for Jesus your Lord. And in all you do, give thanks to God the Father through Jesus.

Reflection

- When you have finished reading, remain silent for one or two minutes.
- Read the entire passage again. If you have an audio Bible, listen through the passage.
  - *Personal Reflection:* Journal your thoughts on the following questions:
    - What words or phrases from the passage stand out to you?
    - How do these words or phrases connect with your life right now?
    - How might God be inviting you to respond to this passage?

Movement 2: *Lectio*

Scripture Study

- Read or listen to **Colossians 3:1-17**.

- Answer the following study questions:

  1. What does the Scripture say about the believers' lives (vs. 1-4)?

  2. What do you think it means to live for what is in heaven (vs. 1)?

  3. Why should we think only about "what is up there, not what is here on earth (vs. 2)?

  4. Where is our new life kept (vs. 3)?

5. What do you think it means that we will "share in his glory" (vs. 4)?

6. What are the things that we are to put out of our lives (vs. 5-9)?

7. Paul uses the imagery of clothing (vs. 9-10). Why is that a fitting image for the point Paul is trying to make?

8. What does Paul say we are growing in our understanding of (vs. 10)?

9. What do you think that means? What difference does it make for you?

10. What does the new life look like in the community of believers (vs. 11)?

11. In what ways do you think you could reflect that new life in your church or community?

12. What has God done for us (vs. 12)?

13. As you consider what God has done for his people, how do you respond? What is surprising, comforting, challenging, or encouraging about that truth for you?

14. What should our new life look like (vs. 12-17)?

15. Reflect upon your missional community: How can this new life continue to emerge in your leadership-in-community?

16. What are action steps your community can take to strengthen or grow deeper into that new life?

Reading
What is the Imago Dei?

When the Triune God created the man and woman, he gave them a calling distinct from the other creatures. God's command to the man and the woman, called the Cultural Mandate, anticipated that God's redemptive mission, the *missio Dei*, will be carried out through his image bearers:[21]

> So God created humans in his own image. He created them to be like himself. He created them male and female. God blessed them and said to them, "Have many children. Fill the earth and take control of it.

---

[21] McConnell, *Cultural Insights for Christian Leaders*, p. 3.

55

Rule over the fish in the sea and the birds in the air. Rule over every living thing that moves on the earth. (Gen. 1:27-28)

As God's creative regents, the humans' mission is to extend the reign of God over the entire cosmos, pushing back the "formless and empty" that threatens to make it a barren wasteland. The Cultural Mandate features three themes regarding the purpose of the *imago Dei*: worship, work, and rest. Together, these themes increase human flourishing. As humans flourish through worship, work, and rest, they advance the good reign of God throughout the cosmos!

Worship. The *imago Dei* reflects God to the world and the world back to God.[22] After the first five days of creation in the Genesis 1 account, the phrasing of "let there be…" or "let the…" made a notable change on the sixth day to "let *us* make" (Gen. 1:26). When we read that new phrase, we sense that it reveals something profoundly unique about the creation of humans. They were created within a context of relationship. There is a trinitarian conception in the creation and calling of humans! The *imago Dei* is rooted in trinitarian theology.[23] God created humans out of the depth of intimate communion existing between the three persons of the Trinity – Father, Son, and Holy Spirit.[24] Because of this, humans have a unique capacity to relate to God, others, and the world.

In the ancient world, people were not considered autonomous from the networks of relationships in which they lived.[25] They were "images" of their parents, families, tribes, villages, or other primary communities.[26] Their responsibility was to live out the values, behaviors, and ethics that "imaged" respectably upon their community and its leaders.[27] God intended his image-bearers to live in fruitful relationships with himself, other humans, and the creation. But even more, he endowed them with the creative capacity to shape those networks of relationships so that they image him as a loving and creative ruler in the world.[28] In fact, the Genesis text explicitly expresses for humans what is presumed for the other creatures – that they were created as male and female (Gen. 1:27). Andreas Schuele believes that human gender

---

[22] Wright, *After You Believe*, p. 14.
[23] Jessica Joustra, "An Embodied *Imago Dei*," *Journal of Reformed Theology* 11 (2017), p. 12.
[24] Johnson, "The Image of God in Colossians," p. 10.
[25] Schuele, "Uniquely Human," p. 10.
[26] Ibid. p. 10-11.
[27] Malina, *The New Testament World*, p. 58-59.
[28] Schuele, "Uniquely Human," p. 10.

differences function beyond mere reproduction or maintenance of the human species.[29] Humans are meant to live in such harmonic and fruitful relationships with each other that, through their multiplication, they extend the peaceful rule of God throughout the cosmos (Gen. 1:28).[30]

Work. An important priestly function of the *imago Dei* is to create cultures, which involves both relationships and context. Humans shape their networks of relationships within their contexts so that they may rule the earth as regents of the God they image. Humans rule by cultivating the earth, like gardeners tilling the soil to produce fruit.[31] They take the raw material of the earth and tend, care for, and shape it into new possibilities.[32] Crouch defines culture-making as "what we make of the world."[33] He says:

> And those who are made in [God's] image will also be both creators and rulers. They will have a unique capacity to create – perhaps not to call something out of nothing in quite the way that God does in Genesis 1:1, but to reshape what exists into something genuinely new. And they will have a responsibility to care for what God has made…. They will sort out the cultivated from the wild.[34]

While the earth God created was "very good" (Gen. 1: 31), it was not finished. God made it with a raw potential for humans to cultivate for growth and development.[35] Abraham Kuyper said, "The whole creation is nothing but the visible curtain behind which radiates the exalted working of [God's] divine thinking."[36] He articulated that the human vocation to rule the earth is the culture-creative process of unlocking from the world the "thoughts of God" and reflecting them back to God in worship.[37]

This means that culture making is more than merely "making stuff." Culture making gives meaning to the world in which we live. In other words, humans give meaning to the world when they make something of it.[38] Kuyper

---

[29] Ibid.

[30] Ibid. p 12.

[31] Crouch, *Culture Making*, p. 96.

[32] Ibid. p. 35.

[33] Ibid. p. 23.

[34] Ibid. p. 22.

[35] Ben Witherington III, *Work: A Kingdom Perspective of Labor* (Grand Rapids: William B. Eerdmans Publishing Company, 2011), p. 2-3.

[36] Abraham Kuyper, *Wisdom & Wonder: Common Grace in Science & Art* (Grand Rapids: Christian's Library Press, 2011), p. 39.

[37] Ibid.

[38] Crouch, *Culture Making*, p. 24.

states this beautifully: "…in the creation God has revealed, embedded, and embodied a rich fullness of his thoughts…. God created in human beings, as his image-bearers, the capacity to understand, to grasp, to reflect, and to arrange within a totality these thoughts expressed in creation."[39]

The human capacity to create meaning, otherwise called "sensemaking," is a uniquely relational dynamic within a community of people. According to organizational culture expert Edgar H. Schein, culture is the "accumulated shared learning of a group" as the group interacts with the world in which it lives and adapts to it with new perceptions, thoughts, feelings, customs, and behaviors.[40] In the context of Genesis 1, this means that the embodied nature of the *imago Dei* is good and purposeful. Humans need relationships and physical contexts to exercise their priestly calling as God's image-bearers.[41] Physical and relational contexts establish the boundaries of formative spaces in which humans can make sense of the world they inhabit by creating cultures within them.[42]

Rest. The beginning of Genesis 2 points to the goal (or in Greek, the *telos*) of the worship and work of the *imago Dei*:

> So the earth, the sky, and everything in them were finished. God finished the work he was doing, so on the seventh day he rested from his work. God blessed the seventh day and made it a holy day. He made it special because on that day he rested from all the work he did while creating the world. (Gen. 2:1-3)

The worship and work of the *imago Dei* moves forward with vision and in anticipation of its fulfillment in the rest of God. James K. A. Smith argues, "To be human is to be *for* something, directed toward something, oriented toward something. To be human is to be on the move, pursuing something, *after* something."[43] In this spirit, Smith believes that we are oriented primarily by love – what we desire, what we treasure.[44] The ultimate hope of the image of God is God himself. We were created out of the intimate love of our triune God. And so, our work and worship aim toward our fulfillment in him (Heb. 4:1-7). We long for *shalôm*, that through our worship and work, the world we

---

[39] Kuyper, *Wisdom & Wonder*, p. 41-42.
[40] Edgar H. Schein with Peter Schein, *Organizational Culture and Leadership* 5th ed. (Hoboken: John Wiley & Sons, Inc., 2017), p. 6.
[41] Joustra, "An Embodied *Imago Dei*," p. 17.
[42] Schuele, "Uniquely Human," p. 11-12.
[43] Smith, *You Are What You Love*, p. 8.
[44] Ibid. p. 8-9.

rule as God's image-bearers becomes the place where all creation flourishes in God's presence.[45]

Paul continues the theme of the *imago Dei* in his letter to the Colossians. He reminded the Christians of Colossae that "God has made us free from the power of darkness. And he brought us into the kingdom of his dear Son" (Col. 1:13). As in *The Matrix*, we have been rescued from a spiritual darkness that hides the glorious reality of the Kingdom of God breaking into the cosmos. This Kingdom is led by Jesus Christ, the image of the invisible God (Col. 1:15). He "paid the price to make us free" from the sin and darkness that distorts his image in us and frustrates our longing for his rest (Col. 1:14). Paul wanted us to remember that Jesus is exalted over the cosmos, despite what we experience around or inside us. He invites us to let that truth transform our lives and relationships so that we may honor him once again as his image bearers (Col. 1:9-10).[46]

Colossae and the Roman Empire

To understand Paul's vision of the *imago Dei* in his letter to the Colossian Christians, we must consider the context of Colossae in which Paul wrote. After the last king of Pergamum bequeathed his kingdom to the Romans in 133 BCE, Colossae and the Lycus river valley became a hub for east-west transportation in the Roman empire.[47] Consequently, the Lycus valley was a melting pot of religions, philosophies, and cultic practices.[48] Various regional cults occupied Colossae: Isis, Sarapis, Mithras, Demeter, Helios (the sun), Selene (the moon), Artemis (the Greek goddess of wild animals, the hunt, chastity, and childbearing), and the local Phrygian religion of Men Karou (a cult of the moon god).[49] These cultic practices involved the worship of astral bodies (the sun and the moon) and the four elements (fire, water, earth, and air).[50] They also included worship of the gods they believed promised to satisfy the human need for food, health, pleasure, and nature.[51] Colossae was the center for the cult of Cybele, the mother goddess, which

---

[45] Miroslav Volf & Matthew Croasmun, *For the Life of the World: Theology That Makes a Difference* (Grand Rapids: Brazos Press, 2019), p. 11.

[46] DeSilva, *An Introduction to the New Testament*, p. 690.

[47] Wright & Bird, *The New Testament in Its World*, p. 456.

[48] Ibid. p. 456-457.

[49] Ibid. p. 691.

[50] Ibid.

[51] Ibid. p. 457.

included fertility rites, ascetic practices, and ritual mutilation.[52] Anthropologists also believe that Zeus was the patron deity of Colossae because they discovered there many cultic hymns to Zeus composed by ancient poets.[53] As we will see, Paul seems to have alluded to many of these local influences in his letter to the Colossians.

A sizeable Jewish community also lived in the Lycus valley because the Greek ruler Antiochus III relocated many Jews here from Babylon around 200 BCE.[54] Scholars believe that, by the time Paul's letter to the Colossians was written, the majority of Jews in the region were fully Hellenized having combined their religious practices with the local cultic customs and cultures around them.[55] With such a proliferation of religions and idolatries surrounding it, the small Colossian church had to be vigilant against these ideas and practices creeping into their lives.

Furthermore, the presence of the Roman Empire was felt everywhere. Its symbols and images of Caesar adorned the markets, city squares, public baths, theaters, temples, houses, and even clothing.[56] The Christians of Colossae were confronted daily by the reality of the Rome's dominance.[57] And this empire did not suffer disloyalty and sedition! All were expected to worship Caesar as the divine lord of the empire. He was the "father supreme" within a centralized patriarchal power structure that served to secure his rule and authority over everything.[58] The economic and military power of Rome was legitimized by the powerful myth of the *Pax Romana* that praised the rule of Caesar as the hope of peace, prosperity, and human flourishing.[59] A regular cadence of public festivals and thanksgiving feasts reinforced this myth in celebration of Rome's victory over its enemies and the blessings of the gods.[60] The Romans sang hymns to reinforce the cultural, political, and religious values of the emperor and his *Pax Romana*.[61] This is a significant background

---

[52] DeSilva, *An Introduction to the New Testament*, p. 690.

[53] James R. McConnell, "Colossians: Background and Contexts," *Review and Expositor* 116, no. 4 (2019), p. 401.

[54] DeSilva, *An Introduction to the New Testament*, p. 691.

[55] Ibid. p. 691.

[56] Brian J. Walsh & Sylvia C. Keesmaat, *Colossians Remixed: Subverting the Empire* (Downers Grove: IVP Academic, 2004), p. 63.

[57] Ibid. p. 58.

[58] Ibid. p. 59.

[59] Ibid. p. 61.

[60] Ibid. p. 61-62.

[61] Mark S. Medley, "Subversive Song: Imagining Colossians 1:15-20 as a Social Protest Hymn in the Context of the Roman Empire," *Review and Expositor* 116, no. 4 (2019), p. 428.

to Paul's letter because Paul repurposes these imperial themes to laud the rule and reign of Christ.

In the swirl of ideologies, idolatries, and deities around them, the Colossian believers apparently began to doubt the sufficiency of Christ.[62] They were influenced by "those who have nothing worth saying and only plan to deceive [them]" (Col. 2:8). They began to embrace empty philosophies that promoted asceticism, feasts, holy days, and the worship of angels as the gateway into ecstatic experiences that falsely claimed to reveal knowledge about the mysteries of God (Col. 2:16-23).[63] These practices emerged from Jewish traditions syncretized with the pagan philosophies predominant at the time.[64] Greek philosophy supported the idea that the cosmos was made up of three realms: the upper air, the physical world, and the atmosphere between them.[65] The upper air contained astral deities (the sun, moon, and stars) that they believed controlled human destiny.[66] The atmosphere between the physical world and the upper air was filled with powerful spirits, such as angels (Col. 2:18) and the "powers that influence this world" (Col. 2:20).[67] People were required to venerate these spirits in order to pass into the "fullness" of the divine realms.[68] And so they tried to keep their souls pure through ascetic practices and ritual cleaning.[69]

Paul was eager to protect the fledgling church in Colossae from these destructive ideas. He knew that the believers needed to have a solid grounding in Jesus Christ so that they would not be seduced by the spiritually charged environment around them:

> You accepted Christ Jesus as Lord, so continue to live following him. You must depend on Christ only, drawing life and strength from him. Just as you were taught the truth, continue to grow stronger in your understanding of it. And never stop giving thanks to God. (Col. 2:6-7)

---

[62] Marianne Meye Thompson, *Colossians & Philemon* (Grand Rapids: William B. Eerdmans Publishing Company, 2005), p. 8.

[63] Ibid. p. 7.

[64] Ibid. p. 7-8.

[65] DeSilva, *An Introduction to the New Testament,* p. 693.

[66] Ibid.

[67] Ibid.

[68] Ibid.

[69] Ibid.

In his letter, Paul expressed persuasively that Jesus Christ is the center of God's activity in the world.[70] He explained that Jesus is superior to every other power and authority and that he is sufficient for the fullness of life God intends for his people.[71] Ironically, Paul did so by use of the poetic form typically reserved for the public exaltation of the greatness of Caesar or the gods! However, in his hymn of worship, Paul praises Jesus Christ, *the* image of God, who is superior to all other lords and rules over everything.

The Son of God is the Same as God

[15]No one can see God,
  but the Son is exactly like God.
  He rules over everything that has been made.
[16]Through his power all things were made:
  things in heaven and on earth, seen and not seen—
  all spiritual rulers, lords, powers, and authorities.
  Everything was made through him and for him.

[17]The Son was there before anything was made.
  And all things continue because of him.
[18]He is the head of the body, which is the church.
  He is the beginning of everything else.
And he is the first among all who will be raised from death.
  So in everything he is most important.

[19]God was pleased for all of himself to live in the Son.
  [20]And through him, God was happy to bring all things back to
    himself again—
  things on earth and things in heaven.
God made peace by using the blood sacrifice of his Son on the cross.
  (Col. 1:15-20)

A Subversive Hymn: Colossians 1:15-20

Alasdair MacIntyre famously said, "I can only answer the question 'What am I to do?' if I can answer the prior question 'Of what story or stories

---

[70] Ben C. Blackwell, "You Are Filled in Him: Theosis and Colossians 2-3," *Journal of Theological Interpretation* 8, no. 1 (2014), p. 118.
[71] N. T. Wright, *Paul for Everyone: The Prison Letters* (Louisville: Westminster John Knox Press, 2004), p. 147, 150.

do I find myself a part?'"[72] We are meant to live out a story to tell. We intend for our lives to move in a meaningful direction, like an unfolding plotline. And so, we create ways-of-being that we believe will advance those stories.[73] In this vein, Smith describes humans as *teleological* creatures:

> We are the sorts of [creatures] whose love is aimed at different ends or goals (Greek: *teloi*). As intentional, love always has a target, something that it intends or aims at. So as we inhabit the world primarily in a noncognitive, affective mode of intentionality, implicit in that love is an end, or *telos*. In other words, what we love is a specific vision of the good life, an implicit picture of what we think human flourishing looks like. Such a picture of human flourishing will have all sorts of components: implicit in it will be assumptions about what good relationships look like, what a just economy and distribution of resources look like, what sorts of recreation and play we value, how we ought to relate to nature and the nonhuman environment, what sorts of work count as good work, what flourishing families look like, and much more… *Our ultimate love is oriented by and to a picture of what we think it looks like for us to live well, and that picture then governs, shapes, and motivates our decisions and actions.*[74]

In a *Matrix* world where we are lulled and seduced by competing stories of the good life, we must continually remember and rehearse the stories that we most desire to live. Smith continues, "…we are, ultimately, *liturgical* [creatures] because we are fundamentally desiring creatures. We are what we love, and our love is shaped, primed, and aimed by liturgical practices that take hold of our gut and aim our heart to certain ends."[75] In Colossians 1:15-20, Paul gave the Colossians a beautiful liturgical hymn which they could sing and teach to one another (Col. 3:16) so that their hearts and minds would be continually shaped by the story of Jesus. Paul's purpose in Colossians was to shape the collective imagination of the Christian community, both in Colossae and in us today.[76]

---

[72] Alasdair MacIntyre, *After Virtue: A Study of Moral Theory* 2nd ed. (Notre Dame: University of Notre Dame Press, 1984), p. 216.

[73] James K. A. Smith, *Desiring the Kingdom: Worship, Worldview and Cultural Formation* (Grand Rapids: Baker Academic, 2009), p. 40, italics added. Kindle.

[74] Ibid. p. 52.

[75] Ibid. p. 40.

[76] Walsh & Keesmaat, *Colossians Remixed*, p. 84.

Paul's hymn resisted the powerful narratives of empire and idolatry surrounding the Colossian church.[77] While it echoed the language and expressions reserved for Caesar in the larger Roman society, Paul repurposed them for Jesus Christ who he proclaimed supreme over "all spiritual rulers, lords, powers, and authorities."[78] According to Mark S. Medley, the hymn "co-opted one of the empire's key devices of cultural and political propaganda in order to advocate and support a worldview that challenged it with the revolutionary confession of Jesus Christ as Lord and Savior of the universe."[79] The Colossian hymn was a liturgy useful to forge a newly constituted people of God, a redeemed *imago Dei*, whose allegiance was exclusive to a new King, Jesus Christ, whom the hymn celebrated and worshipped. What does this hymn say in praise of the Lord Jesus?

He is the Image of the Invisible God (Col.1:15). The Greek word *eikon* (from which we get the English word *icon*) refers to a visible image of something that is invisible.[80] Jesus Christ embodied the invisible God within the physical creation.[81] New Testament scholar Marianne Meye Thompson says, "But to say that Christ is the *image* of God means that, in some way, the unseen or invisible God becomes visible, moves into our sphere of sense perception, in the life of this human being."[82] The images of the empire were everywhere the Colossian believers looked constantly reminding them who was in power.[83] But this first phrase of the Colossian hymn directly challenged the authority of the empire and reminded believers that the Kingdom of God has come with its true King, Jesus Christ.[84]

Sensual images of all manner of deities also filled the air around the Colossian experience. These cults required asceticism, ritual cleansing, and veneration of the spirit-powers so that devotees could purify their souls and pass through the spheres into the realm of the gods.[85] But in the Colossian hymn, Paul exalted the invisible God whose *eikon* came into our physical world.

---

[77] Medley, "Subversive Song," p. 427.
[78] Walsh & Keesmaat, *Colossians Remixed*, p. 84.
[79] Medley, "Subversive Song," p. 428.
[80] Johnson, "The Image of God in Colossians," p. 10.
[81] Ibid.
[82] Thompson, *Colossians & Philemon*, p. 28.
[83] Walsh & Keesmaat, *Colossians Remixed*, p. 83.
[84] Arthur M. Wright, Jr., "Disarming the Rulers and Authorities: Reading Colossians in its Roman Imperial Context," *Review and Expositor* 116, no. 4 (2019), p. 453.
[85] DeSilva, *An Introduction to the New Testament*, p. 693.

In first-century honor-shame contexts, image was everything! An individual's imaging of the kinship group to whom he or she belonged impacted their social, political, and economic status.[86] "Kinship" refers to the social norms that regulate relationships within a family or community to advance its values.[87] People and groups lived in continual interaction between society's norms and how they "imaged" those norms in specific behavior.[88] If they perceived that their actions reproduced the norms of society, then they expected public grants of honor from others.[89] As Bruce Malina describes it:

> Thus a person's claim to honor requires a grant of reputation by others before it becomes honor in fact. If a person's claim to honor because of some action results in no social grant of reputation, then the person's action (and frequently the person him/herself) is labeled ridiculous, contemptuous, or foolish, and treated accordingly.[90]

But honor was also a limited resource.[91] Acquiring honor required that a person or group challenge and excel over the honor of another person or group.[92] Paul's claim that Jesus is the "image of the invisible God" (Col. 1:15, NIV) challenged the other images of power and worship that demanded the Colossians' loyalty. Jesus Christ, the *eikon* of God, is the head of a new kinship group, a Kingdom of redeemed *eikons*. And Jesus challenges the honor of every other image.

He is the Firstborn of All Creation (Col. 1:15). The phrase "firstborn" was a title that referred to the preeminence of a person over others.[93] Medley explains, "Jesus' cosmic and political sovereignty is remembered by singing of him as the 'firstborn of all creation.'"[94] In the creation story, God commanded humans to rule the earth he created (Gen. 1:26-28). He placed them in the garden to "work the soil and take care of the garden" (Gen. 2:15). God's intent for their image-bearing was to worship him *through* their rule over the earth.[95] But, according to David H. Johnson, by Genesis 3, they "are

---

[86] Malina, *The New Testament World*, p. 29.
[87] Ibid. p. 134.
[88] Ibid. p. 31.
[89] Ibid.
[90] Ibid. p. 32.
[91] Ibid. p. 33.
[92] Ibid.
[93] Johnson, "The Image of God in Colossians," p. 10.
[94] Medley, "Subversive Song," p. 431.
[95] Johnson, "The Image of God in Colossians," p. 10.

not ruling creation, rather it is rebelling against them (vv. 17-20); and humans are not worshipping and obeying, they are cut off from the place of fellowship with God (v. 24)."[96] But the Colossian hymn declares brilliantly that Jesus is the firstborn of a *new* creation. He redeems the *imago Dei* and restores its vocation to rule and cultivate the earth.

Scot McKnight clarifies the significance of Jesus as the firstborn over all creation. He explains that an important aspect of the *imago Dei's* rule was its relational "oneness" with God, with the self, with other image-bearers, and with the creation.[97] But sin "cracked" that image. McKnight states:

> What we learn in Genesis 3 is that sin distorts oneness because the *Eikon* is now cracked. What we learn is profoundly common to all human experience: humans do bad things to one another because humans are curved in on themselves instead of curved toward God.[98]
>
> Oneness has given way to "otherness" because of sin.[99]

But Jesus as the firstborn of a new creation redeems the *imago Dei*, the cracked *eikon*, to the oneness it was meant to experience from the beginning.[100] McKnight continues, "The Bible's story has a plot headed in the direction of a *person*. And that same story is headed in the direction of a *community* 'in' that person."[101] Jesus Christ is the head of a new humanity restored to oneness in both their status and in their mission in the world.

He is the Fullness of God (Col. 1:19). "For God was pleased to have all his fullness dwell in him" (Col. 1:19, NIV). The language of fullness that Paul used has the same reference to God's *shekinah* glory in the Old Testament. The *shekinah* glory was his presence living with his people in the temple.[102] But now, this glory is the fullness of God present with his people *in Jesus Christ*. In contrast to the "hollow and deceptive philosophy" to which the Colossians were enticed (Col. 2:8, NIV), Jesus is sufficient for the life of his people because "God lives in Christ fully, even in his life on earth" (Col. 2:9). The divine nature is not abstract or intangible; it is incarnate in a person, Jesus

---

96 Ibid.
97 McKnight, *The Blue Parakeet*, p. 75-78.
98 Ibid. p. 78.
99 Ibid. p. 79.
100 Ibid. p. 79, 83.
101 Ibid. p. 83.
102 Blackwell, "You are Filled in Him," p. 105.

the Firstborn, through whom God reconciled all things through his embodied death and life (Col. 1:20).[103]

Paul's letter tells us, "And because you belong to Christ you are complete, having everything you need. Christ is ruler over every other power and authority" (Col. 2:10). We are filled with God's glory because Christ Jesus lives in us by his Spirit. Again, this is not an otherworldly, spiritual experience of the divine or some secret knowledge reserved for only an elite few – Paul was careful to refute that idea! We who are in Christ participate in the divine image in an embodied way.[104] Ben C. Blackwell argues:

> For Paul, we cannot access God and his fullness without first and foremost looking to the embodied work of Christ, a sentiment that simply extends Paul's previous argument in [Colossians] 1:13-20: the redemption of creation was achieved through an embodied death and resurrection."[105]

The *imago Dei* is reoriented to God and to the world through a relationship with and in Christ.[106] We participate in the fullness of God as we embody the life, death, resurrection, and rule of Christ in our lives.[107] Blackwell summarizes this powerfully:

> The story of true humanity is humility and a recognition of creatureliness, but humans have sought a self-deification that, ironically, led to a dehumanization. Paul, however, calls believers to an [in-Christ] experience: by embodying Christ's death believers return to their creaturely humility that draws them into the life of God. Through resurrection life, believers are fully transformed into the image of Christ, the true human, as they participate in the life and glory of God.[108]

The fullness of God in Jesus alters the reality of the cosmos. We are saved from the deceptive *Matrix*, "made free from the powers that influence this world" (Col. 2:20) and raised from death with Christ into new life (Col. 3:1-4). He is the *telos* of the new creation that he has liberated from bondage to

---

103 Ibid. p. 108, 111.
104 Ibid. p. 112-113.
105 Ibid. p. 111.
106 Ibid. p. 112.
107 Ibid.
108 Ibid. p. 119.

violence and death into a new reality where life flourishes.[109] Participation in Christ – embodying his story – will be an important theme for our leadership-in-community.

Movement 3: *Meditatio*

The Colossian hymn exalts Jesus as supreme over all other "spiritual rulers, lords, powers, and authorities" (Col. 1:15-20). Some scholars believe the early church sang this hymn during the baptism sacrament as a confession of their deliverance from the power of death into a new life joined together with Christ.[110] Baptism symbolized their participation in the death and resurrection of Christ. They have died to their allegiance to all other lords, including themselves, and are now an entirely new people identified by their allegiance to Jesus as their King.[111] Paul reminded them of their new identity in Jesus:

> You were raised from death with Christ. So live for what is in heaven, where Christ is sitting at the right hand of God. Think only about what is up there, not what is here on earth. Your old self has died, and your new life is kept with Christ in God. Yes, Christ is now your life, and when he comes again, you will share in his glory. (Col. 3:1-4)

They were now called to live out a story of Good News, one that countered those which dominated the culture around them.

Paul explained what this counter-narrative means for those whose lives are hidden in Christ: "God has chosen you and made you his holy people" (Col. 3:12). Christ is restoring the *imago Dei* in us, his people, so that we live out his honor and glory in the world. Medley agrees, "Jesus Christ is the *cantus firmus*, the centering melody, the fixed song of wisdom, truth, unity, and reconciliation, not only for Christian living and community, but also the whole realm of creation."[112] The world offers us numerous false stories entrenched in empty philosophies.[113] But we are people of *the* story, the Gospel.[114] So, Paul tells us to take off those things that conform to the false

---

[109] Medley, "Subversive Song," p. 432.
[110] DeSilva, *An Introduction to the New Testament*, p. 696.
[111] Gerhard Swart, "Eschatological Vision or Exhortation to Visible Christian Conduct? Notes on the Interpretation of Colossians 3:4," *Newtestamentica* 33, no. 1 (1999), p. 173.
[112] Medley, "Subversive Song," p. 435.
[113] McKnight, *The King Jesus Gospel*, p. 169.
[114] Ibid.

narratives of this world (Col. 3:5-9). In Jesus, we are "renewed in knowledge in the image of [our] Creator" (Col. 3:10, NIV). He is putting new clothes on us – that which reflects the values and beauty of our God (Col. 3:10-17). God loves us (Col. 3:12) and so, above all, we must put on the new clothes of love. His love worked out in our community creates the cultures – new mindsets and practices – that expand the good reign of God to the entire cosmos.[115]

Missiological Themes

The restored *imago Dei* in Christ Jesus highlights five missiological themes that will shape our leadership-in-community: communities of participation, the Gospel, election, embodiment, and human flourishing.

Communities of Participation. In leadership development, communities of practice are used as a form of collective learning.[116] Communities of practice are "groups of people informally bound together by shared expertise and passion for a joint enterprise."[117] They contain three essential elements: a domain of knowledge, people who care about and are involved in this domain, and the shared practices they have developed to be effective in that domain.[118] But the concept of communities of practice is inadequate for our purposes in missional leadership. Because we are people now identified by our *participation* in Jesus Christ, we must also *participate* in a worldwide community that is "growing in our understanding of the one who made [us]" and is "becoming more and more like him" (Col. 3:10). Communities of *participation* embrace the three elements of communities of practice, but push us more deeply into the relational, spiritual, teleological, and ethical realities of our common mission, the *missio Dei.*

To participate in Christ Jesus as redeemed image-bearers is to reimagine the world around us as sacred and beautiful, enchanted with the thoughts of God, and full of potential.[119]

We are not naïve that the "formless and empty" has made a resurgence in the world because of human sin and suppression of the knowledge of God (Rom. 1:18-23). Indeed, we live in a *Matrix* world, a dynamic that cultural

---

115 Terrell Carter, "Love is the Appropriate Response: Colossians 3:12-17," *Review and Expositor* 116, no. 4 (2019), p. 476.

116 Ronan Carbery, "Organizational Learning," in *Human Resource Development: A Concise Introduction,* Eds. Ronan Carbery & Christine Cross (London, UK: Palgrave, 2015), p. 94.

117 Ibid.

118 Ibid. p. 95.

119 Paul M. Gould, *Cultural Apologetics: Renewing the Christian Voice, Conscience, and Imagination in a Disenchanted World* (Grand Rapids: Zondervan, 2019), p. 27.

anthropologist Paul Gould describes this way: "When we fail to acknowledge God, this failure has catastrophic effects, corrupting our perception of reality. Everything goes wrong. Reality is turned on its head, and 'the world is put out of joint.'"[120] But we also confidently hope in God's redemptive work through Christ! God is re-enchanting the world through his restored *imago Dei* that participates in Christ. Paul says:

> This message is the secret truth that was hidden since the beginning of time. It was hidden from everyone for ages, but now it has been made known to God's holy people. God decided to let his people know just how rich and glorious that truth is. That secret truth, which is for all people, is that Christ lives in you, his people. He is our hope for glory. (Col. 1:26-27)

As a community of participation in Christ Jesus, we must maintain a re-enchanted perception of the world through practices that strengthen our relational and spiritual vitality.

First, we must rehearse the story of the Gospel through embodied habits that aim our hearts and imaginations toward the Kingdom of God. Gould asserts, "We are shaped by what we value as great and good. We are moved by what we think is lovely."[121] Our habits and rituals form us into certain kinds of people, for good or bad.[122] As a community of participation in Christ, we need to cultivate communal and individual practices that inscribe his story on our hearts so that our desires aim for God and his expanding rule over the renewed world. We have many resources available to help us cultivate such habits: most especially the Scriptures, but also traditions, our Spirit-informed reason, and Christian experience.[123] With help of the Holy Spirit working through those practices in our lives and communities, we can start to perceive the world anew. As Gould says, "we begin to see God and the world the way Jesus does and then to invite others to see God in the same way. In other words, re-enchantment is a work of the Holy Spirit."[124]

Second, we must engage with changing social and cultural contexts so that the Gospel story speaks to the issues present in those contexts.[125] We do

---

[120] Ibid. p. 16.

[121] Ibid. p. 45.

[122] Smith, *Desiring the Kingdom*, p. 83.

[123] Ircel Harrison, "A Word About...Equipping Leaders for Twenty-First Century Ministry," *Review and Expositor* 116, no. 4 (2019), p. 392.

[124] Gould, *Cultural Apologetics*, p. 40-41.

[125] Harrison, "A Word About...Equipping Leaders," p. 392.

this primarily in community – by learning from and valuing the contributions of others within our community of participation. Paul declared:

> In this new life [in Christ] it doesn't matter if you are Greek or a Jew, circumcised or not. It doesn't matter if you speak a different language or even if you are a Scythian. It doesn't matter if you are slave or free. Christ is all that matters, and he is in all of you. (Col. 3:11)

All ethnic, social, and class distinctions no longer separate us. As a community of participation in Christ, all are included, and our differences become a richly diverse expression of our worship and work. Because Christ is in all of us, we can learn and grow together as we carry our mission into a diverse and changing world.

Finally, communities of participation include both gathering and scattering.[126] We gather to worship, learn, and grow together.[127] But then, we scatter to fulfill God's mission.[128] We are sent by Jesus to share the Gospel story with others, to rescue others from the *Matrix* and invite them to participate in the re-enchanted world of God's Kingdom. This essential worship-and-work dynamic gives health to a community of participation.

The Gospel. To appreciate the Gospel as a story, rather than as a set of doctrinal beliefs, is to affirm that humans are made for a world enchanted by the thoughts of God. The restored *imago Dei* is called to participate in the grand narrative of God's redeeming movement throughout history. Gould eloquently describes that grand narrative:

> God wants to be known. And as God reveals himself to us through the storyline of the Bible, we learn that he pursues us in love, even as we run from him.... In the Bible we find not only the greatest story ever told but the greatest *possible* story ever told. It features man's tragedy, a divine comedy, and a fairy-tale ending. It's an inviting story that points us, relentlessly, to the deep and abiding love of a God who creates, pursues, redeems, and restores all that he has made.[129]

The Gospel should not be reduced to merely personal salvation – that Jesus died to save sinners from hell – as important as personal salvation is within

---

126 Ibid.
127 Ibid.
128 Ibid.
129 Gould, *Cultural Apologetics*, p. 40-41.

the grander narrative.[130] Rather, *salvation flows out of the Gospel*.[131] The Gospel is about a King (the image of the invisible God) who has come at last to rescue his people from their sins by his death and resurrection. He recreates them into a new society of his redeemed image-bearers, empowered by his Holy Spirit to serve him in love, peace, justice, and holiness.[132] And it is a story that is moving somewhere very good! One day, this King will be exalted over all the cosmos so that, under his good reign, it is transformed into a place of rest and fullness, of *shalôm*, where God lives forever with his people.[133]

Election. Paul said that the redeemed community of Jesus is God's chosen people (Col. 1:12). While much debate surrounds the nature of God's election, an important take-away for our purposes is that when God chooses people to be *his own* people, he gives them a mission for the sake of the world. Through our communities of participation in Jesus, we are compelled to tell people the Gospel in the hope that the mystery of the Kingdom will break into their lives (Col. 1:28). Vinoth Ramachandra states, "Thus for Paul, as for all the other New Testament writers, it is the universality of God's saving love which is the ground of his choosing and calling a community to be the messengers of his truth and bearers of his love for all peoples."[134] Throughout the Scriptures, God carried out his plans for the universal blessing of all people through his choice of particular people.[135] This truth gets to the heart of the *imago Dei's* essential nature as "relatedness-in-love," as Lesslie Newbigin describes it.[136] God does not intend for the Gospel of Jesus Christ to be revealed in abstract terms, but in the embodied and loving oneness of diverse people who participate in Jesus as Lord.[137] This truth repels any elitism of the "chosen" and calls us all to humble participation in the real-life contexts and communities which God places us.[138]

Embodiment. While the resurrection of Christ radically alters reality for us who now belong to him, we still live in particular social, cultural, and

---

[130] McKnight, *The King Jesus Gospel*, p. 37-41.
[131] Ibid. p. 51
[132] Ibid. p. 167-168.
[133] Ibid. p. 168.
[134] Ramachandra, *The Recovery of Mission*, p. 235.
[135] Lesslie Newbigin, *The Open Secret: An Introduction to the Theology of Mission* Revised Edition (Grand Rapids: William B. Eerdmans Publishing Company, 1995), p. 68.
[136] Ibid. p. 69.
[137] Ibid. p. 68-69.
[138] Ibid. p. 68.

political contexts. But there lies our mission field! Ramachandra agrees, "...all rationality is socially embodied; so that neither truth nor love can be communicated except as they are embodied in a community which reasons and loves."[139] So, while God's chosen and holy people must live within these spaces, they are not identified by them. They develop a new identity by drawing from the nutrients of Jesus Christ and the empowering presence of his Holy Spirit who lives in them.[140] Furthermore, they embody that identity in their ethics that they work out in their specific contexts. Newbigin articulates well what embodiment looks like for God's people:

> Human life from its beginning is a life of shared relationship in the context of a task – a task that is continuous with God's creative work in the natural world. In contrast to those forms of spirituality that seek the 'real' self by looking within, the Bible invites us to see the real human life as a life of shared relationships in a world of living creatures and created things, a life of mutual personal responsibility for the created world, its animal and vegetable life and its resources of soil and water and air. This, and no other, is the real human life, which is the object of God's primal blessing and of his saving purpose.[141]

In the first-century honor-shame contexts, a group's way of life either defended or destroyed the honor of the group and its leadership. By embodying the values and ethics of the Kingdom of God in our various contexts, we show that Jesus *really is* King and that life in his Kingdom is to be desired as a treasure above all else (Col. 2:3).

Human Flourishing. To say that human flourishing is at the heart of the Gospel may at first sound like one of the human-centered philosophies that Paul condemns as "hollow" in Colossians. However, it is in fact the hope of the entire cosmos. Read carefully what Paul writes to the Romans:

> Everything that God made is waiting with excitement for the time when he will show the world who his children are. The whole world wants very much for that to happen. Everything God made was allowed to become like something that cannot fulfill its purpose. That was not its choice, but God made it happen with this hope in view: That the creation would be made free from ruin – that everything God made would have the same freedom and glory that belong to God's children.

---

[139] Ramachandra, *Recovery of Mission*, p. 235.
[140] Sigmon, "Homiletical Possibilities and Challenges in Colossians," p. 459.
[141] Ibid. p. 69.

We know that everything God made has been waiting until now in pain like a woman ready to give birth to a child. Not only the world, but we also have been waiting with pain inside us. We have the Spirit as the first part of God's promise. So we are waiting for God to finish making us his own children. I mean we are waiting for our bodies to be made free. We were saved to have this hope. If we can see what we are waiting for, that is not really hope. People don't hope for something they already have. But we are hoping for something we don't have yet, and we are waiting for it patiently. (Romans 8:19-25)

In the fullness that we have in Christ Jesus (Col. 2:10), our new life as restored image-bearers advances the wholeness (*shalôm*) of the entire creation. Our fullness in Christ is lived out in loving oneness with God, ourselves, others, and the creation. Terrell Carter, Chief Diversity Officer at Greenville University, states:

> An individual has the responsibility to exhibit the love quality of Christ, but cannot do so in a personal vacuum. Loving is a challenge the whole body, the Church, faces together. This foundational idea of love and how it is lived out within community is not only for the benefit of one person, but for that of the entire community.[142]

Love is resurrection behavior. It is the driving concern of a holy people called to bear witness to the greatness of King Jesus in a broken cosmos. It is bearing the image of Jesus whose "love-making is the revelation of God to those who know that the image of God that they are is broken, perhaps tortured, into powerlessness and fear."[143] The Gospel is a story of wholeness. Theologian Ellen T. Charry agrees:

> Jesus' actions in his life, death, and afterlife reveal God as the consummate lover who takes the broken shards, like the dry bones in Ezekiel's valley, and brings them bone upon bone into wholeness with sinews, flesh, skin, and breath.[144]

Among the futile narratives that imprison the creation in brokenness, the Gospel story, courageously embodied in us, radiates brilliantly the hope of

---

[142] Carter, "Love is the Appropriate Response," p. 477.
[143] Ellen T. Charry, *God and the Art of Happiness* (Grand Rapids: William B. Eerdmans Publishing Company, 2010), p. 261-262.
[144] Ibid. p. 262.

redemption through our reigning King Jesus. For this reason, Paul directed the Colossian believers, and us today, to love: "…the most important part of your new life is to love each other. Love is what holds everything together in perfect unity" (Col. 3:14). And so, to conclude our reflections of the *imago Dei*, may the words of Paul be a prayer over your life and leadership:

> *This is what we pray: that God will make you completely sure of what he wants by giving you all the wisdom and spiritual understanding you need; that this will help you live in a way that brings honor to the Lord and pleases him in every way; that your life will produce good works of every kind and that you will grow in your knowledge of God; that God will strengthen you with his own great power, so that you will be patient and not give up when troubles come. (Col. 1:9-12)*

Movement 4: *Oratio*

Heavenly Father,

Your kingdom seems far away today. We see death and disaster in the news, and everywhere, people are arguing, always arguing. And yet Jesus said that your domain – the only true and enduring reality – is also among us.

May your kingdom come in the midst of our despair.

Even in my own heart, I hold grudges, nurse anxieties, withhold compassion, and put myself first. Too often, my heart is not a hospitable place for your Spirit. I resist your rightful rule there, too.

May your kingdom come first in my heart.

Empower your people to see where your way of life is already showing up. Help us to become passionate agents in this continuing unfolding of your will for all things.[145]

In Jesus' name, Amen.

Movement 5: *Imitatio*

+ Individual Reflection
  o Journal your responses to the following questions:

---

[145] Prayer adapted from the ancient spiritual practice of the Prayer Wheel. Dodd, Riess, & Van Biema, *The Prayer Wheel*, p. 35.

- What key points of the *missio Dei* is God leading you to embrace and grow into?

- How can you live this out in your life and leadership?

- How can your missional leadership group pray for you in living this out?

+ Group Reflection
  o In your missional leadership group, share your individual reflections with each other.

  o Pray for one another.

Movement 6: *Missio*

+ Experiencing Mission
  o Level 1 *Awareness*

    - Pray each day that the Lord sends you into his mission that day.

    - At the end of each day, reflect on or journal about one experience you had that day where you witnessed the *missio Dei* personally. Describe what happened. What was significant about that experience for you?

  o Level 2 *Personal Commitment*

    - Ask the Lord where he may be sending you to be his witness on a regular basis.

    - Make a commitment to serve in that way.

Movement 7: *Communio*

+ Experiencing Mission
  o Level 3 *Group Experience*

    - If possible, the small group may consider performing a mission or service project together to experience mission as a community.

+ Group Reflection

o   Where did you see the *missio Dei* in action this past week?

o   What were the most significant or surprising observations you made about your experience?

o   What did you learn about God from that experience? What did you learn about yourself from that experience?

o   What difference does that make in your leadership? How will you apply what you have learned?

Movement 8: *Contemplatio*

Each week in your small group, spend time reflecting and celebrating the ways that you have seen "God on the move" in the past week.

✦ Spend some time in prayer or singing in thanksgiving and praise to our missionary God.

Section 2:

The Community of Leadership-in-Community

Chapter 3

Communitas

God is a missionary God. He is on the move! On his great mission, the *missio Dei*, he crosses the boundaries from faith to the formless and empty places of "no faith" to redeem his image-bearers, the *imago Dei*, and reclaim their priestly vocation of work and worship. Through their restored culture-making, God renews the hope of *shalôm* where the entire creation participates in his good reign.

The essence of this mission is trinitarian. God, the Father, *sent* his Son Jesus Christ, the firstborn image of the invisible God, to redeem his people by his death and resurrection. The Father and the Son *sent* the Holy Spirit to empower his redeemed people to carry on this mission in community with each other. This is the story God calls us to live into every day! Following Jesus is an amazing adventure of mission.

The concepts of the *missio Dei* and the *imago Dei* provide the missiological framework that distinguishes missional leadership as *essentially* leadership-in-community. They emphasize that our mission begins and ends with God. Those who follow Christ participate in that mission. Our Triune God calls us first to participate in the trinitarian communion of his redeeming love overflowing with the intent to save. From out of that communion emerges the character of our leadership and the nature of our mission. And so, we begin our exploration of leadership-in-community by reflecting on the Triune God whose image we bear in our community of faith.

The doctrine of the Trinity asserts that God, who is one substance, exists in three persons: Father, Son, and Holy Spirit.[1] Each person exists in and for each other as one being in an intimate relationship of reciprocal love, dedication, and purpose.[2] In God's work of creation and salvation, the three persons of the Trinity are united in a perfectly harmonious dance.[3] The "logic" (Greek *logos*) of the Trinity is oneness from which creativity, life, and growth spring.[4] God exists not as three independent entities that come into relationship with one another, but as a wholly-constituted relationality.[5] Graham Hill explains:

---

[1] Hill, *Salt, Light, and a City: Volume 1*, p. 266.
[2] Ibid. The Greek word *perichoresis* expresses that the three persons of the Trinity exist as one being in a relationship of intersubjectivity, mutuality, and reciprocity.
[3] James Montgomery Boice, *Foundations of the Christian Faith: A Comprehensive & Readable Theology* (Downers Grove: InterVarsity Press, 1986), p. 115.
[4] Hill, *Salt, Light, and a City: Volume 1*, p. 267, 280.
[5] Ibid. p. 280.

The triune God *is* relations…. The redemptive mission of Jesus Christ connects with his deep love for the Father. This mission emerges from his longing to fulfill his Father's purposes. In the Godhead, we see the highest example of self-sacrifice and mutual dedication. Three divine persons exist in perfect harmony and unity, sharing the same divine faculties and power.[6]

In the "divine trinitarian dance of God,"[7] the people of God participate in the love and communion of the Godhead.[8]

Participation in the trinitarian communion nuances the meaning of bearing God's image: God's people look like him when they embrace self-sacrificing love and mutual service in their lives and work. Hill says, "When a trinitarian vision grips the missional imagination of the church, it transforms that church."[9] The trinitarian logic of oneness characterizes our worship and work. Hill explains:

> The church's communion and nature are a direct result of the gospel. So, while we consider the joy of communion with each other and with God, we must never forget the correct progression. The perfect, triune God reaches out to humanity according to his grace and purpose. He reaches out in the historical movements of the Father, Son, and Spirit. He redeems humanity through the historical life, death, resurrection, and final glorification of Jesus Christ. Because of the triune God's actions in history, and of his willingness to invite us into his "own self-originating life," human beings can be redeemed and sanctified. We can enjoy communion with each other and with God.[10]

Leadership-in-community images the trinitarian logic of communion that *energizes* our gospel witness and *governs* our mission (including its leadership, forms, and structures) in unity and multiplicity.[11]

The trinitarian logic of oneness compels us to favor forms of leadership that reflect the communion and loving mutuality of our Triune God who sends us. Leadership-in-community prioritizes relationship as the driver of creative enterprise within teams and organizations. In other words,

---

[6] Ibid. p. 267.
[7] Pete Ward, *Liquid Church* (Peabody: Hendrickson, 2002), p. 49-55.
[8] Hill, *Salt, Light, and a City: Volume 1*, p. 265, 267.
[9] Ibid. p. 262.
[10] Ibid. p. 268.
[11] John B. Webster, *Confessing God: Essays in Christian Dogmatics II* (London: T. & T. Clark, 2005), p. 153-193.

relational processes, rather than pragmatic skills, techniques, or structures, achieve those outcomes that all leaders hope for: a unified team with a common direction, alignment, and commitment.[12] Leadership expert Debashis Chatterjee agrees, "Wise leaders transform the quality of relationships within organizations. They ask what we are able to create together. In a transformational system monologue becomes *multilogue*."[13] As we saw before, humans have a remarkable ability to shape and influence their networks of relationships to create new cultures that expand mission opportunities.[14] Communities (e.g. committees, organizations, teams, or communities of practice) that embody the love and mutuality of the Trinity are centers of social interaction and support where members can safely share their cultural differences and, in the context of their mutual mission, create new meanings and horizons for their work together.[15] This is *multilogue*: when all member contributions are validated, they deepen the collective understanding of the task and, consequently, enhance the team's effectiveness.[16]

A common identity further unifies a diverse team around its central mission. Social integration is strongest when all members welcome one another and share a group identity forged from the multilogue – the diversity of expressions, perspectives, and cultures embedded within the group.[17] For this to happen, the group needs trust. Leadership-in-community establishes and maintains trust, sometimes vigorously, so that nothing gets in the way of the open sharing and dialogue that promote the group's integration and learning.[18] Quite simply, leadership-in-community seeks out friendships![19] When we invite others into authentic friendship, especially others who are different than we are, we represent the Kingdom ethos of the *missio Dei*. This is *communitas*: an intimate, diverse community with a shared identity and mission forged through periods of change and invigorated by the *agape* love of God.

---

[12] Drath, *The Deep Blue Sea*, Chapter 5 Relational Dialogue, "People Make Sense of reality Through Relational Processes," para. 1.

[13] Debashis Chatterjee, "Wise Ways: Leadership as Relationship," *Journal of Human Values* 12 (2006), p. 154.

[14] Schuele, "Uniquely Human," p. 10-12.

[15] McConnell, *Cultural Insights for Christian Leaders*, p. 174.

[16] Ibid.

[17] Ibid. p. 702.

[18] Ibid. p. 710.

[19] Ibid. p. 178.

The *communitas* of leadership-in-community "starts with the desire for any mission movement or structure to become a community of trust, with friendship as an expression of the unity of believers."[20] *Communitas* embraces the trinitarian logic of oneness – friendships of interdependence as the source of creative energy and cohesion within the team. We will explore *communitas* by looking at the story of the Jerusalem Council in Acts 15. This is a rich story of leadership-in-community that set the course of the global Christian movement throughout the ages even down to our day.

Movement 1: *Adspecto*

Prayer

✦ Pray for the Holy Spirit to speak to you through the Scripture. Use the following words of Psalm 122 as a prayer:

> *I was happy when the people said,*
> > *"Let us go to the LORD's Temple."*
> *Here we are, standing at the gates of Jerusalem.*
> *This is New Jerusalem!*
> > *The city has been rebuilt as one united city.*
> *This is where the tribes come, the tribes who belong to the LORD.*
> > *The people of Israel come here to praise the LORD's name.*
> *The kings from David's family put their thrones here.*
> > *They set up their thrones to judge the people.*
>
> *Pray for the peace in Jerusalem:*
> > *"May those who love you find peace.*
> *May there be peace within your walls.*
> > *May there be safety in your great buildings."*
>
> *For the good of my family and neighbors,*
> > *I pray that there will be peace here.*
> *For the good of the Temple of the LORD our God,*
> > *I pray that good things will happen to this city.*

Scripture Reading

✦ **Read Acts 15:1-35.** Listen for words or phrases from the passage that stand out to you.

---

[20] Franklin, *Towards Global Missional Leadership*, p. 85.

The Meeting at Jerusalem

[1]Then some men came to Antioch from Judea and began teaching the non-Jewish believers: "You cannot be saved if you are not circumcised as Moses taught us." [2]Paul and Barnabas were against this teaching and argued with these men about it. So the group decided to send Paul, Barnabas, and some others to Jerusalem to talk more about this with the apostles and elders.

[3]The church helped them get ready to leave on their trip. The men went through the countries of Phoenicia and Samaria, where they told all about how the non-Jewish people had turned to the true God. This made all the believers very happy. [4]When the men arrived in Jerusalem, the apostles, the elders, and the whole church welcomed them. Paul, Barnabas, and the others told about all that God had done with them. [5]Some of the believers in Jerusalem had belonged to the Pharisees. They stood up and said, "The non-Jewish believers must be circumcised. We must tell them to obey the Law of Moses!"

[6]Then the apostles and the elders gathered to study this problem. [7]After a long debate, Peter stood up and said to them, "My brothers, I am sure you remember what happened in the early days. God chose me from among you to tell the Good News to those who are not Jewish. It was from me that they heard the Good News and believed. [8]God knows everyone, even their thoughts, and he accepted these non-Jewish people. He showed this to us by giving them the Holy Spirit the same as he did to us. [9]To God, those people are not different from us. When they believed, God made their hearts pure. [10]So now, why are you putting a heavy burden around the necks of the non-Jewish followers of Jesus? Are you trying to make God angry? We and our fathers were not able to carry that burden. [11]No, we believe that we and these people will be saved the same way—by the grace of the Lord Jesus."

[12]Then the whole group became quiet. They listened while Paul and Barnabas told about all the miraculous signs and wonders that God had done through them among the non-Jewish people. [13]When they finished speaking, James said, "My brothers, listen to me. [14]Simon Peter has told us how God showed his love for the non-Jewish people. For the first time, God accepted them and made them his people. [15]The words of the prophets agree with this too:

16'I will return after this.
   I will build David's house again.
   It has fallen down.
   I will build again the parts of his house that have been pulled down.
   I will make his house new.

17Then the rest of the world will look for the Lord God—
   all those of other nations who are my people too.
The Lord said this.
   And he is the one who does all these things.' *Amos 9:11-12*

18'All this has been known from the beginning of time.'

19"So I think we should not make things hard for those who have turned to God from among the non-Jewish people. 20Instead, we should send a letter telling them only the things they should not do:

Don't eat food that has been given to idols. This makes the food unclean.

Don't be involved in sexual sin.

Don't eat meat from animals that have been strangled or any meat that still has the blood in it.

21They should not do any of these things, because there are still men in every city who teach the Law of Moses. The words of Moses have been read in the synagogue every Sabbath day for many years."

The Letter to the Non-Jewish Believers

22The apostles, the elders, and the whole church wanted to send some men with Paul and Barnabas to Antioch. The group decided to choose some of their own men. They chose Judas (also called Barsabbas) and Silas, men who were respected by the believers. 23The group sent the letter with these men. The letter said:

From the apostles and elders, your brothers,

To all the non-Jewish brothers in the city of Antioch and in the countries of Syria and Cilicia.

Dear Brothers:

24We have heard that some men have come to you from our group. What they said troubled and upset you. But we did not tell them to do this. 25We have all agreed to choose some men and send them to you. They will be with our dear friends, Barnabas and Paul. 26Barnabas and Paul have given their lives to serve our Lord Jesus Christ. 27So we have sent Judas and Silas with them. They will tell you the same things. 28We agree with the Holy Spirit that you should have no more burdens, except for these necessary things:

29Don't eat food that has been given to idols.

Don't eat meat from animals that have been strangled or any meat that still has the blood in it.

Don't be involved in sexual sin.

If you stay away from these, you will do well.

We say goodbye now.

30So Paul, Barnabas, Judas, and Silas left Jerusalem and went to Antioch. There they gathered the group of believers together and gave them the letter. 31When the believers read it, they were happy. The letter comforted them. 32Judas and Silas, who were also prophets, said many things to encourage the believers and make them stronger in their faith. 33After Judas and Silas stayed there for a while, they left. They received a blessing of peace from the believers. Then they went back to those who had sent them.21

35But Paul and Barnabas stayed in Antioch. They and many others taught the believers and told other people the Good News about the Lord.

Reflection

+ When you have finished reading, remain silent for one or two minutes.

+ Read the entire passage again. If you have an audio Bible, listen through the passage.

  o *Personal Reflection:* Journal your thoughts on the following questions:

---

21 Some Greek copies add verse 34: "But Silas decided to remain there."

- What words or phrases from the passage stand out to you?

- How do these words or phrases connect with your life right now?

- How might God be inviting you to respond to this passage?

Movement 2: *Lectio*

Scripture Study

➕ Read or listen to **Acts 15:1-12**.

➕ Answer the following study questions:

1. Who came to Antioch to teach the non-Jewish believers (vs. 1)?

2. What were they teaching the non-Jewish believers (vs. 1)?

3. Why do you think Paul and Barnabas were against this teaching (vs. 2)?

4. What does the Antioch church do in response to this controversy (vs. 2)?

5. Why do you think the Antioch church took this approach to resolve the controversy?

6. What happened in Phoenicia and Samaria (vs. 3)?

7. Why do you think Luke includes this point about Paul and Barnabas' journey on their way to Jerusalem?

8. What happened once Paul and Barnabas arrived in Jerusalem (vs. 4)?

9. How does Luke describe those who present the opposing view to the council (vs. 5)?

10. What do the believers who "had belonged to the Pharisees" think non-Jewish believers must do (vs. 5)?

11. Why do you think they insist that non-Jewish believers should do these things?

12. What does Peter remind the council (vs. 7)?

13. How does Peter describe the non-Jewish people (vs. 8-9)?

14. What is Peter's counter argument to those who think that non-Jewish believers should be circumcised and obey the Law of Moses (vs. 10-11)?

15. What are some ways that you think a "heavy burden" may be put on new believers today?

16. What does Paul and Barnabas share with the council (vs. 12)?

17. Why do you think they share this?

18. Imagine you are present during the Jerusalem Council. What impressions do you have of everything that is going on around you?

19. Peter said in his closing argument, "...we and these people will be saved the same way – by the grace of the Lord Jesus" (vs. 11). What do you think the grace of the Lord Jesus looks like in the community of God's people?

20. How might God be challenging existing beliefs or perspectives in your community? Describe that experience.

21. What lessons do you think God is speaking into your community through this story of the Jerusalem Council? Or what values do you think God is embedding in your community?

Reading
The Context of Acts

Tradition identifies Luke, a travel companion of Paul and a physician, as the author of both the Gospel of Luke and the Acts of the Apostles (Luke-Acts) as a two-part volume.[22] One of the most significant themes throughout Luke-Acts can be summarized in one word: salvation.[23] Wright and Bird expand, "Luke-Acts is the story of the 'Saviour', the story of 'those who are being saved', and traces how salvation extends from Israel to the ends of the earth."[24] Luke himself articulates his purpose for writing:

Most Honorable Theophilus: Many others have tried to give a report of the things that happened among us to complete God's plan. What they have written agrees with what we learned from the people who

---

[22] Wright & Bird, *The New Testament in Its World*, p. 607.
[23] Ibid. p. 605.
[24] Ibid.

saw those events from the beginning. They also served God by telling people his message. I studied it all carefully from the beginning. Then I decided to write it down for you in an organized way. I did this so that you can be sure that what you have been taught is true. (Luke 1:1-4)

Luke's history of Jesus and the early church served as a defense of the Christian faith as the continuation of Israel's story through the reign of Jesus Christ and out into the larger world.[25] New Testament scholar David deSilva agrees, "Acts is an authenticating document. It locates the Christian movement squarely within the unfolding drama of God's chosen people, effecting a smooth transition from the usual authorities of Judaism to the new authorities of the new community."[26]

In particular, Luke wanted to assure his patron, Theophilus, who sponsored his literary work, and other believers (especially Gentile believers) that they were now part of God's people through Jesus Christ.[27] In his writing, he asserted that Jesus, the prophesied Messiah, restored the broken Davidic kingdom and brought salvation to his people, both Jews and Gentiles.[28] Luke presented the apostle Peter at Pentecost expressing this revolutionary truth. Carefully read his speech to the crowd.

My brothers, I can tell you for sure about David, our great ancestor. He died, was buried, and his tomb is still here with us today. He was a prophet and knew something that God had said. God had promised David that someone from his own family would sit on David's throne as king. David knew this before it happened. That is why he said this about that future king:

'He was not left in the place of death.
His body did not rot in the grave.'

David was talking about the Messiah rising from death. So Jesus is the one God raised from death. We are all witnesses of this. We saw him. Jesus was lifted up to heaven. Now he is with God, at God's right side. The Father has given the Holy Spirit to him, as he promised. So Jesus

---

[25] Ibid. p. 607, 615.
[26] DeSilva, *An Introduction to the New Testament*, p. 348.
[27] Ibid.
[28] Wright & Bird, *The New Testament in its World*, p. 614.

has now poured out that Spirit. This is what you see and hear. David was not the one who was lifted up to heaven. David himself said,

'The Lord God said to my Lord:
Sit at my right side,
Until I put your enemies under your power.'

So, all the people of Israel should know this for certain: God has made Jesus to be Lord and Messiah. He is the man you nailed to the cross. (Acts 2:29-36)

Peter further testified before the Jewish High Council that only King Jesus has the power to save people (Acts 4:12). The book of Acts testifies to the advancing reign of Jesus as his witnesses shared the Good News throughout the world all the way to Rome.

Leading up to the Jerusalem Council, the Good News about Jesus had spread from Judea to Samaria and into the Gentile world just as Jesus said it would (Acts 1:8). As the Gospel moved outward from Jerusalem, Luke depicted a pioneering shift regarding who God authorized to speak on his behalf.[29] No longer was it the temple priests and the Sanhedrin. In fact, Luke presented these as the chief antagonists of the faith.[30] Instead, as we saw from Peter's speech to the crowd at Pentecost above, the apostles and disciples were now empowered by God's Spirit to give bold witness to all that God was doing.[31] These men had "no special training" but had "been with Jesus" and were "not afraid to speak" (Acts 4:13). Luke carefully positioned them in the narrative as those with legitimate authority to define the identity and way of life for the community of God's people.[32] The power struggle between the Jewish leaders and the nascent leaders of the early church culminated in severe persecution in Jerusalem, orchestrated by Saul, that scattered the disciples throughout Judea and Samaria (Acts 8:1-3).

The persecution was the catalyst God used to send out his witnesses to all parts of the Roman world and to spread the Gospel wherever they went (Acts 8:4). As the Gospel began to encounter different people and places, new tensions emerged that increasingly strained traditional views of who

---

[29] DeSilva, *An Introduction to the New Testament*, p. 355.
[30] Ibid.
[31] Ibid.
[32] Ibid. p. 359.

belonged to the covenant community. This tension climaxed with the Jerusalem Council, a pivotal moment in the history of salvation that forever altered the ongoing story of God's people.

The Conflict

At the Jerusalem Council, the main disputants were a sect of Jewish Christians, called Judaizers, who insisted that Gentiles could not belong to God's covenant community unless they came within the boundary lines that had long separated the in-group from those outside (Acts 15:1).[33] For centuries, circumcision and the Law of Moses demarcated the Jews as God's holy people and set them apart from all the surrounding nations.[34] To the faithful Jew, it was unfathomable that Gentiles – those unclean outsiders to the covenant – could also become God's people *as Gentiles*.[35] The Judaizers especially insisted that the Gentiles must first become faithful, Torah-adhering Jews before they belonged to the covenant.[36] But when God began to pour out his Spirit on Gentile believers, even though they were not circumcised, he was clearly on the move in new and surprising ways! These events needed to be interpreted by God's newly anointed spokespeople – the apostles and elders – to define and direct what they meant for God's people and his purposes in the world. The old answers no longer applied.

Luke did not merely present the history of these events in Acts. He used a rhetorical strategy intended to persuade the theological and missiological perspectives of his readers.[37] First, he seems to purposely distance the Judaizer's views from those of the main body of believers in the text.[38] He described the Judaizers with the nameless monikers of "some men" (Acts 15:1, 24) and "some of the believers" (Acts 15:5). And because Luke connected them to the Pharisees (vs. 5), he insinuated that their viewpoints aligned more closely with the principal antagonists in Luke's narrative than with the apostles and elders.[39] Ultimately, the apostles and elders unanimously

---

[33] Hyung Dae Park, "Drawing Ethical Principles from the Process of the Jerusalem Council: A New Approach to Acts 15:4-29," *Tyndale Bulletin* 61, no. 2 (2010), p. 275.

[34] C. K. Robertson, "Proto-Conciliarism in Acts 15," *Sewanee Theological Review* 61, no. 2 (2018), p. 418.

[35] DeSilva, *An Introduction to the New Testament*, p. 348.

[36] Ibid.

[37] Michal Beth Dinkler, "New Testament Rhetorical Narratology: An Invitation Toward Integration," *Biblical Interpretation* 24 (2016), p. 214-215.

[38] Timothy Gervais, "Acts 15 and Luke's Rejection of Pro-Circumcision Christianity," *Journal of Theta Alpha Kappa* 41, no. 2 (2017), p. 9.

[39] Ibid. p. 10-11.

rejected the position of these men, articulating unequivocally to the Antioch believers that the Judaizer's troubling message did not come from them (Acts 15:24).

Luke employed an interesting dynamic between silence and debate in the narrative. In the Hellenistic culture of which Luke's readers were fully immersed, silent and respectful listening was celebrated as a Roman ideal for public manners.[40] But in the narrative, Luke associated the Judaizers with argument and debate (Acts 15:2, 7). What they said "troubled and upset" the Gentile believers (Acts 15:24). The readers would have associated such discord with other dissenters in Acts.[41] Opponents of the Way were portrayed as disruptive violators of conversational decorum.[42]

On the other hand, after the long debate (Acts 15:7), Luke depicted an orderly procession of speakers from Peter, to Paul and Barnabas, and finally ending with James (Acts 15:7-21). A respectful silence fell as these men addressed the council in turn (Acts 15:12-13). The silence gave weight to their position that Gentiles ought to be welcomed in without circumcision.[43] Essentially, Luke followed Roman rhetorical ideals to set decisive boundaries between these two conflicting worldviews.[44] In the end, Luke succeeded in minimizing the strength of the opposing view.[45] The silence was not passive! It was a very productive element in the narrative that accentuated for the readers a new theological appreciation for God's activity in the church.[46] Through deep listening, the council discerned the guidance of the Holy Spirit (Acts 15:28) that renewed the identity of God's covenant people forever.[47]

And the result? The Antioch believers were *very happy* when they heard the letter that gave them great comfort (Acts 15:31)! This resonates with the joy of the believers in Phoenicia and Samaria who were also very happy that the Gentiles were turning to God (Acts 15:3). Luke wanted his readers to fully embrace the unity of God's people, both Jews and Gentiles, who now have a common hope of salvation through Jesus Christ.[48] George Goldman clarifies, "Gentile conversion does not annul God's promise of a restored and

---

[40] Dinkler, "New Testament Rhetorical Narratology," p. 224-227.
[41] Ibid. p. 225.
[42] Ibid. p. 226.
[43] Gervais, "Acts 15 and Luke's Rejection," p. 11.
[44] Dinkler, "New Testament Rhetorical Narratology," p. 226.
[45] Gervais, "Acts 15 and Luke's Rejection," p. 11.
[46] Dinkler, "New Testament Rhetorical Narratology," p. 35.
[47] Ibid.
[48] Park, "Drawing Ethical Principles," p. 286.

redeemed Israel, but rather expands it; nor does faith (rather than Torah observance) as the condition of Gentile conversion contradict God's plan of salvation, but rather confirms it."[49] What the Jerusalem Council modeled in this process was the spirit of *communitas*.

The *Communitas*

Communitas is the deep sense of community that emerges among people as they go through "a chaotic, unpredictable, liminal period of change and transformation."[50] The social change and upheaval transforms them from a group of individuals to the true oneness of a community with shared identity, values, and mission.[51] Acts shows how Christ's cosmic supremacy so radically reconstituted the identity and mission of God's people. But now that redefinition had to be worked out in the community. It inevitably led to friction between the old guard and the new Jesus community.

By the time of the Jerusalem Council, the rising tension reached a critical moment where the church had to resolve the question "could the Gentiles now be included in the 'messianically renewed Israel' without becoming Jews?"[52] Lamin Sanneh describes how revolutionary it was that Gentiles could be assured of their full immersion in God's salvation *as Gentiles*. "...that assurance calls up a troubling fact, for trust in the forms in which the law was devoutly enshrined must now be so massively drained of the element of exclusivity as to create a defining breach."[53] What happened at the Jerusalem Council would set the precedent of *communitas* for the Christian movement throughout the coming ages.

Through the upheaval, God deepened the communion of the disciples as they displayed his love in their life and mission together.[54] Graham Hill explains:

> This acute experience of community – which occurs when a church is going through chaotic, transformative, missional change – is an

---

[49] Robert Wall, "Israel and the Gentile Mission in Acts and Paul: A Canonical Approach," in *Witness to the Gospel: The Theology of Acts*, Eds. I. Howard Marshall & David Peterson (Grand Rapids: William B. Eerdmans Publishing Company, 1998), p. 449-450.

[50] Hill, *Salt, Light, and a City: Volume 1*, p. 281.

[51] Ibid.

[52] Park, "Drawing Ethical Principles," p. 276.

[53] Lamin Sanneh, *Translating the Message: The Missionary Impact on Culture* Revised and Expanded (Maryknoll: Orbis Books, 2009), p. 31.

[54] Hill, *Salt, Light, and a City: Volume 1*, p. 281.

expression of the communion within the Trinity.... [God] uses these periods of upheaval to shape a people in the image of the Trinity.[55]

Communitas is the creaturely reflection of the intimate love that originates in the Trinity and manifests itself in mutual submission, self-sacrifice, and servanthood.[56] It favors *power for and with* that nourishes communal life and mission against the *power over* of institutionalism and leadership hierarchies.[57] *Communitas* is the picture of true humanity, the restored *imago Dei*, that is celebrated and embraced in the Kingdom of God.[58]

Movement 3: *Meditatio*

Communitas is the necessary interpersonal dynamic of our leadership-in-community as we make sense of our common mission. When we encounter the unsettling mysteries of changing environments, our *communitas* generates the mission's form, substance, direction, motivation, and vision. The *communitas* of God's *imago Dei* bears fruit that extends the good reign of God to the cosmos.[59] In the beginning, God blessed his image-bearers with the power to shape their networks of diverse relationships and create cultures that move the creation toward *shalôm*.[60] *Communitas* spends that power in love, self-sacrifice, and learning to truly create something new and better, something life-giving for creation, together.

Community Themes

The story of the Jerusalem Council highlights five community themes that will shape our leadership-in-community: covenant, change, context, compel, and create.

Covenant. When people share a common task, they bring their own cultural perspectives, expressions, worldviews, and experiences into the task.[61] While such diversity is a beautifully rich resource for the group's

---

[55] Ibid.
[56] Ibid. p. 276, 281.
[57] Ibid. p. 278.
[58] Ibid. p. 281-282.
[59] Wright, *After You Believe*, p. 74.
[60] Schuele, "Uniquely Human," p. 10-11.
[61] Lingenfelter, *Leading Cross-Culturally*, p. 80.

performance, it can lead to misunderstanding, frustration, and conflict.[62]
Sherwood Lingenfelter says:

> People learn patterns and priorities of work, sharing, self-interest,
> competition, and conflict as children, and form habits for life while
> growing up in their families and communities. We have seen how
> adults can and do learn many new ways of relating to others as well as
> skills for work and relationship. Yet in situations of stress, people
> default to those habits and behaviors acquired early in their life
> experience, habits of the "flesh" rather than habits of the "spirit."[63]

When the group is focused primarily on accomplishing the task, rather than
on the relationships necessary for accomplishing the task, inclusion of diverse
perspectives and ways of working will feel like inconvenient obstacles.
Leadership habits "of the flesh" will take over as leaders abuse power and
authority to minimize differences to get the job done.

Leadership-in-community prioritizes the relationships that, when
fruitful, generate rich and productive mission. People make sense of the task
through relational processes.[64] This means that, in missional leadership,
people *belong* before they *perform*! The concept of *covenant* captures this
important commitment. A covenant is a three-way relationship between God,
us, and others.[65] The idea of covenant, so prominent throughout Scripture,
reveals the intention of God to make a community of people who reflect his
love:

> But you are his chosen people, the King's priests. You are a holy
> nation, people who belong to God. He chose you to tell about the
> wonderful things he has done. He brought you out of the darkness of
> sin into his wonderful light. (1 Pet. 2:9)

In covenant, the priority of leadership-in-community is to build relationships
of trust strong enough to navigate the complexities of change. Covenant
relationships embody love for one another and hope in God who will carry
forward his mission through the community. Lingenfelter agrees, "Leaders
must help the group center on their new identity in Christ and lead them in a

---

[62] Ibid. p. 70-72.
[63] Ibid. p. 80.
[64] Drath, *The Deep Blue Sea*, Chapter 5 Relational Dialogue, "People Make Sense of Reality
Through Relational Processes."
[65] Lingenfelter, *Leading Cross-Culturally*, p. 74.

process of commitment to Christ and to one another to be the people of God on mission together."[66] They shift the focus from accomplishing the task to *being God's people* in the context of accomplishing the task together.[67]

Change. As discussed in the introduction to this curriculum, many contemporary ideas about leadership are based on a Newtonian worldview that says that the world is a certain and predictable place.[68] Apply the right formula of skills, behaviors, or traits and we should get the results we planned. But how often are our plans frustrated by the circumstances we could not predict or the results that we did not intend? Intuitively and experientially, we know that the world is a complex place. It consists of innumerable social, political, economic, cultural, and religious exchanges that interact endlessly in open systems.[69] No one can fully grasp all the random connections they make nor predict where they will end up.[70] Leaders cannot simply apply the prescribed formula and cause certain outcomes to happen. Indeed, leaders are themselves embedded within this complex interplay of forces like pawns in a game of chess.[71]

Chess is not won in the beginning or at the end of the game. It is won in the "mid-game" where opponents continually assess and react to the moves of each other. Similarly, mission success is not gained through elaborate strategic plans and budgets (the beginning) or achievement of "predictable" outcomes (the end). Success occurs in the mid-game where leaders, in community, assess and respond wisely to the changing conditions of the environments around them in which they are trying to advance their mission.[72]

Complexity Leadership Theory captures this dynamic "chessboard" reality of leadership. First, it expresses that leader need strong learning, creativity, and adaptive capacities to succeed within complex environments.[73]

---

[66] Ibid. p. 80.

[67] Ibid. p. 80.

[68] Marquardt, *Building the Learning Organization*, p. 17.

[69] Anselm Schneider, Christopher Wickert, and Emilio Marti, "Reducing Complexity by Creating Complexity: A Systems Theory Perspective on How Organizations Respond to Their Environments," *Journal of Management Studies* 54, no. 2 (March 2017), p. 183.

[70] Ibid.

[71] Mary Uhl-Bien, Russ Marion, & Bill McDelvey, "Complexity Leadership Theory: Shifting Leadership from the Industrial Age to the Knowledge Era," *The Leadership Quarterly* 18 (2007), p. 302.

[72] Hardin Tibbs, "Making the Future Visible: Psychology, Scenarios, and Strategy." Paper presented to the Australian Public Service Futures Group, Canberra (1999), p. 3.

[73] Uhl-Bien et al., "Complexity Leadership Theory," p. 304.

Second, it emphasizes that leadership within a community must then be highly collaborative, interactive, and emergent as it develops "mid-game" strategies to adapt to changes in the environment.[74] The most powerful tools of leadership-in-community are relationship and dialogue! Through "relational dialogue," leadership-in-community constructs a common direction as group members "interact through thought, word, and action to bring into being what is important, worthy, real, and actual."[75] The more skilled a group is in dialogic processes, the more capable it is to make sense of what is happening around them. As it does so, it can effectively align the group's knowledge, resources, and commitment toward a common direction.[76]

Leadership-in-community is more formally known as a *complex adaptive system*. A complex adaptive system is a web of interdependent "agents" (leaders) who adapt to changing circumstances (the chessboard) by continually reorganizing themselves to address specific issues.[77] These reorganized structures, called "containers," are improvised and fluid. They are not controlled by any person or body, and so they have the flexibility to meet, disband, regroup, or reorganize as fitting for the situation at hand.[78] As a complex adaptive system, leadership-in-community is a team of interdependent leaders empowered to respond adaptively to changing environments so that it can sustain the mission. The components essential for our leadership-in-community to function effectively as a complex adaptive system include:

- **Agents:** Agents are the building blocks of complex systems. Agents can be individuals, teams, or whole organizations. Within a complex adaptive system, agents are interconnected – the actions of one affect the others. But agents also have some degree of power to intervene within their networks in order to influence their courses of actions.[79] Emerging leaders are often very difficult

---

[74] Ibid. p. 306.
[75] Drath, *The Deep Blue Sea*, "People Make Sense of Reality Through Relational Processes," para. 2.
[76] Drath et al., "Direction, Alignment, Commitment," p. 636.
[77] Thomas Y. Choi, Kevin J. Dooley, & Manus Rungtusanatham, "Supply Networks and Complex Adaptive Systems: Control Versus Emergence," *Journal of Operations Management* 19 (2001), p. 352-353.
[78] Ibid.
[79] Ibid. p. 353

to identify in complex environments.[80] So, what is vital in leadership development is the ability to recognize when individuals begin to distinguish themselves as agents.[81] Agents are those people who not only participate in the community but become *shapers* of the community.[82] They are gaining valuable experiences and developing essential skills that allow them to balance between thinking and acting independently while participating cooperatively within the group.[83]

- **Mental Models:** Mental models are the "deeply ingrained assumptions, generalizations, or even pictures or images that influence how we understand the world and how we take action."[84] These mental models drive the agents' behaviors.[85] More will be said about mental models in the next section on context.

- **Self-Organization:** Self-organization is the initiative of the agents to cluster together in ad hoc groups or subgroups, called containers, to define what and how work will happen in the group.[86] Containers set semi-permeable boundaries so that they may adapt to changes as they occur.[87]

- **Emergence:** Emergence is the result of self-organizing behavior.[88] As agents interact through a process of trial and error, with feedback, they produce new knowledge and systematic patterns very different from what they started with.[89]

- **Coherence:** Coherence in the system occurs when the interaction between agents produces new patterns around which containers

---

[80] Alan Weaver, "Activating Kingdom Agents: Toward a Model of Awakening and Releasing God's People for Ministry and Leadership," in *Devoted to Christ: Missiological Reflections in Honor of Sherwood G. Lingenfelter*, Ed. Christopher L. Flanders (Eugene: Pickwick Publications, 2019), p. 94.

[81] Ibid.

[82] Ibid.

[83] Ibid.

[84] Peter M. Senge, *The Fifth Discipline: The Art & Practice of the Learning Organization* (New York: Currency, 2006), p. 8.

[85] Choi et al., "Supply Networks," p. 353.

[86] Edwin E. Olson & Glenda H. Eoyang, *Facilitating Organization Change: Lessons from Complexity Science* (San Francisco: Jossey-Bass/Pfeiffer, 2001), Chapter 1 An Emerging Paradigm of Organization Change, "The Self-Organizing Process." Kindle.

[87] Ibid. "Conditions for Self-Organization."

[88] Choi et al., "Supply Networks," p. 354.

[89] James E. Innes & David E. Booher, "Consensus Building and Complex Adaptive Systems: A Framework for Evaluating Collaborative Planning," *Journal of the American Planning Association* 65, no. 4 (1999), p. 417.

organize.[90] These interactions are transformative: the agents share and build upon their resources (i.e., information, power, money, or energy) in order to co-construct new possibilities.[91]

- **Environment:** Because the boundaries of the container are semi-permeable, the group exists in continual interaction with its external environment in a continuous flow of information, energy, and other resources.[92] Consequently, the container and the environment continually influence and impact one another.

When these components come together, leadership-in-community functions more like a living organism that learns from and adapts to its environment.[93] It is not like a machine that is programmed to accomplish a task within a defined context.[94] Leadership-in-community reads its context and responds.

Context. The important function of leadership-in-community is *sense-making.* The community reads the environment and, through relational dialogue, co-constructs meaning that forms its response. The community's mission will continually be re-negotiated as it engages with its context. Gordon T. Smith says:

> Mission is always contextual – for this time and this situation. It is often heard that mission remains static and fixed and vision is dynamic and fluid. And yet surely we need to insist that mission *does* change. People who argue that we are "faithful" if we are faithful to the mission fail to appreciate that we are not faithful to the original vision or mission until and unless the mission is changing – for the rather simple and obvious reason that the situation is different. We change to stay the same. Or better put, we change so that we can be faithful stewards of our vocation – our institutional calling. Context is fluid and thus mission must be dynamic and responsive.[95]

---

90 Olson & Eoyang, *Facilitating Organizational Change*, "Transforming Exchanges."
91 Ibid.
92 Rika Preiser, Reinette Biggs, Alta De Vos, & Carl Folke, "Social-Ecological Systems as Complex Adaptive Systems: Organizing Principles for Advancing Research Methods and Approaches," *Ecology and Society* 23, no. 4 (2018), p. 48.
93 Innes & Booher, "Consensus Building," p. 417.
94 Ibid.
95 Gordon T. Smith, *Institutional Intelligence: How to Build an Effective Organization* (Downers Grove: InterVarsity Press, 2017), p. 43.

Our mission, then, is contextually determined.[96] Global and local influences interconnect and inform one another in an interactive process called "glocalization."[97] Graham Hill further clarifies the dynamic of glocalization:

> The local is a dimension of the global and the global shapes the local. The two are interdependent. They enable each other. They form each other, reciprocally. While tensions exist, the global and local are not opposing forces. They connect – deeply and inextricably.[98]

Leadership-in-community reads the global and local dimensions through dialogue to make sense of its context and respond with adaptive strategies to move the mission forward.

Contextualization requires missional leaders to consider the mental models that influence team behaviors. Reading the context well means that the group must be adept at surfacing, testing, and improving the mental models that actively shape what the group sees.[99] Implicit mental models can inhibit learning if they are not evaluated against the group's experiences of their changing context.[100] Surfacing mental models requires leaders to instill habits of reflection and inquiry within group practice. The group must occasionally slow down to reflect.[101] When they do, they become aware of the underlying mental models influencing their attitudes or actions.[102] Then, they can evaluate whether those mental models are helping or hindering their success.[103]

In addition, contextualization requires missional leaders to recognize mysteries. Mysteries are phenomena that enter our awareness, elude our understanding, but arouse our curiosity.[104] These mysteries prompt groups to explore their meaning through questioning and experimentation.[105] Eventually, the experimentation and consequent experiential learning begins to build stronger mental models as the mysteries transform into new knowledge and effective practices for the mission.

---

[96] Preiser et al. "Social-Ecological Systems," p. 50.

[97] Hill, *GlobalChurch*, p. 26.

[98] Ibid.

[99] Senge, *The Fifth Discipline*, p. 163.

[100] Ibid. 167.

[101] Ibid.

[102] Ibid. p. 175.

[103] Ibid.

[104] Roger Martin, *The Design of Business: Why Design Thinking is the Next Competitive Advantage* (Boston: Harvard Business Press, 2009), p. 9.

[105] Ibid. p. 11.

Compel. The *missio Dei* originates from the trinitarian love of God that compelled him to send his Son to redeem the world.[106] That same love compels the Father and Son to send the Spirit to continue that work of redemption and reconciliation.[107] And now God sends us, his people filled by his Spirit. The love of God compels our mission and leadership. Douglas McConnell articulates, "We begin by affirming that human beings are an integral part of creation, physically embodied persons interacting with the world in which we are embedded, and most importantly in a partnering relationship with God."[108] The people with whom we work are not merely "cogs in a machine." They are agents that reflect the image of the loving God who created them. Therefore, the great task of leadership-in-community is to care for people – both those on the team and those the team serves.[109]

The Greek language used different words to describe various kinds of love. *Agape* love described the kind of love that comes from God.[110] It is the self-sacrificial concern for the good of others and emerges in us as we live in God's love for us.[111] We learn about love most especially by watching how God loves! Jesus taught the meaning of *agape* love most explicitly in his Sermon on the Mount (Matt. 5-7) in which he epitomizes it as the essence of the right kind of life in contrast to, and even in contention with, the world around us.[112] Leadership-in-community displays *agape* love first by deep listening to understand and appreciate the perspectives, feelings, and thoughts of others.[113] Anthropologists recognize that a distinctly human sense of self, what they term the "narrative self," is derived by individuals' "active thought processes, volition, and understanding of themselves in relation to the world around them."[114] People often reveal their sense of self by the stories they tell. Our stories reveal our values, histories, thought processes, and what is sacred to us. Storytelling is an important aspect to leadership and the transmission of culture.[115] We love people the way God does when we take

---

[106] McConnell, *Cultural Insights for Christian Leaders*, p. 2-3.
[107] Ibid.
[108] Ibid. p. 52.
[109] Ibid. p. 52, 76.
[110] Dallas Willard, *The Divine Conspiracy: Rediscovering Our Hidden Life in God* (London: William Collins, 1998), p. 153.
[111] Ibid. p. 203-204
[112] Ibid. p. 156, 161-162, 203-204.
[113] McConnell, *Cultural Insights for Christian Leaders*, p. 76.
[114] Ibid. p. 55.
[115] Ibid. p. 76.

the time to truly listen to their stories. Our commitment as Christian leaders is to show *agape* love that fosters empathy for others within the community.[116]

And empathy compels mission! Scot McKnight says that *agape* love is not only a deep commitment to be *for* others, but also to be *unto* God's perfect design for us: "God loves us, and God's kind of love transforms us into loving and holy, God-glorifying and other-oriented people in God's kingdom."[117] *Agape* love makes deep friendships between "differents" and builds the trust that leads to transforming mission. Jesus told his disciples on the night he was betrayed:

> I have loved you as the Father has loved me. Now continue in my love. I have obeyed my Father's commands, and he continues to love me. In the same way, if you obey my commands, I will continue to love you. I have told you these things so that you can have the true happiness that I have. I want you to be completely happy. This is what I command you: Love each other as I have loved you. The greatest love people can show is to die for their friends. You are my friends if you do what I tell you to do. I no longer call you servants, because servants don't know what their master is doing. But now I call you friends, because I have told you everything that my Father told me.
>
> You did not choose me. I chose you. And I gave you this work: to go and produce fruit – fruit that will last. Then the Father will give you anything you ask for in my name. This is my command: Love each other. (John 15:9-17)

Leadership-in-community obeys the Lord when it prioritizes *agape* love through friendships that compel mission.

Chris Lowney, writing about what has sustained the Jesuit order for over 450 years, describes the central tenet of its mission as love-driven leadership.[118] He states:

> Leaders face the world with a confident, healthy sense of themselves as endowed with talent, dignity, and the potential to lead. They find exactly these same attributes in others and passionately commit to honoring and unlocking the potential they find in themselves and in

---

[116] Ibid.

[117] Scot McKnight, *A Fellowship of Differents: Showing the World God's Design for Life Together* (Grand Rapids: Zondervan, 2014), p. 57-60.

[118] Chris Lowney, *Heroic Leadership: Best Practices from a 450-Year-Old Company that Changed the World* (Chicago: LoyolaPress, 2003), p. 31.

others. They create environments bound and energized by loyalty, affection, and mutual support.[119]

May the same love-driven leadership characterize our leadership-in-community.

Create. Leadership-in-community fueled by *agape* love generates mission within changing contexts. It is essentially creative. An inherent creative energy exists in the space between where a group is (the now) and where it wants to go (the not yet). The mysterious phenomena that occur in that in-between space – phenomena that defies the accepted wisdom – produces a highly oxygenated environment for creativity.[120] Much of leadership-in-community is not accomplishing the goal *per se* as it is leading through that in-between space to discover innovations that extend the horizons of the mission.[121] The kind of dialogue and resource sharing that occurs in the in-between frees the group from the bounds and blinders of current ways of seeing the world.[122] It unleashes new ways of thinking that enables the group to respond well to its changing context.[123]

To ignite the creative spark in the in-between, power within the group needs to be distributed and shared. All members must be *equally* informed and enabled to contribute before the dialogue can be truly creative.[124] In group collaboration, power is a resource that, when shared through *agape* love, generates the group's expanding capacity to create new cultural horizons.[125] From the beginning, God empowered his *imago Dei* to rule his creation in community so that it would flourish, extending the good reign of God to the cosmos.[126] There is a dance that occurs within teams when power is shared through relational dialogue – when one person shares his or her power to increase the power of others.[127] This dance raises the creative potential of the whole team and extends it outward in concentric circles to make something

---

[119] Ibid.
[120] Andrew Johnston, *Fired Up: Kindling and Keeping the Spark in Creative Teams* (Nashville: SALT Conferences, 2017), p. 27-30.
[121] Ibid. p. 30-31.
[122] Innes & Booher, "Consensus Building," p. 418.
[123] Ibid.
[124] Ibid.
[125] Andy Crouch, *Playing God: Redeeming the Gift of Power* (Downers Grove: InterVarsity Press, 2013), p. 51.
[126] Ibid. p. 35.
[127] Ibid. p. 41-44.

beautiful and new in the world for which it is on mission.[128] Andy Crouch summarizes this dance:

> All true being strives to create room for more being and to expend its power in the creation of flourishing environments for variety and life, and to *thrust back the chaos that limits true being.* In doing so it creates other bodies and invites them into mutual creation and tending of the world, building relationships where there had been none: thus they then cooperate together in creating more power for more creation. And the process goes on.[129]

While power can be corrupted in order to "power over" others in ways that repress freedom, leadership-in-community uses power to nourish and deepen life on mission so that the *imago Dei* is empowered to rule and flourish with creativity.[130]

Movement 4: *Oratio*

Heavenly Father,

> You are holy. May your sacred presence in all people and all living things be known and revered throughout the world.

> You are our Father. You care for us as the most loving mothers and fathers care for their children. May we rest today in your care.

> You grant wisdom to all who ask. May your wisdom guide us and shape us in all we do. We are the work of your hand – help us to flourish in insight, common sense, and discretion.

> You, Lord Jesus, are the Prince of Peace. Wherever there is strife in the world today – in relationships, in communities, between races and religions, between nations – may peace, not violence, prevail. And may your children be the first to love peace and pursue it, so that we can bring some heaven to earth.

> Thank you that none of these requests – nothing we could ever ask or imagine or need – is alien to you, because you know what it is like to be human.

---

[128] Ibid. p. 16-19.
[129] Ibid. p. 51, italics added.
[130] Hill, *Salt, Light, and a City: Volume 1*, p. 278.

Thank you, God, for dwelling among us, and for showing us the way home.[131]

In Jesus' name, Amen.

Movement 5: *Imitatio*

- Individual Reflection
  - Journal your responses to the following questions:
    - What key points is God leading you to embrace and grow into?
    - How can you live this out in your life and leadership?
    - How can your missional leadership group pray for you in living this out?

- Group Reflection
  - In your missional leadership group, share your individual reflections with each other.
  - Pray for one another.

Movement 6: *Missio*

- Experiencing Mission
  - Level 1 *Awareness*
    - Pray each day that the Lord sends you into his mission that day.
    - At the end of each day, reflect on or journal about one experience you had that day where you witnessed the *missio Dei* personally. Describe what happened. What was significant about that experience for you?
  - Level 2 *Personal Commitment*

---

[131] Prayer adapted from the ancient spiritual practice of the Prayer Wheel. Dodd, Riess, & Van Biema, *The Prayer Wheel*, p. 29.

- Ask the Lord where he may be sending you to be his witness on a regular basis.

- Make a commitment to serve in that way.

Movement 7: *Communio*

+ Experiencing Mission

  o Level 3 *Group Experience*

    - If possible, the small group may consider performing a mission or service project together to experience mission as a community.

+ Group Reflection

  o Where did you see the *missio Dei* in action this past week?

  o What were the most significant or surprising observations you made about your experience?

  o What did you learn about God from that experience? What did you learn about yourself from that experience?

  o What difference does that make in your leadership? How will you apply what you have learned?

Movement 8: *Contemplatio*

Each week in your small group, spend time reflecting and celebrating the ways that you have seen "God on the move" in the past week.

+ Spend some time in prayer or singing in thanksgiving and praise to our missionary God.

Chapter 4

Jesus Communities

The center of Christian community is Jesus. While this may seem an obvious and harmless statement, it is a scandalous truth that has gotten Christians in trouble so many times! Wherever the Christian movement spread, it carried with it the claim that Jesus is Lord universally. Communities that formed around Jesus endeavored to live out his lordship against all other allegiances. Historically, the Christian church has been persecuted, misunderstood, marginalized, and excluded because of its insistence that Jesus is Lord. Very few have criticized the moral or ethical teachings of Jesus. Many are, in fact, content to describe him as a prophet, religious guru, great moral teacher, or even a visionary leader. But what many others find so repugnant about Jesus is his exclusive claim *to be God* who has come in one decisive and unrepeatable moment.[1]

To illustrate the scandal of Jesus, Lesslie Newbigin, former missionary in India, described the reaction of a typical Hindu:

> I have referred in passing to this scandal of particularity, and now we must face it squarely. To a devout Hindu, heir to four thousand years of profound religious and philosophical experience, there is something truly scandalous in the suggestion that, to put it crudely, he or she must import the necessities for salvation from abroad. "Is it really credible," the Hindu will ask, "that the Supreme Being whom I and my ancestors have loved and worshipped for forty centuries is incapable of meeting my soul's need, and that I must await the coming of an agent of another tradition from Europe or North America if I am to receive his salvation? What kind of a god are you asking me to believe in? Is he not simply the projection of your own culture-bound prejudices? Come! Let us be reasonable! Let us open our treasures and put them side by side, and we shall see that your symbols and mine are but the differing forms of one reality shaped according to our different histories and cultures. If God is truly God – God of all people and all the earth – then surely God can and will save me where I am with the means he has provided for me in the long experience of my own people."[2]

The attitude this man expressed is the epitome of the pluralist world that the Gospel confronts. The supremacy and exclusiveness of Jesus, extoled in Paul's Christ hymn (Col. 1:15-20), seems unreasonable and abrasive among the myriad of cultures, religions, and lifestyles of the world. In such a world,

---

[1] Ramachandra, *The Recovery of Mission*, p. 145.
[2] Newbigin, *The Open Secret*, p. 66-67.

Jesus had a lot of gall commanding his disciples to go and "make followers of all people in the world" (Matt. 28:19).

But history reveals that Christianity has reproduced and sustained itself in the hearts of people *because of* its cross-cultural engagement. Andrew Walls described this reality as the "translatability" of the Christian faith.[3] He said:

> Christianity…has throughout its history spread outwards, across cultural frontiers, so that each new point on the Christian circumference is a new potential Christian centre. And the very survival of Christianity as a separate faith has evidently been linked to the process of cross-cultural transmission. Indeed, with hindsight, we can see that on several occasions this transmission took place only just in time; that without it, the Christian faith must surely have withered away. Nor has its progress been steadily outwards, as Muslims may claim of their faith. Its progress has been serial, with a principal presence in different parts of the world at different times.[4]

When the Gospel encountered people at the frontiers, its transmission succeeded only as they made sense of its claims in light of their own cultural and historical contexts. This is, indeed, how Christianity grew and was sustained generation after generation.

But Christianity's translatability inevitably leads to conflict as the Gospel presents itself as a universal message. When the Gospel meets various worldviews, it confronts the perceptions and mental models of both receiving and sending cultures. Cultural context is not a blank slate! It is filled with its own biases that will resist any counter claims that confronts it.[5] Culture prescribes for the community what is sacred and ultimate, while deviance is resisted and purged. But, as missiologist Lamin Sanneh explains, "… all cultural expressions remain at the periphery of truth, all equal in terms of access, but all equally inadequate in terms of what is ultimate and final."[6] The scandal of the Gospel is its insistence that Jesus Christ must displace those cultural pre-sets and take the place of highest honor within Christian community.[7] Jesus communities are those gathered by and around Christ.

---

[3] Walls, *The Missionary Movement in Christian History*, p. 22.

[4] Ibid.

[5] Lamin Sanneh, *Whose Religion is Christianity? The Gospel Beyond the West* (Grand Rapids: William B. Eerdmans Publishing Co., 2003), p. 5.

[6] Lamin Sanneh, "The Gospel, Language and Culture: The Theological Method in Cultural Analysis," *International Review of Mission* 84, no. 332/333 (1995), p. 61.

[7] Ibid.

And his universal lordship is demonstrated in Jesus communities by their love of enemies, pursuit of reconciliation, generous welcome of diversity, mutual submission and service, and gracious forgiveness.[8]

Because of their welcome of people with vastly different cultural, social, and economic backgrounds, Jesus communities challenge social conformity based on particular cultural ideals.[9] Historically, so much of the Gospel's transmission across cultures was enforced by what Sanneh describes as "mission by diffusion."[10] Mission by diffusion is the unexamined belief that the Gospel *must* be accompanied by the assumptions and traditions of missionaries and their home cultures.[11] Craig Keener gives an example from his African friends:

> Some African friends have expressed surprise to learn that their cultures' traditional customs of bride wealth and family-arranged marriages are more like the Jewish marriage arrangements of Jesus's day than are expensive church weddings and wedding rings. This insight proved valuable because some African Christians were living together for years while saving money for a church wedding. In this case, the problematic custom was partly imported by Western missionaries who assumed that their cultures' customs were de facto Christian.[12]

Regrettably, Christian mission has too often carried cultural chauvinism on its back as it enforced a brand of Christianity upon the very people it intended to "reach," people with different cultural values and lifestyles.[13] Besides the social, political, and economic injustices of such approaches, mission by diffusion fails to proclaim King Jesus in ways that capture the hearts and imaginations of people.[14]

In contrast to mission by diffusion, "mission by translation" respects the recipient culture as a valid and even necessary locus of the transmission of the faith.[15] Jesus communities are comprised of those people *called out from* the world and *called into* a community loyal to Jesus Christ as Lord. Mission

---

[8] Jason Goroncy, "Ethnicity, Social Identity, and the Transposable Body of Christ," *Mission Studies* 34 (2017), p. 224.

[9] Ibid.

[10] Sanneh, *Translating the Message*, p. 33.

[11] Ibid.

[12] Keener, *Spirit Hermeneutics*, p. 79.

[13] Hill, *GlobalChurch*, p. 34-35.

[14] Ibid. p. 34.

[15] Sanneh, *Translating the Message*, p. 33-34.

by translation, then, is the proclamation of the Gospel so that members of the recipient culture can apprehend the significance of Jesus as God's exalted King and translate that reality that into their cultural contexts.[16] More simply, mission by translation is dialogue between the Gospel and the recipient culture.[17] It removes the cultural blinders that impede our ability to see the enormity of God's movements in other cultural contexts.[18] Sanneh says:

> As missionaries of the modern era found, encountering evidence of God's reality outside the familiar terms of one's culture overthrows reliance on that culture as universal and exclusive. A fresh criterion of discernment is introduced by which the truth of the gospel is unscrambled from one cultural yoke in order to take firm hold in another culture.[19]

We have seen this in Jesus' encounter with the Samaritan woman (John 4). Jesus broke through centuries of "formless and empty" divides to *translate* himself into this Samaritan context as the Messiah and living water.

As the Samaritans believed in Jesus through the woman's testimony, Jesus told his disciples, "But I tell you, open your eyes, and look at the fields. They are ready for harvesting now" (John 4:35). God is already on the move in diverse cultural contexts of this pluralistic world. We only need to open our eyes and see! Jesus communities authenticate the Gospel in this pluralistic world when they translate it faithfully into their day-to-day lives within their various cultural contexts. Sanneh says,

> Whatever the question about the essence of the message, the specific and the concrete foundations of mission are set in cultural particularity and historical specificity. Christianity is a religion of historical events that are decisive in the meaning people ascribe to them. That process of attaching meaning to events contains the seeds of personal as well as cross-cultural engagement, and it defines the task of mission. It was not only that these events occurred that interested the apostles *but the fact that individuals wrestled with the meaning of the events.* History is not merely a circular chronicle of things that happened when, where, and by whom; there is an overarching logic of purpose that is intrinsic to the surface parade of events. Human events do not just go nowhere.[20]

---

[16] Ibid. p. 19.
[17] Ibid. p. 35.
[18] Ibid.
[19] Ibid. p. 29.
[20] Ibid. p. 33, italics added.

The Jerusalem Council demonstrated how the earliest Jesus community wrestled with and made sense of the Gospel as they witnessed God's saving activity among Samaritans and Gentiles. During its dialogue and debate, the community read Scripture anew as they witnessed firsthand God's salvation purposes to the ends of the earth. And they wrestled with its implications for the transmission of the faith. In other words, they practiced mission by translation! Let's continue our exploration of this intriguing story.

Movement 1: *Adspecto*

Prayer

✦ Pray for the Holy Spirit to speak to you through the Scripture. Use the following words of Psalm 37 as a prayer:

> *God, show mercy to us and bless us.*
> *Please accept us!*
>
> *Let everyone on earth learn about you.*
> *Let every nation see how you save people.*
>
> *May people praise you, God!*
> *May all people praise you.*
>
> *May all nations rejoice and be happy because you judge people fairly.*
> *You rule over ever nation.*
>
> *May the people praise you, God!*
> *May all people praise you.*
>
> *God, our God, bless us.*
> *Let our land give us a great harvest.*
>
> *May God bless us,*
> *And may all people on earth fear and respect him.*

Scripture Reading

✦ **Read Acts 15:1-35.** Listen for words or phrases from the passage that stand out to you.

The Meeting at Jerusalem

[1]Then some men came to Antioch from Judea and began teaching the non-Jewish believers: "You cannot be saved if you are not circumcised as Moses

taught us." ²Paul and Barnabas were against this teaching and argued with these men about it. So the group decided to send Paul, Barnabas, and some others to Jerusalem to talk more about this with the apostles and elders.

³The church helped them get ready to leave on their trip. The men went through the countries of Phoenicia and Samaria, where they told all about how the non-Jewish people had turned to the true God. This made all the believers very happy. ⁴When the men arrived in Jerusalem, the apostles, the elders, and the whole church welcomed them. Paul, Barnabas, and the others told about all that God had done with them. ⁵Some of the believers in Jerusalem had belonged to the Pharisees. They stood up and said, "The non-Jewish believers must be circumcised. We must tell them to obey the Law of Moses!"

⁶Then the apostles and the elders gathered to study this problem. ⁷After a long debate, Peter stood up and said to them, "My brothers, I am sure you remember what happened in the early days. God chose me from among you to tell the Good News to those who are not Jewish. It was from me that they heard the Good News and believed. ⁸God knows everyone, even their thoughts, and he accepted these non-Jewish people. He showed this to us by giving them the Holy Spirit the same as he did to us. ⁹To God, those people are not different from us. When they believed, God made their hearts pure. ¹⁰So now, why are you putting a heavy burden around the necks of the non-Jewish followers of Jesus? Are you trying to make God angry? We and our fathers were not able to carry that burden. ¹¹No, we believe that we and these people will be saved the same way—by the grace of the Lord Jesus."

¹²Then the whole group became quiet. They listened while Paul and Barnabas told about all the miraculous signs and wonders that God had done through them among the non-Jewish people. ¹³When they finished speaking, James said, "My brothers, listen to me. ¹⁴Simon Peter has told us how God showed his love for the non-Jewish people. For the first time, God accepted them and made them his people. ¹⁵The words of the prophets agree with this too:

> ¹⁶'I will return after this.
> I will build David's house again.
> It has fallen down.
> I will build again the parts of his house that have been pulled down.
> I will make his house new.
> ¹⁷Then the rest of the world will look for the Lord God—

all those of other nations who are my people too.
The Lord said this.
And he is the one who does all these things.' *Amos 9:11-12*

18'All this has been known from the beginning of time.'

19"So I think we should not make things hard for those who have turned to God from among the non-Jewish people. 20Instead, we should send a letter telling them only the things they should not do:

Don't eat food that has been given to idols. This makes the food unclean.

Don't be involved in sexual sin.

Don't eat meat from animals that have been strangled or any meat that still has the blood in it.

21They should not do any of these things, because there are still men in every city who teach the Law of Moses. The words of Moses have been read in the synagogue every Sabbath day for many years."

The Letter to the Non-Jewish Believers

22The apostles, the elders, and the whole church wanted to send some men with Paul and Barnabas to Antioch. The group decided to choose some of their own men. They chose Judas (also called Barsabbas) and Silas, men who were respected by the believers. 23The group sent the letter with these men. The letter said:

From the apostles and elders, your brothers,

To all the non-Jewish brothers in the city of Antioch and in the countries of Syria and Cilicia.

Dear Brothers:

24We have heard that some men have come to you from our group. What they said troubled and upset you. But we did not tell them to do this. 25We have all agreed to choose some men and send them to you. They will be with our dear friends, Barnabas and Paul. 26Barnabas and Paul have given their lives to serve our Lord Jesus Christ. 27So we have sent Judas and Silas with them. They will tell you the same things. 28We agree with the Holy Spirit that you should have no more burdens, except for these necessary things:

29Don't eat food that has been given to idols.

Don't eat meat from animals that have been strangled or any meat that still has the blood in it.

Don't be involved in sexual sin.

If you stay away from these, you will do well.

We say goodbye now.

³⁰So Paul, Barnabas, Judas, and Silas left Jerusalem and went to Antioch. There they gathered the group of believers together and gave them the letter. ³¹When the believers read it, they were happy. The letter comforted them. ³²Judas and Silas, who were also prophets, said many things to encourage the believers and make them stronger in their faith. ³³After Judas and Silas stayed there for a while, they left. They received a blessing of peace from the believers. Then they went back to those who had sent them.²¹

³⁵But Paul and Barnabas stayed in Antioch. They and many others taught the believers and told other people the Good News about the Lord.

Reflection

- When you have finished reading, remain silent for one or two minutes.
- Read the entire passage again. If you have an audio Bible, listen through the passage.
  - Personal Reflection: Journal your thoughts on the following questions:
    - What words or phrases from the passage stand out to you?
    - How do these words or phrases connect with your life right now?
    - How might God be inviting you to respond to this passage?

Movement 2: *Lectio*

Scripture Study
- Read or listen to **Acts 15:12-35**.

---

21 Some Greek copies add verse 34: "But Silas decided to remain there."

✦ Answer the following study questions:

1. Imagine that you are in the room during the Jerusalem Council. You hear the debate, and you listen to Paul, Barnabas, and Peter share their testimonies. Describe what is happening around you. How are you experiencing this event?

2. How would you react to everything that is happening?

3. Why do you think the whole room became quiet after Peter spoke (vs. 12)?

4. What do Paul and Barnabas tell the Council (vs. 12)?

5. Why was it important for them to share these testimonies?

6. What does Peter say God has done for the non-Jewish people (vs. 14)?

7. What does James present as the evidence of what God has done (vs. 15-18)?

8. What do you think "David's house" refers to (vs. 16)?

9. What does God promise to do for David's house (vs. 16)?

10. What will be the result of God's actions (vs. 17)?

11. Why is that important for the non-Jewish people?

12. Why is that important for us today?

13. What does James propose should be the answer to the church in Antioch (vs. 19-21)?

14. Why do you think he recommends that non-Jewish believers should follow the four prohibitions (vs. 20, 29)?

15. How do the believers in Antioch respond to the letter read by Paul, Barnabas, Judas, and Silas (vs. 31)?

16. As you read through this story, what impresses you about the way the Jerusalem Council came to make this decision?

17. What are some lessons in this story about leadership-in-community that may be applied in your church, organization, or ministry?

Reading
The Context of the Jerusalem Council

In this text, the Jerusalem Council was responding to a conflict that erupted in Antioch regarding the requirements of membership into God's special, covenantal people. The Holy Spirit was moving in unprecedented ways among people who were historically alien to (and in some cases, enemies of) the Jewish nation: Samaritans (Acts 8:5-25), the Ethiopian eunuch (Acts 8:26-40), and now Gentiles (Acts 10; 11:19-21). We saw how the Lord used this conflict to instill his trinitarian logic of *communitas*, or oneness, in the early church. God was reconstituting them into a Jesus community of very diverse people upon whom the Lord was pouring out his Spirit. In essence, the traditional narratives about God's salvation needed to be reinterpreted for a new time and place in which God was moving in surprising and even controversial ways.

If we accept traditional scholarship's position that the author of Acts was Luke, then the Luke-Acts volumes were most likely written around 80-90 CE.[22] This is approximately 50 years after the death of Jesus[23] and at least a decade after the destruction of the Jerusalem temple in 70 CE.[24] At this point in church history, the Jerusalem church ceased to be the nerve center of the Christian movement. Jesus communities were spreading to every part of the Roman empire. Luke may have written Acts to legitimize Christianity as it became a predominantly Gentile movement after Jerusalem's destruction.[25] He was eager to confirm to these Jesus communities that the Christian movement was, indeed, the legitimate continuation of God's covenant inherited from Judaism.[26]

Prior to the destruction of the Jerusalem temple, the leaders of the church envisioned that Israel's redemption, the restoration of its ethnic and national honor, was at hand.[27] They anticipated the immediate return of Christ to establish his political theocracy in Jerusalem (Acts1:6).[28] However, after 70 CE, the narrative of God's purposes for his people needed to be updated to reflect their new reality. People from different cultural contexts

---

[22] Wright & Bird, *The New Testament in Its World*, p. 607-612.

[23] Malina, *The New Testament World*, p. 198.

[24] Wright & Bird, *The New Testament in Its World*, p. 612.

[25] DeSilva, *An Introduction to the New Testament*, p. 354.

[26] Ibid. p. 355.

[27] Malina, *The New Testament World*, p. 202.

[28] Ibid.

were experiencing the risen Lord Jesus![29] They were organizing into new kinship groups who centered their worship and lives in obedience and honor to Jesus.[30] These diverse believers dispersed throughout the world now had a "common birth, a new beginning in a new family with a new Father" (John 1:12-13).[31]

What would transpire during the Jerusalem Council would have monumental consequences for the extension of God's covenant people that now included very diverse people. The definition of "God's people" shifted from a primarily ethnic and national identity centered in Jerusalem to a global family centered in Jesus Christ. The church needed to make sense of God's mysterious work because it had significant implications for how the community of God's people would understand itself now and forever. It needed to remember the Scripture and interpret it for God's new order.

Remembering Scripture

At the Jerusalem Council, after all the debate and testimonials, James gave the capstone speech to the assembly (Acts 15:13-21). James "the Just," a brother of the Lord, was recognized as a leader in the Jerusalem church as well as its senior spokesman.[32] Luke seems to have provided James with a place of prominence in the Jerusalem church because he gave James the final word prior to the council's decision.[33] James' words had weight within the community. When he spoke to the council, he argued that the words of the Old Testament prophets agreed with Peter's testimony about "how God showed his love for the non-Jewish people" (Acts 15:14-15). This is extraordinary! James recalled the words of Amos whose prophecy dated about 765-760 BCE and spoke of impending judgement against the northern kingdom of Israel at the hands of Assyria.[34] He re-appropriated the prophecy in support of God's saving activity that was now pouring out among the Gentiles.

James quoted the portion of Amos' prophecy in which God promised to restore and bless Israel after the severe judgment that would fall upon it

---

[29] Ibid. p. 204.
[30] Ibid.
[31] DeSilva, *An Introduction to the New Testament*, p. 436.
[32] J. Paul Tanner, "James's Quotation of Amos 9 to Settle the Jerusalem Council Debate in Acts 15," *Journal of the Evangelical Theological Society* 55, no. 1 (2012), p. 65, 69.
[33] Ibid. p. 69.
[34] Ibid. p. 66.

for its covenantal unfaithfulness (Amos 9:11-12).[35] Amos foretold that God would rebuild the Davidic kingdom, David's "tent" or "house," which will thereafter "possess the remnant of Edom and all the nations that bear [God's] name" (Amos 9:12, NIV). The Masoretic text, the authoritative Hebrew-Aramaic translation of the Old Testament, gives the sense of Amos' prophecy that the royal house of David will be restored and will once again reign over the territory that was once part of David's empire.[36] Up until the first century CE, readers of Amos would have understood that Israel, as a restored nation state, would "possess" these former enemies either by military conquest[37] or, more positively, by their inclusion into Israel's covenant relationship with God by means of the traditional Jewish rites.[38] But instead, James applied the prophecy according to God's current saving activities testified to by Peter (Acts 15:7-11). He suggests that the prophecy's fulfillment had two parts: first, the restoration of David's house was the resurrection and exaltation of Jesus Christ (who is in the line of David) as the King of a reconstituted Israel in his worldwide followers; and second, the possession of the remnant of Edom, Israel's historic enemy,[39] was the inclusion of believing Gentiles along with believing Jews in the new Israel, the church.[40]

By the time of the Jerusalem Council, the Greek translation of the Masoretic text, the Septuagint, had translated Amos 9:12 from "that they may possess the remnant of Edom" to "that the remnant of men may seek (me)."[41] This textual change was not a mistake made by the Septuagint's translators. Rather, they were motivated by concerns of interpretation.[42] They may have used a Jewish method of interpretation (*gezerah shavuah*) in which they linked together two different texts that shared a common word or phrase.[43] These different texts might even have been addressing similar issues.[44] By linking

---

35 Ibid. p. 77.

36 F. F. Bruce, *The Book of Acts: New International Commentary on the New Testament* (Grand Rapids: William B. Eerdmans Publishing Co., n. d.), p. 310, quoted in Kenneth R. Cooper, "The Tabernacle of David in Biblical Prophecy," *Bibliotheca Sacra* 168 (2011), p. 405.

37 W. Edward Glenny, "The Septuagint and Apostolic Hermeneutics: Amos 9 in Acts 15," *Bulletin for Biblical Research* 22, no. 1 (2012), p. 4.

38 Tanner, "James's Quotation of Amos 9," p. 69.

39 Ibid. p. 68.

40 F. F. Bruce, quoted in Kenneth R. Cooper, "The Tabernacle of David in Biblical Prophecy," p. 405.

41 Glenny, "The Septuagint and Apostolic Hermeneutic," p. 6.

42 Karen H. Jobes & Moisés Silva, *Invitation to the Septuagint* (Grand Rapids: Baker, 2000), p. 195.

43 Ibid. p. 8.

44 Ibid.

them together, the translators were using one text to explain the meaning of the other.[45] For example, scholars believe that the Septuagint translators linked Zechariah 8:22 ("And many peoples and powerful nations will come to Jerusalem to seek the LORD Almighty") to Amos 9:12 thus rendering their translation of "possess" as "seek."[46] The translators may have also used a translation technique in which they inferred an interpretation from the major sense to the minor or vice versa (*qal wahomer*).[47] For example, they rendered "remnant of Edom" to "the remnant of men" reasoning that if God can save Edomites as Edomites, then he can certainly save Gentiles as Gentiles.[48]

James himself went beyond the work of the Septuagint translators and interpreted Amos' prophecy for the church's first-century context in the light of Jesus Christ. James did not merely quote Amos 9:11-12 word for word. He also applied interpretive license for the Jerusalem Council. Scholars note that James drew from other Old Testament texts in his application of Amos to the current circumstances, summarized in the following chart:

Prophecy	James' Rendering	Cross-reference	Interpretation
Amos 9:11 "at that time"	Acts 15:16 "after this"	Hosea 3:5 "After this"	Hosea spoke of Israel's captivity in Hosea 3:4. In verse 5, Hosea said, "*After this*, the people of Israel will come back and look for the LORD their God and for David their king."[49]
Amos 9:11 "I will restore" (NIV)	Acts 15:16 "I will return"	Jeremiah 12:15 "I will bring each family back"	Prior to verse 15, Jeremiah prophesied that God would abandon the temple and judge his people. Then, he would uproot Israel's wicked neighbors who took possession of

---

[45] Ibid.
[46] Ibid.
[47] Ibid.
[48] Ibid. p. 9.
[49] Glenny, "The Septuagint and Apostolic Hermeneutics," p. 12.

			their land. In 12:15, the prophecy stated that the Lord will have compassion on his people and will return them to their land. *And* he will establish the former pagan peoples as part of his people if they learn the ways of God's people and live by God's name.[50]
Isaiah 45:21 "Who told you about this before it happened? Who told you this so long ago?"	Acts 15:18 "All this has been known from the beginning of time."		The context of Isaiah 45 described those who were saved out of the nations and, "in faraway places," turned to the Lord (vs. 20-22). James used this prophecy to prove that God's plan from eternity was to bring the Gentiles in as his covenant people.[51]

By connecting these Old Testament prophecies together, James interpreted their meaning in Jesus Christ and the new covenant established in his name.[52] He demonstrated a consistent message across the Old Testament and into the New Testament. The prophecies came together in harmony with the recent events depicted in Acts.[53]

The Translatability of the Christian Faith

What James demonstrated is the translatability of the Christian faith. As Christianity spread, the story of God's saving work in the life of his people needed to be remembered and updated for new contexts. If Luke and Acts were indeed written after the fall of Jerusalem in 70 CE, then the recollection

---

[50] Ibid. p. 13.
[51] Ibid. p. 14.
[52] Ibid.
[53] Ibid. p. 15.

of the Jerusalem Council was significant for Jesus communities that saw the destruction of Jerusalem and the dispersion of its people.[54] These believers would have had serious questions about the validity and future of their faith. In fact, many of the New Testament books reapplied the story of Jesus for new circumstances so that the Jesus communities they were written to would be confident about their history, identity, and continuation as God's people.[55] The Gospels, for example, were composed after many Jesus communities were sprouting up across the empire.[56] They were written to help these communities remember what Jesus said and did, but in ways that made sense in new and very different contexts.[57] The interests of the communities required the translation of the story of Jesus directly into their contextual concerns.[58]

This implies that the act of remembering is not simply the retrieval of the objective facts of history from an archive of fixed memories.[59] According to psychologists, memory is more like "a process involving bits and pieces of information that are continually interpreted and reconstructed during the course of remembering."[60] In other words, we update our memories as we interpret them through current circumstances.[61] Bruce Malina says, "…remembering is the production of an articulated narrative understanding of one's life story refashioned at various times. Hence it produces a sort of updated, edited narrative truth."[62] For Jesus communities, remembering the story of Jesus had the purpose of shaping their identity as members of God's covenant people as that story continued onward. Referring to Jesus communities as "post-Jesus" groups that emerged after the ascension of Christ, Malina states:

> What of post-Jesus groups? It seems that the awareness of the need for change derived from "experiencing the Risen Lord." All traditions that mention the point trace the rise of post-Jesus groups to the experience of the Risen Lord… For these persons, it was an experience of Jesus interpreted through a shared story of Jesus that led them to

---

[54] Malina, *The New Testament World*, p. 200.
[55] Ibid.
[56] Ibid. p. 202.
[57] Ibid. p. 200.
[58] Ibid. p. 202.
[59] Ibid. p. 198.
[60] Ibid.
[61] Ibid. p. 199.
[62] Ibid.

believe some specific situation should be changed. The situation here dealt with that divine, cosmic rescue called "salvation." The change sought here was something that would guarantee God's salvation. And the guarantee was accepting God's call to join the group rooted in Jesus as Israel's Messiah to come.[63]

Now as then, the Holy Spirit united Jesus communities across cultures and generations as they experienced the risen Lord and, through his guidance, made sense of their various contexts in relationship to his resurrection and eternal reign. It shaped their ethics and aimed their hearts toward a common hope (*telos*), the consummated reign of God over the entire cosmos!

In the resolution to the Jerusalem Council, the apostles and elders agreed to write a letter to the Gentiles in Antioch and affirm their inclusion into the community of faith without the requirement of circumcision (Acts 15:19-29). They only asked that these Gentiles follow four prohibitions:

1. Do not eat food that has been given to idols,
2. Do not eat meat from animals that have been strangled,
3. Do not eat meat that still has the blood in it, and
4. Do not be involved in sexual sin. (Acts 15:29)

Some scholars argue that these prohibitions were given to the Gentile believers as a compromise to accommodate cultural sensitivities or conservative views.[64] However, more likely, the Council was once again "remembering" Scripture for the current circumstances. These four prohibitions, in fact, connected to those given in Leviticus 17-18 in the context of worship within the covenant community.[65] They were intended for Jewish citizens as well as any Gentile "foreigner living among you" (Lev. 17:8, 10, 12, 13, 15; 18:26). Essentially, the Council used these prohibitions to emphasize the unity of both Jewish and Gentile believers.[66] The Gentile believers' observance of these prohibitions demonstrated that they belonged to the covenant people of God *as Gentiles* based on the Levitical code.[67]

---

63 Ibid. p. 203.

64 Cornelius Bennema, "The Ethnic Conflict in Early Christianity: An Appraisal of Bauckham's Proposal on the Antioch Crisis and the Jerusalem Council," *Journal of the Evangelical Theological Society* 56, no. 4 (2013), p. 760.

65 Park, "Drawing Ethical Principles From the Process of the Jerusalem Council," p. 285.

66 Ibid. p. 285-286.

67 Bennema, "The Ethnic Conflict in Early Christianity," p. 760.

In the end, the Jerusalem Council remembered the narrative of Scripture in the light of God's saving activity through Jesus Christ among the Gentiles. They updated the story of God's covenant people for a new day in which God's Kingdom was moving outward to many different contexts. W. Edward Glenny articulates this well:

> ...the reason given from Scripture as the basis for Gentile inclusion in the people of God, as Gentiles, is the restoration of the reign of the Davidic dynasty in fulfillment of the promises to David. This reign is not as it would have been envisioned in the time of Amos; it is accomplished by the dynamic of the new covenant, a covenant not known to Amos, which has been inaugurated by the ultimate Davidite. Jesus Christ, the Spirit-anointed Son of David, instituted the new covenant in his blood, and God raised him from the dead and established him in his rightful place as universal Lord. From this place of authority, he administers the new covenant and dispenses its blessings to all, Jew or Gentile, who come to God by him.[68]

By recording the Jerusalem Council, Luke "remembered" its significance for the Jesus communities spread throughout the empire after Jerusalem's destruction. What the Jerusalem Council demonstrated is that Jesus communities are "hermeneutical" communities. They continually interpret Scripture, under the guidance of the Holy Spirit, for their ever-changing contexts so that they may live faithfully as God's people wherever they are.

It Seemed Good to the Holy Spirit and to Us

The Jerusalem Council resolved all the debate and discussion by stating, "It seemed good to the Holy Spirit and to us not to burden you with anything beyond the following requirements..." (Acts 15:28, NIV). This is the core of a hermeneutical community: The Spirit speaking through the Scriptures within a community as they make sense of their contexts in regard to Jesus Christ. Kevin Vanhoozer affirms, "...the Spirit speaking in Scripture about what God was/is doing in the history of Israel and climactically in Jesus Christ is the supreme rule for Christian faith, life, and understanding."[69] This, he believes, includes the "faithful contextualization or application of

---

[68] Glenny, "The Septuagint and Apostolic Hermeneutics," p. 24.
[69] Kevin J. Vanhoozer, "'Rule to Rule Them All?' Theological method in an Era of World Christianity," in Craig Ott and Harold A. Netland Eds., *Globalizing Theology: Belief and Practice in an Era of World Christianity* (Grand Rapids: Baker Academic, 2006), p. 108.

canonical truth to shifting cultural contexts."[70] By the Spirit's leading, the hermeneutic community comes to fresh understandings of God's mission according to the revelation of Jesus Christ, especially when it experiences God's movements in new and surprising ways![71]

Context is a very important consideration for faithful biblical interpretation and theological reflection on the life and mission of God's people. God is on the move! And so, God's people must be aware of how God is moving so that they can follow faithfully as his image-bearers. Jesus communities need to continually read and interpret Scripture in regard to their contexts and their contexts in regard to Scripture in order to follow where God is leading and embody his presence there.[72] Orlando Costas explains:

> The purpose of revelation is the true knowledge of God and ourselves. This knowledge is made available in the communion of faith. The church is the community that has appropriated this knowledge and bears witness to it in the world.
>
> Revelation is divine speech – God's Word. This is not to be understood simply as a codification of concepts or propositions, but as history-making creative events, pregnant with meaning... For Christians, the clearest, most concrete and definitive expression of God's Word is Jesus of Nazareth in his life and work (Heb. 1:2; John 1:1-3, 14). The meaning and significance of Jesus, God's Incarnate Word, continue to make themselves known to us... It can be argued that the self-disclosure that comes through God's Word has not yet concluded, although we have sufficient "light" to come to a certain (though open) saving knowledge of God through the revelation that has already been made available in Jesus of Nazareth. He is, therefore, the norm of Christian theology.[73]

The hermeneutical community *needs* a context to discover and appropriate the self-disclosure, the incarnation, of God's Word as it bears his image as its King. Context provides the psychological and social space that makes possible communication to occur between people – communication that

---

[70] Brent Neely, "Kevin Vanhoozer's Theodramatic Improvisation and the Jerusalem Council of Acts 15," *Evangelical Review of Theology* 43, no. 1 (2019), p. 6.

[71] Ibid. p. 12.

[72] Ibid.

[73] Orlando E. Costas, *Liberating News: A Theology of Contextual Evangelization* (Eugene: Wipf and Stock Publishers, 1989), p. 3.

helps them make sense of their world.[74] When people inhabit this space together, they can share information, feelings, experiences, ideas, and values. And they can weave them together to form new meanings. Costas agrees, "Because knowledge is contextual, it is also practical. It is human sensorial activity, shaped by reality and geared toward its transformation."[75] This is the creative capacity of the *imago Dei*.

The Jesus community's faithful contextualization requires an interpretive ethos beyond merely a "principlizing" approach to Scripture.[76] Principlizing attempts to identify principles within the Scripture text that stand outside of the text's genre and its historical and cultural contexts. Its goal is to extract those principles from the text as abstract "truths" so that they can be applied universally unconditioned by the particularities of any context (i.e., culture, history, circumstances, worldviews).[77] Principlizing promises to deliver the "objective truth" to which all faithful Christians ought to subscribe.[78] It presumes that the text presents meaning without any interpretive mediation.[79]

However, according to cognitive scientists, meaning emerges as human minds construct it through relationship and dialogue with the text, each other, and their environments.[80] In reality, no one can avoid the interpretive grid of their specific cultural context. Everyone lives within a context that unavoidably shapes their worldviews. While God is the eternal and universal God over all cultures and contexts, Christian faith simply cannot be practically experienced without a context.[81] People can only experience it within the historical and culturally conditioned forms that it takes in their local situations.[82]

We discovered how the Jerusalem Council re-appropriated various Scriptures for a new context that was quite different from those in which those Scriptures were originally given. But they did so to remain faithful to

---

[74] Orlando Costas, *Christ Outside the Gate: Mission Beyond Christendom* (Eugene: Wipf & Stock Publishers, 1982), p. 4.

[75] Ibid.

[76] John Sanders, *Theology in the Flesh: How Embodiment and Culture Shape the Way We Think about Truth, Morality, and God* (Minneapolis: Fortress Press, 2017), p. 119.

[77] Ibid.

[78] Ibid. p. 119-120.

[79] Ibid. p. 118, 121.

[80] Ibid.

[81] Walls, *The Missionary Movement in Christian History*, p. 235.

[82] Ibid.

the *127eSilva Dei*. They changed in order to stay the same! Theologian John Sanders affirms:

> God's words are revised by other writers speaking in God's name, suggesting that the Bible itself exemplifies how communities of faith reflect on God's word and even change it where necessary. These revisions are not made casually. They were done in order to assist the present community to remain faithful to the purposes and *telos* of God as the people journeyed with God.[83]

The Jerusalem Council expressed the hallmark of the hermeneutic community: "It seemed good to the Holy Spirit and to us!" We read our experiences in light of Scripture.[84] But our experiences also influence how we read Scripture.[85] The hermeneutical community invites the Holy Spirit to help it read both Scripture and context faithfully. And it trusts him to lead it so that the eternal truth of Jesus Christ can be contextualized into the "formless and empty" places where God is on the move.

Movement 3: *Meditatio*

Within a Jesus community, contextualization is a deeply communal process of prayer, reflection, dialogue, and commitment through which the Holy Spirit forms the community into a true reflection of God's image within its specific time and space.[86] Wise contextualization does not compromise the Gospel to the moods of any culture's shifting values. Instead, it *embodies* the universal reality of God's Kingdom within the contingent contexts of our temporal lives.[87] Lesslie Newbigin states:

> True contextualization happens when there is a community which lives faithfully by the gospel and in the same costly identification with the people in their real situations as we see in the earthly ministry of Jesus. Where these conditions are met, the sovereign Spirit of God does his own surprising work.[88]

---

[83] Sanders, *Theology in the Flesh*, p. 132.
[84] Keener, *Spirit Hermeneutics*, p. 26.
[85] Ibid.
[86] Craig Ott & Gene Wilson, *Global Church Planting: Biblical Principles and Best Practices for Multiplication* (Grand Rapids: Baker Academic, 2011), p. 111.
[87] Paul G. Hiebert, *The Gospel in Human Contexts: Anthropological Explorations for Contemporary Missions* (Grand Rapids: Baker Academic, 2009), p. 26.
[88] Lesslie Newbigin, *The Gospel in a Pluralist Society* (Grand Rapids: William B. Eerdmans Publishing Company, 1989), p. 154.

Leadership-in-community is a hermeneutical community. It interprets both Scripture and context in order to discern wisely how the group ought to live, work, and relate faithfully as redeemed bearers of the image of its King Jesus.[89] Newbigin continues, "And since the gospel does not come as a disembodied message, but as the message of a community which claims to live by it and which invites others to adhere to it, the community's life must be so ordered that it 'makes sense' to those who are so invited."[90]

Community Themes

The Jerusalem Council highlights four community themes regarding Jesus communities that will shape our leadership-in-community: Scripture, spiritual formation, learning, and the Holy Spirit.

Scripture. Scripture is the primary source of God's revelation to us.[91] In it, we find the faithful record of God's saving activity throughout the ages, first in ancient Israel and then in the early Jesus communities.[92] In the canon of Scripture, God has given us his divinely inspired "measuring stick"[93] by which all other claims to revelation are evaluated, especially those claims that call us to live in a manner befitting God's people (2 Tim. 3:14-17).[94]

The Bible is not merely a timeless set of principles which we retrieve and apply to our very different situations.[95] The content of the canon of Scripture was drafted over centuries of time to different audiences facing different situations, and in multiple literary genres meant to produce a certain rhetorical effect on its audiences. When we define the Gospel in propositional terms and seek to transmit it unchanged and uncontaminated by historical or cultural circumstances, we lose something very significant in its meaning.[96] We fail to let it speak as the word of God to those times and places. The "principlizing" approach decontextualizes Scripture from its original forms, including its languages, cultures, literary forms, and interpretations, and sets it in formless (or "abstract") propositional statements that can be dropped

---

[89] Ott & Wilson, *Global Church Planting*, p. 111-112.
[90] Newbigin, *The Gospel in a Pluralist Society*, p. 141.
[91] Costas, *Liberating News*, p. 3-4.
[92] Ibid. p. 4.
[93] "Measuring stick" is the literal meaning of the word "canon."
[94] Keener, *Spirit Hermeneutics*, p. 107-118.
[95] McKnight, *The Blue Parakeet*, p. 25.
[96] Hiebert, *The Gospel in Human Contexts*, p. 21.

into any context.[97] But, quite frankly, this approach to Scripture is untenable. Even the best of us tend to pick and choose what Scriptures have relevance to our lives and churches at any given moment.[98] The purpose of the Scripture's various forms is, in fact, to communicate significant meaning about God, the creation, his mission, humans, sin, and redemption through Christ – the Bible's *metanarrative* – in ways that cannot simply be captured in mere propositions.[99] They help us make sense of the Bible's message and its relevance for our contextual concerns.

In Acts 15, we saw that the apostles and elders read Scripture to make sense of their experiences. They interpreted the Scripture in light of the redemptive story of God throughout the history of Israel, the life and ministry of Jesus, and the outpouring of the Holy Spirit on the Gentiles. And they communicated what they discerned God was doing now so that others could live in the fullness of the Gospel. In the same way, our leadership-in-community must read and interpret Scripture for our contextual concerns. But it must do so in a way that honors God and welcomes the Scripture as his Word for all times.[100] We must learn to read Scripture *canonically* and *contextually*. The Scripture is canonical in the sense that it contains a theological unity across its entirety.[101] All of its various parts come together to tell the overarching metanarrative of God and his redeeming love. But it is also contextual in the sense that it speaks that story into our day-to-day realities.[102] Reading Scripture canonically and contextually reflects our priestly function as the *imago Dei* – that we represent God to the world, and we create meaningful cultures that extend the good reign of God to the formless and empty places of this world.

Therefore, the task of leadership-in-community as a hermeneutical community is *discernment*. Leadership-in-community contemplates Scripture as the grand story that our mission is caught up in. It is the story of God's revelation of himself and his redemptive acts throughout history. Orlando Costas agrees:

---

[97] Sanders, *Theology in the Flesh*, p. 116.
[98] McKnight, *The Blue Parakeet*, p. 13.
[99] Sanders, *Theology in the Flesh*, p. 115-116.
[100] Ibid.
[101] Darrell L. Bock, *Cultural Intelligence: Living for God in a Diverse, Pluralistic World* (Nashville: B&H Academic, 2020), p. 101.
[102] Ibid.

[The Bible] testifies to God's self-disclosure as witnessed to and interpreted by the people of God through music and poetry, prayers and liturgies, historical narratives, religious instruction, and preaching – materials recorded, edited, and integrated into a library (Bible) of authorized writings (canon). Christians recognize the Bible as God's Word insofar as it is the written record of God's revelation and the product of the inspirational activity of the Holy Spirit (who "breathed" inspiration into its complex list of collaborators), God's saving word amidst the frail and fallible reality of human history. As God's written Word, it is confirmed by the power of the Holy Spirit, manifested in the proclamation and teaching of the gospel and its saving effect in the life and mission of the community of faith. This explains why many Christians consider the Bible to be a rule of faith and practice: it instructs, reproves, corrects, and guides in the practice of faith (cf. 2 Tim. 3:16-17).[103]

When we read the Bible as the story of God and his people, we interpret it with discernment through dialogue and prayer so that the story shapes our identity and ethics as the people of God in our specific contexts.[104]

Scot McKnight simplifies the overarching story of the Bible as "creation, fall, *and then covenant community* – page after page of community – *as the context* in which our wonderful *redemption* takes place."[105] He continues:

That redemptive story about the covenant community gains its shape from the King and His Kingdom Story: our focus is to be on God, who at this point in the Story is the sole King.... This King designs immediately a way for cracked *Eikons* [God's image bearers] to experience communion with the King and with others in the covenant community called Israel, called "the kingdom" often enough in the Bible.[106]

Covenant community is how we, as God's people, experience the blessings of His redemption.[107] Therefore, the interpretive work of leadership-in-community is strongly focused on restoring and maintaining the unity of those within the covenant community.[108] When we read Scripture, we must take a relational approach. We interpret within the covenant community that

---

103 Costas, *Liberating News*, p. 4.
104 McKnight, *The Blue Parakeet*, p. 139.
105 Ibid. p. 80.
106 Ibid.
107 Ibid. p. 81.
108 Ibid. p. 81.

includes God, his people throughout time, and ourselves. First, we approach Scripture in the conviction that behind it is a God that wants to relate with us and communicate to us.[109] Second, we recognize that we participate in a historical conversation about the meaning of Scripture as God's revelation to his people.[110] We explore the Scripture's meaning in the original context and we engage with how the people of God have historically applied its meaning for different times and places.[111] And finally, out of love for God and each other, we respectfully dialogue with and listen to others in our Jesus communities to make sense of the Scripture for our diverse contexts.[112] McKnight says, "We have learned to discern how to live out the Bible in our world today; we have discerned what to do and what not to do, what to keep as permanent and what to see as 'that was then.' We do more than read and apply; we read, we listen, and we (in connection with God's Spirit and God's people) discern."[113]

We also interpret Scripture in relation to the world around us. We are on mission because our God is on the move! As a covenant community, we are called to embody God's redemption story in our lives and ethics so that we may be witnesses of Christ in all the world (Acts 1:8). McKnight argues that "any method of Bible study that doesn't lead to transformation abandons the missional path of God and leaves us stranded."[114] While the Spirit illuminates the minds and hearts of the community of believers to understand Scripture, he also empowers the community for his mission.[115] Knowledge that does not compel mission in the covenant community is useless. Costas agrees:

> Indeed, the knowledge of God does not come merely or even primarily as the result of intellectual effort. For God is not an object that can be analyzed and dissected like a plant or a body. Nor... is God a pure concept that can be studied abstractly. *The knowledge of God is, above all else, communion with God, the experience of God's presence, the fulfillment of God's will, and participation in God's mission.* It is a holistic knowledge because it is relational, experiential, ethical, and missional.[116]

---

[109] Ibid. p. 100-101.
[110] Ibid. p. 100.
[111] Ibid.
[112] Keener, *Spirit Hermeneutics*, p. 66
[113] McKnight, *The Blue Parakeet*, p. 133.
[114] Ibid. p. 115.
[115] Keener, *Spirit hermeneutics*, p. 43.
[116] Costas, *Liberating News*, p. 7, italics added.

Leadership-in-community stands in the crossroads between God's mission and the world in which God's people are called to be his witnesses. Reading Scripture missionally necessitates faithful contextualization. The people of God live out the eternal story of God's salvation in their own time and place.[117] In doing so, the covenant community is a real-life witness to Jesus Christ, who has made his home among us and whose inbreaking Kingdom is restoring all creation to the flourishing life he intends.[118]

Spiritual Formation. Leadership-in-community that embodies the story of God's redemption is not primarily taught through skill development or training programs. It grows organically in the life of the covenant community through spiritual formation. Spiritual formation is growing into the fullness of Christ: our lives kept with him, our minds set on him, and our earthly natures put to death (Col. 3:1-4). Paul wrote to the Corinthians:

> The Lord is the Spirit, and where the Spirit of the Lord is, there is freedom. And our faces are not covered. We all show the Lord's glory, and we are being changed to be like him. This change in us brings more and more glory, which comes from the Lord, who is the Spirit." (2 Cor. 3:17-18)

Spiritual formation is becoming more like Jesus. Graham Hill states:

> Discipleship and conformity go hand in glove. They're inseparable....
> We must submit to Christ and receive his sonship and glory. Through the death and resurrection of Christ, and in the power of the Spirit, the church participates in Jesus's sonship and in his just and righteous rule over all creation – so that God's shalom and glory might fill the whole earth. We shared in the Son's glory.[119]

The implication of this is that we must recognize that our organizations are spaces of spiritual formation. The day-to-day routines, policies and procedures, organizational structures, and the work responsibilities and tasks – all of it is part of God's great work of shaping us into a people compelled by his mission! While many assume it is inappropriate to talk about spiritual formation in today's organizations, leadership-in-community needs to embrace spiritual formation as an indispensable aspect of our mission.

---

[117] McKnight, *The Blue Parakeet*, p. 265.
[118] Volf & Croasmun, *For the Life of the World*, p. 75-80.
[119] Hill, *Salt, Light, and a City: Volume 2*, p. 209.

Spiritual formation practices in the organization embed the values of God's Kingdom in the hearts, imaginations, and behaviors of the covenant community. Values are defined as:

> Central desires or beliefs regarding final states or desirable conducts that transcend specific situations, guide the choice and evaluation of our decisions and, therefore, of our conducts, becoming an integral part of our way of being and acting to the point of shaping our character.[120]

For this reason, organizational values emerge from the narrative in which the community understands itself and its mission. Our values are the answers to our most basic, intrinsic questions, including:

- What is our identity?
- Who do we understand ourselves to be?
- What preserves our unity as a community?
- What do we hope for (our *telos*)?

These are the questions that illuminate the story we believe we are living out. Robert Roberts calls them "constitutive narratives" and they surface our values and drive our ethics.[121] In the story of Scripture, Jesus Christ reconstitutes God's covenant people and leads them as their King toward the renewal (*133eSilv*) of all things through his good reign. Leadership-in-community incorporates spiritual formation practices in the organization that rehearse that story so that its Kingdom values become embedded in the community's imagination, priorities, ethics, and decisions.

A key problem in the principlizing approach to Scripture is that its decontextualized propositions do not capture the missional hearts and imaginations of people. As we have seen, Scripture is not a set of principles or rules, but is a "comprehensive understanding of reality" that includes "all life originating from God, the nature of God and man, and life's meaning."[122] Spiritual formation allows people to use *all* their faculties to discern from Scripture the narratives and values of the Kingdom that *ought to* guide their actions.[123]

---

120 Antonio Argandoña, "Fostering Values in Organizations," *Journal of Business Ethics* 45, no. 1/2 (2003), p. 16.

121 Robert Roberts, "Narrative Ethics," *Philosophy Compass* 7, no. 3 (2012), p. 180.

122 David Kim, Dan Fisher, & David McCalman, "Modernism, Christianity, and Business Ethics: A Worldview Perspective," *Journal of Business Ethics* 90 (2009), p. 119.

123 Ibid.

Spiritual formation is fostered by personal and organizational habits that build the corporate culture desired by leadership-in-community. Habits are learned behaviors, generally associated with past successes, that become embedded practices in the organization.[124] The more these habits are practiced, the more they reinforce the community's identity so that alternative actions seem less acceptable or practical.[125] James K. A. Smith argues that "a desire for and orientation to a particular vision of the good life (the kingdom) becomes operative in us (motivating actions, decisions, etc.) by becoming an integral part of the fabric of our *dispositions* – our precognitive tendencies to act in certain ways and toward certain ends."[126] Thus, our spiritual formation habits shape our values, behaviors, and cultures toward the vision of flourishing that burns in our hearts.

Indeed, our organizations are sacred spaces that God uses to develop our souls.[127] They are the contexts in which we interact with other people in love and service in the hope of achieving common goals. Gordon Smith says, "Institutions are spheres of human involvement and influence where we can grow in wisdom, learn what it means to love the other, foster a capacity for vocational and personal integrity and, of course, learn to live with joy and peace in the midst of difficulty and, not infrequently, turmoil."[128] We need to view our organizations as places of rich spiritual formation. Even its structures, policies, and procedures ought to be the lived-out reflections of our community's values.

Learning. Within complex and changing environments, leadership-in-community requires contextualization to live out its values faithfully. Consequently, learning is a vital concern for missional leadership. Much of the focus of leadership-in-community is to continually develop shared meaning within the group so that it may wisely discern the way forward.

Learning within a group asks the question, "How do we know what we know?" The Newtonian vision of knowledge idealizes objective truth – just the facts derived from empirical processes emptied of feelings or morals.[129] And so, our knowledge commitments become validated on purely

---

[124] Phillippa Lally & Benjamin Gardner, "Promoting Habit Formation," *Health Psychology Review* 7, no. 1 (2013), p. 137.

[125] Ibid.

[126] Smith, *Desiring the Kingdom*, p. 55.

[127] Smith, *Institutional Intelligence*, p. 207.

[128] Ibid.

[129] Heibert, *The Gospel in Human Contexts*, p. 20.

rational and objectives grounds.[130] However, the true work of theology is the deep reflection on our faith in the light of our historical and cultural contexts.[131] We can only know reality in part, not in its entirety, because we can only live within contingent, or temporal, contexts (1 Cor. 13:8-10).[132] Our knowledge, according to missiological anthropologist Paul Hiebert, is more like a road map:

> Maps must correspond to reality in what they claim to affirm, but they are mental images that are schematic, approximate, and – of necessity – limited and selective. A road map does not make truth claims about property boundaries or economic variables. Moreover, to be useful it must be simple, not showing every bend in the road or every pothole or bridge. However, it must get drivers to their intended destinations.[133]

Our knowledge is an embodied human understanding of much deeper realities. It will always be temporal and perspectival, and it arises in response to the questions that we raise considering our contextual circumstances.[134] We use various signs (including language, gestures, sounds, and images), all with their own contextual and subjective forms, in our efforts to construct and share the meaning of these realities for our times and places.[135]

According to Heibert, we need a "community-based hermeneutics in which dialogue serves to correct the biases of individuals. On the global scale, this calls for both local and global theologies."[136] Leadership-in-community learning is a social dynamic in which the members of the group share their resources (skills, knowledge, perspectives, finances, and power) through exchanges of trust. These exchanges create new forms of social, intellectual, and political capital necessary to solve problems.[137] Through collaboration, team members build new and stronger relationships that enhance communication, learning, and problem solving.[138] The highest form of

---

[130] Ibid.
[131] Costas, *Christ Outside the Gate*, p. 3.
[132] Heibert, *The Gospel in Human Contexts*, p. 28.
[133] Ibid. p. 28.
[134] Ibid. p. 29.
[135] Ibid. p. 27-29.
[136] Ibid. p. 29.
[137] Innes & Booher, "Consensus building and Complex Adaptive Systems," p. 414.
[138] Ibid.

learning in collaboration is "double loop learning," defined as the more creative type of learning that occurs when:

> ...a group, stymied by its differences, reassesses its purposes and changes its task. In this process, individual participants may discover ways to accommodate others' interests without damaging their own. They may learn how all participants' interests are interconnected and come to see the problem as a joint one in which each has a stake. They may even change their understanding of their interests. They may conclude that [collaboration] can work more effectively for them than confrontational tactics, and in the future they may seek out dialogue rather than bringing lawsuits or creating opposing legislative proposals.[139]

Leadership-in-community works to build the atmosphere where such generative collaboration can occur. Especially within teams of diverse members, collaboration enhances team learning and performance by welcoming the resources of different team members.

Collaboration is essential for contextualization. As teams attempt to make sense of their contexts, they need the opportunities to slow down and reflect on their experiences. When a team collaborates, they can grasp the phenomena, or "mysteries," they experience and transform them into real learning.[140] Experiential learning is a four-stage process, as illustrated by the Experiential Learning Cycle Model in Figure 1:

---

[139] Ibid. p. 415.
[140] Kok-Yee Ng, Linn Van Dyne, & Soon Ang, "From Experience to Experiential Learning: Cultural Intelligence as a Learning Capability for Global Leader Development," *Academy of Management Learning & Education* 8, no. 4 (2009), p. 513.

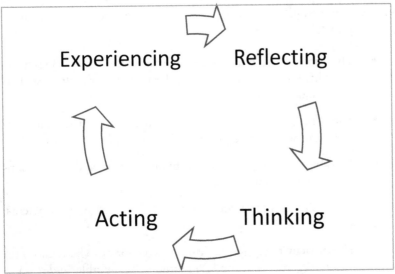

Figure 1: Experiential Learning Cycle[141]

The four stages of the Experiential Learning Cycle are:

- **Experiencing** – The team experiences concrete and tangible events,
- **Reflecting** – The team reflects on their observations about these experiences,
- **Thinking** – The team transforms those observations into conceptual interpretations, and
- **Acting** – The team experiments with their interpretations through more concrete actions.[142]

The actions that the team takes lead to new experiences that further process into new learning. With a commitment to experiential learning, leadership-in-community transforms its relationships, resources, and contexts into fields of new knowledge with the capacity to expand its cultural horizons.

In experiential learning, spiritual formation remains an overall focus. Organizational research has shown that, despite rising secularity in organizational life, spiritual values are, in fact, a central driving force in adult

---

141 David A. Kolb, *Experiential Learning: Experience as the Source of Learning and Development* (Englewood Cliffs: Prentice-Hall, 1984), quoted in Ng et al., "From Experience to Experiential Learning," p. 512-514.
142 Ibid.

learning and development.[143] The research considers the following components of "spiritual intelligence" that lead to stronger team performance:

- The capacity for transcendence such as the ability to envision one's life and work within a grander purpose or picture, such as the Kingdom of God,

- The ability to enter into heightened spiritual states of consciousness such as prayer, reflection, and meditation,

- The ability to invest everyday activities, events, and relationships with a sense of the sacred,

- The ability to utilize spiritual resources to solve life problems, and

- The capacity to engage in virtuous behavior or to be virtuous (to show forgiveness, express gratitude, be humble and display compassion).[144]

Within Christian mission organizations, this secular research challenges leadership-in-community to prioritize relational and spiritual dynamics of the mission because these promote healthy team collaboration. The research agrees that spirituality is a vital component of leadership-in-community because it creates vision and a sense of calling for all team members. Also, it establishes a team culture of *agape* love: a culture of genuine care, concern, and appreciation for others.[145]

Holy Spirit. The most important community theme is the presence and work of the Holy Spirit. Jesus communities are created, nourished, and sustained by the Holy Spirit as missional communities. The Holy Spirit "creates, leads, and teaches the church to live as the distinctive people of God."[146] He points us continually to Jesus Christ and makes him present and central in our community life.[147] He graces the community with gifts to share

---

[143] Arshad Mahmood, Mohd Anuar Arshad, Adeel Ahmed, Sohail Akhtar, & Shahid Khan, "Spiritual Intelligence Research within Human Resource Development: A Thematic Review," *Management Research Review* 41, no. 8 (2018), p. 990.

[144] Ibid. p. 989.

[145] Ibid. P. 991.

[146] Craig Van Gelder, *The Essence of the Church: A Community Created by the Spirit* (Grand Rapids: Baker, 2000, p. 31.

[147] J. I. Packer, *Keep in Step with the Spirit: Finding Fullness in Our Walk with God* 2nd ed. (Grand Rapids: Baker Books, 2005), p. 192.

for service and mission.[148] By trust and reliance on the Holy Spirit, leadership-in-community has the confidence to interpret the Scripture faithfully and wisely for its contexts. We need to listen prayerfully to the Spirit who inspired the text in the first place so that our communities will grow in the knowledge of "one who made us" (Col. 3:10) and our reflection of him in this world.[149] In this confidence, we offer the following prayer to the Holy Spirit:

Movement 4: *Oratio*

Holy Spirit,

> You've promised the gift of understanding. Yet I am so often blind to your presence, your will, and your ways.
>
> Teach me to see you and live. I cry out today for help to see beyond my limitations.
>
> Teach me to seek for understanding as if it were a buried treasure that's waiting and available to me if I keep digging, keep asking.
>
> Show me your presence, your will, and your ways — in the Scriptures, in my ordinary day…in the beauty of faith.
>
> Hear my cry for insight.[150]

In Jesus' name, Amen.

Movement 5: *Imitatio*

✛ Individual Reflection

   o Journal your responses to the following questions:

   ▪ What key points is God leading you to embrace and grow into?

   ▪ How can you live this out in your life and leadership?

   ▪ How can your missional leadership group pray for you in living this out?

---

148 Hill, *GlobalChurch*, p. 123.
149 Keener, *Spirit Hermeneutics*, p. 258.
150 Prayer adapted from the ancient spiritual practice of the Prayer Wheel. Dodd, Riess, & Van Biema, *The Prayer Wheel*, p. 37.

🔸 Group Reflection

  ○ In your missional leadership group, share your individual reflections with each other.

  ○ Pray for one another.

Movement 6: *Missio*

🔸 Experiencing Mission

  ○ Level 1 *Awareness*

    ▪ Pray each day that the Lord sends you into his mission that day.

    ▪ At the end of each day, reflect on or journal about one experience you had that day where you witnessed the *eSilva Dei* personally. Describe what happened. What was significant about that experience for you?

  ○ Level 2 *Personal Commitment*

    ▪ Ask the Lord where he may be sending you to be his witness on a regular basis.

    ▪ Make a commitment to serve in that way.

Movement 7: *Communio*

🔸 Experiencing Mission

  ○ Level 3 *Group Experience*

    ▪ If possible, the small group may consider performing a mission or service project together to experience mission as a community.

🔸 Group Reflection

  ○ Where did you see the *140 Missio Dei* in action this past week?

  ○ What was the most significant or surprising observations you made about your experience?

  ○ What did you learn about God from that experience? What did you learn about yourself from that experience?

o What difference does that make in your leadership? How will you apply what you have learned?

Movement 8: *Contemplatio*

Each week in your small group, spend time reflecting and celebrating the ways that you have seen "God on the move" in the past week.

+ Spend some time in prayer or singing in thanksgiving and praise to our missionary God.

Chapter 5

Witness

The apostles could not stay out of trouble! They kept talking boldly about Jesus, that unsettling rabbi that the Jewish leaders thought had finally been silenced with Rome's help. Yet, these uneducated men would not stop preaching in his name! They had the audacity to proclaim that Jesus is Savior and Lord, a brazen challenge against the rule of Caesar, whom the Romans worshiped as savior and lord. There had already been a series of anti-Roman revolutionaries in Palestine. And the Jewish leaders in Jerusalem were eager to keep such fomenting rebellion under control so that Rome would stay out of their business. But the followers of Jesus just would not stay silent. They were gaining more popular attention all the time.

In Acts 5, the apostles stood before the Jewish high council. "We told you never again to teach using that name," accused the high priest (Acts 5:28). "But look at what you have done! You have filled Jerusalem with your teaching. And you are trying to blame us for his death." Peter retorted, "We must obey God, not you!" (Acts 5:29). He continued,

> You killed Jesus by nailing him to a cross. But God, the same God our fathers had, raised Jesus up from death. *Jesus is the one God honored by giving him a place at his right side. He made him our Leader and Savior.* God did this to give all the people of Israel the opportunity to change and turn to God to have their sins forgiven. We saw all these things happen, and we can say that they are true. The Holy Spirit also shows that these things are true. God has given this Spirit to all those who obey him. (Acts 5:30-32, italics added)

Peter's insubordination was inflammatory! The council erupted in anger and tried to find a way to kill the apostles. But Gamaliel, a Pharisee and member of the council, advised them to leave the apostles alone (Acts 5:34-39). He recounted the many failed Jewish nationalist revolutions of their recent history and warned, "If their plan is something they thought up, it will fail. But if it is from God, you will not be able to stop them. You might even be fighting against God himself!" (Acts 5:38-39).

Gamaliel did not realize how prophetic his words would prove to be. Shortly after, persecution swept through Jerusalem (Acts 8:1-4). Many Jewish Christians fled the city and scattered to various parts of the empire. Everywhere they went, they told people about the good news of Jesus. As a result, Jesus communities popped up everywhere! Jesus' words were coming true: "But the Holy Spirit will come on you and give you power. You will be my witnesses. You will tell people everywhere about me – in Jerusalem, in the rest of Judea, in Samaria, and in every part of the world" (Acts 1:8).

This movement was the work of God and could not be stopped by any human authority. Yet, everywhere the movement spread, as it crossed the frontiers of faith to the places of "no faith" – to the formless and empty – it encountered resistance and opposition from the surrounding cultures. What the world found so detestable was the Gospel's insistence that, as Peter put it, "Jesus is the one God honored by giving him a place at his right side. He made him our Leader and Savior" (Acts 5:31). As Lord and Savior, Jesus demands the allegiance of the whole world! The Gospel as it was lived out by these Jesus communities disrupted the social and political order around them. It was dangerously subversive! Rome could be very tolerant and hospitable to a pantheon of regional deities that *quietly* claimed their adherents' private worship.[1] But it would not tolerate the flagrant claim that Jesus was Lord over all rulers, nations, and thrones.

Even as they proclaimed Jesus as Savior and Lord, Jesus communities did not seem to present an obvious threat to the empire. Yes, Rome needed to manage this movement…but how? In some ways, they seemed to be better citizens because of their allegiance to Christ.[2] Pliny the Younger, the Roman governor of Bithynia between 111 and 113 CE, wrote to emperor Trajan asking for his guidance on what to do with these Christians.[3] His letter is quoted here in full to underscore the perplexing nature of this strange bunch:

It is my practice, my lord, to refer to you all matters concerning which I am in doubt. For who can better give guidance to my hesitation or inform my ignorance? I have never participated in trials of Christians. I therefore do not know what offences it is the practice to punish or investigate, and to what extent. And I have been not a little hesitant as to whether there should be any distinction on account of age or no difference between the very young and the more mature; whether pardon is to be granted for repentance, or, if a man has once been a Christian, it does him no good to have ceased to be one; whether the name itself, even without offenses, or only the offenses associated with the name are to be punished.

---

[1] Ramachandra, *The Recovery of Mission*, p. 226.
[2] DeSilva, *An Introduction to the New Testament*, p. 844.
[3] Wright & Bird, *The New Testament in Its World*, p. 774-775.

Meanwhile, in the case of those who were denounced to me as Christians, I have observed the following procedure: I interrogated these as to whether they were Christians; those who confessed I interrogated a second and a third time, threatening them with punishment; those who persisted I ordered executed. For I had no doubt that, whatever the nature of their creed, stubbornness and inflexible obstinacy surely deserve to be punished. There were others possessed of the same folly; but because they were Roman citizens, I signed an order for them to be transferred to Rome.

Soon accusations spread, as usually happens, because of the proceedings going on, and several incidents occurred. An anonymous document was published containing the names of many persons. Those who denied that they were or had been Christians, when they invoked the gods in words dictated by me, offered prayer with incense and wine to your image, which I had ordered to be brought for this purpose together with statues of the gods, and moreover cursed Christ – none of which those who are really Christians, it is said, can be forced to do – these I thought should be discharged. Others named by the informer declared that they were Christians, but then denied it, asserting that they had been but had ceased to be, some three years before, others many years, some as much as twenty-five years. They all worshipped your image and the statues of the gods, and cursed Christ.

They asserted, however, that the sum and substance of their fault or error had been that they were accustomed to meet on a fixed day before dawn and sing responsively a hymn to Christ as to a god, and to bind themselves by oath, not to some crime, but not to commit fraud, theft, or adultery, not to falsify their trust, nor to refuse to return a trust when called upon to do so. When this was over, it was their custom to depart and to assemble again to partake of food – but ordinary and innocent food. Even this, they affirmed, they had ceased to do after my edict by which, in accordance with your instructions, I had forbidden political association. Accordingly, I judged it all the more necessary to find out what the truth was by torturing two female slaves who were called deaconesses. But I discovered nothing else but depraved, excessive superstition.

I therefore postponed the investigation and hastened to consult you. For the matter seemed to me to warrant consulting you, especially because of the number involved. For many persons of every age, every rank, and also of both sexes are and will be endangered. For the contagion of this superstition has spread not only to the cities but also to the villages and farms. But it seems possible to check and cure it. It is certainly quite clear that the temples, which had been almost deserted, have begun to be frequented, that the established religious rites, long neglected, are being resumed, and that from everywhere sacrificial animals are coming, for which until now very few purchasers could be found. Hence it is easy to imagine what a multitude of people can be reformed if an opportunity for repentance is afforded.[4]

Pliny's letter demonstrates the baffling disruption that the community of faith causes in a dark world. Jesus communities are a peculiar people because of their proclamation of and commitment to Jesus as Lord. While many attempts have been made throughout history to domesticate Christian faith within the values and power structures of this world, true faithfulness as the covenant community of God will always make us strangers and exiles: "God's chosen people who are away from their homes…" (1 Pet. 1:1).

Even today, as God's people who are scattered throughout the world, we are no less strangers within our own native lands. But it is *because* we are "aliens and strangers in the world" (1 Pet. 2:11 NIV), not *in spite of* it, that we are called to be Christ's witnesses…to "tell about the wonderful things he has done" (1 Pet. 2:9). In Peter's first pastoral letter to the believers scattered around Asia Minor (modern-day Turkey), he reminded them of the rich heritage they had in a great lineage of God's holy people chosen to receive the blessings of his salvation (1 Pet. 1:1-5). He reframed their suffering for the sake of Christ, not as the shame that their neighbors intended upon them, but as the honor of their privileged identity in Christ (1 Pet. 1:6-7). Today, we are in the same lineage of faith as those to whom Peter wrote. Jesus, whom we proclaim as Lord, calls us to live in this world as a chosen people, set apart as his witnesses to "be holy in everything [we] do, just as God is holy" (1 Pet. 1:15). As we consider our witness to Jesus within our leadership-in-community, let us listen to the pastoral wisdom Peter gave to us.

Movement 1: *Adspecto*

Prayer

+ Pray for the Holy Spirit to speak to you through the Scripture. Use the following words of Psalm 96 as a prayer:

---

[4] Ibid.

Sing a new song to the LORD!
Let the whole world sing to the LORD!
Sing to the LORD and praise his name!
Tell the good news every day about how he saves us!
Tell all the nations how wonderful he is!
Tell people everywhere about the amazing things he does.
The LORD is great and worthy of praise.
He is more awesome than any of the "gods."
All the "gods" in other nations are nothing but statues,
but the LORD made the heavens.
He lives in the presence of glory and honor.
His Temple is a place of power and beauty.
Praise the LORD, all people of every nation;
praise the LORD's glory and power.
Give the LORD praise worthy of his glory!
Come, bring your offerings into his courtyard.
Worship the LORD in all his holy beauty.
Everyone on earth should tremble before him.
Tell the nations that the LORD is King!
The world stands firm and cannot be moved.
He will judge all people fairly.
Let the heavens rejoice and the earth be happy!
Let the sea and everything in it shout for joy!
Let the fields and everything in them be happy!
Let the trees in the forest sing for joy
when they see the LORD coming!
He is coming to rule the world.
He will rule all the nations of the world
with justice and fairness.

Scripture Reading

✚ **Read 1 Peter 2:1-12.** Listen for words or phrases from the passage
that stand out to you.

The Living Stone and the Holy Nation

[1]So then, stop doing anything to hurt others. Don't lie anymore and stop trying to fool people. Don't be jealous or say bad things about others. [2]Like newborn babies hungry for milk, you should want the pure teaching that feeds your spirit. With it you can grow up and be saved. [3]You have already tasted the goodness of the Lord.

[4]The Lord Jesus is the living stone. The people of the world decided that they did not want this stone. But he is the one God chose as one of great value. So come to him. [5]You also are like living stones, and God is using you to build a spiritual house. You are to serve God in this house as holy priests, offering him spiritual sacrifices that he will accept because of Jesus Christ. [6]The Scriptures say,

> "Look, I have chosen a cornerstone of great value,
>   and I put that stone in Zion.
> Anyone who trusts in him will never be disappointed." *Isaiah 28:16*
>   [7]So, that stone brings honor for you who believe. But for those who don't believe he is
> "the stone that the builders refused to accept,
>   which became the most important stone." *Psalm 118:22*
>   [8]For them he is also
> "a stone that makes people stumble,
>   a rock that makes people fall." *Isaiah 8:14*

People stumble because they don't obey what God says. This is what God planned to happen to those people.

[9]But you are his chosen people, the King's priests. You are a holy nation, people who belong to God. He chose you to tell about the wonderful things he has done. He brought you out of the darkness of sin into his wonderful light.

> [10]In the past you were not a special people,
>   but now you are God's people.
> Once you had not received mercy,
>   but now God has given you his mercy.

Live for God

[11]Dear friends, you are like visitors and strangers in this world. So I beg you to keep your lives free from the evil things you want to do, those desires that fight against your true selves. [12]People who don't believe are living all around you. They may say that you are doing wrong. So live such good lives that they will see the good you do, and they will give glory to God on the day he comes.

Reflection

+ When you have finished reading, remain silent for one or two minutes.

+ Read the entire passage again. If you have an audio Bible, listen through the passage.

   o *Personal Reflection:* Journal your thoughts on the following questions:

      ▪ What words or phrases from the passage stand out to you?

      ▪ How do these words or phrases connect with your life right now?

      ▪ How might God be inviting you to respond to this passage?

Movement 2: *Lectio*

Scripture Study

+ Read or listen to **1 Peter 2:1-12**.

+ Answer the following study questions:

   1. What does Peter say we must stop doing (vs. 1)?

   2. What does Peter say that we should want instead (vs. 2)?

   3. Why does Peter say that we should want this (vs. 2)?

   4. What is the effect of pure teaching (vs. 2-3)?

   5. What does Peter mean when he says that pure teaching lets us "grow up and be saved" (vs. 2)?

   6. Peter describes Jesus as a "living stone" (vs. 4). What do you think he means by "living stone?"

   7. Who else does he describe as living stones (vs. 5)?

8. Why are they living stones?

9. What does it mean to be a spiritual house (vs. 5)?

10. How are we to serve in the spiritual house (vs. 5)?

11. What does it mean to be a holy priest (vs. 5)?

12. What happens to those who believe in the cornerstone and those who do not (vs. 6-8)?

13. Why do you think Peter says that those who trust in Jesus will never be disappointed (vs. 6)?

14. What do you think it means that those who do not trust in Jesus stumble (vs. 8)?

15. How does Peter describe believers (vs. 9-10)?

16. For what purpose has God chosen believers (vs. 9)?

17. What does it mean to you to be chosen for that purpose?

18. What does Peter say that makes believers a "special people" (vs. 10)?

19. Why do you think that distinguishes believers as a "special people" (vs. 10)?

20. In what other ways does Peter describe believers (vs. 11)?

21. How does Peter instruct believers to live (vs. 11-12)?

22. Why does Peter want us to live this way (vs. 12)?

23. As leadership-in-community, how can we live so that others will give glory to God on the day he comes?

Reading
The Indigenous and Pilgrim Principles of the Gospel

Missiologist Andrew Walls made a powerful observation, quoted here at length, about two apparent tensions that have pushed the Jesus movement forward throughout history – the *indigenous principle* and the *pilgrim principle* of the Gospel:

> Church history has always been a battleground for two opposing tendencies; and the reason is that each of the tendencies has its origin in the Gospel itself. *On the one hand it is of the essence of the Gospel that God accepts us as we are, on the ground of Christ's work alone, not on the ground of what we have become or are trying to become.* But, if He accepts us "as we are"

150

that implies He does not take us as isolated, self-governing units, because we are not. We are conditioned by a particular time and place, by our family and group and society, by "culture" in fact. In Christ God accepts us together with our group relations; with that cultural conditioning that makes us feel at home in one part of human society and less at home in another. But if He takes us with our group relations, then surely it follows that He takes us with our "dis-relations" also; those predispositions, prejudices, suspicions, and hostilities, whether justified or not, which mark the group to which we belong. He does not wait to tidy up our ideas any more than He waits to tidy up our behavior before He accepts us sinners into His family....

But throughout Church history there has been another force in tension with this indigenizing principle, and this also is equally of the Gospel. Not only does God in Christ take people as they are: *He takes them in order to transform them into what He wants them to be.* Along with the indigenizing principle which makes his faith a place to feel at home, *the Christian inherits the pilgrim principle, which whispers to him that he has no abiding city and warns him that to be faithful to Christ will put him out of step with his society*; for that society never existed, in East or West, ancient time or modern, which could absorb the word of Christ painlessly into its system. Jesus within Jewish culture, Paul within Hellenistic culture, take it for granted that there will be rubs and frictions – not from the adoption of a new culture, but from the transformation of the mind toward that of Christ.[5]

The dialogue, and sometimes argument, between the Gospel's indigenizing and pilgrim principles creates a tension that propels the community of faith forward in mission. Sometimes the church has erred on the side of compromise or syncretism (becoming too at home in this world) and sometimes on the side of seclusion and detachment (becoming too strange in this world). But the tension is necessary because it compels forward movement! Christian witness exists on the frontline of mission where the Gospel's indigenizing and pilgrim principles meet at the formless and empty spaces where God calls us.

In Peter's encouragement to God's "chosen exiles," both then and now, he revealed that God is building us into a "spiritual house," a temple of which its cornerstone is Jesus Christ (1 Pet. 2:4-5). Quoting directly from the prophet Isaiah, Peter wrote, "See, I lay a stone in Zion, a chosen and precious

---

5 Walls, *The Missionary Movement in Christian History*, p. 7-8.

cornerstone, and the *one who trusts in him will never be put to shame*" (1 Pet. 2:6, NIV, italics added; cf. Isaiah 28:16). God builds us together as living stones into his new global temple which takes its plumb line and levels from Jesus.[6] The community's participation in Jesus determines the contours and dimensions of their Christian witness. As God constructs our community life upon Jesus, we are not put to shame as we witness to his glory in the formless and empty places of this dark world.

In the Isaiah text Peter quoted, the word "trust" (Greek *pisteuō*) has a much deeper connotation than merely an intellectual belief in God.[7] It carries a profound sense of covenantal allegiance to God in whom one trusts with one's whole life.[8] This term was used in political and military contexts to indicate mutual and harmonious relationships between groups.[9] For those who pledge their trust to King Jesus, they are placing their whole lives in his hands in confidence that he will save them from all disgrace.[10]

The Christians to whom Peter wrote faced such shame and disgrace from their neighbors and societies because of their trust in Jesus. Their dedication to only one God, and their commitment to his new kinship group, put them at odds with their former communities.[11] David 152e Silva described their situation:

> A major cause of distress is the disrepute into which the believers have fallen in the eyes of their neighbors. Insult, slander and other forms of verbal abuse are prominent in this letter (1 Pet 2:12, 15; 3:16; 4:4, 14). The Christians find themselves maligned as though they were deviant and vice-ridden, unworthy elements of society. They have fallen victim to their society's social-control techniques of shaming, labeling and marginalizing, all reflective of their neighbors' attempts to cajole them back into conformity with the local customs and values (see especially 1 Pet 4:1-4).[12]

---

[6] Nathan Wheeler, "For a Holy Priesthood:" A Petrine Model for Evangelical Cultural Engagement," *Journal of Evangelical Theological Society* 59, no. 3 (2016), p. 530.

[7] "Honor and Shame as (New) Covenant Language," HonorShame (blog), Honorshame.com, June 3, 2020, http://honorshame.com/honor-and-shame-as-new-covenant-language/.

[8] Ibid.

[9] Ibid.

[10] Ibid.

[11] DeSilva, *An Introduction to the New Testament*, p. 841.

[12] Ibid. p. 843.

Many scholars believe that most of the believers to whom Peter wrote were Gentiles. It was the former way of life of the Gentile believers that Peter described as "evil" and "useless" (1 Pet. 1:14, 18) and a waste of time "doing what those who don't know God like to do" (1 Pet. 4:3). Peter said that formally these Gentile believers were "not a special people" (1 Pet. 2:10), unlike their Jewish brethren who could claim the rich heritage of Israel. He ascribed shame to the old ways of life these believers once lived, even as their neighbors who still lived that way attempted to shame them back into solidarity with them and their "useless" values and gods.[13] The Gentile Christians were now considered by their neighbors atheistic and antisocial because they snubbed the civic festivals and endangered the community's favor with the gods.[14]

Amid such overwhelming pressure, the believers may have started to think that some compromises would be prudent. Having left their former kinship groups to join their new community in Christ, a community that was facing intensifying societal disfavor, these believers most likely questioned the value of their commitment to Christ.[15] Pliny's letter to Trajan confirms that many admitted that they had once been Christians but had ceased to be so because of social and political pressure.[16] In his letter, Peter expressed his pastoral concern for these believers that they would endure this harsh treatment and embrace their new identity as a holy nation in Christ (1 Pet. 1:7; 2:9). But Peter's message is also for us, the inheritors of the faith of those early Jesus communities. We share in the same living hope and anticipate the same salvation they did (1 Pet. 1:3, 9). Like them, we have something of immense value to offer in the formless and empty places of this world: a faith that is "worth more than gold" and will "result in praise and glory and honor when Jesus Christ comes" (1 Pet. 1:7). We carry on their legacy of faith as witnesses of Jesus who put our trust entirely in him.

God's Special People

Peter's letter addressed Christians who were formerly excluded from the covenant of God.[17] They were not a "special people" and their previous lives were "useless," passed onto them from their forefathers (1 Pet. 1:18;

---

[13] Ibid. p. 844.
[14] Ibid. 843-844.
[15] DeSilva, *An Introduction to the New Testament*, p. 844.
[16] Wright & Bird, *The New Testament in Its World*, p. 774-775.
[17] Peter H. Hobbie, "1 Peter 2:2-10," *Interpretation* 47, no. 2 (1993), p. 170.

2:10).[18] They "did not have understanding" and so they "did the evil things [they] wanted to do" (1 Pet. 1:14). They wasted time living immoral lives, getting drunk, having wild parties, and worshipping shameful idols (1 Pet. 4:3). But now, God had grafted them into his covenant people through Jesus Christ who formed them, like living stones, into a spiritual house. They are now a special people, a holy nation, chosen by God to declare all the good things he has done (1 Pet. 2:9-10). Their witness to God's glory was their identity, their priesthood, and their honor.

Identity. Because God included Gentile believers into his special people through Christ, Peter encouraged them to live in community in such a way that looks like Jesus: to live together in peace, understand each other, love each other as family, be kind to one another, bless one another, and share in Christ's sufferings together (1 Pet. 3:8-16). Peter declared that they now bear the identity formerly used of Israel: "a chosen people, a royal priesthood, a holy nation, a people belonging to God" (1 Pet. 3:9, NIV). He appropriated this imagery to describe what it means to be the Jesus community we call the church.[19]

At the crux of this identity change is the mercy of God: "Once you had not received mercy, but now God has given you his mercy" (1 Pet. 2:10). Because of the mercy of God, they belonged to the rich heritage of God's people, a great lineage of faith that bestowed on them incredible honor:

> Praise be to the God and Father of our Lord Jesus Christ. God has great mercy, and because of his mercy he gave us a new life. This new life brings us a living hope through Jesus Christ's resurrection from death. Now we wait to receive the blessings God has for his children. These blessings are kept for you in heaven. They cannot be ruined or be destroyed or lose their beauty. (1 Pet. 1:3-4)

Their affiliation with this new kinship group was not centered on the pride of nation, history, and culture. These fleshly identity markers separate and exclude. But mercy is inclusive! Their participation in the covenant people of God was opened to them only by the mercy of God.[20]

---

[18] DeSilva, *An Introduction to the New Testament*, p. 842-843.

[19] Valdir R. Steuernagel, "An Exiled Community as a Missionary Community: A Study Based on 1 Peter 2:9,10," *Evangelical Review of Theology* 40, no. 3 (2016), p. 200.

[20] Ibid. p. 199.

God's mercy flows from his love that originates in the Trinity, his *agape* love that seeks out authentic relationship in community.[21] It is that trinitarian love that begets our identity and births our mission as God's chosen people.[22] The doctrine of election – of being God's chosen people as Peter emphasized – is insufficient if it does not compel the witness of God's people. Valdir Steuernagel asserts, "...a healthy identity is always an invitation for companionship."[23] So, while Peter's readers were tempted to either confine themselves from (an over-reaction of the "pilgrim" impulse) or compromise with (an over-reaction of the "indigenizing" impulse) their pagan societies, Peter's reminded them of their rich heritage in God's mercy and how that compelled their witness:[24] "[God] chose you to tell about the wonderful things he has done. He brought you out of the darkness of sin into his wonderful light" (1 Pet. 2:9).

Priesthood. Peter further described the believers as the "King's priests" (1 Pet. 2:9). Because our identity flows from God's mercy, our witness is a priestly vocation – reflecting God's mercy to the world he sends us to inhabit. And we inhabit that world at the nexus of the Gospel's indigenizing and pilgrim principles. This means that we must participate in the families and societies in which we are embedded, even while we remain a holy and "strange" people in those same contexts.[25] Jason Goroncy agrees,

> This is part of what it means for the church to not abandon the world – to live in the world while discerning the presence of the Word in common life; the Word who makes us free for 'versatile involvement in the turmoil and travail of the world's everyday existence', for intercession for the sake of the world, and for service of the world in the name and style of Christ. Christians, in other words, 'must live in the world – and not for their own sake, and not for the sake of the Church, much less for the sake of any of the churches, *not even for God's sake*, but for the sake of the world. That is to say, the Christian must live in this world, where Christ lives: the Christian must live in this world *in* Christ.[26]

---

[21] Hobbie, "1 Peter 2:2-10," p. 170.
[22] Steuernagel, "An Exiled Community," p. 202.
[23] Ibid.
[24] Ibid.
[25] Ibid. p. 201.
[26] Goroncy, "Ethnicity, Social Identity, and the Transposable Body of Christ," p. 235, with quotes from William Stringfellow, *A Private and Public Faith* (Grand Rapids: William B. Eerdmans Publishing Co., 1962), p. 74, italics added.

Peter captured this priestly witness by his imagery of the temple (1 Pet. 2:4-8). Just as the Lord Jesus is the living stone rejected by the world, so now also his followers are rejected from the families and other kinship groups to which they once belonged (1 Pet. 2:4-5). Yet Jesus is God's chosen cornerstone of great value! On him, his followers are built as living stones into a "spiritual house" in which they serve as "holy priests, offering him spiritual sacrifices that he will accept because of Jesus Christ" (1 Pet. 2:5). Peter turned the rejection on its head. What the world intended for their shame God redeemed for their honor. He transformed their separation from their previous kinship groups into their acceptance by God as a holy ("separate") nation (1 Pet. 2:6-7). Now, as the King's priests, they make spiritual sacrifices in the temple pleasing to God because of Jesus Christ (1 Pet. 2:5)

The temple was the place where God's people gathered to worship him. The priests in the temple were dedicated to his service, performing spiritual sacrifices on behalf of the people so that God would accept them. In the reconstituted temple of God's people, the priestly task is carried out through essentially Christian community, including acts of goodness, fellowship, self-sacrifice, and service for others and the common good.[27] Because Jesus Christ determines the lines and angles of this spiritual house,[28] the community of priests reflect the goodness of Jesus to the world around them. As Peter said, "People who don't believe are living all around you. They may say that you are doing wrong. So live such good lives that they will see the good you do, and they will give glory to God on the day he comes" (1 Pet. 2:12). The Christian community in its priestly vocation stands, as Peter Hobbie states, "as a lighthouse of mercy to the society beyond its doors."[29] Mission is, indeed, the task that must be exercised in community, because only a community rich in mercy can proclaim and demonstrate the glory of Jesus.[30]

The Jerusalem temple in Jesus' day included a large Court of the Gentiles designed so that even Gentiles could experience the praise of God.[31] Psalm 96 expressed God's intention that his temple would be a place where all the nations would experience and worship him:

---

[27] Hobbie, "1 Peter 2:2-10," p. 172.
[28] Ibid. p. 171.
[29] Ibid. p. 173.
[30] Steuernagel, "An Exiled Community," p. 203.
[31] John Dickson, *The Best Kept Secret of Christian Mission: Promoting the Gospel with More than Our Lips* (Grand Rapids: Zondervan, 2010), p. 28.

> Sing a new song to the LORD!
>> Let the whole world sing to the LORD!
> Sing to the LORD and praise his name!
>> Tell the good news every day about how he saves us!
> Tell all the nations how wonderful he is!
>> Tell people everywhere about the amazing things he does.
> The LORD is great and worthy of praise.
>> He is more awesome than any of the "gods."
> All the "gods" in other nations are nothing but statues,
>> but the LORD made the heavens.
> He lives in the presence of glory and honor.
>> His Temple is a place of power and beauty.
> Praise the LORD, all people of every nation;
>> praise the LORD's glory and power. (Psalm 96:1-7)

This was the witness of the Old Testament community of faith. John Dickson comments on the temple's witness, "The proclamation of salvation and God's glory is intended for those for whom it is 'news,' the pagan nations around Israel. Israel's praise of God – in the temple and the synagogue – was meant to be overheard by the pagans round about."[32]

Now, as a renewed temple built upon Jesus Christ, we continue this witness through our community life. Our mission as the King's priests is to be a sign of the Kingdom of God.[33] We offer our "spiritual sacrifices" (1 Pet. 2:5) – our gifts and prayers – in the community as worship so that our witness to the surrounding nations resounds clearly. Peter encouraged us:

> The time is near when all things will end. So keep your minds clear, and control yourselves. This will help you in your prayers. Most important of all, love each other deeply, because love makes you willing to forgive many sins. Open your homes to each other and share your food without complaining. God has shown you his grace in many different ways. So be good servants and use whatever gift he has given you in a way that will best serve each other. If your gift is speaking,

---

[32] Ibid p. 29
[33] Wheeler, "'For a Holy Priesthood,'" p. 524.

your words should be like words from God. If your gift is serving, you should serve with the strength that God gives. Then it is God who will be praised in everything through Jesus Christ. Power and glory belong to him forever and ever. Amen. (1 Pet. 4:7-11)

As we saw in Chapter Two, the redeemed *imago Dei* is a priestly vocation. We mediate between God and the world: we unlock the thoughts of God in creation and offer them back to him in worship.[34] The priestly task of witness, the offering of our gifts and services in the temple, results in the "glorification of God for his excellence in redemption" so that the whole world will know him.[35]

Even our suffering for Christ is our priestly offering. The suffering that the covenant community faces for its allegiance to Christ has a redemptive purpose. Peter explained that when we suffer for doing good, we imitate Christ who suffered to "bring all of you to God" (1 Pet. 3:17-18). God is glorified when his people offer themselves for the sake of others who are presently in darkness so that they also experience the mercy of Christ.[36] For this reason, the community of faith is one of both priests (indigenous principle) and strangers (pilgrim principle). We participate in the world, even to the point of suffering, so that we are witnesses in this world to the reality and values of the Kingdom of God.[37]

Honor. Peter's pastoral strategy was to redeem the honor of Jesus communities even as they faced intense shaming from their former kinship groups. Because they no longer participated in the religious festivals that celebrated the pagan values of their former kinship groups, they were marginalized as antisocial, atheistic, and nonconformist.[38] Their neighbors used hostility and shaming tactics to provoke them into returning to a more "respectable" way of life with their former groups.[39] But Peter's retort was that those former ways of life were, in fact, what was truly shameful. Instead, he declared that Jesus communities have tremendous honor as those who have inherited the rich heritage of God's covenant people and will receive God's blessings that cannot be ruined, destroyed, or lose their beauty (1 Pet. 1:4). Jesus Christ, the living cornerstone of great value, brings honor to those

---

[34] Ibid. p. 525.
[35] Ibid. p. 532.
[36] Ibid.
[37] Steuernagel, "An Exiled Community," p. 204.
[38] DeSilva, *An Introduction to the New Testament*, p. 844.
[39] Ibid. p. 844.

who trust in him (1 Pet. 2:4-7). But Jesus brings shame to those who do not believe. He is "a stone that makes people stumble, a rock that makes people fall" (1 Pet. 2:8).

The honor-shame social dynamics of the first century Roman world were a powerful force upon the lives of people. But even in today's pluralistic societies, the desire for honor and glory is a powerful motivator. Steven Hawthorne explains:

> We desire glory. Actually, God made us that way. Three features mark humans as creatures of glory: We perceive glory, we celebrate glory together, and we desire glory... Anything truly worthy is also praiseworthy. That is, we don't just behold what is beautiful or exceptional. We call for the attention of others to see and celebrate it together. There is something deeply satisfying about celebrating, with others, someone or something of worth. Perhaps the only thing we find even more satisfying is to be the object of praise and celebration. We are formed with an intrinsic yearning, an essential desiring, to be named, to be recognized, to be loved.[40]

The problem is not that we desire honor. Rather, the problem is that we seek honor in the wrong places! Peter did not chastise the Gentile believers because of their desire for honor. Instead, he reoriented their desire for honor so that it was found only in Jesus Christ. He was emphatic that the idols of the culture around them, to which they were pressured to return, were worthless and shameful (the Hebrew word for idols, *elilim*, essentially means worthlessness or nothingness).[41] Instead, Peter called them to trust in Jesus Christ, the cornerstone of great value who brings honor to those who believe in him (1 Pet. 2:6-7).

Jesus is worthy of our patient endurance until we obtain the honor that our hearts truly desire. Peter's words speak even to us today:

> You have not seen Christ, but still you love him. You can't see him now, but you believe in him. You are filled with a wonderful and heavenly joy that cannot be explained. Your faith has a goal, and you are reaching that goal – your salvation. (1 Pet. 1:8-9)

---

[40] Steven C. Hawthorne, "The Honor and Glory of Jesus Christ: Heart of the Gospel and the Mission of God," in *Honor, Shame, and the Gospel: Reframing Our Message and Ministry*, Eds. Christopher Flanders & Werner Mischke (Littleton: William Carey Publishing, 2020), p. 4.

[41] Dickson, *The Best Kept Secret of Christian Mission*, p. 31.

The good news of Jesus does not remove our desire for honor. Rather, it reorients us toward the One who is truly worthy of all honor, Jesus Christ.[42] Only he can give us the honor for which we long.[43] Therefore, our mission of witness is more than merely a "rescue mission." It is, in fact, more profoundly a "reality mission" as we invite people to respond to the Lord's mercy and to belong to his great kinship group that trusts in him and will never be put to shame.[44] St. Augustine agreed, "The thought of you stirs [man] so deeply that he cannot be content unless he praises you, because you made us for yourself and our hearts find no peace until they rest in you."[45]

Honor is an indispensable component of witness. In both the proclamation and the demonstration of the Gospel, the honor of both God and other people is at stake. The *proclamation* of the Gospel is the community's witness to the honor and glory of our great Lord and Savior, who is worthy of everyone's allegiance. Dickson articulates the driving force of our proclamation of the Gospel: "If there is one Lord to whom all people belong and owe their allegiance, the people of that Lord must promote this reality everywhere."[46]

The *demonstration* of the Gospel, on the other hand, connects God's honor to the restoration of the honor of people. The Gospel is good news to the extent that our witness, as the King's priests, restores the honor and dignity of people by God's mercy.[47] The salvation of Christ reverses a person's status from a position of shame to that of great honor.[48] Witness demonstrates the beauty, worth, and value the King gives his people when they turn from worthless idols and shameful behaviors and wholly trust in him. We must, therefore, be vigilant in our witness to reflect the honor of our merciful King by showing honor to one another and to others.

Witnessing Communities

Witness frames the entire way-of-being for leadership-in-community. While we may come together for different tasks and occasions, the overriding

---

[42] Hawthorne, "The Honor and Glory of Jesus Christ," p. 4-6.
[43] Ibid. p. 6.
[44] Dickson, *The Best Kept Secret of Christian Mission*, p. 35.
[45] St. Augustine, *Confessions of a Sinner* translated by R. S. Pine-Coffin (London: Penguin Group, 2004), p.1.
[46] Dickson, *The Best Kept Secret of Christian Mission*, p. 31.
[47] Jayson Georges & Mark D. Baker, *Ministering in Honor-Shame Cultures: Biblical Foundations and Practical Essentials* (Downers Grove: IVP Academic, 2016), p. 168.
[48] Ibid.

concern for our leadership-in-community is to proclaim and demonstrate the goodness of our God in whatever we do. Missional leadership creates a witnessing community whose priestly vocation extends God's mercy into this dark world.

Witness as a Community Identity. Peter reinforced that, even while we may be strangers and aliens, we are honored inheritors of the great promises of the covenant. We are in the same lineage of faith as the believers in Asia Minor to whom Peter wrote. God is raising us up as a spiritual house in which we also offer our gifts and services as spiritual sacrifices (1 Pet. 2:4-6). Why? So that we can tell others about the wonderful things God has done (1 Pet. 2:9)! We are a special people, chosen by his mercy, *so that* we may be witnesses to his glory throughout the earth.

While individual witness is important, God's purpose remains to raise up a people – a covenant community – that proclaims and demonstrates the mercy and honor of the Lord within the contexts where they live. Rick Richardson agrees:

> God is far more committed to raising up witnessing *communities* than to raising up witnessing *individuals....* Though individual witness is certainly important, the Holy Spirit fills a Christian community and uses the community as a body in witness. Each member has its own particular contribution to make, according to the gifts each person has been given. More important than each of us doing the same thing to witness to others, we each must do our particular part. Then our witness together will be much greater than the sum of our parts.[49]

A traditional view of evangelism that stresses our individual responsibility to share the Gospel verbally constrains the kind of witness that Peter envisioned. The core message of Jesus was that the Kingdom of God was at hand, that God's rule through Jesus his Son is setting the whole world to rights.[50] Witness, then, is more rightfully understood as the reign of Jesus demonstrated through the life and love of the community of Jesus. Whenever the community demonstrates the reality of God's reign, whether in word or deed, the Gospel has been proclaimed.[51] And so, Peter instructs us to "use whatever gift [God] has given [us] in a way that will best serve each other" (1

---

[49] Rick Richardson, *Reimagining Evangelism: Inviting Friends on a Spiritual Journey* (Downers Grove: InterVarsity Press, 2006), p. 27.
[50] Ibid. p. 29.
[51] Ibid. p. 28.

Pet. 4:10). This act of spiritual sacrifice in the temple demonstrates the reign of God to the world around us: "If your gift is speaking, your words should be like words from God. If your gift is serving, you should serve with the strength that God gives. Then it is God who will be praised in everything through Jesus Christ. Power and glory belong to him forever and ever. Amen" (1 Pet. 4:11).

Gospel as a Community Story. If witness is the community identity, then the Gospel is the community story. Essentially, evangelism tells the story of God's saving message, the Gospel, as it has become an integral part of our lives in community. [52] People *belong* before they *believe*.[53] So then, evangelism is not merely getting people to agree to a certain set of doctrinal beliefs or propositional truth statements inadequately described as "the Gospel."[54] Evangelism is about helping people to belong to the community so that they can experience the goodness of God in Christ, the cornerstone of that community.[55]

Furthermore, when people convert, they do not merely change their beliefs, but even more profoundly, they change their primary communities![56] They embrace a new group identity as their allegiance transfers from one lord to another.[57] Richardson states, "Whenever people embrace a new identity – a transformation that is at the heart of conversion – they are embracing the community that makes that identity possible."[58] The Gospel must be so embedded in the life, worship, and leadership of this community that its new and seasoned members continually experience the goodness of God and grow into the likeness of Jesus through their participation in that community (Col. 3:10-11).

Narrative is, in fact, necessary for the formation and continuation of community.[59] Richardson states:

> …stories (are) the only containers big enough to carry truth, because stories convey not just the facts but also the feelings and nuances of truth. Stories are a bigger and better container for the whole of the

---

[52] Costas, *Liberating News*, p. 71.

[53] Ibid. p. 27.

[54] Ibid. p. 28.

[55] Ibid. p. 27.

[56] Georges & Baker, *Ministering in Honor-Shame Cultures*, p. 184.

[57] Ibid.

[58] Richardson, *Reimagining Evangelism*, p. 52.

[59] Andrew Leslie, "How Stories Argue: The Deep Roots of Storytelling in Political Rhetoric," *Storytelling, Self, Society* 11, no. 1 (2015), p 68.

truth than propositions, concepts and dogmas. Propositions are wonderful when filled out by story, but abstract and skeletal when divorced from story.[60]

Through storytelling, the community reinforces the values, ideals, images, heroes, villains, and ethics by which it understands itself as a particular people.[61] Stories also indicate where the community has come from, where it is going, and what it hopes for.[62] A person's identity is formed principally through the significant stories shared through their community.[63] The more salient, richer, deeper, and pronounced those stories are within the community, the more they capture the hearts and imaginations of people and orient their desires toward the ultimate hope that community embraces.[64] Essentially, they become a certain kind of people – a Kingdom people.

Rehearsing the Gospel continually through ritual, liturgy, and ethical practices is essential for effective witness. The culture of a community is developed as its stories take on meaning through the habits and practices the community cultivates.[65] Culture develops and grows as the community's stories become tangible, institutional realities through participants' behaviors and actions.[66] According to Richardson, people are won over, not by dogmas or beliefs, but by an "experiential reality of God" proclaimed *and* demonstrated in the life of the community.[67]

Evangelism as a Community Ethic. If God is highly interested in developing witnessing communities, then witness must be a collaborative enterprise. Richardson says, "The writers of Scripture thought more in terms of *corporate* witness. Each of us, filled with the Holy Spirit, does our part to live like Jesus and minister in Jesus' name. Together, we contribute according to the gifts the Spirit gives us."[68] Collaborative witness is animated by the Holy Spirit within a community that welcomes the contributions of all

---

[60] Richardson, *Reimagining Evangelism*, p. 84.

[61] Leslie, "How Stories Argue," p. 68.

[62] Martha Montello, "Narrative Ethics: The Role of Stories in Bioethics," *The Hastings Center Report* 44 (2014), p. S3.

[63] Roberts, "Narrative Ethics," p. 175.

[64] Smith, *Desiring the Kingdom*, p. 65-71.

[65] Mariana Sueldo & Dalia Streimikiene, "Organizational Rituals as Tools of Organizational Culture Creation and Transformation: A Communicative Approach," *Transformations In Business & Economics* 15, no. 2 (2016), p. 91.

[66] Ibid. p. 92.

[67] Richardson, *Reimagining Evangelism*, p. 28.

[68] Ibid. p. 55.

members' gifts and services. The role of leadership within collaborative witness is to recognize and call to life the gifts of all members in the community for the purpose of God's mission.[69] Some may serve while some may speak (1 Pet. 4:11). But all have a part to play in their community's witness to the reality and reign of Jesus Christ. Only collaborative witness is fruitful witness.[70]

Movement 3: *Meditatio*

Witnessing communities are the "province of the Spirit," in the words of Orlando Costas.[71] At the last supper, Jesus taught his disciples about the work of the Holy Spirit who he refers to as the Helper:

> When the Helper comes, he will show the people of the world how wrong they are about sin, about being right with God, and about judgment. He will prove that they are guilty of sin, because they don't believe in me. He will show them how wrong they are about how to be right with God. The Helper will do this, because I am going to the Father. You will not see me then. And he will show them how wrong their judgment is, because their leader has already been condemned. (John 16:8-11)

The Holy Spirit is the ultimate witness to Jesus, the "teacher par excellence of the truth of Christ's saving work."[72] He convicts people of sin and their alienation from God, and he calls people to repent in anticipation of the inbreaking reign of God in Christ.[73] The Holy Spirit makes the witnessing community a sign of hope for the world![74] And so, Peter encouraged us with these words:

> But keep the Lord Christ holy in your hearts. Always be ready to answer everyone who asks you to explain about the hope you have. But answer them in a gentle way with respect. Keep your conscience clear. Then people will see the good way you live as followers of Christ, and those who say bad things about you will be ashamed of what they said. (1 Pet. 3:15-16)

---

[69] Ibid. p. 57.
[70] Ibid. p. 36.
[71] Costas, *Liberating News*, p. 77.
[72] Ibid. p. 78.
[73] Ibid.
[74] Ibid. p. 79.

Community Themes

Peter's instructions highlight four community themes that will shape our leadership-in-community: vision, ethics, honor, and service.

Vision. A witnessing community is a hermeneutic community. As discussed in chapter four, the hermeneutic community contextualizes the eternal truths of Scripture for the community's real time and place. The community's witness emerges from "incarnating" the reality of Jesus in its life. Consequently, witness is not relegated only to specialists, those with particular gifts or charisma for evangelism.[75] A false dichotomy exists between "missionaries" and "ordinary Christians." Ordinary Christians are those who presume to enjoy the blessings of participation in the community of faith but are somehow exempt from witness.[76] The *missio Dei* decommissions this presumption. All believers are called to participate in the witness of the community.

In fact, witness is unavoidable! In both our words and our actions, we constantly communicate to those around us who or what we worship. If we are a new creation in Christ, then "people will see the good way [we] live as followers of Christ..." (1 Pet. 3:16). Richardson states:

> At the heart of who we are as Christians is a new being, a new creation, produced by the union of God's Spirit with our spirit. This new creation is the determining fact of our existence and the basic ground of our identity. We get it as a gift. Now we need to become as adults what we already are in infancy. The life energy is there. The new identity is there. We merely choose to see it, to embrace it, to live in the reality of what we already are and have already been given.[77]

The responsibility of leadership-in-community is to fan this vision to life for all its members. Leaders cast the vision and set the pace for witness.[78] They influence all members to embrace a shared vision of witness that builds unity and brings coherence to their diverse activities.[79] That shared vision sustains their identity and animates their witness as the living testimony that Jesus is Lord.[80]

---

[75] Ibid. p. 86.
[76] Padilla, "What is Integral Mission?"
[77] Rick Richardson, *Evangelism Outside the Box: New Ways to Help People Experience the Good News* (Downers Grove: InterVarsity Press, 2000), p. 143.
[78] Richardson, *Reimagining Evangelism*, p. 57.
[79] Senge, *The Fifth Discipline*, p. 194.
[80] Ibid.

Ethics. Leadership-in-community fosters a vision for witness by enrolling its members in an ethic of witness. Enrollment is the process of becoming part of something by choice, rather than by compliance.[81] Leaders encourage member commitment to the vision by demonstrating their own sincere and contagious enthusiasm for the mission while also giving others the time and space to "buy in" at their own pace.[82] As members enroll in the vision and come to truly desire its fulfillment, they begin to participate in the community and allow their worldviews, behaviors, and values to be shaped by that participation.[83] They become evangelists of the community's vision as it become etched upon their identities.

Corporate spiritual disciplines are essential in the enrollment and commitment process. Liz Warren and Stephanie Luz Cordel agree, "Storytelling is the most fundamental and profound way in which humans preserve and share information. Stories are used to convey meaning, transmit history and tradition, entertain, instruct, to build empathy and community, and to motivate people to act."[84] Leadership-in-community develops the spiritual disciplines that enable the community to continually rehearse the Gospel story so that it embodies it as a temple of God's presence in the world.

The Virtuous Cycle of Corporate Spiritual Disciplines (Figure 2) is a compelling framework for corporate spiritual disciplines.[85] The Virtuous Cycle creates a community rhythm that engages all members in their shared vision. Through the practice of these spiritual disciplines, members infuse their daily, mundane tasks with "soul-stirring ideals, such as honor, truth, love, justice, and beauty," according to the cycle's creators, Bruno Dyck and Kenman Wong.[86] The Virtuous Cycle presents four practices, one flowing into the next, that build the community ethic of witness.[87]

---

[81] Ibid. p. 203.

[82] Ibid. p. 206.

[83] Ibid.

[84] Liz Warren & Stephanie Luz Cordel, "Storytelling as a Catalyst for Systems Change," Vitalyst Health Foundation, August 2018. https://vitalysthealth.org/wp-content/uploads/2018/08/Storytelling-Brief.pdf.

[85] Bruno Dyck & Kenman Wong, "Corporate Spiritual Disciplines and the Quest for Organizational Virtue," *Journal of Management, Spirituality & Religion* 7, no. 1 (2010), p. 8.

[86] Ibid. p. 8.

[87] Ibid. p. 14.

	Organizational Structures & Systems	Face-to-Face Relationships
Listening	**PHASE 1: Confession** ⟶ - Embrace a "we" fellowship - Identify systematic injustices	**PHASE 2: Worship** - Find God - Resist temptation to blame
Responding	**PHASE 4: Celebration** ⟵ - Try new ideas/structures - Challenge the status quo	**PHASE 3: Guidance** - Ask for help/prayer - Gather information/ideas

Figure 2: Virtuous Cycle of Corporate Spiritual Disciplines[88]

In the Virtuous Cycle, the community begins with practices of confession in which its members embrace a "we" fellowship.[89] A "we" fellowship calls all members to share responsibility for the mission and, in humility, for the structural or systematic injustices that keep the community from progressing toward its vision.[90] Confession then releases people to worship. In worship, the community acknowledges the lordship and goodness of its God as each member offers his or her gifts or services (1 Pet. 2:5).[91] Worship of God also compels us to value and welcome the image of God in others and welcome them to participate with us in the mission.[92] Then, the community waits in "holy expectancy" for God to speak and work among them.[93]

Corporate guidance is "all about discerning ideas *in community*."[94] First, guidance embraces corporate habits of prayer as the community seeks for God's leading. Second, guidance includes others in the decision-making process.[95] As a spiritual discipline, guidance seeks the wisdom, perspectives, knowledge, and counsel of others, and consequently, actively includes diverse

---

[88] Adapted from Dyck & Wong's Virtuous Cycle Model of Spiritual Disciplines. Dyck & Wong, "Corporate Spiritual Disciplines," p. 14.
[89] Ibid. p. 15-16.
[90] Ibid.
[91] Ibid. p. 16-17.
[92] Ibid. p. 17.
[93] Ibid. p. 16.
[94] Ibid.
[95] Ibid. p. 18.

voices in community dialogue.[96] Third, guidance welcomes innovation and creativity that challenges the status quo while discerning how new ideas fit or necessitate change within corporate systems and structures.[97]

Following guidance, celebration is an important response to positive changes within the community as it advances toward its corporate vision.[98] Celebration is often overlooked in "business-as-usual" practices. But truly positive change that expands the horizons of the group's vision should be celebrated! The community delights in the joy that God brings as he blesses the work of their hands.[99] Celebration honors the Lord by rejoicing in hope of the new creation that his Kingdom brings. This kind of celebration generates witness!

Honor. Restoring honor is at the heart of witness. In the late 1990s, at InterVarsity Christian Fellowship's Urbana Missions Conference, a contingent of Japanese Christian students publicly apologized to other Asian students in attendance for the sins that Japan committed against their nations before and during World War II.[100] Katie Rawson, InterVarsity's International Student Ministry Senior Resource Developer, describes this beautiful scene: "By recognizing and appropriately responding to acts of shaming, the Japanese students opened doors to reconciliation, and nonbelievers saw God's glory in Christ, which is what Jesus prayed for in John 17:20-21."[101] Witness and honor are inextricably woven together in the message of the Gospel.

In his letter to the Christians of Asia Minor, Peter instructs the community of believers in a new honor code founded on Christ:

So all of you should live together in peace. Try to understand each other. Love each other like brothers and sisters. Be kind and humble. Don't do wrong to anyone to pay them back for doing wrong to you. Or don't insult anyone to pay them back for insulting you. But ask

---

[96] Ibid.
[97] Ibid.
[98] Ibid.
[99] Ibid. p. 19.
[100] Katie J. Rawson, "A Gospel That Reconciles: Teaching about Honor-Shame to Advance Racial and Ethnic Reconciliation," in *Honor, Shame, and the Gospel: Reframing Our Message and Ministry*, Christopher Flanders & Werner Mischke, Eds. (Littleton: William Carey Publishing, 2020), p. 175.
[101] Ibid.

God to bless them. Do this because you yourselves were chosen to receive a blessing. The Scriptures say,

> "If you want to enjoy true life and have only good days,
> then avoid saying anything hurtful, and never let a lie come out of your mouth.
>
> Stop doing what is wrong, and do good.
> Look for peace, and do all you can to help people live peacefully.
>
> The Lord watches over those who do what is right,
> and he listens to their prayers.
> But he is against those who do evil."

If you are always trying to do good, no one can really harm you. But you may suffer for doing right. If that happens, you have God's blessings. "Don't be afraid of the people who make you suffer; don't be worried." But keep the Lord Christ holy in your hearts. Always be ready to answer everyone who asks you to explain about the hope you have. But answer them in a gentle way with respect. Keep your conscience clear. Then people will see the good way you live as followers of Christ, and those who say bad things about you will be ashamed of what they said. (1 Pet. 3:8-16).

Witnessing communities are grounded in the honor they receive from the Lord *and* the honor they bestow on others. The Gospel is "deeply rooted in Jesus' shame-removing and honor-restoring life."[102] When believers in Jesus recognize the way that sin distorts the honor of people made in God's image, they can restore honor through a witness that demonstrates that the Gospel is truly good news because it sets people free. Witness that does not respect or restore honor is a false witness. Witness seeks to honor Christ as Savior and Lord by restoring honor for God's image-bearers who are broken and lost in the shame of sin.

Service. Peter connected the community's witness to the priestly service in the temple (1 Pet. 2:5; 4:10). The Old Testament priestly service was often described with the Hebrew verb *Sharah*, translated into the Greek *leitourgein*

---

102 Georges & Baker, *Ministering in Honor-Shame Cultures*, p. 204.

from which we get the English word *liturgy*.[103] *Sharah* connoted the exclusive ministry of the select priestly class.[104] However, Peter used the Greek verb *diakoneō* that was used in the context of menial service.[105] This has a profound implication for our worship and witness. Because we are the King's priests in his reconstituted temple, God accepts *all* our gifts of services (1 Pet. 2:5, 9). Even menial services offered in the name of Jesus Christ result in praise to God. Costas states, "The church exists to celebrate and call the world to honor and revere God in the freedom of the Holy Spirit in response to Christ's great redemptive work."[106] The offering of our gifts of service in the *missio Dei* follows from the great liturgical tradition of priestly service in the temple.[107] Every moment of our lives is a sacred moment! Our witness to Christ in every moment is our priestly service that God accepts and uses to glorify Christ in the dark world we inhabit. Steven Hawthorne agrees, "The church declares publicly to the world everything that it communicates to its own members – namely, that the good news of salvation that God has offered in Christ is now available for all to hear and believe."[108]

Movement 4: *Oratio*

Father of glory,

> We rejoice to behold, through the eyes of our expectant hearts, the abounding glory that you have given your Son. You have raised him from death, exalted him to your right hand, and now, by your Spirit, you are drawing people from every nation to lavish obedient love upon him. In these days, in which Christ is both hated and praised as never before, we aspire to follow him fully, tasting the honor of bearing shame for his greater glory. We call on you to subdue our wayward, jealous ambitions. Guide us in your ways so that the gospel would swiftly bear the fruit of Christ's beauty amid each of the peoples.[109]

In Jesus' name, Amen.

---

[103] Ibid. p. 3.
[104] Ibid.
[105] Robert Deffinbaugh, "The Work of the Ministry: The Meaning of New Testament Ministry," Bible.org, October 7, 1979, p. 5,
[106] Costas, *Liberating News*, p. 137.
[107] Ibid.
[108] Ibid.
[109] Hawthorne, "The Honor and Glory of Jesus Christ," p. 18-19.

Movement 5: *Imitatio*

- Individual Reflection
    - o Journal your responses to the following questions:
        - What key points is God leading you to embrace and grow into?
        - How can you live this out in your life and leadership?
        - How can your missional leadership group pray for you in living this out?

- Group Reflection
    - o In your missional leadership group, share your individual reflections with each other.
    - o Pray for one another.

Movement 6: *Missio*

- Experiencing Mission
    - o Level 1 *Awareness*
        - Pray each day that the Lord sends you into his mission that day.
        - At the end of each day, reflect on or journal about one experience you had that day where you witnessed the *missio Dei* personally. Describe what happened. What was significant about that experience for you?
    - o Level 2 *Personal Commitment*
        - Ask the Lord where he may be sending you to be his witness on a regular basis.
        - Make a commitment to serve in that way.

Movement 7: *Communio*

- Experiencing Mission
    - o Level 3 *Group Experience*

- If possible, the small group may consider performing a mission or service project together to experience mission as a community.

+ Group Reflection
  - Where did you see the *missio Dei* in action this past week?

  - What was the most significant or surprising observations you made about your experience?

  - What did you learn about God from that experience? What did you learn about yourself from that experience?

  - What difference does that make in your leadership? How will you apply what you have learned?

Movement 8: *Contemplatio*

Each week in your small group, spend time reflecting and celebrating the ways that you have seen "God on the move" in the past week.

+ Spend some time in prayer or singing in thanksgiving and praise to our missionary God.

Chapter 6

Imitatio Dei

In 1 Peter, we saw that witness is our priestly responsibility. As a temple-people, our community witness is our priestly responsibility to "tell about the wonderful things he has done" (1 Pet. 2:5, 9). We are a special people who have received mercy to live good lives so that others "will see the good [we] do, and they will give glory to God on the day he comes" (1 Pet. 2:12). The temple was a very visible and prominent center of life for God's people.[1] It was the place where God promised to meet with them, hear their prayers, and receive the sacrifices of worship that covered their sins and secured their well-being as a nation.[2] Now, in Christ, we are his temple! He lives in us and makes himself known through us. Wherever we are located, we are the King's priests, a holy nation, offering spiritual sacrifices that God accepts (1 Pet. 2:5, 9). And so, Peter instructs us:

> So prepare your minds for service. With complete self-control put all your hope in the grace that will be yours when Jesus Christ comes. In the past you did not have the understanding you have now, so you did the evil things you wanted to do. But now you are children of God, so you should obey him and not live the way you did before. *Be holy in everything you do, just as God is holy.* He is the one who chose you. In the Scriptures God says, "Be holy, because I am holy." (1 Pet. 1:13-16, italics added)

In this chapter, we look closely at Peter's instruction to be holy just as God is holy. As a holy nation, we are called to imitate God's holiness in our lives, our witness, and our service. This is our *imitatio Dei* – the imitation of God.

Peter's call to the *imitatio Dei* is rooted in the Old Testament book of Leviticus, the ancient code that prescribed the appropriate rules and forms of temple worship befitting Israel's covenantal relationship with God.[3] Leviticus is a complex and difficult book that detailed how the people of Israel needed to deal with sin and impurity in the community so that their holy God could live among them.[4] But its ethical and cultic content is summed up in the Lord's command to all of Israel, "I, the LORD, brought you out of Egypt so that you could be my special people and I could be your God. I am holy, so you must be holy too" (Lev. 11:45, cf. 19:2). Because God delivered them from slavery and called them out from Egypt, Israel's life, worship, and ethics

---

[1] DeSilva, *An Introduction to the New Testament*, p. 75.
[2] Ibid.
[3] ESV Study Bible, "Introduction to Leviticus" (Wheaton: Crossway Bibles, 2008), p. 211-213.
[4] Ibid.

were immersed in the holiness of their God – to bear his image among the nations (Lev. 20:26).[5]

What does that holiness look like? In his classic tale *Les Misérables*, Victor Hugo introduced the main character, Jean Valjean, as a hardened man laboring in prison for 19 years for the crime of stealing bread to feed his sister's seven starving children. Upon parole, he is issued a passport that identifies him as a former convict. He must carry that identity with him everywhere he goes. He is refused shelter, food, and work by all who inspect his passport. He is rejected by society, and he becomes increasingly angry and embittered to the point that he is no more than an animal sleeping on the streets.

But the kindly old bishop of Digne (in French, *digne* means "worthy"), Monseigneur Myriel Bienvenu (*bienvenue* means "welcome"), offers Valjean food and shelter without raising any questions. However, in the night, Valjean steals precious silverware from the bishop and flees. The police capture Valjean and return him to Digne. But the bishop does not demand the recompense and justice due from Valjean that would further engrave his identity as a convict. Instead, the bishop insists to the police that he gave the silverware to Valjean as a gift. In this act of overwhelming mercy (in which the priest also added to Valjean silver candlesticks), the priest gives Valjean a new identity that forever changes the trajectory of his life:

"My friend," resumed the Bishop, "before you go, here are your candlesticks. Take them."

He stepped to the chimneypiece, took the two silver candlesticks, and brought them to Jean Valjean. The two women looked on without uttering a word, without a gesture, without a look that could disconcert the Bishop.

Jean Valjean was trembling in every limb. He took the two candlesticks mechanically, and with a bewildered air.

"Now," said the Bishop, "go in peace. By the way, when you return, my friend, it is not necessary to pass through the garden. You can always enter and depart through the street door. It is never fastened with anything but a latch, either by day or by night."

---

[5] Daniel C. Timmer, *A Gracious and Compassionate God: Mission, Salvation and Spirituality in the Book of Jonah* (Downers Grove: IVP Academic, 2011), p. 147. Kindle.

Then, turning to the gendarmes, "You may retire, gentlemen."

The gendarmes retired.

Jean Valjean was like a man on the point of fainting.

The Bishop drew near to him, and said in a low voice:

"Do not forget, never forget, that you have promised to use this money in becoming an honest man."

Jean Valjean, who had no recollection of ever having promised anything, remained speechless. The Bishop had emphasized the words when he uttered them. He resumed with solemnity:

"Jean Valjean, my brother, you no longer belong to evil, but to good. It is your soul that I buy from you; I withdraw it from black thoughts and the spirit of perdition, and I give it to God."[6]

Valjean's life was remade by mercy. The bishop gave him an unmerited *welcome* (*beinvenue*) that restored his *worth* (*digne*) as a child of God. Throughout the rest of the story, Valjean's actions are compelled by the mercy that redeemed his life, even when such mercy would compromise his freedom and security to live a "safe" life.

The Holiness of God's Mercy

Valjean's story beautifully depicts what the imitation of God means for us. God's holy people are *first* the people of God's mercy. His mercy has made us his people. The overall arc of the biblical narrative reveals how God chooses people by his mercy to declare his glory throughout the world. In the Old Testament, the LORD revealed his glory to Moses in the wake of the Israelites' faithless worship of the golden calf:

Then the LORD came down to him in a cloud, stood there with Moses, and spoke his own name. That is, the LORD passed in front of Moses and said, "YAHWEH, the LORD, is a kind and merciful God. He is slow to become angry. He is full of great love. He can be trusted. He shows his faithful love to thousands of people. He forgives people for the wrong things they do, but he does not forget to punish

---

[6] Victor Hugo (Translated by Isabel F. Hapgood), *Les Misérables* (San Diego: Canterbury Classics, 2015), p. 93-94.

the guilty people, but their children, their grandchildren, and their great-grandchildren will also suffer for the bad things these people do." (Exod. 34:5-7)

The Lord spoke these words to reconfirm his covenant with Israel after its terrible idolatrous breach. He revealed that he is YAHWEH, which is his special name he reserved for his covenant people whom he has delivered out of the nations to be his own.[7] YAHWEH commanded Israel to turn away from the worship of false gods and to reject political alliances with those nations that did not (Exod. 34:10-17). They were to trust only in him. They were to be a holy people, just as YAHWEH their Savior was holy.

YAHWEH also revealed the special character of his holiness: he is kind, merciful, slow to anger, full of great love, trustworthy, forgiving, and just (Exod. 34:6-7). What did Israel do to merit such kindness and mercy from God? Nothing! Listen to what the Lord told them:

> This is what you must do to those nations: You must smash their altars and break their memorial stones into pieces. Cut down their Asherah poles and burn their statues. Do this because *you are the LORD's own people. From all the people on earth, the LORD your God chose you to be his special people – people who belong only to him.* Why did the LORD love and choose you? It was not because you are such a large nation. You had the fewest of all people! But the LORD brought you out of Egypt with great power and made you free from slavery. He freed you from the control of Pharaoh, the king of Egypt. The LORD did this because he loves you and he wanted to keep the promise he made to your ancestors. (Deut. 7:5-8, italics added)

Just like Monseigneur Bienvenu, YAHWEH's mercy *welcomed* the Israelites as his people and restored their *worth* by freeing them from slavery. Now they are his temple-people declaring and demonstrating the goodness of their God to all the nations.

The Old Testament songbook of temple worship declared this covenantal theme with liturgic majesty:

Praise the LORD!
Great blessings belong to those who fear and respect the LORD,

---

7 Timmer, *A Gracious and Compassionate God*, p. 59.

who are happy to do what he commands.
Their descendants will be given power on earth.
Those who do right will be greatly blessed.
Their family will be very rich,
and their goodness will continue forever.
A light shines in the dark for those who are good,
for those who are merciful, kind, and fair.
It is good for people to be kind and generous
and to be fair in business.
Such good people will never fall.
They will always be remembered.
They will not be afraid of bad news.
They are confident because they trust in the LORD.
They remain confident and without fear,
so they defeat their enemies.
They freely give to the poor.
Their goodness will continue forever.
They will be honored with victory.
The wicked become angry when they see this.
They grind their teeth in anger, but then they disappear.
They will never get what they want most. (Psalm 112)

The *imitatio Dei* is the *imago Dei's* witness of God's good and merciful reign over all the nations (Exod. 19:5-6). Old Testament scholar John Goldingay agrees, "In most of its forms, at least, Israel is designed to be a working model of what it means to be a human community and to be a means of blessing to other human communities, not least because the way God blesses it makes other communities pray to be blessed as it is blessed (e.g., Gen. 12:1-3; 22-17-18)."[8] God's people are a Kingdom of priests who convey to all the nations by their worship the goodness of God: how excellent is his character, how he has dealt with sin through Christ, and how he invites and welcomes all people into a flourishing life under his good reign.[9]

---

[8] John Goldingay, *Old Testament Ethics: A Guided Tour* (Downers Grove: IVP Academic, 2019), p. 152.
[9] Timmer, *A Gracious and Compassionate God*, p. 24.

In this chapter, we will explore the *imitatio Dei* by looking at one prophet's bad example of it! All Sunday school children know the story about Jonah and the whale (or more appropriately, the "big fish"). But Jonah also serves as a counterexample of the good purposes of Yahweh, the compassionate and gracious God, for the salvation of the entire world. Let's spend some time in his company.

Movement 1: *Adspecto*

Prayer

✛ Pray for the Holy Spirit to speak to you through the Scripture. Use the following words of Psalm 111 as a prayer:

> *¹Praise the LORD!*
> *I thank the LORD with all my heart*
> *in the assembly of his good people.*
> *²The LORD does wonderful things,*
> *more than anyone could ask for.*
> *³The things he does are great and glorious!*
> *There is no end to his goodness.*
> *⁴He does amazing things so that we will remember*
> *that the LORD is kind and merciful.*
> *⁵He gives food to his followers.*
> *He remembers his agreement forever.*
> *⁶He has shown his people how powerful he is*
> *by giving them the land of other nations.*
> *⁷Everything he does is good and fair.*
> *All his commands can be trusted.*
> *⁸His commands will continue forever.*
> *They must be done with truth and honesty.*
> *⁹He rescued his people and made his agreement with them forever.*
> *His name is awesome and holy.*
> *¹⁰Wisdom begins with fear and respect for the LORD.*
> *Those who obey him are very wise.*
> *Praises will be sung to him forever.*

Scripture Reading

✦ **Read Jonah 3:10 – 4:11.** Listen for words or phrases from the passage that stand out to you.

---

¹⁰God saw what the people did. He saw that they stopped doing evil. So God changed his mind and did not do what he planned. He did not punish the people.

God's Mercy Makes Jonah Angry

¹Jonah was not happy that God saved the city. Jonah became angry. ²He complained to the LORD and said, "LORD, I knew this would happen! I was in my own country, and you told me to come here. At that time I knew that you would forgive the people of this evil city, so I decided to run away to Tarshish. I knew that you are a kind God. I knew that you show mercy and don't want to punish people. I knew that you are kind, and if these people stopped sinning, you would change your plans to destroy them. ³So now, LORD, just kill me. It is better for me to die than to live."

⁴Then the LORD said, "Do you think it is right for you to be angry?"

⁵Jonah went out of the city to a place near the city on the east side. He made a shelter for himself and sat there in the shade, waiting to see what would happen to the city.

The Gourd Plant and the Worm

⁶The LORD made a gourd plant grow quickly over Jonah. This made a cool place for Jonah to sit and helped him to be more comfortable. He was very happy because of this plant.

⁷The next morning, God sent a worm to eat part of the plant. The worm began eating the plant, and the plant died.

⁸After the sun was high in the sky, God caused a hot east wind to blow. The sun became very hot on Jonah's head, and he became very weak. He asked God to let him die. He said, "It is better for me to die than to live."

⁹But God said to Jonah, "Do you think it is right for you to be angry just because this plant died?" Jonah answered, "Yes, it is right for me to be angry! I am angry enough to die!"

[10]And the LORD said, "You did nothing for that plant. You did not make it grow. It grew up in the night, and the next day it died. And now you are sad about it. [11]If you can get upset over a plant, surely I can feel sorry for a big city like Nineveh. There are many people and animals in that city. There are more than 120,000 people there who did not know they were doing wrong."

Reflection

- When you have finished reading, remain silent for one or two minutes.

- Read the entire passage again. If you have an audio Bible, listen through the passage.

  o *Personal Reflection:* Journal your thoughts on the following questions:

    - What words or phrases from the passage stand out to you?

    - How do these words or phrases connect with your life right now?

    - How might God be inviting you to respond to this passage?

Movement 2: *Lectio*

Scripture Study

- Read or listen to **Jonah 3:10 - 4:11**.

- Answer the following study questions:

  1. How does Jonah feel about God not punishing Nineveh (vs. 3:10-4:1)?

  2. Why do you think he feels this way?

  3. What does Jonah do in response (vs. 2)?

  4. What is your impression of Jonah's prayer?

  5. What would you say is Jonah's chief complaint (vs. 2)?

  6. Do you think it was appropriate for Jonah to pray this way? Why or why not?

181

7. What does Jonah want God to do (vs. 3)?

8. Why do you think he wants God to do this?

9. What question does God ask Jonah (vs. 4)?

10. Why do you think God asks him this question?

11. Where does Jonah go (vs. 5)?

12. Why does he go there?

13. What does God do for Jonah (vs. 6)?

14. How does Jonah feel about what God does for him (vs. 6)?

15. What does God do the next morning (vs. 7)?

16. Why do you think God does this?

17. How does Jonah feel about this turn of events (vs. 8)?

18. What question does God repeat to Jonah (vs. 9)?

19. What is Jonah's response (vs. 9)?

20. Why does Jonah think he is right to feel this way (vs. 9)?

21. What does God want to teach Jonah (vs. 10-11)?

22. What does God want to teach us through Jonah's story?

23. Is there someone or some group that God is challenging you/us to change your/our attitude about?

24. What would it mean to imitate God's compassion and mercy to these people?

Reading
The Context of Jonah

Most of us would most likely prefer to worship a God who is kind and merciful. So, we may be shocked to find in the Bible a story about a man – notably, a prophet of God – who is angry *because of* the mercy and compassion of God to the extent that he wanted to die! God's mercy creates tension in the book of Jonah precisely because it is *that mercy* that God expects his people to imitate. Now, showing mercy to those who are part of "our group" – our people, our ethnicity, our culture, our family, our friends – is the easy part (although sometimes even that can be challenging). But to love those who are not part of our group – people with a different culture, worldview, ethnicity, political persuasion, power status, and *even* our enemies – is something that Jonah, and often we, cannot accept.

But Jesus taught us to love our enemies because, if we do, we will be "children who are truly like [our] Father in heaven" (Matt. 5:45). It was within the same context that Jesus repeated the ancient Levitical command: "What I am saying is that you must be perfect, just as your Father in heaven is perfect" (Matt. 5:48). Our perfection as God's covenant people is inextricably related to the mercy and compassion that we show to those on the outside. While enemies may be the most extreme case, Jesus' teaching extends to all manner of people who are outside of our natural affinities. He calls us to show mercy to those who are "not us."

This is exactly what the prophet Jonah was running away from. Interestingly, Jonah is unusual as a book of prophecy because of its surprising lack of prophetic material.[10] His entire prophetic message is summarized in one, short sentence: "After 40 days, Nineveh will be destroyed!" (Jonah 3:4). And he only proclaimed this message after a lot of resistance. Because his mission required him to warn his enemies of their impending doom due to their evil, Jonah ran away from it. Even in the turmoil of a great storm where the pagan men around him were crying out to their gods to save them, Jonah remained either asleep or silent until he was compelled to speak up so they, not he, could pray to his God to save them (Jonah 1:4-13).[11]

But, in striking contrast, Jonah was very articulate in prayer about his own deliverance as he wallowed in the belly of the big fish (Jonah 2:1-9)! Twice in the prayer, he pointed to the temple in Jerusalem where God's presence can be appealed to for help (Jonah 2:4, 7). Daniel Timmer notes that "Jonah seems to equate God's presence with life, something that the temple and its strict rules for access into God's presence made abundantly clear to Israelites…"[12] Jonah praised Yahweh for delivering him and exclaimed in terms related to temple worship, "I will give sacrifices to you, and I will praise and thank you. I will make special promises to you, and I will do what I promise" (Jonah 2:9). We find that Jonah celebrated the gracious and compassionate God when he was the beneficiary, but he lamented God's kindness and mercy to the Gentiles in passive-aggressive terms.

---

[10] Timmer, *A Gracious and Compassionate God*, p. 96.
[11] Alan Jon Hauser, "Jonah: In Pursuit of the Dove," *Journal of Biblical Literature* 104, no. 1 (1985), p. 22-27.
[12] Timmer, *A Gracious and Compassionate God*, p. 85.

In further contrast, the book of Jonah noted remarkable distinctions between Jonah's response to God and that of the Gentile characters in the story. That contrast is emphasized by the author's use of two different names for God: *Yahweh* (the name of God associated with his deliverance of and covenantal relationship with Israel) in reference to Jonah, and *Elohim* (the general Hebrew word for God) in reference to the Gentiles.[13] When faced with impending calamity, Jonah did not relent of his disobedience in running from Yahweh's commission to go to Nineveh.[14] And yet, he praised Yahweh for delivering him from death (Jonah 2:2-9). Jonah understood Yahweh to be *his* God, whose compassion was the exclusive benefit for *his people*.[15] But, as Hans Walter Wolff explains, "fearing or revering Yahweh 'describes a living relationship of obedience and trust,' but neither of these elements is evident in Jonah's behavior."[16] Instead of going to Nineveh obediently on God's mercy mission, Jonah criticized those who "worship useless idols" (Jonah 2:8) and separated himself from those who did (Jonah 1:5; 4:5).[17]

But it is these idolators who readily repented and called on the name of *Yahweh*, not *Elohim*, to save them from the calamity coming upon them! In the great storm, the Gentile sailors, at first, called on each of their own gods to save them (Jonah 1:5). But after these gods failed to respond, and they discovered that it was Jonah's God who brought this calamity upon them. They cried out to Yahweh: "We know you are the LORD, and you will do whatever you want" (Jonah 1:14). This is the only occasion in the story in which the name of Yahweh is associated with Gentiles. These pagan men even tried to save Jonah's life! They attempted to row to shore rather than throw him overboard even though they knew his guilt was responsible for the storm (Jonah 1:12-14). These non-Israelites showed more mercy to Jonah than Jonah, the prophet of God, showed toward them (Jonah 1:7-12).[18]

The repentance of the Gentile sailors foreshadowed the even more significant repentance of the Ninevites (Jonah 3:5-9). The table below displays

---

[13] Ibid. p. 128.

[14] Ibid. p. 70.

[15] John H. Walton, "The Object Lesson of Jonah 4:5-7 and the Purpose of the Book of Jonah," *Bulletin for Biblical Research* 2 (1992), p. 51-52.

[16] Hans Walter Wolff, *Obadiah and Jonah: A Commentary*, trans. By Margaret Kohl (Minneapolis: Augsburg, 1986), quoted in Timmer, *A Gracious and Compassionate God*, p. 70.

[17] Mary Donovan Turner, "Jonah 3:10-4:11," *Interpretation* 51, no. 4 (1998), p. 412.

[18] Timmer, *The Gracious and Compassionate God*, p. 70.

the expressions that vividly contrast Jonah's disobedience with the complete obedience of the Ninevites:[19]

Jonah's Disobedience		Nineveh's Obedience	
Verse	Expression	Verse	Expression
Jonah 1:3	"tried to run away"	Jonah 3:5	*The Ninevites*
	"went to Joppa"		"believed God"
	"found a boat that was going to the faraway city		"decided to stop eating…to think about their sins"
	"paid money for the trip"		"put on special clothes to show they were sorry"
	"He wanted to travel with the people on this boat…and run away from the Lord"		"all the people did this"
Jonah 1:5	"had gone down into the boat"	Jonah 3:6-7	*The king of Nineveh*
	"went to sleep"		"left his throne"
			"removed his robe"
			"put on special clothes to show that he was sorry"
			"sat in ashes"
			"wrote a special message and sent it throughout the city"

While it is difficult to capture the emotional force of these expressions, they would have been disturbing to an 8th century BCE Israelite audience to hear of an Israelite prophet cast in such a negative light compared to the Ninevites. Nineveh was the royal city of ancient Assyria, an evil empire built upon "violence and God-defying self-aggrandization."[20] Prior to destroying the kingdom of Israel (the northern kingdom) in 722 BCE, Assyria was the

---

[19] Ibid. p. 90.
[20] Ibid. p. 92.

perennial enemy of Israel. Several prophets railed against its bloodlust, idolatry, and immorality.[21] Chesung Justin Ryu notes:

> Scholars have made various negative observations regarding Israelite attitudes toward Nineveh, casting the city as 'the most despised foreign city,' the memory of which was 'a bitter and longlasting yoke' evoking 'thoughts of anger and retribution,' and 'the archenemy,' serving as 'a most poignant example of a great city, a capital of a powerful empire, that was not only utterly destroyed but also never rebuilt.'[22]

Certainly, Jonah's hatred for this foreign people was justifiable. Nineveh deserved its prophesied destruction.

But God was undeterred from Jonah's mission to warn Nineveh, the city that God refers to twice in the text as that "great city" (Jonah 1:2; 3:2, NIV). The Hebrew expression for "great city" includes a reference to *elohim* implying that, indeed, Nineveh was a city very important to Israel's God.[23] He sent Jonah to warn them of impending judgment and calamity so that they might repent, which is one of biblical prophecy's main functions.[24] Jonah well understood this and despaired that, instead of destroying Nineveh as it deserved, Yahweh would be kind and merciful to it. Goldingay characterizes Jonah's attitude very well: "[Jonah] didn't invite Nineveh to repent, but to his disgust it did so, and his awful fear was fulfilled. God relented."[25] So lamentable is Yahweh's mercy that Jonah wanted to die!

The story of Jonah, with all its irony and satire, presents a caricature to its readers of who they *should not* wish to imitate.[26] But the saga of Jonah and Nineveh does not end with Nineveh's repentance as we would expect. Rather, Yahweh, the gracious and compassionate God, has more to teach Jonah, and us, about how he expects his people to imitate him.

The Object Lesson: The Plant, the Worm, and the East Wind

By the end of the third chapter of Jonah, the Ninevites had repented of their sins and God "changed his mind" and "did not punish the people" (Jonah 3:10). And they all lived happily ever after…right? Wrong!

---

[21] See 2 Kings 17:5; 2 Chron. 32:9-32; the whole book of Nahum; and Zeph. 2:13-15.
[22] Chesung Justin Ryu, "Silence as Resistance: A Postcolonial Reading of the Silence of Jonah in Jonah 4:1-11," *Journal for the Study of the Old Testament* 34, no. 2 (2009), p. 202-203.
[23] Timmer, *A Gracious and Compassionate God*, p 95.
[24] Ibid. p. 97.
[25] Goldingay, *Old Testament Ethics*, p. 170.
[26] Ibid. p. 147.

At the beginning of the next chapter, we find Jonah sulking because God saved Nineveh:

> He complained to the LORD [Yahweh] and said, "LORD, I knew this would happen! I was in my own country, and you told me to come here. At that time I knew that you would forgive the people of this evil city, so I decided to run away to Tarshish. I knew that you are a kind God. I knew that you show mercy and don't want to punish people. I knew that you are kind, and if these people stopped sinning, you would change your plans to destroy them. So now, LORD, just kill me. It is better for me to die than to live." (Jonah 4:2-3)

To summarize Jonah's complaint in modern language: "I just *knew* this would happen...I knew it, I knew it, I KNEW IT!" At least we can appreciate Jonah's honesty! Perhaps implicitly, this text contrasts Jonah with Moses who, after Israel's grievous sin with the golden calf, interceded passionately and selflessly on behalf of Israel, even to the extent of asking that his own name be erased from Yahweh's book (Exod. 32:30-33:23). For Jonah, Yahweh's grace given to those outside of the covenant "in-group" was simply unacceptable. He did not even want to live in a world where God showed compassion and mercy to the enemies of his people.

The irony of the story of Jonah and Nineveh is even more pronounced by the fact that Israel, at the time of the writing of Jonah, was itself an apostate nation.[27] Prophets contemporary to Jonah, including Hosea, Micah, and Amos, condemned Israel's idolatry and faithlessness to Yahweh and warned of impending judgment and destruction (cf. Amos 7).[28] This makes it even more remarkable that Jonah depicts the Ninevites, the enemies of Israel who "did not know they were doing wrong" (Jonah 4:11), as willing to admit that they had violated the moral standards against Israel's God.[29] Not even Israel was willing to do that! Timmer states:

> Even if Nineveh's response to Jonah's message included significant repentance but stopped short of full faith in Yahweh, as seems to be the case, it is difficult to imagine an account better calculated to overthrow the assumption that heathens could not or would not respond to God's word. *It simultaneously condemns Israel's lack of repentance in an unprecedented way:* 'By their response to a prophetic warning, however ephemeral it may have been, the Ninevites put hard-hearted

---

27 Timmer, *A Gracious and Compassionate God*, p. 100.
28 Ibid.
29 Ibid.

Israel to shame.' Moreover, even a response so qualified met with a demonstration of God's mercy that surely would have shocked many Israelites of Jonah's day. While a similar picture was painted with only a few characters in chapter 1, here 120,000 people and their cattle form an immense demonstration of the far-reaching mercy of God. Nineveh, as incredible as it seemed to Jonah, had turned from her wickedness and been spared.[30]

God decided to drive the point home for Jonah with an object lesson. As Jonah sat outside the city in a makeshift shelter "waiting to see what would happen to the city" (presumably holding out hope that the city would backslide and he would be proven right[31]), the Lord made a gourd plant to grow over Jonah (Jonah 4:5-6).

The gourd plant provided shelter to Jonah that "[eased] his discomfort" and made him very happy (Jonah 4:6, NIV) in much the same way that God's earlier rescue of him from the storm and sea prompted a prayer of praise (Jonah 2). The word for "discomfort" is a translation of the same Hebrew word from which "calamity" is translated in the context of Nineveh's impending destruction.[32] So far, the object lesson comports with Jonah's expectation of how his God, Yahweh, works in salvation for his covenant people. As we have seen, the name of God, *Yahweh,* is associated with Jonah, whereas *Elohim* is associated with the Gentiles. More specifically, Yahweh is portrayed as the one who acted to deliver Jonah from danger and hardship (Jonah 1:17; 2:10).[33] Jonah praised God by saying "Salvation only comes from the LORD [Yahweh]!" (Jonah 2:9). By this, he meant that only God's special people benefit from Yahweh's compassion and mercy, not foreigners.[34] He understood that Yahweh punished those who worship useless idols that can never help them (Jonah 2:8).[35]

The author, however, used a compound form of God's name, *Yahweh Elohim,* to introduce the object lesson (Jonah 4:6).[36] Thereafter, the author reverted to *Elohim* throughout the rest of the object lesson.[37] This name

---

[30] Ibid. p. 110-111.
[31] Pinchas Khan, "The Epilogue to Jonah," *Jewish Bible Quarterly* 28, no. 3 (2000), p. 150.
[32] Ibid. 131.
[33] Ibid. p. 128.
[34] Simon Oxley, "Certainties Transformed: Jonah and Acts 10:9-35," *The Ecumenical Review* 56, no. 3 (2004), p. 324.
[35] Ibid.
[36] Walton, "The Object Lesson," p. 48.
[37] Ibid.

change signaled to Jonah's readers that Jonah will discover something significant about the character of God's compassion and mercy.

Following the joy of Jonah's comfort from the gourd plant, Elohim appointed both a worm to eat the plant and a hot east wind to blow (Jonah 4:7-8). Jonah became very weak as this discomfort/calamity came upon him (Jonah 4:8). Elohim treated Jonah in the same way Jonah believed Yahweh should treat the Nineveh that he so hates![38] Timmer notes:

> When the author of the book changes his pattern of usage [from Yahweh to Elohim] in chapter 4, therefore, and connects Jonah with 'God', he has most probably done so in order to show that the God who has shown mercy and compassion toward the Gentiles is the same God Jonah knows, the same God Israel has known from her very beginning.[39]

Once again, Jonah was angry and asks for death, but this time because of the plant's destruction (Jonah 4:8-9). In the Hebrew, the author used the same verb-preposition, "to have pity on," to describe both Jonah's sentiments regarding the plant and Yahweh's compassion for Nineveh.[40] Jonah had pity for the dead plant. And he believed he was right to be so angry because it died (Jonah 4:9).[41] Jonah received a gracious benefit from the plant for which he did nothing to deserve (Jonah 4:10).[42] Yahweh Elohim graciously provided it for him to deliver him from his "calamity."[43] Jonah's pity was derived not from the plant but from the benefit he received from the plant. When God took that grace away from him, Jonah's worldview – his preconception of how God's grace and deliverance ought to work out in the world – was severely shaken. Timmer agrees:

> …God's grace per se is not onerous to Jonah: he simply hates grace shown to those he thinks don't deserve it, especially non-Israelites (the issue of merit, though it overturns grace in proper theological terms, seems necessary to Jonah's understanding of it). But in taking upon his lips the divine self-revelation of Exodus 34 [in Jonah 4:2-3] Jonah

---

[38] Ibid.
[39] Timmer, *A Gracious and Compassionate God*, p. 128.
[40] Ibid. p. 130.
[41] Ibid. p. 130.
[42] Ibid.
[43] Ibid. p. 130.

unwittingly and ironically condemns his own critique of Yahweh's indiscriminate grace.[44]

Jonah wanted to receive God's grace without being changed by it. But at the same time, he expected God's grace to be removed from "outsiders" who, in fact, did respond to it with a ready repentance.[45]

The object lesson is infused with themes about both grace and deliverance.[46] In the epilogue to Jonah (Jonah 4:10-11), Elohim called out Jonah because Jonah was angrier over the destruction of a gourd plant than of the potential destruction of a whole city God cared about. What is striking is that God's closing response (Jonah 4:10-11) parallels Jonah's opening complaint (Jonah 4:2-3). In the Hebrew, both are presented in a 39-word parallel structure called a chiastic structure.[47] Jonah and Nineveh are put side-by-side and Jonah is found wanting. As Alan Jon Hauser states:

> The repentance of the Ninevites and their instantaneous obedience to God stand in stark contrast to Jonah, who never repented and became obedient only under extreme duress. The Ninevites might have asked "Who is this God?" or "Why should we obey Him?" but they do not. They might have threatened Jonah in order to get him to be quiet, but they do not. They might have responded with sullen silence, as Jonah does, but they do not. Or they might even have fled, like Jonah. Instead, their obedience is immediate and wholehearted, and there is never the slightest hesitation in their commitment to humbling themselves, turning from their evil ways, and seeking God's forgiveness. With Jonah, a maximum amount of effort on God's part produced only a minimal and grudging response, whereas with the Ninevites a minimal amount of effort (Jonah's five words of 3:4... "Yet forty days until Nineveh is overthrown") produces maximum response.[48]

As readers of Jonah, we are left with the question of what Yahweh desires for us to learn. Will we be hard-hearted, receiving God's grace with joy while denying it to those who are different and far away from us? Or will we imitate Yahweh, the gracious and compassionate God, whose deliverance is available to us *as well as* the world to which he calls us to be his witnesses?

---

[44] Ibid. p. 122.
[45] Ibid. p. 132.
[46] Ibid. p. 130.
[47] Khan, "The Epilogue to Jonah," p. 152.
[48] Hauser, "Jonah: In Pursuit of the Dove," p. 33.

Mary Donovan Turner states that "compassion literally means to 'suffer with' or 'suffer together.'"[49] And so she asks:

> Where are the limits of our own expressions of compassion? With whom and for whom are we willing to suffer? Do we live with an us-versus-them mentality? Who are our people?... As we overhear this conversation between [Yahweh] and Jonah, we pause to ask ourselves: For whom do we wish life? Who are the foreigners to whom we are sent and what message do we carry?[50]

The *imitatio Dei* invites us to be holy because our God is holy. Even more, God calls us to reflect his image in this dark and evil world:

> You are God's dear children, so try to be like him. Live a life of love. Love others just as Christ loved us. He gave himself for us — a sweet-smelling offering and sacrifice to God.... So be very careful how you live. Live wisely, not like fools. I mean that you should use every opportunity you have for doing good, because these are evil times. So don't be foolish with your lives, but learn what the Lord wants you to do. Don't be drunk with wine, which will ruin your life, but be filled with the Spirit. Encourage each other with psalms, hymns, and spiritual songs. Sing and make music in your hearts to the Lord. Always give thanks to God the Father for everything in the name of our Lord Jesus Christ. (Eph. 5:1-2, 15-20)

Movement 3: *Meditatio*

The *missio Dei* pushes us beyond the comfort and familiarity of our own contexts to bring the Gospel to the formless and empty places of "no faith." God is on the move and that is the direction he is moving toward. He intends for the entire cosmos to flourish under his good reign:

> Christ must rule until God puts all enemies under his control. The last enemy to be destroyed will be death. As the Scriptures say, "God put everything under his control." When it says that "everything" is put under him, it is clear that this does not include God himself. God is the one putting everything under Christ's control. After everything has been put under Christ, then the Son himself will be put under God. God is the one who put everything under Christ. And Christ will be put under God so that God will be the complete ruler over everything. (1 Cor. 15:25-28)

---

[49] Turner, "Jonah 3:10-4:11," p. 414.
[50] Ibid.

Everything will be fulfilled and immersed in the great trinitarian dance of love from which everything was created!

The *imitatio Dei* is the mandate that emerges from the trinitarian logic of the *missio Dei*: Be holy because the Lord our God is holy.[51] He is Yahweh, "The LORD, the LORD, the compassionate and gracious God, slow to anger, abounding in love and faithfulness, maintaining love to thousands, and forgiving wickedness, rebellion and sin" (Exod. 34:6-7, NIV). Because he has shown mercy to us, he expects us to show mercy to others. This is the lesson Jonah had to learn the hard way. May we be so humble not to run from mercy's call, but to embrace it as the mark of our family name.

But God is rich in mercy, and he loved us very much. We were spiritually dead because of all we had done against him. But he gave us new life together with Christ. (You have been saved by God's grace.) Yes, it is because we are a part of Christ Jesus that God raised us from death and seated us together with him in the heavenly places. God did this so that his kindness to us who belong to Christ Jesus would clearly show for all time to come the amazing richness of his grace.

I mean that you have been saved by grace because you believed. You did not save yourselves; it was a gift from God. You are not saved by the things you have done, so there is nothing to boast about. God has made us what we are. In Christ Jesus, God made us new people so that we would spend our lives doing the good things he had already planned for us to do. (Eph. 2:4-10)

The mercy of God that marks us as his covenant people is hospitable. It welcomes those who are far away to find a home in the family. As God sends us out on mission, we will encounter cultural worlds that are far away from what we know. The people that live there may not be enemies, like the Ninevites were to Jonah, but they will challenge the ethnocentric barriers that limit our vision of where God is on the move. We will encounter the mysterious cultural divides that God calls us to bridge so that we may invite

---

[51] See Lev. 11:44, 45; 19:2; 20:7, 26; 21:8; Deut. 23:14; Matt. 5:48; Luke 6:36; and 1 Pet. 1:16-17.

others to his banqueting table.[52] We will misunderstand and find others perplexing. But these are the frontiers of cultural worlds where God calls us to be holy just as he is holy.

Community Themes

The story of Jonah highlights five community themes regarding the *imitatio Dei* that will shape our leadership-in-community: communities of trust, cross-centered leadership, cultural worlds, cultural intelligence, and cultural transformation.

Communities of Trust. Leadership-in-community that imitates God pursues friendship with others, especially those who are different than we are.[53] Friendship is the fertile ground in which the seeds of creativity are planted, where they are nurtured and emerge as new cultural horizons that extend the good reign of God into our contexts. In our study on the *imago Dei*, we learned that humans have a unique, God-given capacity to shape our relationships so that we make something of the world. Creating culture is the *imago Dei's* priestly function and it involves worship, work, and rest – all of which necessitate meaningful relationships within the community of God's covenant people.

But if the community of faith does not include diversity, then its ability to create cultures is undermined. Cross-cultural specialist Patty Lane explains, "Because culture establishes what is appropriate, living in homogeneous culture groups reinforces our belief that our behavior is right. It also enhances our perception that behavior of those outside the group is wrong."[54] Multicultural friendships provide the creative energy the community needs to explore mysteries, test assumptions, challenge mental models, and innovate new ideas that lead to transforming change. A community that values and pursues multicultural friendships develops the skills necessary to cross cultural frontiers, appreciate cultural differences, and build the relationships that God uses to welcome others into his family.[55] Remember: people *belong* before they *believe*.[56]

---

[52] Hiebert, *The Gospel in Human Contexts*, p. 47.
[53] Franklin, *Towards Global Missional Leadership*, p. 78-79.
[54] Patty Lane, *A Beginner's Guide to Crossing Cultures: Making Friends in a Multicultural World* (Downers Grove: InterVarsity Press, 2002), p. 136.
[55] Ibid. p. 137.
[56] Richardson, *Reimagining Evangelism*, p. 27.

Leadership-in-community is adamantly committed to building communities of trust as networks of multicultural friendships. Within communities of trust, members learn values, worldviews, and appropriate behaviors through imitation.[57] Human cognitive studies have researched the power of imitation in personal and spiritual formation.[58] In fact, the discovery of perception-action reciprocity was a breakthrough in cognitive studies. This research proved that a person's brain will code in a similar way actions that the person observes others perform and actions that the person performs him or herself.[59] Douglas McConnell explains:

> To illustrate, think of the axiom often applied in medical education, "See one, do one, teach one," and relate it to a worship service. A person sees an unfamiliar action or a different practice in a familiar event (such as intinction of the bread into the wine in the Eucharist or kneeling at the rail for prayer) and constructs a mental image of how it is done, even a perception of the motivation and rationale for doing it, without any verbal communication. It is purely an observation of an action. This often results in imitation, doing it oneself. This may be the immediate response, such as joining the line of congregants to participate in the Communion service, or it may be to contemplate the reasons for particular actions while waiting one's turn to go forward. Normally, the person observes and practices until the task is mastered, after which they may well become the person others imitate – for better or for worse, since this process works with deviant behavior as well as appropriate behavior. The important point is that imitation is a natural ability including both observation for understanding and production for skill.[60]

Because the core of culture is shared meanings, culture creation requires human interaction, imitation, and reciprocity so that members learn the community's way-of-being in relationship with one another and the world around them.[61]

Love-driven leadership sees the potential in others and commits to unlocking it through loyalty, affection, and mutual support.[62] Only through

---

[57] McConnell, *Cultural Insights for Christian Leaders*, p. 83-84.
[58] Ibid. p. 81.
[59] Ibid.
[60] Ibid.
[61] Hana Shepherd, "Culture and Cognition: A Process Account of Culture," *Sociological Forum* 29, no. 4 (2014), p. 1007-1008.
[62] Lowney, *Heroic Leadership*, p. 31.

authentic friendship does a community unlock its culture-creating potential. Love-driven leadership in communities of trust captures the hearts and imaginations of members so that they *desire* to emulate the values of the community. James K. A. Smith states:

> The body of Christ should be a testimony to the kingdom that is coming, bearing witness to how the world will be otherwise. Our work and our practices should be foretastes of that coming new city and thus should include protest and critique. Our engagement with God's world is not about running the show or winning a culture war. We are called to be witnesses, not necessarily winners....

> This requires being regularly recentered in the Story.... Yes, God's affirmation of the goodness of creation tells us that everything matters; and you will learn that over and over again *in the church*. It is in the worship of the Triune God that we are restored by being restoried. It is the practices of Christian worship that renarrate our imagination so that we can perceive the world as God's creation and thus hear his *call* that echoes within it.

> This now intersects with our core theme because our (culture-) making, our work, is generated as much by what we *want* as by what we believe. We are made to be makers, but as makers we remain lovers. So if you are what you love, then you *make* what you love. Your cultural labor – whether in finance or fine arts, as a fireman or a first-grade teacher – is animated less by "principles" that you carry in your head and more by habits of desire that operate under the hood of consciousness.[63]

We "image" the community to which we belong: what it loves, what it values, and what story it is living into. By inclusion and celebration of diversity within the community of trust, we unlock the potential of the community to image the glory of our covenant-making God, and we orient our mission toward the King we love and his coming Kingdom that we look for.

The Six Dimensions of Multicultural Organizations, developed by diversity management consultant Taylor Cox, Jr., are useful for building communities of trust. These dimensions provide a framework that teams and organizations can use to plan strategies and initiatives that strengthen diversity in their leadership-in-community.

---

[63] Smith, *You Are What You Love*, p. 174-175.

1. **Acculturation:** The appreciation of cultural pluralism and the creation of an environment where minority cultural voices and perspectives can positively influence organizational norms and values.

2. **Structural Integration:** The ability to conform the organizational structures to that which encourage and enable organizational diversity.

3. **Informal Integration:** The integration of cultural diversity into informal social networks.

4. **Cultural Bias:** The elimination of cultural discrimination and prejudice through in-service training, proactive recruitment and advancement policies, and ongoing research and evaluation.

5. **Organizational Identification:** The organizational identification and image which publicly promotes a positive view of diversity.

6. **Inter-group Conflict:** The resolution of intergroup conflict where efforts are made to handle conflict in a balanced way.[64]

Leadership-in-community that invests in their teams and organizations along these six dimensions clears space for a rich social context in which multicultural friendships can begin, grow, and thrive. Healthy and flourishing culture making needs a context – a real time and place – to happen. Like a gardener clearing the ground overrun by toxic, life-killing weeds, leadership-in-community clears its social and organizational contexts of structural or systemic bias so that diverse members can generate genuine friendships.

Cross-centered Leadership. Within Christian communities of trust that prioritize multicultural friendships, the character of leadership-in-community is defined by the Cross of Christ. As Jesus was approaching Jerusalem knowing that he would be crucified there, the mother of James and John approached him to ask that her sons sit on his right and left sides in his Kingdom (Matt. 20:20-21). In response, Jesus called his disciples together and told them:

> You know that the rulers of the non-Jewish people love to show their power over the people. And their important leaders love to use all their authority over the people. But it should not be that way with you. Whoever wants to be your leader must be your servant. Whoever wants

---

[64] Taylor Cox, Jr. "The Multicultural Organization," *Academy of Management Executive* 5, no. 2(1991), p. 39-47.

to be first must serve the rest of you like a slave. Do as I did: The Son of Man did not come for people to serve him. He came to serve others and to give his life to save many people. (Matt. 20:25-28)

Leadership in communities of trust exercise authority, not to power over others, but to build healthy trust that fosters creative, generative friendships.[65] Trust is correlated strongly with dependence and risk. It builds when leaders use their power to call to life the giftedness of others so that the whole community benefits.[66] McConnell agrees:

> One of the significant insights arising out of the study of culture and human nature is that we are embodied through creation with natural abilities predetermined by virtue of our physicality, and we are embedded in a cultural context that gives us what we need to become what God intends us to be. It is truly a wonder of creation. As we develop from childhood through adulthood, our natural abilities engage with our cultural experiences, shaping us in response to the world God places us in. Our formation is an interconnected process physically, culturally, and spiritually. And the wonderful truth that we have affirmed often is that all of this is in the providence of God.
>
> Such a strong affirmation should cause us to consider more deeply our role as leaders in discerning the gifts of those we lead and equipping them according to the mission God has given our organization. Each person with whom we serve is also loved, called, and being equipped by God in the same way we are as leaders. So when it comes to selecting and equipping leaders, we must start with discerning the gifting of the Holy Spirit in the individuals we are considering.[67]

When all members of the community of trust freely exercise their gifts and services, new cultural horizons are truly possible for the community's mission. Cultural innovation occurs when all members contribute to new shared meanings.[68]

Therefore, cross-centered leadership focuses on the proper exercise of power in service to others and unto the mission of the community. In his seminal research on enduring "great" organizations, Jim Collins noted that

---

[65] McConnell, *Cultural Insights,* p. 116.
[66] Ibid. p. 117, 121.
[67] Ibid. p. 121.
[68] Harrison M. Trice & Janice M. Beyer, "Cultural Leadership in Organizations," *Organization Science* 2, no. 2 (1991), p. 152.

they were led by leaders who "channel their ego needs away from themselves and into the larger goal of building a great company… They are incredibly ambitious – but their ambition is first and foremost for the institution, not themselves."[69] These leaders exhibited a "compelling modesty" that was "quiet, humble, modest, reserved, shy, gracious, mild-mannered, self-effacing, understated…"[70] They did not aspire to be put on a pedestal, but to pour their energies and power into the enduring success of their company's mission.[71] At the same time, they exercised an "unwavering resolve" to do what was necessary to make their companies successful.[72] In the final analysis, Collins says this of these leaders:

> [They] look out the window to apportion credit to factors outside themselves when things go well (and if they cannot find a specific person or event to give credit to, they credit good luck). At the same time, they look in the mirror to apportion responsibility, never blaming bad luck when things go poorly.[73]

How much more, then, should Christian leaders-in-community exhibit a cross-centered humility and resolve in their mission? In Colossians, Paul instructs us to "put to death" everything that destroys Christian community and "clothe" ourselves with compassion, kindness, humility, gentleness, and patience (Col. 3:5-12). In culturally diverse communities, these qualities imitate our God who chose us as his holy and dearly loved people (Col. 3:11-12, NIV).

Cultural Worlds. An important aspect of the *imitatio Dei* in leadership-in-community is our awareness of and appreciation for the different cultural worlds with which we interact in the community. A cultural world is the "lived reality of a group of people" who have created that world through the "process of establishing, constructing, and maintaining" the group's "way of inhabiting" its environment.[74] A cultural world includes the aspects of worldview, such as beliefs, values, and feelings.[75] But it also incorporates

---

[69] Jim Collins, *Good to Great: Why Some Companies Make the Leap…and Others Don't* (New York: Harper Business, 2001), p. 21.
[70] Ibid. p. 27.
[71] Ibid.
[72] Ibid. p. 30.
[73] Ibid. p. 35.
[74] McConnell, *Cultural Insights for Christian Leaders*, p. 130.
[75] Ibid.

contextual realities of time, place, and relationships.[76] As group members come to the table, they carry with them the various cultural worlds within which they have learned to function from their families or societies.[77] In their effort to create new cultural horizons for their mission, they do not simply begin from a neutral, cultureless position.[78] Therefore, the task of leadership-in-community is threefold:

1. To look for the cultural worlds at play in group dynamics,[79]

2. To appreciate the contributions those cultural worlds provide for knowledge creation and the development of shared meaning in the team,[80] and

3. To channel the interaction of cultural worlds within the team (i.e., sharing, learning from, and adapting valuable insights from different cultural worlds[81]) so that the team truly integrates into a community of trust with shared direction, alignment, and commitment.[82]

Essentially the task of leadership-in-community is to "exegete humans," to unpack their contextual realities and understand how they affect organizational life and leadership.[83] In order to do so in a way that builds relational integration between members, leaders must be careful not to sacrifice depth for area.[84] They must take the valuable time necessary to listen, ask questions, study, reflect, and assimilate all team members into a cohesive community ready to respond wisely to the variables their environments throw at them.[85]

   Cultural Intelligence. The awareness of different cultural worlds on the team is the beginning of cultural intelligence. Cultural intelligence is "the capability to function effectively across national, ethnic, and organizational cultures."[86] Leadership-in-community must exegete well the human contexts

---

[76] Ibid.

[77] Ibid. p. 156.

[78] Ibid. p. 139, 156.

[79] Ibid.

[80] Ibid. p. 175-176.

[81] Ibid. p. 139.

[82] Drath et al., "Direction, Alignment, Commitment," p. 636.

[83] McConnell, *Cultural Insights for Christian Leaders*, p. 156.

[84] Ibid. p. 155-156.

[85] Ibid.

[86] David Livermore, *Leading with Cultural Intelligence: The Real Secret to Success* 2nd ed. (New York: AMACON, 2015), p. 4.

that shape its mission. Cultural intelligence is the ability to do so *and* take appropriate actions so that the team can create new cultural horizons. It includes four capabilities that leadership-in-community must continually assess and develop within their teams or organizations:

1. **Drive (Motivation):** Having the interest, confidence, and drive to adapt cross-culturally,

2. **Knowledge (Cognition):** Understanding intercultural norms and differences,

3. **Strategy (Metacognition):** Making sense of culturally diverse experiences to make strategic plans for engaging cultural differences effectively, and

4. **Action (Behavioral):** Changing verbal and nonverbal actions appropriately when interacting cross-culturally.[87]

These four capabilities reveal that cultural intelligence is more than merely cultural competency, which is the ability to understand, appreciate, and interact with others from different cultural backgrounds.[88] It involves experiential learning that leads the team or organization to new discoveries, new knowledge, and new strategies for moving the mission forward.[89]

One person cannot possibly comprehend all the forms and nuances of cultural norms he or she encounters. Nor can anyone suspend his or her own cultural worldviews when encountering different cultural worlds. Cultural intelligence recognizes that all team members approach teamwork from their own cultural starting points. Rather than deny or disparage those cultural assumptions, cultural intelligence *appreciates* them as a human resource that each member shares with the team for the purpose of constructing shared meaning of its common mission. Leadership-in-community cultivates the four capabilities so that the team can leverage its different cultural worlds productively to respond with agility to any cross-cultural mystery it encounters as it carries out its mission.

While some people may be more naturally adept at cross-cultural engagement, cultural intelligence can be learned through training and leadership development.[90] Certainly, leadership-in-community needs a

---

[87] Ibid. p. 26-31.
[88] Ibid. p. 33-34.
[89] Ibid. p. 29, 33.
[90] Ibid. p. 37.

healthy curiosity about people that motivates continual learning about them and their cultures.[91] But as it develops and applies experiential learning skills (see Chapter 4), leadership-in-community transforms that curiosity into meaningful engagement with cultural worlds that expands the cultural horizons of its mission.

Cultural Transformation. Drawing close to others in authentic friendship is the beginning of culture making. We saw how Jonah's indictment against the Ninevites is nowhere more contemptuous than in his personal separation from them (Jonah 4:5). When we withdraw from others and cloister in our cultural enclaves, we resist our priestly vocation as the *imago Dei* that creates new cultural horizons and expands the good reign of God over the entire cosmos. Even more, we resist the command of God to be holy as he is holy – the *imitatio Dei.*

Our imitation of God in our cross-cultural friendships reflects his kindness, mercy, patience, love, trustworthiness, and forgiveness (Exod. 34:6-7). In his cultural mandate (Gen. 1:26-28), God commanded his image-bearers to create cultures that extend his good reign over the earth. He intended our culture-making to resist and push back any force that threatens to undo his good creation into the formless and empty. Political science author and professor Patrick Deneen labels these forces "anticulture" and points to pervasive self-interest and autonomous individuality as its source.[92] They are essentially the sin and evil that fractures the fruitfulness of self-giving relationships between God, us, and our neighbors. God intended his *imago Dei* to fill the earth through these fruitful relationships and demonstrate his goodness and mercy. But the anticulture of sin and evil separates us from God, others, and even ourselves! It destroys culture-making by destroying our community.

But Yahweh, our covenant-making God who has delivered us from slavery to our "anticulture," has given us a new life through the compassion and kindness he demonstrated in his Son, Jesus Christ! 1 Peter reminds us:

> Praise be to the God and Father of our Lord Jesus Christ. God has great mercy, and because of his mercy he gave us a new life. This new life brings us a living hope through Jesus Christ's resurrection from death. Now we wait to receive the blessings God has for his children.

---

[91] Ibid. p. 35.
[92] Patrick J. Deneen, *Why Liberalism Failed* (New Haven: Yale University Press, 2018), p. 66.

These blessings are kept for you in heaven. They cannot be ruined or be destroyed or lose their beauty. (1 Pet. 1:3-4)

When Jesus restores our relationships with God and with others, he also restores our culture-making. We have a living hope that our culture-making is going somewhere good. It will not be fruitless but will extend the good reign of God. And he promises to bless us with blessings that cannot be ruined, destroyed, or lose their beauty. Transforming culture is the goal of our imitation of God. Our witness as God's restored *imago Dei* aims at the greater vision of God's restoration of the entire cosmos.

Christian anthropologist Paul Hiebert asks the key question of missiology: "How can the gospel of Jesus Christ be incarnated in human contexts so that people understand and believe, societies are transformed, and the kingdom of God is made manifest on earth as it is in heaven?"[93] This is the central concern for our missional leadership-in-community. We explored the inherent tension between the indigenizing and pilgrim principles of the Gospel. While effective witness finds ways to make the Gospel at home in particular cultures, it is not content to leave culture as it is. The pilgrim principle asserts that God in Christ takes people where they are *in order to* transform them into who he wants them to be.[94]

H. Richard Niebuhr describes cultural transformation in his classic work on faith and ethics, *Christ & Culture*:

> The conversionist, with his view of history as the present encounter with God in Christ, does not live so much in expectation of a final ending of the world of creation and culture as in awareness of the power of the Lord to transform all things by lifting them up to himself. His imagery is spatial and not temporal; and the movement of life he finds to be issuing from Jesus Christ is an upward movement, the rising of men's souls and deeds and thoughts in a mighty surge of adoration and glorification of the One who draws them to himself. This is what human culture can be – a transformed human life in and to the glory of God. For man it is impossible, but all things are possible to God, who has created man, body and soul, for Himself, and sent his Son into the world that the world through him might be saved.[95]

---

[93] Hiebert, *The Gospel in Human Contexts*, p. 33.

[94] Walls, *The Missionary Movement in Christian History*, p. 8.

[95] H. Richard Niebuhr, *Christ & Culture* 50th Anniversary Expanded Edition (New York: HarperOne, 1951, 2001), p. 195-196.

What a compelling vision of cultural transformation for our leadership-in-community to embrace! God himself is the goal of all creation, including human life.[96] Humans, as the *imago Dei*, are called to care for creation and cultivate it into a place where life may flourish, and God is glorified.[97]

Leadership-in-community reflects the mercy of God by unlocking human creativity from anticultural forces. It focuses on human resources in a way that nurtures the commitment, communication, empowerment, teamwork, trust, participation, and flexibility of all members.[98] In this way, the love of God is on full display within the community! It is these elements that build the relational capacities necessary for creativity and innovation in complex environments.[99] Senge defines the learning organization as one "where people continually expand their capacity to create the results they truly desire, where new and expansive patterns of thinking are nurtured, and where collective aspirations are set free."[100] The learning organization is a culture-transforming organization. It harnesses the power of authentic friendship that draws together diverse people into a community of love that imitates their God and expands his good reign by creating new cultural horizons.

Movement 4: *Oratio*

Heavenly Father,

Sometimes I am afraid of you,
or at least of my idea of you –
afraid of being exposed; afraid of being punished.
But this fear pushes me away from you,
Whose nearness is my good.

Open my eyes to who you really are, to what
a Spirit-born fear is supposed to elicit in my life.

Dismantle my small, self-centered, convenient ideas about you.
Replace the illusions with glimpses of your true glory.

---

[96] Benno Van Den Toren, "God's Purpose for Creation as the Key to Understanding the Universality and Cultural Variety of Christian Ethics," *Missiology: An International Review* 30, no. 2 (2002), p. 218.

[97] Ibid.

[98] Christopher M. Branson, "Achieving Organisational Change through Values Alignment," *Journal of Educational Administration* 46, no. 3 (2008), p. 377.

[99] Ibid. p. 378.

[100] Senge, *The Fifth Element*, p. 3.

Bring forth my deepest reverence.
Build in me a lifestyle of praise.

You, Lord, are like an ocean – too deep to fathom,
too wonderful to comprehend.
You are greater than all matter, all energy, all time.
Your very name is the essence of mystery and might.

Today I ask you to grace me with an abiding, life-shaping fear
of you. By your Spirit, reveal your divine nature so I can
trust you more fully,
seek your best with my whole heart, and
serve you with joy.[101]

In Jesus' name, Amen.

Movement 5: *Imitatio*

- Individual Reflection

  - Journal your responses to the following questions:

    - What key points is God leading you to embrace and grow into?

    - How can you live this out in your life and leadership?

    - How can your missional leadership group pray for you in living this out?

- Group Reflection

  - In your missional leadership group, share your individual reflections with each other.

  - Pray for one another.

Movement 6: *Missio*

- Experiencing Mission

  - Level 1 *Awareness*

---

[101] Prayer adapted from the ancient spiritual practice of the Prayer Wheel. Dodd, Riess, & Van Biema, *The Prayer Wheel*, p. 117.

- Pray each day that the Lord sends you into his mission that day.

- At the end of each day, reflect on or journal about one experience you had that day where you witnessed the *missio Dei* personally. Describe what happened. What was significant about that experience for you?

  o Level 2 *Personal Commitment*
  - Ask the Lord where he may be sending you to be his witness on a regular basis.

  - Make a commitment to serve in that way.

Movement 7: *Communio*

+ Experiencing Mission

  o Level 3 *Group Experience*

  - If possible, the small group may consider performing a mission or service project together to experience mission as a community.

+ Group Reflection

  o Where did you see the *missio Dei* in action this past week?

  o What was the most significant or surprising observations you made about your experience?

  o What did you learn about God from that experience? What did you learn about yourself from that experience?

  o What difference does that make in your leadership? How will you apply what you have learned?

Movement 8: *Contemplatio*

Each week in your small group, spend time reflecting and celebrating the ways that you have seen "God on the move" in the past week.

+ Spend some time in prayer or singing in thanksgiving and praise to our missionary God.

Section 3:

The Ethics of Leadership-in-Community

Chapter 7

Hospitality

From May 1889 to May 1890, Dutch painter Vincent van Gogh was hospitalized at the Saint-Paul de Mausole asylum in Saint-Rémy-de-Provence, France. He sought treatment at the sanitarium because of his escalating mental illness. Prior to his stay at Saint-Rémy, he had suffered from alcoholism, smoker's cough, depression, and a rapid mental deterioration.[1] He experienced frequent hallucinations and mental breakdowns to the extent that the townspeople of Arles, where he was living, labeled him a madman.[2] Besides his prolific artwork, he is well-remembered for cutting off part of his ear during one of his delirious altercations.[3] He was hearing voices and purportedly attacked his friend and fellow artist, Paul Gaugin, with a razor.[4] He eventually turned the razor on himself. His psychotic bouts became so frequent that 30 townspeople petitioned the village of Arles to close his house.[5] Shortly thereafter, he voluntarily entered the asylum in Saint-Rémy.

During the winter of 1890 when the weather was too cold for him to leave his cell and paint outside, he spent his time inside creating a series of paintings based on the works of other artists.[6] He reinterpreted them in his own distinct style much like a musician produces different arrangements of familiar songs.[7] One such work was Eugene Delacroix's 1889 painting *The Good Samaritan* that Van Gogh painted from a black-and-white lithograph.[8]

Van Gogh might have found himself drawn to the image of the Good Samaritan. He was a broken, fragile, spent man. His helplessness surrounded him within the confines of his small room with barred windows.[9] On July 27, 1890, shortly after leaving the asylum and within a few months of completing

---

[1] Jan Greenberg & Sandra Jordan, *Vincent van Gogh: Portrait of an Artist* (New York: Dell Yearling, 2001), p. 90-94. Kindle.

[2] Leo Jansen, Hans Luijten, & Nienke Bakker (Eds.), "Report drawn up by Joseph d'Ornano, Chief of Police, in response to the petition from local residents, Arles, 27 February 1889," *Vincent van Gogh – The Letters* (Amsterdam: Van Gogh Museum & Huygens ING, 2009). Accessed January 18, 2021, http://vangoghletters.org/ vg/documentation.html.

[3] Greenberg & Jordan, *Vincent van Gogh*, p. 90.

[4] Ibid.

[5] Jansen, Luijten, & Bakker (Eds.), "Report drawn up by Joseph d'Ornana."

[6] Bible Odyssey, "The Good Samaritan," accessed December 7, 2020, https://bibleodyssey.org/tools/image-gallery/g/good-samaritan-van-gogh.

[7] Ibid.

[8] Hovak Najarian, "The Good Samaritan: Art for Proper 10C," Hear What the Spirit is Saying (blog), St. Hugh's Episcopal Church, Idyllwild, CA, accessed December 6, 2020, https://smecsundaymorningforum.org/tag/the-good-samaritan.

[9] The University of Notre Dame Alumni Association, "The Good Samaritan – Van Gogh," Faith ND, accessed December 7, 2020, http://faith.nd.edu/s/1210/faith/interior.aspx?sid=1210&gid=609&pgid=44542&cid=85960&ecid=85960&crid=0&calpgid=44241&calcid=85766.

his own rendition of *The Good Samaritan*, with "sadness and extreme loneliness,"[10] he took his own life by a gunshot to his chest. His disease, it seemed, had robbed him of his last remnant of humanity.

Take a few moments to look at Van Gogh's *The Good Samaritan*. What do you see? What grabs your attention and draws you in? What emotions does it evoke for you? Reflect on it, not as an outside observer, but as a participant in it immersed in the drama, color, and emotions of the scene:

Figure 3: The Good Samaritan, oil on canvas, 1890, Vincent van Gogh[11]

---

[10] Van Gogh would describe the wheatfields he was painting in *Wheatfield with Crows* as representing his "sadness and extreme loneliness." He painted this piece prior to his suicide in July 1890. Leo Jansen, Hans Luijten, & Nienke Bakker (eds.). "898: To Theo van Gogh and Jo van Gogh-Bonger. Auvers-sur-Oise, on or about Thursday, 10 July 1890." *Vincent van Gogh – The Letters* (Amsterdam: Van Gogh Museum & Huygens ING., 2009), accessed December 7, 2020, http://vangoghletters.org/vg/letters/let898/letter.html.

[11] Van Gogh, Vincent, "The Good Samaritan (after Delacroix)," Oil on Canvas Painting, 1890, Kröller-Müller Museum, Otterlo, The Netherlands.

Even though Van Gogh was rapidly declining mentally and physically between 1888 and 1890, his work during this period has been acclaimed by art experts as his most masterful and prolific. As his own humanity was ebbing away, Van Gogh portrayed the scene of *The Good Samaritan* with such vibrancy and vitality. The muted figures of the priest and Levite diminish off in the background with their backs turned upon the Samaritan and the injured man. While in the foreground, an incredible act of compassion is on full display with such energy, intensity, and profusion of color. The Samaritan and the injured man are locked in an intimate embrace as the Samaritan strains to hoist the man onto his horse. Painted from the depth of Van Gogh's pain-filled longing, this scene invites us to see the humanity of both men, the Samaritan's profound hospitality restoring the dignity and worth of the injured man.

We have considered how leadership-in-community welcomes the diverse voices of all team members. In our unpredictable and complex world, we will experience mysterious phenomena that refuses to fit our prescribed formulas. We must listen and learn from one another! The *communitas* of leadership-in-community prizes the diversity and differences of our team members as beautiful gifts that God has given us. They help us make sense of this world and create new cultural horizons in it that witness to God's good reign.

But to listen and learn well, we need to slow down, suspend judgment, and contemplate with wonder and respect what "the other" brings to our dialogue. We must welcome the innovative ideas (no matter how crazy they initially seem!), unique perspectives, important values, expertise, and experiences our diverse team members offer. Leadership-in-community requires deep hospitality.[12]

Hospitality is an essential leadership ethic for our priestly vocation as the renewed *imago Dei*. To welcome others is to honor their humanity. It reveres the image of God they bear. And it embraces them as a fellow living stone who God is fitting together with us into his temple (1 Pet. 2:5). Pastor Luke Richards of Pocono Lake Wesleyan Church spoke this same vision of hospitality over his congregation:

---

[12] Gina Grandy & Martyna Sliwa, "Contemplative Leadership: The Possibilities for the Ethics of Leadership Theory and Practice," *Journal of Business Ethics* 143 (2017), p. 425, 435.

We're family. We might be one of the strangest families around, but that's what we are. My prayer for this church is not that we would grow to become the biggest and coolest church around. Honestly, it's not necessarily my goal to add numbers to our Sunday attendance. What I would rather have is for us to look around this sanctuary one day and think, "how on earth did *that guy* become my brother?" I want us to be the biggest collections of misfits, messes, and failures around. I don't want a church full of church people, I want a church full of people who could never possibly deserve to be here, and they know it, and they're grateful that Christ has brought them back from the brink. I want a church full of people who are so radically different from one another that we can't possibly get along, much less love one another, and the only thing we have going for us is that we're one in Christ's name, and that's all it takes for us to be family. And I want the world to look at us and be so amazed that such a bizarre assortment of people have built a community together that they can't help but know that we had help from above.[13]

This radical welcome of "the other" into our communities of trust is a brilliant witness to the glory of our compassionate and merciful God. Ultimately, our mission is hospitality. As we extend the welcome of Christ to others who are lost in the formless and empty, he restores their dignity and humanity as his *imago Dei*. He sets them free to participate in the *imago Dei's* priestly vocation of creating life-giving cultures that expand God's good reign to the cosmos.

In this chapter, we will look deeply at the Parable of the Good Samaritan and what it teaches us about our leadership-in-community ethic of hospitality.

Movement 1: *Adspecto*

Prayer

+ Pray for the Holy Spirit to speak to you through the Scripture. Use the following words of Psalm 23 as a prayer:

> [1]*The LORD is my shepherd.*
> *I will always have everything I need.*

---

[13] Luke Richards, "Deep Community and Beautiful Hospitality (Sermon)," Pocono Lake Wesleyan Church, accessed December 8, 2020, https://poconolakewesleyan.org/uploads/1/5/3/9/15395128/5_deep_community_and_beautiful_hospitality_2.pdf.

> *²He gives me green pastures to lie in.*
>> *He leads me by calm pools of water.*
> *³He restores my strength.*
>> *He leads me on right paths to show that he is good.*
> *⁴Even if I walk through a valley as dark as the grave,*
>> *I will not be afraid of any danger, because you are with me.*
>> *Your rod and staff comfort me.*
> *⁵You prepared a meal for me in front of my enemies.*
>> *You welcomed me as an honored guest.*
>> *My cup is full and spilling over.*
> *⁶Your goodness and mercy will be with me all my life,*
>> *and I will live in the LORD's house a long, long time.*

Scripture Reading

✦ **Read Luke 10:25-37.** Listen for words or phrases from the passage that stand out to you.

A Story About the Good Samaritan

²⁵Then an expert in the law stood up to test Jesus. He said, "Teacher, what must I do to get eternal life?"

²⁶Jesus said to him, "What is written in the law? What do you understand from it?"

²⁷The man answered, "'Love the Lord your God with all your heart, all your soul, all your strength, and all your mind.' Also, 'Love your neighbor the same as you love yourself.'"

²⁸Jesus said, "Your answer is right. Do this and you will have eternal life."

²⁹But the man wanted to show that the way he was living was right. So he said to Jesus, "But who is my neighbor?"

³⁰To answer this question, Jesus said, "A man was going down the road from Jerusalem to Jericho. Some robbers surrounded him, tore off his clothes, and beat him. Then they left him lying there on the ground almost dead.

³¹"It happened that a Jewish priest was going down that road. When he saw the man, he did not stop to help him. He walked away. ³²Next, a Levite came

near. He saw the hurt man, but he went around him. He would not stop to help him either. He just walked away.

33"Then a Samaritan man traveled down that road. He came to the place where the hurt man was lying. He saw the man and felt very sorry for him. 34The Samaritan went to him and poured olive oil and wine on his wounds. Then he covered the man's wounds with cloth. The Samaritan had a donkey. He put the hurt man on his donkey, and he took him to an inn. There he cared for him. 35The next day, the Samaritan took out two silver coins and gave them to the man who worked at the inn. He said, 'Take care of this hurt man. If you spend more money on him, I will pay it back to you when I come again.'"

36Then Jesus said, "Which one of these three men do you think was really a neighbor to the man who was hurt by the robbers?"

37The teacher of the law answered, "The one who helped him."

Jesus said, "Then you go and do the same."

Reflection

✚ When you have finished reading, remain silent for one or two minutes.

✚ Read the entire passage again. If you have an audio Bible, listen through the passage.

  o *Personal Reflection:* Journal your thoughts on the following questions:

    ▪ What words or phrases from the passage stand out to you?

    ▪ How do these words or phrases connect with your life right now?

    ▪ How might God be inviting you to respond to this passage?

Movement 2: *Lectio*

Scripture Study
✚ Read or listen to **Luke 10:25-37.**

✦ Answer the following study questions:

1. What did the expert in the law (the lawyer) ask Jesus (vs. 25)?

2. What was the lawyer's intention in asking Jesus this question (vs. 25)?

3. How did Jesus answer the question (vs. 26)?

4. Why do you think Jesus answers him this way?

5. What did the lawyer understand is the law's requirement to get eternal life (vs. 27)?

6. Jesus responded to the lawyer, "Your answer is right. Do this and you will have eternal life" (vs. 28). How do you think the lawyer felt hearing this response from Jesus?

7. Why do you think the lawyer was not satisfied with Jesus' response?

8. What did the lawyer ask Jesus as a follow-up question (vs. 29)?

9. What was the lawyer's intent in asking Jesus this question (vs. 29)?

10. Why do you think Jesus responds by telling a story?

11. In the story Jesus tells, what happened to the man traveling from Jerusalem to Jericho (vs. 30)?

12. What do the priest and the Levite do as they come near the place where the man was (vs. 31-32)?

13. Why do you think they take these actions?

14. What does the Samaritan man do when he comes near the place where the man was (vs. 33-35)?

15. Why do you think he takes these actions?

16. What impresses you the most (positively or negatively) about the actions of the priest, the Levite, and the Samaritan?

17. How do you think Jesus' story answers the lawyer's question, "Who is my neighbor?" (vs. 36)?

18. The lawyer quoted from two Old Testament commands: "You must love the LORD your God with all your heart, with all your soul, and with all your strength" (Deut. 6:5) and

"Forget about the wrong things people do to you. Don't try to get even. Love your neighbor as yourself. I am the LORD" (Lev. 19:18). How do you think Jesus understood the law compared to how the lawyer understood the law?

19. What did Jesus finally tell the lawyer (vs. 37)?

20. How does Jesus' story of the Good Samaritan impact you?

21. If Jesus told this story to your missional community, what difference would it make for its leadership-in-community?

Reading
The Context of Luke

One of the central concerns of Luke's Gospel is the interpretation of the Old Testament Scriptures in light of their fulfillment in Christ and the reconstitution of God's people in the church (Luke 24:44-49).[14] This was especially important to the early church as it made sense of how the inclusion of the Gentiles comported with God's continuing faithfulness to Israel after the destruction of Jerusalem in 70 CE.[15] Throughout the Gospel, Luke elevated the place of mercy and compassion as most essential for God's people in reading and interpreting Torah.[16] Mercy and compassion trumped the purity regulations that had been handed down by the Jewish leaders for generations.[17]

The religious leaders understood *purity* as the measure by which they were set apart as God's people, separate and uncontaminated by the surrounding nations. Bruce Malina states:

> Traditional Israelite ideology was pivoted on the awareness of the holiness of the God of Israel. Holiness is social exclusivity, and the God of Israel demanded such exclusivity from the people who were chosen to be exclusively God's – or so went Israel's story line.[18]

Accordingly, the storyline that Israel used as its interpretive grid of Torah presumed that the welfare and prosperity of God's holy nation required that

---

[14] DeSilva, *An Introduction to the New Testament*, p. 320.
[15] Ibid. p. 316, 318).
[16] Torah is the word for the Law as recorded in the first five books of the Old Testament. Ibid. p. 320.
[17] Ibid. p. 321-322.
[18] Malina, *The New Testament World*, p. 170-171.

they remain sacred and exclusive.[19] It set rigid boundaries between the sacred and profane, the clean and unclean, based on its strict interpretation of Torah.[20] To be welcomed by God, they reasoned, they must also stay pure from anything that defiles.

But Jesus kept blurring the lines between the sacred and the profane, much to their indignation! Luke presented many stories of Jesus offering provocative hospitality to the unclean: eating with tax collectors and sinners, healing on the Sabbath, and touching the unclean. This really rankled the experts in the law! In his Gospel, Luke presented lawyers as the narrative's chief antagonists.[21] Their interpretation of the Law was in constant conflict with that of Jesus.[22] Jesus reprimanded the teachers of the law who over-emphasized purity while neglecting "justice and the love of God" (Luke 11:42, NIV; cf. Matt. 23:23). He shamed those who prioritized purity over mercy and compassion (Luke 13:17). He taught that the fulfillment of God's law was not rigid separation from anyone that would defile. Instead, he demonstrated that the true rhythm of life in God's Kingdom was the compassion that welcomed others.[23]

By introducing the character of the expert of the law, Luke signaled to his readers that conflict with Jesus over a matter of the law was imminent.[24] When the lawyer stood up to test Jesus (Luke 11:25), readers would have assumed that he was looking for evidence to discredit Jesus. In fact, the Greek word Luke used for "test" (*ekpeirazō*) was powerfully negative, used only one other time in both Luke and Acts when Satan tested Jesus in the wilderness (Luke 4:12).[25] The lawyer was not a "seeker" who honestly desired to learn from this rabbi. He was an "expert in the law" who desired to justify his interpretation publicly before the onlookers.[26]

---

[19] Ibid. p. 171.

[20] Ibid.

[21] Joshua Marshall Strahan, "Jesus Teaches Theological Interpretation of the Law: Reading the Good Samaritan in Its Literary Context," *Journal of Theological Interpretation* 10, no. 1 (2016), p. 72.

[22] Ibid.

[23] DeSilva, *An Introduction to the New Testament*, p. 321-322.

[24] Strahan, "Jesus Teaches Theological Interpretation," p. 72.

[25] Colin M. Ambrose, "Desiring to Be Justified: An Examination of the Parable of the Good Samaritan in Luke 10:25-37," *Sewanee Theological Review* 54, no. 1 (2010), p. 19.

[26] Ronald Burris, "Another Look at the Good Samaritan: Luke 10:25-37," *Review and Expositor* 114, no. 3 (2017), p. 458.

The interaction between Jesus and the lawyer was a game of social push-and-shove called "challenge and response."[27] It was played often in the honor and shame cultures of the ancient Mediterranean world.[28] Honor was the pivotal value of these societies. It was the claim to public worth, and it guaranteed a person's success, welfare, and status in his or her community.[29] Honor was publicly ascribed to the person who belonged to the right group and had the right relationships.[30] But honor was not in unlimited supply.[31] A person could not acquire more honor without taking it from someone else. And so, the game was afoot. Individuals would hassle one another according to socially defined rules in order to excel over them and gain their honor.[32]

Challenge and response was won on the battleground of public opinion.[33] If a person claimed honor for winning the challenge, but the witnesses did not also grant honor to that person, then he or she won no honor.[34] In fact, such a person would have been thought of as presumptuous, ridiculous, and contemptuous.[35]

In our story, the lawyer's question was intended to challenge Jesus. If he bested Jesus in the eyes of the public, Jesus along with his teaching would be discredited. The lawyer's interpretation of the Law would be honored as the legitimate interpretation of Torah. So much was riding on the outcome of the conversation that was about to transpire.

What Must I Do to Get Eternal Life?

The lawyer began the challenge by asking, "Teacher, what must I do to get eternal life?" (Luke 10:25). Even though the lawyer gave Jesus some social courtesies (standing as a sign of respect and addressing him as "teacher"), he most likely intended these gestures contemptuously because his true purpose was to test Jesus.[36] The lawyer was not interested in Jesus' prescribed "plan of salvation" to get into heaven.[37] Such was not the overriding concern of first-century Judaism that was, in fact, largely

---

[27] Malina, *The New Testament World*, p. 33.

[28] Ibid. p. 29.

[29] Ibid. p. 29, 33.

[30] Ibid. p. 29.

[31] Ibid. p. 30, 33.

[32] Ibid. p. 33.

[33] Ibid. p. 40.

[34] Ibid. p. 32.

[35] Ibid.

[36] Ambrose, "Desiring to be Justified," p. 19.

[37] Ibid. p. 26.

preoccupied with Israel's restoration as a political nation unyoked from the subjugation of Rome or any other "unclean" foreign power.[38] Judaism presumed this would happen according to its strict interpretation of the covenant as well as the historic prophetic promises of redemption that it viewed through the lens of privilege and exclusivity.[39] So much of one's religious observance was practiced to demonstrate that he or she indeed belonged to the covenant community.[40] We see this in the lawyer's desire to "show that the way he was living was right" (Luke 10:29). N. T. Wright explains, "Justification in this setting…is not a matter of how someone enters the community of the true people of God, but of how you tell who belongs to that community."[41] And purity was the measure of faithfulness. Through rigid purity codes, the Jewish leaders, teachers, and lawyers demarcated between who was in and who was out of God's special people.

In true rabbinic style, Jesus answered the question by asking questions in return: "What is written in the law? What do you understand from it?" (Luke 10:26). New Testament scholar Philip Esler believes Jesus' response here is sharp and dismissive, as if to say, "You're a lawyer, what do you think?"[42] Jesus called upon the lawyer to answer his own question and, in doing so, exposed the inadequacy of the lawyer's own thinking. The lawyer answered Jesus' first question by quoting from Torah (Luke 10:27; see Deut. 6:5 and Lev. 19:18). But he failed to answer the second question about how he interprets the Law he just recited. So, Jesus caught the lawyer in his own game! Again, he responded dismissively, as if to say "Good answer! Go do that!" (Luke 10:28). Jesus won this challenge, and his response brilliantly exposed the inauthenticity of the lawyer's question.[43] The lawyer lost face and now sought to "justify himself" (Luke 10:29, NIV).

Who Is My Neighbor?

And so, the lawyer attempted a counterpunch: "But who is my neighbor?" (Luke 10:29). Again, his question was not motivated by a sincere

---

[38] Ibid.

[39] Ibid.

[40] Ibid. p. 26-27.

[41] N. T. Wright, *What Saint Paul Really Said: Was Paul of Tarsus the Real Founder of Christianity?* (Grand Rapids: Eerdmans, 1997), p. 118.

[42] Philip E. Esler, "Jesus and the Reduction of Intergroup Conflict: The Parable of the Good Samaritan in Light of Social Identity Theory," *Biblical Interpretation* 8 (2000), p. 333.

[43] Peter N. Rule, "The Pedagogy of Jesus in the Parable of the Good Samaritan: A Diacognitive Analysis," *HTS Teologiese Studies/Theological Studies* 73, no. 3 (2017), p. 4.

altruism. He was after public vindication.[44] He wanted to discredit Jesus right at the central issue of contention: *who belongs to God's elected community?*[45] The lawyer seemed to rightly understand that Torah is appropriately interpreted within a relational context, that of loving God and loving neighbors.[46] So, he "wanted to show that the way he was living was right" within that relational context (Luke 10:29). But his faithfulness to Torah now hinged on what Torah meant by "neighbor." He was eager to prove that his interpretation, rather than that of Jesus, was right and justified him in the context of Israel's exclusive relationship with its covenant God.

Justification is a central theme of the discussion between Jesus and the lawyer. In the Old Testament, the concept of justification, which shares the same Hebrew word family as righteousness, does not primarily refer to a person's obedience to an objective standard or law.[47] More precisely, justification refers to taking correct actions within the context of a given relationship.[48] For example, in some cultural contexts, children may care for their aging parents by placing them in an assisted living facility. However, in other cultural contexts, this action may be perceived as dishonoring and disrespectful to parents. In these cases, adult children are expected to care for their aging parents by welcoming them to live with them in their homes. No law may indicate that either action is right or wrong. Rather, the relational context *justifies* the appropriate actions to take. Hermann Cremer explains, "Every relationship brings with it certain claims upon conduct, and the satisfaction of these claims, which issue from the relationship and in which alone the relationship can persist, is described by our term [justification]..."[49] While Jesus and the lawyer agreed on what the law said, they diverged in their interpretation of what it meant. How each interpreted "neighbor" had significant implications for what was justified as faithful living before God.

The lawyer's interpretation established boundaries between who was his neighbor and who was not. He wanted to delineate clearly who he must love as a fellow member of God's elect people and who he needed to exclude

---

44 Ambrose, "Desiring to Be Justified," p. 27.

45 Ibid.

46 Ibid. p. 28.

47 Ibid. p. 25.

48 Ibid.

49 Hermann Cremer, *Biblisch-theologisches Worterbuch*, 7th ed. (Gotha: F. A. Perthes, 1893), 273-275, quoted in Gerhard von Rad, *Old Testament Theology*, trans. D. M. G. Stalker, vol.1 (San Francisco: Harper, 1965), p. 370.

as unclean.[50] He believed that the command to love neighbors (Lev. 19:18b) applied unquestionably to members of the covenant community but not to all people.[51] He wanted to be clear on this point because he was concerned that if he associated with the wrong people, he would be unfaithful in his relationship with God and God's covenant community.[52]

However, Jesus interpreted the law by telling a story about an extreme act of hospitality. The Parable of the Good Samaritan was not a disarming moral tale of exemplary virtuous behavior. It was a provocative story that unhinged the law from exclusionist shackles and reclaimed the identity of God's people as those who imitate him by "doing" mercy (Luke 10:37). Jesus was a teacher of wisdom, a genre of instruction focused on such content as the character of God, what is valuable or important, and how one should live.[53] He used parables to engage his listeners into active thought.[54] His teaching did not merely convey information or provide instruction on the right virtues. Instead, he often told open-ended stories to compel his listeners to work out the meaning and application for themselves.[55] His parables drew material from common life that would be familiar to his listeners.[56] But he used this material to make surprising comparisons to the spiritual wisdom he wanted to impart to them. Such wisdom would arrest the attention of his listeners by its strangeness.[57] It was a brilliant teaching strategy. It oriented his listeners in common experiences they could relate to, but then it challenged their assumptions with unexpected turns in the story.[58] These surprising twists awoke his listeners to grand new spiritual truths about God, themselves, or the world.[59]

Jesus used a typical triadic format of storytelling in the Parable of the Good Samaritan.[60] This format was usually structured around a priest, a

---

[50] Ambrose, "Desiring to be Justified," p. 28.

[51] Johannes Fichtner, "πλησίον in the LXX and the Neighbour in the Old Testament," in *Theological Dictionary of the New Testament*, Ed. Gerhard Kittel & Gerhard Friedrich (Grand Rapids: William B. Eerdmans Publishing Company, 1977), 6:315.

[52] Ambrose, "Desiring to be Justified," p. 28.

[53] Rule, "The Pedagogy of Jesus," p. 1.

[54] Ibid. p. 2.

[55] Ibid.

[56] Ibid.

[57] Ibid.

[58] Ibid.

[59] Ibid.

[60] Mark A. Proctor, "'Who Is My Neighbor?' Recontextualizing Luke's Good Samaritan (Luke 10:25-37)," *Journal of Biblical Literature* 138, no. 1 (2019), p. 207-208.

Levite, and an Israelite layman.[61] After the priest and the Levite failed to help the injured victim, the audience would have expected an Israelite to emerge to fulfill the duty of love.[62] They may have even given a pass to the priest and Levite on the potential grounds that they were constrained by religious purity rules.[63] However, in the story, they were heading away from Jerusalem where their temple service was performed. Purity obligations should not have prevented them from helping the injured man.[64]

But Jesus shocked his listeners by introducing a Samaritan in the place of the Israelite. Even more, the Samaritan was the story's hero who saved the life of the injured man![65] In the story of Jesus and the Samaritan woman (John 4), we learned that Samaritans were despised by the Jews for historic, cultural, and religious reasons. To make matters worse, evidence from the story suggests, according to Ernest van Eck, that this Samaritan was "one of the most despised figures in the 1st-century advanced agrarian world, namely a merchant."[66] Merchants had a reputation for being dishonest, envious, cowardly, unmerciful, lazy, and idle.[67] They were perceived as godless thieves who grew rich by taking advantage of common people.[68] The first-century Mediterranean person regarded the accumulation of wealth as an unrighteous act of betrayal against the relational obligations he or she had to the community.[69] In an agrarian economy, peasant production was primarily used for subsistence living and not for exchange.[70] The resources available to them for production were limited.[71] A person only amassed wealth at the expense of others.[72] Van Eck explains, "For peasants, it was therefore 'unnatural' to use money to buy commodities which one then resold at a profit.

---

[61] Ibid.

[62] Ibid. p. 207.

[63] Strahan, "Jesus Teaches Theological Interpretation of the Law," p. 76.

[64] Ibid.

[65] Ernest van Eck, "A Samaritan Merchant and His Friend, And Their Friends: Practicing Life-Giving Theology," *HTS Teologiese Studies/Theological Studies* 75, no. 1 (2019), p. 6.

[66] Van Eck argues that the Samaritan is a merchant because he is traveling, he carries oil and wine (which were common items of trade), he has an animal to carry his wares, and he seems to know the innkeeper well enough that he is able to establish a tab with him for the injured man's welfare. Van Eck, "A Samaritan Merchant and His Friend," p. 5.

[67] Ibid.

[68] Ibid. p. 6.

[69] Ibid.

[70] Ibid.

[71] Ibid.

[72] Malina, *The New Testament World*, p. 89.

Profitmaking was seen as evil and socially destructive..."[73] It threatened the community's delicate social balance.[74] But nevertheless, Jesus presented a Samaritan merchant as the hero of this story. It was this hated, unclean person that fulfilled the Law's requirement to love his neighbor. And he did so in the most lavish and generous manner (Luke 10:34-35).

According to the social rules of antiquity, no act of hospitality went unreciprocated.[75] The Samaritan's hospitality created an indebtedness of reciprocity for the injured man.[76] Gustav Stählin describes this obligation:

> The two relations of neighbourliness and hospitality carry with them a sacred duty. The friend as neighbour and host must be available for a friend... Friendship means service, concern, and sacrifice even to the point of life itself... Whether in terms of hospitability or of neighbourliness, the friend can expect help from his friend even when it is inconvenient.[77]

The injured man was now bound to the Samaritan in a reciprocal relationship of hospitality that secured the equitable welfare of both men.[78] The Samaritan's act of mercy transformed an enemy into a neighbor.[79]

This surprising reversal in the story challenged Jesus' listeners to identify with the injured man left half-dead on the side of the road, and not with any of the other characters.[80] Jesus shifted the focus from the injured man to the one who helped him. While the lawyer asked about *who he should love* as a neighbor, Jesus answers with *who loves* as a neighbor.[81] Jesus presented the Samaritan as the exemplar of love. This would have acutely offended his Jewish listeners.[82] In essence, Jesus' answer was, according to Peter Rule, "Not 'love your enemy' but 'my enemy loves me; I should be like him'."[83]

---

[73] Van Eck, "A Samaritan Merchant and His Friend," p. 6.

[74] Malina, *The New Testament World*, p. 97.

[75] Proctor, "Who Is My Neighbor?" p. 208.

[76] Ibid. p. 206.

[77] Gustav Stählin, "φίλος, φίλη, φιλία," in *Theological Dictionary of the New Testament*, Eds. Gerhard Kittel & Gerhard Friedrich (Grand Rapids: William B. Eerdmans Publishing Company, 1977), 9:146-171.

[78] Ibid. p. 212.

[79] Ibid. p. 219.

[80] Strahan, "Jesus Theological Interpretation," p. 85.

[81] Rule, "The Pedagogy of Jesus," p. 7.

[82] Ibid. p. 7.

[83] Ibid. p. 7.

Throughout the Gospel of Luke, compassion and mercy characterize God.[84] In the parable, the Good Samaritan represents God. Its message is that, because God had shown mercy to his people, they are obligated to reciprocate by showing mercy to others. Jesus challenged the lawyer, and us today, that to be in right standing with God – to be justified in the context of our relationship with God – we must show welcome and mercy to others, even to the "outsiders," just as God our Savior showed lavish mercy to us.[85] Colin Ambrose agrees:

> Jesus is stating that the purpose of the law is not to define who is in and who is out of covenant relationship, but rather to give identity to God's covenant people. In response to the lawyer's desire to define who is justified by being part of God's covenant people, Jesus tells him what it means to be part of God's covenant people. Thus the primary message of the parable is not that all men are our neighbors, though this is implied, but rather that *the intent of the law, the law of God's covenant people, is not to define who is a member, but rather to define what it means to be a member.* The law is not primarily about who God's people are, but how to be God's people.[86]

Generous hospitality is the mark of God's people. It reflects his glory because it imitates his character and actions. Our leadership-in-community must reflect his generous hospitality by our gracious welcome of others.

Hospitality and the Gospel

In the Parable the Good Samaritan, Jesus created for his listeners a vision of the Kingdom of God that sets hospitality above the purity regulations.[87] When faced with the dilemma between rescuing the half-dead man or maintaining ritual purity, only the Samaritan outsider fulfilled the law of God by extending hospitality to the stranger.[88] Joshua Jipp says:

---

[84] Strahan points to the two songs that open Luke's Gospel, the first from Mary who "proclaims that God shows mercy to everyone, from one generation to the next," (Luke 1:50) and the second from Zechariah, "who prophecies that God 'has shown the mercy promised to our ancestors'" (Luke 1:72). Strahan, "Jesus Theological Interpretation," p. 81-82.

[85] Ibid. p. 82.

[86] Ambrose, "Desiring to be Justified," p. 28.

[87] Joshua W. Jipp, *Saved by Faith and Hospitality* (Grand Rapids: William B. Eerdmans Publishing Company, 2017), p. 162.

[88] Ibid.

God's relationship to his people is fundamentally an act of hospitality to strangers, as God makes space for "the other," for his people, by inviting humanity into relationship with him. This experience of God's hospitality is at the very heart of the church's identity. We are God's guests and friends. And it is because of God's extension of hospitality and friendship to us that the church can offer hospitality to one another *and* to those seeming outside the reach of our faith communities.[89]

The primary problem presented in Luke and Acts is alienation from God and others caused by sin.[90] Sin had separated us from life-giving relationships with God and others for which we were created.[91] But at the inauguration of Jesus' public ministry, he declared the reversal of this curse with Isaiah's proclamation of "the year of the Lord's favor" (Luke 4:19, NIV):

> The Spirit of the Lord is on me.
> He has chosen me to tell good news to the poor.
> He sent me to tell prisoners that they are free
> and to tell the blind that they can see again.
> He sent me to free those who have been treated badly
> and to announce that the time has come for the Lord to show his kindness.
> (Luke 4:18-19)

The good news of Jesus, the Lord's anointed king, is that his reign is one of generous hospitality toward the "outsiders." Jesus welcomes all who are separated by sin into the flourishing life of the "year of the Lord's favor" (Luke 4:19, NIV).[92]

Luke and Acts are replete with language and images of hospitality – food, meals, and houses – that expressed the nature of Jesus' identity as King.[93] He extended welcome to others without distinction: sinners and religious, men and women, rich and poor, Jew and Gentile.[94] The lawyer's question to Jesus was essentially, "Teacher, what must *I do* to be welcomed into God's people?" Jesus responded by telling him a story about what *God*

---

[89] Ibid. p. 2.
[90] Ibid. p. 35.
[91] Ibid.
[92] Ibid.
[93] Ibid. 17.
[94] Ibid. p. 18.

had done to welcome those once alienated by sin into the banquet of his restoring Kingdom.

Hospitality in the Kingdom, in fact, reverses the trajectory of "contamination." The purity tradition asserted that the unclean contaminated the clean.[95] The faithful do not touch anything unclean for fear of becoming unclean. Yet Luke showed that Jesus touched people to heal them – the holy making the unclean pure.[96] The direction of sin is exclusion, contamination, and dehumanization.[97] But the direction of love is inclusion, making friends out of enemies, expanding the boundaries, and restoring the honor of the *imago Dei* in others.[98] This is only possible because of Jesus Christ. Because of his death, resurrection, and eternal reign, the faithful can touch the unclean with his mercy and restore their humanity as God's image-bearers. Through his Gospel people, Jesus extends his welcome to those lost in the formless and empty world.[99] Hans Boersma, reflecting on the significance of Christ's atonement as the foundation of life-giving hospitality, states:

> Union with Christ means that, in a real sense, the Church has been raised up with Christ and has received a place in heaven at the right hand of God (Eph. 2:6; Col. 2:12; 3:1-4). A recovery of the Spirit-given identity between Christ and his Church enables us to identify the continued presence of the prophet, priest, and king in the world and so to explore the continuation of atonement and reconciliation in the life of the Church.

The Gospel compels us to reach out to others and to welcome them into the "eternal life" that the lawyer sought. It is the good news that God, through Christ, has set a banqueting table in his Kingdom and is inviting "the poor, the crippled, the blind, and the lame," everyone on the "highways and country roads" to come (Luke 14:15-24).

---

[95] Richard Beck, *Unclean: Meditations on Purity, Holiness, and Mortality* (Eugene: Cascade Books, 2011), p. 81.
[96] Ibid.
[97] Ibid. p. 122.
[98] Ibid. p. 86, 123.
[99] Hans Boersma, *Violence, Hospitality, and the Cross: Reappropriating the Atonement Tradition* (Grand Rapids: Baker Academic, 2004), p. 208.

Movement 3: *Meditatio*

Leadership-in-community is characterized by the deep hospitality that reflects how God, in Christ, has welcomed us. Paul wrote to the Romans:

> All patience and encouragement come from God. And I pray that God will help you all agree with each other, as Christ Jesus wants. Then you will all be joined together. And all together you will give glory to God the Father of our Lord Jesus Christ. *Christ accepted you, so you should accept each other. This will bring honor to God.* (Rom. 15:5-7, italics added)

At conversion to Christ, a person changes loyalty from his or her given cultural idolatries to the God who transcends all cultures.[100] Think of the example of Abraham who left his home country and people to go to an unfamiliar place God would show him (Gen. 12:1).[101] Theologian Miroslav Volf describes how Abraham rearranged all his former allegiances for the God who called him to leave his homeland:

> Abraham chose to leave. The courage to break his cultural and familial ties and abandon the gods of his ancestors (Joshua 24:2) out of allegiance to a God of all families and all cultures was the original Abrahamic revolution. Departure from his native soil, no less than the trust that God will give him an heir, made Abraham the ancestor of us all (see Hebrews 11:8).[102]

If Abraham is the father of all who believe in the God of all families, then it follows that our ultimate loyalty is to his God, and not to any particular place, culture, or family.[103] Volf continues, "Abraham is a progenitor of a people which 'even when it has a home…is not allowed full possession of that home. It is only a stranger and a sojourner.'"[104] Jesus said:

> If you come to me but will not leave your family, you cannot be my follower. You must love me more than your father, mother, wife, children, brothers, and sisters – even more than your own life! Whoever will not carry the cross that is given to them when they follow me cannot be my follower. (Luke 14:26-27)

---

[100] Miroslav Volf, *Exclusion & Embrace: A Theological Exploration of Identity, Otherness, and Reconciliation* (Nashville: Abingdon Press, 1996), p. 40.

[101] Ibid. 39-40.

[102] Ibid. p. 39.

[103] Ibid.

[104] Ibid., quoting Franz Rosenzweig, *The Star of Redemption* translated by William W. Hallo (New York: Holt, Rinehart, Winston, 1971), p. 300.

It is our "strangeness" as God's special people that distinguishes us in a world that still demands loyalty to our individual, family, cultural, and national deities. This is the pilgrim principle of the Gospel.

But our strangeness is also the basis for hospitality as an ethic of our leadership-in-community. In a formless and empty world from which God calls us out to be his strange, holy people, we cannot survive without the embrace of our fellow sojourners. Hospitality is the will to give ourselves to one another, create space for one another, and identify with one another as the *imago Dei*.[105] It is the welcome of Christ who is building us as living stones into his spiritual house (1 Pet. 2:5). Such hospitality makes friends from enemies and family from strangers! The hospitality of Christ in the community of his people receives diversity and difference as the space of welcome rather than exclusion.

Ethics Themes

The Parable of the Good Samaritan highlights four themes of hospitality as a leadership ethic that will shape our leadership-in-community: cross-centered hospitality, differentiation and relational integration, resource-based viewpoint, empathy, and expansive thinking.

Cross-Centered Hospitality. Central to Christian hospitality is the cross of Christ. The cross is the ultimate and pivotal act of hospitality. Christ's atonement opened the way of God's extravagant welcome of sinners and enemies into his worldwide covenant family. The apostle Paul wrote to the Romans:

> Christ died for us when we were unable to help ourselves. We were living against God, but at just the right time Christ died for us. Very few people will die to save the life of someone else, even if it is for a good person. Someone might be willing to die for an especially good person. But Christ died for us while we were still sinners, and by this God showed how much he loves us. (Rom. 5:6-8)

Through his body and blood, Jesus created a reconciled and united family of diverse people who now *belong* together. The cross is the ultimate hospitality that forges Christian community.[106] Everything else we discuss about hospitality begins with the cross of Jesus Christ.

---

[105] Volf, *Exclusion & Embrace*, p. 29.
[106] Ibid.

As a community welcomed through the cross of Christ, we are characterized by the self-giving love of Christ.[107] We are the extension of the nail-scarred hands and feet of Jesus in this formless and empty world. Take a moment to meditate on Paul's words to the Corinthians about the Body of Christ:

The Body of Christ

[12]A person has only one body, but it has many parts. Yes, there are many parts, but all those parts are still just one body. Christ is like that too. [13]Some of us are Jews and some of us are not; some of us are slaves and some of us are free. But we were all baptized to become one body through one Spirit. And we were all given the one Spirit.

[14]And a person's body has more than one part. It has many parts. [15]The foot might say, "I am not a hand, so I don't belong to the body." But saying this would not stop the foot from being a part of the body. [16]The ear might say, "I am not an eye, so I don't belong to the body." But saying this would not make the ear stop being a part of the body. [17]If the whole body were an eye, it would not be able to hear. If the whole body were an ear, it would not be able to smell anything. [18-19]If each part of the body were the same part, there would be no body. But as it is, God put the parts in the body as he wanted them. He made a place for each one. [20]So there are many parts, but only one body.

[21]The eye cannot say to the hand, "I don't need you!" And the head cannot say to the foot, "I don't need you!" [22]No, those parts of the body that seem to be weaker are actually very important. [23]And the parts that we think are not worth very much are the parts we give the most care to. And we give special care to the parts of the body that we don't want to show. [24]The more beautiful parts don't need this special care. But God put the body together and gave more honor to the parts that need it. [25]God did this so that our body would not be divided. God wanted the different parts to care the same for each other. [26]If one part of the body suffers, then all the other parts suffer with it. Or if one part is honored, then all the other parts share its honor. (1 Cor. 12:12-26)

---

[107] Ibid. p. 48.

Paul is describing a community of hospitality. They mystery of the human body is that it remains one even though it is made up of many interrelated members. The mystery of the Body of Christ is the same! It becomes and remains one through cross-centered hospitality, empowered by God's Spirit, in which one member bleeds into another to sustain life.

Differentiation and Relational Integration. Theologian Cornelius Plantinga points out an important dynamic that occurred in the Genesis portrayal of God's creative activity that he describes as "separating" and "binding together."[108] He states:

> So God begins to do some creative separating: he separates light from darkness, day from night, water from land, the sea creatures from the land cruiser.... At the same time God binds things together: he binds humans to the rest of creation as stewards and caretakers of it, to himself as bearers of his image, and to each other as perfect complements.[109]

This separating-and-binding is the essential dynamic of creativity – a differentiation that produces a pattern of beautiful interdependence.[110] Our human identities are not independent of others. Rather, truly creative enterprise emerges through a relational dance of both connecting to and distinguishing from one another! Volf agrees, "...the boundaries that mark our identities are both barriers and bridges."[111] The hospitality of leadership-in-community, then, balances carefully the barriers and bridges between team members so that flourishing relationships emerge and lead to life-giving creativity for their common mission.

Healthy relational integration on teams is not established by establishing *sameness* among team members. This only results in elevating dominant values, perspectives, and styles while suppressing and silencing others. Rather, relational integration occurs through the full participation of all team members as they learn how their *differences* fit into the functional whole.[112] In their theological and psychological reflections on relational integration, Jeannine Brown and Steven Sandage note that "the goal of God's

---

[108] Plantinga, *Not the Way It's Supposed to Be*, p. 29.

[109] Ibid.

[110] Volf, *Exclusion & Embrace*, p. 65.

[111] Ibid. p. 66.

[112] Jeannine K. Brown & Steven J. Sandage, "Relational Integration, Part II: Relational Integration as Developmental and Intercultural," *Journal of Psychology & Theology* 43, no. 3 (2015), p. 181.

work in Christ is the restoration of a new humanity, not simply the restoration of individual believers."[113] This means that hospitality is reconciliation. The goal of relational integration on diverse teams is the development of *whole persons* oriented toward and participating in the restored humanity of the *imago Dei*.[114]

Because of its welcome of differences in the team, leadership-in-community is distributed leadership. It *cannot* be one leader towering over everyone else, but *must be* many leaders who are willing and able to act together toward one purpose.[115] Relational integration requires deep engagement and dialogue between team members in order to bring their diverse motives into a unity of purpose.[116] Therefore, the hospitality of leadership-in-community is characterized by *multilogue* rather than *monologue*.[117] In multilogue, patterns of meaning emerge as team members engage with one another in the context of their differences.[118] Multilogue amplifies differences within teams rather than strives for consensus.[119]

Consensus only suppresses differences that could lead to creative solutions while amplifying differences generates creative tensions that prompt the team toward change.[120] Consensus tends to drive differences underground. But those differences do not go away! In the shadows, they fester into toxic attitudes and subversive behaviors.[121] By surfacing and appreciating differences, those potential blocks to team performance are removed and new patterns of engagement can emerge that lead to constructive solutions.[122] In the end, the task of leadership-in-community is not to create innovation in individuals per se, but to establish the conditions that spark innovation in the team.[123] This is the task of hospitality: to welcome the "other" into a common space of belonging, fairness, and equity.[124]

---

[113] Ibid.
[114] Ibid.
[115] Chatterjee, "Wise Ways," p. 154.
[116] Ibid. p. 157.
[117] Ibid p. 154.
[118] Ibid. p. 158.
[119] Olson & Eoyang, *Facilitating Organization Change*, chapter 5.
[120] Ibid. Chapter 5, "Differences in a CAS," para. 1.
[121] Ibid. para. 4.
[122] Ibid. Chapter 5, "Differences and Organization Change," para. 1.
[123] Bruce J. Avolio, "Promoting More Integrative Strategies for Leadership Theory-Building," *American Psychologist* 62, no. 1 (2007), p. 31.
[124] Brown & Sandage, "Relational Integration," p. 187.

Resource-Based Viewpoint. The traditional view of organizational strategy includes two central tenets:

- Market positioning through competition, and
- Limited resources.[125]

Traditional strategic planning based on these tenets is all about obtaining, controlling, and leveraging limited physical resources to gain advantages over other competitors in the market.[126] However, this traditional viewpoint breaks down quickly in complex and unpredictable environments.

Adaptive organizational strategies better suited for complex environments require an agile strategic planning process with an expanded appreciation for all its resources. The *resource-based view* of the organization recognizes that the organization's primary resource is the unlimited potential of its human creativity.[127] It starts from a positive premise that the organization already has access to a unique combination of resources – including physical, financial, social, and organizational – that it can access and transform through the ingenuity of its human resources.[128] When team members share their resources openly with one another in creative and trusting exchanges, they can generate new innovations to advance their mission.

This implies that relationship, trust, and dialogue are the key drivers of organizational innovation. Through dialogue, teams discover and appreciate the rich resources they have available to them. These resources may at first be hidden behind a veil of perceptions about the differences that exist between team members – differences that seem disconcerting and disorienting when team members first encounter them. Entrepreneurial experts describe this initial team disorientation as "equivocality" that could potentially divide the team if not carefully handled: "Members of collaborating firms relying on diverse experiences, resources, capabilities, and frames of reference often have competing interpretations of tasks, routines,

---

[125] Nick Marsh, Mike McAllum, & Dominique Purcell, *Strategic Foresight: The Power of Standing in the Future* (Australia: Crown Content, 2002), Chapter 1 "Why Strategic Foresight."

[126] Ibid.

[127] Ibid.

[128] Matias Bronnenmayer, Bernd W. Wirtz, & Vincent Göttel, "Determinants of Perceived Success in Management Consulting: An Empirical Investigation from the Consultant Perspective," *Management Research Review* 39, no. 6 (2016), p. 709.

and information."[129] In order to mitigate these potentially negative outcomes, the team must quickly reframe its differences through a hospitable resource-based viewpoint. It must begin with an appreciation of each team member's differences as valuable resources they can share with each other to create and unleash new cultural horizons for their common mission.

Appreciative inquiry is a positive approach to organizational development that orients leadership-in-community toward the best in their people, the organization, and the world around them.[130] According to organizational development experts David Cooperrider, Diana Whitney, and Jacqueline Stavros:

> [Appreciative inquiry] is based on the assumption that every organization has something that works well, and those strengths can be the starting point for creative positive change. Inviting people to participate in dialogues and share stories about their past and present achievements, assets, unexplored potentials, innovations, strengths, elevated thoughts, opportunities, benchmarks, high-point moments, lived values, traditions, core and distinctive competencies, expressions of wisdom, insights into the deeper corporate spirit and soul, and visions of valued and possible futures can identify a "positive core."[131]

Leadership-in-community's positive core is its resource-based viewpoint – the unique and inimitable core resources God has entrusted to it that can point it in the direction of a vision of possibilities for its mission.[132] Cooperrider, Whitney, and Stavros argue that "human systems grow in the direction of their persistent inquiries, and this propensity is strongest and most sustainable when the means and ends of inquiry are positively correlated."[133] Appreciative Inquiry begins, then, with the assumption that the organization is a *solution to be embraced* rather than a *problem to be solved*.[134] Appreciative Inquiry provides a model of inquiry that helps a team discover

[129] Per Erik Eriksson, Pankaj C. Patel, David Rönnberg Sjödin, Johan Frishammar, & Vinit Parida, "Managing Interorganizational Innovation Projects: Mitigating the Negative Effects of Equivocality Through Knowledge Search Strategies," *Long Range Planning* 49 (2016), p. 691.

[130] David L. Cooperrider, Diana Whitney, & Jacqueline M. Stavros, *Appreciative Inquiry Handbook: For Leaders of Change* 2nd ed. (Brunswick: Crown Custom Publishing, Inc., 2008), p. 3.

[131] Ibid.

[132] Ibid. p. 34.

[133] Ibid.

[134] Ibid. p. 5.

its positive core. The 4-D Cycle of Appreciative Inquiry (Figure 4) is a model that helps a team discover its positive core.

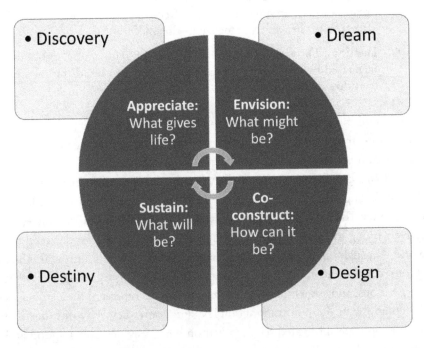

Figure 4: The 4-D Cycle of Appreciative Inquiry[135]

The team begins the process by clearly establishing for all team members the central topic (such as a problem, issue, or opportunity that has presented itself to the team) for which it desires to find organizational solutions.[136] From here, it follows through the four stages of Appreciative Inquiry as follows:

1. **Discovery**: In open dialogue, each team member shares his or her discoveries and thoughts of possibilities for the topic. Through the conversation, "individual appreciation becomes collective appreciation, individual will evolves into group will, and individual vision becomes a cooperative or shared vision for the organization."[137]

---

[135] Ibid. p. 5.
[136] Ibid. p. 5-6.
[137] Ibid. p. 6.

2. **Dream**: The team begins to envision new possibilities and creates a "positive image of a desired and preferred future."[138]

3. **Design**: The team co-constructs the future by designing an organizational architecture that effectively operationalizes daily efforts to progressively actualize its dream.[139]

4. **Destiny**: Through a continual rhythm of innovation and action facilitated by the organizational design, the team builds momentum to realize its dream.[140]

Through this process of appreciative inquiry, the team discovers its resources and shares them through collaboration that transforms them into new realities of mission.

Empathy. The heart of hospitality is empathy. Empathy, in short, is the skill of feeling what another feels.[141] Tim Brown, former CEO of design consultancy IDEO, describes empathy as a mental habit, a discipline, of actively trying to "see the world through the eyes of others, understand the world through their experiences, and feel the world through their emotions."[142] Welcoming those who are different begins by recognizing that their curious, and sometimes nonsensical, behaviors represent their strategies for coping with the confusing, complex, and contradictory world they live in.[143] People are motivated to act based on what they perceive as good and what they think will produce a flourishing life for them. Perhaps those behaviors are ineffective and self-destructive. But empathy begins by suspending judgment and listening attentively to understand what is the perceived good that is motivating the other person. This is where hospitality begins.

By practicing active empathic listening, leadership-in-community gains a deeper appreciation and value for the different perspectives, ideas, and experiences of others.[144] Active listening seeks out the meaning behind the

---

138 Ibid.

139 Ibid. p. 7.

140 Ibid.

141 William Sonnenschein, *The Diversity Toolkit: How You Can Build and Benefit from a Diverse Workforce* (Lincolnwood: Contemporary Books, 1997), p. 59.

142 Tim Brown, *Change by Design: How Design Thinking Transforms Organizations and Inspires Innovation* (New York: HarperCollins, 2019), p. 55-56.

143 Ibid. p. 55.

144 Vijay Kumar, *101 Design Methods: A Structured Approach for Driving Innovation in Your Organization* (Hoboken: John Wiley & Sons, Inc., 2013), p. 4.

words people use.[145] It prompts others to explore their own thoughts and meanings further by asking them sincere, open-ended questions.[146] And it builds awareness of and appreciation for the experiences of others that are different than our own.[147] Active listening includes the following skill set:

- **Paying attention**: adapting a listening frame of mind and attentive body posture that sets a comfortable tone and allows the other person the opportunity to think and speak safely.

- **Suspending Judgment**: embracing a willingness to hear the ideas and perspectives of the other person with an open mind.

- **Reflecting**: reflecting back to the other person, without agreeing or disagreeing, the words and emotions that they used to express their thoughts and perspectives to check with them that you understood them correctly.

- **Clarifying**: asking open-ended and probing questions to clarify any ambiguity, expand ideas, or uncover hidden thoughts.

- **Summarizing**: briefly restating the key ideas or themes from the conversation to confirm your understanding of the other's perspectives or positions.

- **Sharing** – after making sure that you have clearly understood the other person, beginning to share your own ideas, feelings, and suggestions with the aim to begin a collaborative dialogue that seeks out potential solutions or opportunities for the team.[148]

Active, empathic listening skills like these unlock the power of the team to co-construct meaning and release creative new innovations into its mission.

Expansive Thinking. Appreciative Inquiry, empathy, and active listening stimulate a team mindset of expansive thinking that is essential for creativity and innovation. Expansive thinking is the process of "expanding our field of vision, looking as broadly and expansively around us as possible in order not to be trapped by our usual problem framing and pre-existing set of solutions."[149] Unfortunately, most teams focus on the problem to be fixed,

---

[145] Sonnenschein, *The Diversity Toolkit*, p. 54.

[146] Ibid.

[147] Ibid.

[148] Center for Creative Leadership, "The Active Listening Skill Set" in *Active Listening: Improve Your Ability to Listen and Lead* 2nd ed. (Greensboro: CCL Press, 2019).

[149] Jeanne Liedtka & Tim Ogilvie, *Designing for Growth: A Design Thinking Tool Kit for Managers* (New York: Columbia Business School Publishing, 2011), p. 21.

and consequently, limit their field of vision. But innovation requires a *generous hospitality for ideas*, even the crazy, hair-brained ones that seem very ill-advised. Why? Because those ideas expand the field of vision and create a positive team mindset that generates possibilities.

Expansive thinking occurs in the early stages of team dialogue and innovation. Nancy Tennant Snyder and Deborah L. Duarte agree:

> During these early phases, innovators are learning the skills needed for the social networking that occurs in embedded innovation. Diverse teams learn a common set of tools and language. The power of learning is extraordinary. This phase begins a subtle change in the mind-set of innovators. As they work across different boundaries and with new people, they adopt new perspectives and expand their thinking. They begin to gain a sense of how the business works... They develop a bigger view of the world, a view that was once found only at the top of the organization.[150]

Indeed, the time must come for the team to progressively narrow the options generated during expansive thinking to the most promising solutions. But the process that has the most potential for the formation of highly effective diverse teams begins with a rich hospitality toward ideas extended during expansive thinking.

Movement 4: *Oratio*

Heavenly Father,

> *Give us this day our daily bread.*

May this simple prayer flourish in our hearts and minds today. Let it teach us how wholly dependent we are on you for the basics, and how we can trust you for our needs.

Jesus, you asked us to ask.

For the millions who have too little to eat today, have mercy. May all those in positions of power and abundance have mercy, too – mercy that provides for those in need. Show me my necessary part in your provision so those who need food and water can live in health, safety, and dignity.

---

[150] Nancy Tennant Snyder & Deborah L. Duarte, *Unleashing Innovation: How Whirlpool Transformed an Industry* (San Francisco: Jossey-Bass, 2008), p. 142-143.

Jesus, you told us to give.

For the spiritually hungry – may they find deep nourishment in the bread of life. Be present to everyone whose soul is aching. Satisfy and sustain them.

Jesus, only you are the bread of life.

You, Lord, are our provider *and* our provision. You can give us everything we need. And you *are* everything we need.[151]

In Jesus' name, Amen.

Movement 5: *Imitatio*

- Individual Reflection
    - Journal your responses to the following questions:
        - What key points is God leading you to embrace and grow into?
        - How can you live this out in your life and leadership?
        - How can your missional leadership group pray for you in living this out?
- Group Reflection
    - In your missional leadership group, share your individual reflections with each other.
    - Pray for one another.

Movement 6: *Missio*

- Experiencing Mission
    - Level 1 *Awareness*
        - Pray each day that the Lord sends you into his mission that day.

---

[151] Prayer adapted from the ancient spiritual practice of the Prayer Wheel. Dodd, Riess, & Van Biema, *The Prayer Wheel*, p. 67.

- At the end of each day, reflect on or journal about one experience you had that day where you witnessed the *missio Dei* personally. Describe what happened. What was significant about that experience for you?

  o Level 2 *Personal Commitment*

  - Ask the Lord where he may be sending you to be his witness on a regular basis.

  - Make a commitment to serve in that way.

Movement 7: *Communio*

- Experiencing Mission
  o Level 3 *Group Experience*

    - If possible, the small group may consider performing a mission or service project together to experience mission as a community.

- Group Reflection
  o Where did you see the *missio Dei* in action this past week?

  o What was the most significant or surprising observations you made about your experience?

  o What did you learn about God from that experience? What did you learn about yourself from that experience?

  o What difference does that make in your leadership? How will you apply what you have learned?

Movement 8: *Contemplatio*

Each week in your small group, spend time reflecting and celebrating the ways that you have seen "God on the move" in the past week.

- Spend some time in prayer or singing in thanksgiving and praise to our missionary God.

Chapter 8

Servantship

The lavish and costly hospitality of leadership-in-community flows from the conviction that the Gospel truly is good news. The Greek word for gospel (*euangelion*) was a composite of "good" (*eu*) and "declaration" (*angelos*).[1] In the Roman empire, to "gospel" was to declare a message about the military victories and achievements of the Roman emperor.[2] The one who brought good news, or the *euangelos*, would proclaim the message to great joy and acclamation throughout the empire.[3] In God's Kingdom, to gospel is also to declare joyous news! Its witnesses proclaim that God's good reign has overcome the power of the formless and empty through the victory of his anointed King, Jesus Christ! Even Jesus gospeled about himself in his hometown of Nazareth when he announced his Kingdom's welcome to those in the formless and empty places:

> The book of Isaiah the prophet was given to him. He opened the book and found the place where this is written:
>
>> "The Spirit of the Lord is on me.
>> He has chosen me to tell good news to the poor.
>> He sent me to tell prisoners that they are free
>> and to tell the blind that they can see again.
>> He sent me to free those who have been treated badly
>> and to announce that the time has come for the Lord to show his kindness." (Luke 4:17-19)

Jesus' gospel message was quite revolutionary. Rather than proclaiming a political victory that increased the honor and privilege of citizen insiders, he announced the Lord's favor upon the dispossessed and disentitled outsiders. This king leads an "upside-down" Kingdom in which the "the other" – the outsider and the excluded – is truly honored by his kindness and hospitality.

As his witnesses, we gospel the victory of our King Jesus by the same hospitality that marks his Kingdom: the lavish welcome of others into the flourishing life of God's good reign. As we saw in the last chapter, this is a cross-centered welcome that rejects privilege and spends its power so that others may experience the goodness of God. Scot McKnight and Laura Barringer point to the model of goodness that Jesus gives to his people:

---

[1] Scot McKnight & Laura Barringer, *A Church Called Tov: Forming a Goodness Culture* (Carol Stream: Tyndale Momentum, 2020), p. 94.
[2] Wright & Bird, *The New Testament in Its World*, p. 562.
[3] J. Hampton Keathley III, "What is the Gospel?", Bible.org (blog), May 18, 2004, https://bible.org/article/what-gospel.

Pick up your Bible and read Matthew 8-9 and you will see *tov* [Hebrew for "goodness"] in action. Jesus is approachable, willing, compassionate, and humble. He teaches, encourages, admonishes, and challenges. He heals, forgives, and restores because he sees and he listens. He also models *tov* as *resistance* to *ra* ["evil"] – touching the "unclean," dining with tax collectors "and other disreputable sinners," confronting evil in people's hearts, casting out evil spirits "with a simple command," and healing "all the sick." And then this summary statement: "Jesus traveled through all the towns and villages…announcing the Good News about the Kingdom." He did all this because God was *with* him, and *in* him, and working *through* him to accomplish the *tov* gospel for all of us.[4]

The hospitality of King Jesus welcomes his ragamuffin people to a good and flourishing life in his Kingdom where the formless and empty is finally vanquished. This is good news!

His hospitality defines our ethics as "gospel" people. Our whole way-of-being proceeds from his gracious welcome. Latin American theologian Ruth Padilla DeBorst describes gospel people as agents of reconciliation:

> Most communities grant space only to like-minded, like-looking, like-speaking people. But followers of Jesus are called to acknowledge they have been sent as he was into the world, as agents of reconciliation… Once they capture a vision of the table of God's kingdom, submit to Christ's sovereignty and are filled by the Holy Spirit, followers of Jesus are called to celebrate their unmerited inclusion at the table of God's kingdom, and both welcome people who look, think, speak and eat differently than they do, and also take the risk of confronting any power that excludes or deprives people of their rightful presence at the table.[5]

In the upside-down Kingdom, hospitality expends power for the sake of including the other. Research has shown that individuals, when given power, tend to devalue the worth and contributions of others.[6] To include the other when, by any worldly standard, such inclusion would not be expected or even

---

[4] McKnight & Barringer, *A Church Called Tov*, p. 94-95 with quotations from Matt. 8:3, 16 and 9:4, 10.

[5] Ruth Padilla DeBorst, "'Unexpected' Guests at God's Banquet Table: Gospel in Mission and Culture," *Evangelical Review of Theology* 33 (2010), p. 73-74.

[6] Bradley P. Owens, Michael D. Johnson, & Terence R. Mitchell, "Expressed Humility in Organizations: Implications for Performance, Teams, and Leadership," *Organization Science* 24, no. 5 (2013), p. 1520.

accepted is a divestment of power, pride, and identity (including personal, cultural, and national identity). It is costly, but it is necessary to create a space for the other at God's table.

True Kingdom hospitality is intricately connected then to servantship. In fact, hospitality without servantship is mere well-wishing. Servantship expends power, pride, and identity in order to create space for others at the great banqueting table of God's good reign. This is the hallmark of God's upside-down Kingdom where power is spent for the sake of others rather than acquired to lord over others. When the mother of James and John asked Jesus that her sons sit by his side in his Kingdom, Jesus told his disciples what that would really mean for them:

> So Jesus called his followers together. He said, "You know that the rulers of the non-Jewish people love to show their power over the people. And their important leaders love to use all their authority over the people. But it should not be that way with you. Whoever wants to be your leader must be your servant. Whoever wants to be first must serve the rest of you like a slave. Do as I did: The Son of Man did not come for people to serve him. He came to serve others and to give his life to save many people." (Matt. 20:25-28)

Jesus' mission was to live and die for others. His servantship set a place at God's table for all the "wrong" people.[7] Jesus said the Kingdom of God belongs to those who are poor and humble, who mourn, who hunger and thirst for justice, who are merciful and work for peace, those whose hearts are pure and are persecuted for doing right (Matt. 5:3-10). These are first in the Kingdom, not because they exercise power over others, but because they serve so that others may know the goodness of Jesus.

Servantship is an ethic of leadership-in-community. Graham Hill describes servantship with a holistic eloquence:

> Servantship is following Jesus Christ the servant Lord and his mission. It's a life of discipleship to him. It's patterned after his self-emptying, humility, sacrifice, love, values and mission. Servantship is humbly valuing others more than yourself. It's looking out for the interests and well-being of others. Servantship is the cultivation of the same attitude of mind as that of Christ Jesus. It's making yourself nothing. It's being a servant and humbling yourself. And it's submitting yourself to the will and purposes of the triune God. Since servantship is the imitation

---

[7] McKnight & Barringer, *A Church Called Tov*, p. 95.

of Christ, it involves an unreserved participation in his mission. (By this, I mean the *missio Dei* – the trinitarian mission of God.) Servantship recognizes in word and thought and deed that Christian leaders are servants.[8]

Servantship resists ideologies of leadership that emphasize self-interest and control over followers.[9] It embraces genuine care for followers that invests in them as whole persons.[10] It prioritizes relationship with followers while empowering them as partners, or better as friends, in mission.[11] For these reasons, our study together focuses on *servantship*, rather than servant leadership, to highlight that *serving* is the primary character of our leading.

Servantship enables true culture making within teams. Servantship facilitates shared construction and ownership of organizational vision and goals by both leaders and followers.[12] Justin Irving and Mark Strauss agree:

> As important as followership is to organizations, the new, emerging, and complex realities of our time require more expressions of leadership throughout an organization than ever before. Rather than leadership being the responsibility of only a select few at the top of organizations, leadership is a need throughout healthy and thriving organizations.[13]

Servantship calls to life the giftedness of others, and so, stimulates the long-term effectiveness of the whole team.[14] When the relationship between leaders and followers spur on the giftings of one another in mutual service, everyone can joyfully share a vision that is greater than any one person.[15] Leaders and followers inspire one another to work toward their shared goals, even when it comes at the personal sacrifices of time, effort, or inconvenience.[16] In this chapter, we will explore servantship by examining Jesus' Parable of the Talents.

---

[8] Hill, *GlobalChurch*, p. 339.
[9] Justin A. Irving & Mark L. Strauss, *Leadership in Christian Perspective: Biblical Foundations and Contemporary Practices for Servant Leaders* (Grand Rapids: BakerAcademic, 2019), p. 2, 11.
[10] Ibid. p. 28.
[11] Ibid. p. 2.
[12] Ibid. p. 2.
[13] Ibid. p. 27.
[14] McKnight & Barringer, *A Church Called Tov*, p. 176.
[15] Irving & Straus, *Leadership in Christian Perspective*, p. 27.
[16] Ibid.

Movement 1: *Adspecto*

Prayer

+ Pray for the Holy Spirit to speak to you through the Scripture. Use the following words of Psalm 37:1-11 as a prayer:

> *¹Don't get upset about evil people.*
>> *Don't be jealous of those who do wrong.*
> *²They are like grass and other green plants*
>> *that dry up quickly and then die.*
> *³So trust in the LORD and do good.*
>> *Live on your land and be dependable.*
> *⁴Enjoy serving the LORD,*
>> *and he will give you whatever you ask for.*
> *⁵Depend on the LORD.*
>> *Trust in him, and he will help you.*
> *⁶He will make it as clear as day that you are right.*
>> *Everyone will see that you are being fair.*
> *⁷Trust in the LORD and wait quietly for his help.*
>> *Don't be angry when people make evil plans and succeed.*
> *⁸Don't become so angry and upset that you, too, want to do evil.*
> *⁹The wicked will be destroyed,*
>> *but those who call to the LORD for help will get the land he promised.*
> *¹⁰In a short time there will be no more evil people.*
>> *You can look for them all you want, but they will be gone.*
> *¹¹Humble people will get the land God promised,*
>> *and they will enjoy peace.*

Scripture Reading

+ **Read Matthew 25:14-30.** Listen for words or phrases from the passage that stand out to you.

A Story About Three Servants

¹⁴"At that time God's kingdom will also be like a man leaving home to travel to another place for a visit. Before he left, he talked with his servants. He told his servants to take care of his things while he was gone. ¹⁵He decided how much each servant would be able to care for. The man gave one servant five

bags of money. He gave another servant two bags. And he gave a third servant one bag. Then he left. ¹⁶The servant who got five bags went quickly to invest the money. Those five bags of money earned five more. ¹⁷It was the same with the servant who had two bags. That servant invested the money and earned two more. ¹⁸But the servant who got one bag of money went away and dug a hole in the ground. Then he hid his master's money in the hole.

¹⁹"After a long time the master came home. He asked the servants what they did with his money. ²⁰The servant who got five bags brought that amount and five more bags of money to the master. The servant said, 'Master, you trusted me to care for five bags of money. So I used them to earn five more.'

²¹"The master answered, 'You did right. You are a good servant who can be trusted. You did well with that small amount of money. So I will let you care for much greater things. Come and share my happiness with me.'

²²"Then the servant who got two bags of money came to the master. The servant said, 'Master, you gave me two bags of money to care for. So I used your two bags to earn two more.'

²³"The master answered, 'You did right. You are a good servant who can be trusted. You did well with a small amount of money. So I will let you care for much greater things. Come and share my happiness with me.'

²⁴"Then the servant who got one bag of money came to the master. The servant said, 'Master, I knew you were a very hard man. You harvest what you did not plant. You gather crops where you did not put any seed. ²⁵So I was afraid. I went and hid your money in the ground. Here is the one bag of money you gave me.'

²⁶"The master answered, 'You are a bad and lazy servant! You say you knew that I harvest what I did not plant and that I gather crops where I did not put any seed. ²⁷So you should have put my money in the bank. Then, when I came home, I would get my money back. And I would also get the interest that my money earned.'

²⁸"So the master told his other servants, 'Take the one bag of money from that servant and give it to the servant who has ten bags. ²⁹Everyone who uses what they have will get more. They will have much more than they need. But people who do not use what they have will have everything taken away from them.' ³⁰Then the master said, 'Throw that useless servant outside into the darkness, where people will cry and grind their teeth with pain.'

Reflection

- When you have finished reading, remain silent for one or two minutes.

- Read the entire passage again. If you have an audio Bible, listen through the passage.

- Journal your thoughts on the following questions:

  - What words or phrases from the passage stand out to you?

  - How do these words or phrases connect with your life right now?

  - How might God be inviting you to respond to this passage?

Movement 2: *Lectio*

Scripture Study

- Read or listen to **Matthew 25:14-30**.

- Answer the following study questions:

  1. What does the master tell his servants to do while he is traveling to another place (vs. 14)?

  2. How does he decide how much of his wealth each servant will care for (vs. 15)?

  3. What do you think this implies about what God expects of his servants?

  4. What do the first two servants do with their share (vs. 16-17)?

  5. What happens to their share (vs. 16-17)?

  6. What does the third servant do with his share (vs. 18)?

  7. What do you think the example of the three servants means for followers of Jesus today?

  8. When the master returns from his journey, what does he ask the servants (vs. 19)?

  9. How does the master respond to the first two servants (vs. 20-23)?

10. What do you think the master means when he says that he will let the first two servants "care for much greater things" (vs. 21, 23)?

11. What does it mean to you that the master invited the first two servants to share in his happiness (vs. 21, 23)?

12. What does the third servant think of his master (vs. 24-25)?

13. Why do you think this motivated him to take the actions he did with his share of the master's wealth?

14. How does the master respond to the third servant (vs. 26-27)?

15. How do you react to the master's words to the third servant?

16. What does the master tell his other servants to do with the third servant (vs. 28-30)?

17. What you think Jesus' words mean: "Everyone who uses what they have will get more. They will have much more than they need. But people who do not use what they have will have everything taken away from them." (vs. 29)?

18. Why do you think Jesus told his disciples this story?

19. Imagine that Jesus was telling you this story. What do you think he wants you to learn from it?

20. What implications do you think this story has for your group or organization? How can your group or organization apply it to its leadership-in-community?

Reading

The Context for Matthew

Many scholars believe that the Gospel of Matthew was written between 80-100 CE after the fall of Jerusalem in 70 CE.[17] This was a precarious time for Judaism as well as Christianity, which at this point still considered Judaism its parent religion.[18] Both had to reconfigure their beliefs and communities in the wake of the destruction of the Jerusalem temple.[19] The Pharisees and the Jewish Christians were the most influential Jewish groups to have survived the Roman subjugation of Jerusalem.[20] The Pharisees

---

[17] Wright & Bird, *The New Testament World*, p. 579.
[18] DeSilva, *An Introduction to the New Testament*, p. 345, 265-267.
[19] Ibid.
[20] Wright & Bird, *The New Testament World*, p. 584.

had to reconstruct the Jewish way of life around Torah, rather than the Jerusalem temple, as its central symbol.[21] Rabbinic Judaism emerged as the primary expression of religious faithfulness to God's covenant by way of its *halakhah*, its teachings about the way to walk in line with God's law (*halak* is Hebrew for "walk").[22] The Pharisaic-rabbinic *halakhah* emphasized scruples of purity as the measure of faithful law observance. According to N. T. Wright and Michael Bird, "The Pharisees themselves took seriously the task of Israel to be a 'kingdom of priests', adopting the purity regulations originally intended for the priests and Levites: for them, all of life had to be lived as if one were in the Temple, in the very presence of God."[23] The oral teaching of *halakhah* paid close attention to the contaminants – anything believed to make God's holy people "unclean" and unfit for his presence – and what to do to remove such pollution.[24]

Jewish Christians, on the other hand, witnessed an inflow of Gentiles into their communities across the empire.[25] Inevitably, this led to clashes with rabbinic Judaism. The Jewish Christians were progressively expelled from the synagogues in the name of purity.[26] During this time, Judaism was not a religion as much as it was the "activity of zealous propagation of Jewish allegiance and symbolic life," according to Wright and Bird.[27] They explain, "To be excluded from the Jewish world meant a painful break in the network of family, religious, social, and commercial relationships. It frequently entailed a form of social death with all the shame and shunning that went along with that."[28] In this atmosphere, Matthew wrote his Gospel to demonstrate that the emerging communities who followed Jesus as Israel's long-awaited Messiah could legitimately lay claim to Israel's ancestry and heritage.[29] Matthew's Gospel was, in fact, a manifesto by which he set the Christians apart from the parent religion and legitimized their beliefs and practices according to Torah – the same Torah by which Pharisees excluded them as apostates.[30] The Gospel of Matthew presented Jesus as the culmination of

---

[21] Ibid. p. 585.

[22] DeSilva, *An Introduction to the New Testament*, p. 263.

[23] Wright & Bird, *The New Testament and Its World*, p. 117.

[24] Ibid. p. 116-117.

[25] Ibid. p. 579.

[26] Ibid. p. 586.

[27] Ibid. p. 587.

[28] Ibid.

[29] Ibid. p. 579.

[30] DeSilva, *An Introduction to the New Testament*, p. 245.

Israel's story (demonstrated by Jesus' fulfillment of many Old Testament prophecies) and the Davidic Messiah who would, at last, save his people from their present exile due to their sinful unfaithfulness to God's covenant.[31]

The Gospel of Matthew was also a manual of discipleship for Christians living in cultures hostile to the Gospel.[32] One of Matthew's apparent core values was that the character and ethos of the Christians, who were now constituted as the new family of God, reflected that of their God.[33] So, in the Sermon on the Mount (Matt. 5-7), Jesus presented his alternative *halakhah* for God's renewed people, denoted by his repeated phrase "You have heard that it was said... But I tell you..."[34] In fact, Jesus later condemned the Pharisaic-rabbinic tradition as oppressive and impossible to follow (Matt. 23:4).[35] He said to his followers, "I tell you that you must do better than the teachers of the law and the Pharisees. If you are not more pleasing to God than they are, you will never enter God's kingdom" (Matt. 5:20). In contrast to the *halakhah* of the Pharisees, the *halakhah* of Jesus was not based on rigid purity, but on the love of God expressed in mercy to others.[36]

This is most clearly expressed in Jesus' *halakhah* to love enemies based on his Father's character who shows mercy to all people (Matt. 5:43-48). He said, "What I am saying is that you must be perfect, just as your Father in heaven is perfect" (Matt. 5:48). In this text, Matthew took this command from the purity code in the Torah ("I am holy, so you should keep yourselves holy." Lev. 11:44) and reappropriated it for the disciples of Jesus.[37] Some suggest that Matthew may have reworded the command from "holy" to "perfect" out of a concern that the term "holy" placed the wrong emphasis on purity as in the Pharisaic-rabbinic tradition.[38] So instead, Matthew chose to use "perfect," a term similar to "holy" in that it connotes in Torah completeness or wholeness.[39] But "perfect" can also be expanded upon to include the concepts of mercy and love that set the followers of Jesus apart from the

---

[31] Wright & Bird, *The New Testament in Its World*, p. 580-581, 587.
[32] Ibid. p. 589.
[33] DeSilva, *An Introduction to the New Testament*, p. 267.
[34] Ibid. See Matt. 5:21-22, 27-28, 31-32, 33-34, 38-39, 43-44.
[35] Ibid.
[36] Ibid. p. 266.
[37] Ibid. p. 268.
[38] Ibid.
[39] Ibid. p. 269.

Pharisaic community.[40] The disciples of Jesus find their wholeness in God as their Father, so they do not need to pay back "and eye for an eye, and a tooth for a tooth" (Matt. 5:38-39). Rather, they can reflect his love and mercy to others in the hope that others will also be brought into the family of God the Father.[41]

The Olivet Discourse

The Gospel of Matthew was organized around five discourses,[42] the last of which, the Olivet Discourse (Matt. 23-25), was precipitated by the Jewish leaders who questioned the authority of Jesus (Matt. 21:23-27). By the time Jesus told the Parable of the Talents in the Olivet Discourse (Matt. 25:14-30), conflict between Jesus and the teachers of the law had escalated to a fever pitch. They knew by his recent actions that Jesus was claiming authority as the Davidic Messiah: his triumphal entry into Jerusalem (Matt. 21:1-11), his acceptance of praise from the people (Matt. 21:9, 15-16), his cleansing the temple (Matt. 21:12-13), his healing the blind and lame (Matt. 21:14), and his teaching in the temple (Matt. 21:23).[43] Their challenge to Jesus' authority was intended to discredit him publicly. And it launched an extended confrontation that would end with the public legitimation of the *halakhah* of one or the other (Matt. 21:23-22:33).[44] Jesus responded astutely against every tactic they threw at him to test him. In the end, he won the challenge, discredited his opponents, and received the honor of the witnesses who "were amazed at Jesus' teaching" (Matt. 22:22, 33).

At the crescendo of the conflict, the Pharisees asked Jesus which command in the law is the most important (Matt. 22:36). This question went right to the heart of the conflict between the Pharisaic-rabbinic tradition and the new Jesus movement. What may surprise us is that Jesus actually had the most in common with the Pharisees than with any other Jewish sect.[45] Both believed in the resurrection and looked forward to God's coming Kingdom.[46]

---

[40] Ibid.

[41] Ibid.

[42] The five discourses of Matthew include the Sermon on the Mount (Matt. 5-7), the Missionary Discourse (Matt. 9:36-10:42), the Parabolic Discourse (Matt. 13:1-52), the Discourse on the Church or the Rule of the Community (Matt. 18:1-35), and the Olivet Discourse (Matt. 23:1-25:46). Wright & Bird, *The New Testament in Its World*, p. 588.

[43] J. Paul Tanner, "The 'Outer Darkness' in Matthew's Gospel: Shedding Light on an Ominous Warning," *Bibliotheca Sacra* 174 (2017), p. 449-450.

[44] Ibid. p. 450.

[45] Wright & Bird, *The New Testament in Its World*, p. 598.

[46] Ibid.

Many Pharisees even joined the Jesus movement. But they parted ways at how each thought the law was to be interpreted as *halakhah* for the life and ethics of God's people.[47] Jesus answered their question:

> 'Love the Lord your God with all your heart, all your soul, and all your mind.' This is the first and most important command. And the second command is like the first: 'Love your neighbor the same as you love yourself.' *All of the law and the writings of the prophets take their meaning from these two commands.* (Matt. 22:37-40, italics added)

In Jesus' day, religious leaders devoted much time debating the ultimate or "first principles" underlying the law.[48] According to Jesus, the love of God and neighbor, rather than purity, is the interpretive key to the whole law.[49] E. Carson Brisson states:

> For Matthew's community, the greatest of all values or first principles is the life of loving God by loving one's neighbor as oneself (22:36-39). Matthew's community holds this as sincerely taught and sought in the Mosaic Torah (5:17-19), frustrated by Pharisaic development (23:1-36), circumvented by inadequate Christian reductions (7:1-23), and fully realized only in the life and teaching of the one who is its Lord (5:21-48). Matthew's community is now to live in and for this Lord precisely by living for others (7:12; 10:8; 22:40; 25:34-40) even as this Lord lived and died for others (4:23-25; 16:21-23).[50]

In the Kingdom of Jesus the Messiah, the one who is greater than king David (Matt. 22:41-45), those who live out Torah as God's covenant community would do so with the love of God and neighbor as their ultimate concern.

Jesus' Olivet Discourse ensued from this challenge-response exchange between Jesus and the Pharisees. In it, he denounced the old religious forms of the Pharisees and their *halakhah*.[51] First, he declared its forsakenness through a series of "woes" that echoed the Deuteronomy warning of curses upon Israel if it should disobey God's law (Deut. 27 & 28).[52] Pharisaic religion

---

[47] Daniel J. Harrington, S. J., "Polemical Parables in Matthew 24-25," *Union Seminary Quarterly Review* 44 (1991), p. 290.

[48] E. Carson Brisson, "Between Text and Sermon: Matthew 25:14-30," *Interpretation* 56, no. 3 (2002), p. 310.

[49] DeSilva, *An Introduction to the New Testament*, p. 266.

[50] Ibid.

[51] Wright & Bird, *The New Testament in Its World*, p. 598.

[52] Ibid.

had, in fact, became barren and empty because of its hypocrisy, religious showiness, pretention, and predatory behavior (Matt. 23:1-39).

Second, Jesus told his disciples three parables about preparedness regarding his second coming and final judgment (Matt. 24:45-25:30).[53] In these parables, including the Parable of the Talents, Jesus distinguished starkly between the prepared, who are welcomed into blessing, and the unprepared, who are cast out. He presented the final judgment as the time when the Son of Man (the Messianic title for God's anointed king) will come in triumph and hold court with all the nations gathered before him (Matt. 25:31-46).[54] Jesus amplified the cosmic, divine authority that God invested in him to separate the sheep from the goats.[55] And he separates them along the line of mercy according to how they treated the hungry, thirsty, homeless, naked, sick, and imprisoned (Matt. 25:40, 45).[56]

Matthew distinguished the true people of God against the Pharisaic-rabbinic forms whose "house will be left completely empty" (Matt. 23:38). Ultimately, it was left empty through the destruction of the temple in 70 CE. Matthew revealed that the Jesus communities were the legitimate heirs of Israel's heritage according to the Jewish Scriptures that were fulfilled in Jesus as Israel's Messiah.[57] These Jesus communities, comprised of both Jews and Gentiles, were not apostates but were standing squarely in the center of God's saving purposes and the consummation of his Kingdom.[58]

The Parable of the Talents

The ethical teachings of Jesus helped his followers understand how life under the reign of God must be lived out.[59] Jesus taught that the integration of faith and life is the good soil in which the "teachings about God's kingdom" are planted and produce a bountiful harvest (Matt. 13:1-9; 18-23). Jesus told his disciples:

> "Whoever hears these teachings of mine and obeys them is like a wise man who built his house on rock. It rained hard, the floods came, and

---

[53] John B. Carpenter, "The Parable of the Talents in Missionary Perspective: A Call for an Economic Spirituality," *Missiology: An International Review* 25, no. 2 (1997), p. 166.

[54] Richard P. Carlson, "Between Text and Sermon: Matthew 25:13-46," *Interpretation: A Journal of Bible and Theology* 69, no. 3 (2015), p. 345.

[55] Ibid.

[56] Ibid.

[57] Wright & Bird, *The New Testament in its World*, p. 579.

[58] Ibid.

[59] Carpenter, "The Parable of the Talents in Missionary Perspective," p. 167.

the winds blew and beat against that house. But it did not fall because it was built on rock.

"Whoever hears these teachings of mine and does not obey them is like a foolish man who built his house on sand. It rained hard, the floods came, and the winds blew and beat against that house. And it fell with a loud crash."

When Jesus finished speaking, the people were amazed at his teaching. He did not teach like their teachers of the law. He taught like someone who has authority. (Matt. 7:24-29)

Discipleship is the process of integrating faith and practice so that we live out the reign of God fruitfully in the world we inhabit.

Jesus' teachings, especially his parables, illuminated God's ways and his will for the purpose of forming our minds, hearts, actions, and relationships as his gospel people.[60] In the Parable of the Talents, Jesus portrayed life under God's reign as *servantship*. And servantship is preparedness! It is a readiness fostered by integrating Jesus' teachings into our present lives and our hope of Christ's future return.[61] It is a fruitful life that reflects the good reign of God in the present while making ready for his return in the final consummation of his eternal Kingdom.[62] Servantship is entrustment, empowerment, and enactment in the light of a certain future.[63]

Entrustment (The Talents). We observe in the story that the master, before leaving home to travel to another place, entrusted his servants with the care of his things while he was away (Matt. 25:14). He apportioned his wealth in the form of talents (Greek *talanta* appropriately translated in the ERV as "bags of money"). A talent was not a coin but was a measure or weight of money that was paid in either minted coins or in bars of gold or bullion.[64] Talents were used for commercial activities in money economies.[65] The worth of a silver talent varied between US $1,000 to $2,000, while a gold talent could be as high as $30,000.[66] In comparison to the average worker's wage of approximately 15¢ per day, the purchasing power of just one talent

---

[60] Carlson, "Between Text and Sermon: Matthew 25:13-46," p. 344.

[61] Ibid. p. 346.

[62] John F. Walvoord, "Christ's Olivet Discourse on the End of the Age," *Bibliotheca Sacra* 129, no. 515 (1972), p. 206.

[63] Carlson, "Between Text and Sermon: Matthew 25:13-46," p. 345.

[64] R. V. G. Tasker, *Matthew* (London: The Tyndale Press, 1961), p. 235.

[65] Brisson, "Between Text and Sermon: Matthew 25:14-30," p. 308-309.

[66] Walvoord, "Christ's Olivet Discourse on the End of the Age," p. 207.

was significantly greater in Jesus' day than it would be by today's standards.[67] In this light, the parable suggests that the master had great confidence in his servants to entrust them with his wealth, even in the one to whom he entrusted only one talent.[68]

The term "talent" has become associated in modern English with an individual's natural abilities or spiritual gifts.[69] But in the original context of the parable, the talent was money used in commercial activities to generate wealth or a return on investment.[70] We may understand then that the talents in Jesus' parable signify *anything* God has entrusted to us to invest with the purpose of increasing his glory in the formless and empty places where he calls us to serve.[71] We must not take too narrow a view of talents as only natural or spiritual abilities in our application of the parable.[72] Servantship is worship ("worth-ship") that invests all our resources to increase the "worth" of our Master.

An important contextual clue to Jesus' understanding of talents is found in the parable's key verse: "Everyone who uses what they have will get more. They will have much more than they need. But people who do not use what they have will have everything taken away from them" (Matt. 25:29). Earlier Jesus told his disciples, "The knowledge of the secrets of the kingdom of heaven has been given to you" (Matt. 13:11 NIV). Then, with similar language he used in connection to the talents, Jesus revealed to them, "The people who have some understanding will be given more. And they will have even more than they need. But those who do not have much understanding will lose even the little understanding that they have" (Matt. 13:12). In other words, Jesus' disciples, including us today, have been *entrusted* with the knowledge of the secrets of the Kingdom to do something productive with it. That knowledge transforms how we live our lives. As we invest our lives for the glory of God's Kingdom, he reveals it more and more through us to the cosmos around us.

New Testament scholar John Paul Heil believes that the talents are "a rather general and open-ended symbol of all that Jesus has entrusted to his disciples for promoting the reign of the heavens during the time between his

---

[67] Ibid.
[68] Ibid.
[69] Brisson, "Between Text and Sermon: Matthew 25:14-30," p. 308.
[70] Ibid. p. 308-309.
[71] Carpenter, "The Parable of the Talents in Missionary Perspective," p. 167-168.
[72] Ibid. p. 168.

resurrection and final coming." Jesus compared God's Kingdom with a "treasure hidden in a field" and a "very fine pearl" that a person discovers and sells everything else to buy it (Matt. 13:44-46). As servants of *our* Master, King Jesus, we are obliged to invest everything he has entrusted to us – including our knowledge, abilities, money, time, power, and all our resources – to promote God's good reign in the world we inhabit.[73]

Empowerment (The Servants). We also observe that the master entrusted talents to his servants "each according to his ability" (Matt. 25:15, NIV). The servants were not like slaves who had no will of their own and simply did their master's bidding.[74] While the servants were dependent on the master, they also had agency capable of applying their labor and skill to transact business on behalf of their master.[75] The master does not prescribe to the servants exactly what they were to do with his wealth.[76] He entrusted the talents to each servant in the assumption that each knew what was expected of a good and faithful servant.[77] He expected a fruitful return from the talents he entrusted to them.[78]

Enactment (The Investment). Next, we observe that two of the servants invested the money for a return (Matt. 25:16-17) while the third servant buried his share (Matt. 25:18). In the Parable of the Good Samaritan, we learned how first-century peasants felt about the accumulation of wealth. In a primarily subsistence economy with its perspective of limited goods, one person could only accumulate wealth at the expense of others.[79] It was viewed as a dishonorable betrayal of his or her community that maintained its stability and harmony through a carefully balanced social arrangement of status.[80] Within this context, the average peasant would view the master of Jesus' parable as an oppressor who gained his wealth through the exploitation and dehumanization of the poor.[81] John Crossan expounds on this reality, citing pastor and retired Religious Studies professor Richard Rohrbaugh:

---

[73] Ibid. p. 169.

[74] J. Duncan M. Derrett, "Law in the New Testament: The Parable of the Talents and Two Logia," *Zeitschrift für die neutestamentliche Wissenschaft und die Kunde der älteren Kirche* 56, no. 3-4 (1965), p. 185.

[75] Ibid.

[76] Carlson, "Between Text and Sermon: Matthew 25:13-46," p. 344.

[77] Ibid.

[78] Derrett, "Law in the New Testament," p. 189.

[79] Malina, *The New Testament World*, p. 89.

[80] Ibid. p. 90.

[81] George O. Folarin, "The Parable of the Talents in the African Context: An Intercultural Hermeneutics Approach," *Asia Journal of Theology* 22, no. 1 (2008), p. 104.

In the peasant world of imposed limitation, with the ethic of family subsistence and village security rather than imperial exploitation and commercial wealth, one experienced rich people as "inherently evil…because to have gained, to have accumulated more than one started with, is to have taken over the share of someone else." In that peasant morality, the first two servants would be exploiters who probably increased their master's money by loans and foreclosures (of peasant farms) and it would be the third servant who acted honorably and ethically by refusing to enter into such oppressive activity.[82]

The third servant characterized the master as a "very hard man" who would "harvest what [he] did not plant" and "gather crops where [he] did not put any seed" (Matt. 25:24). So, he buried his portion because he was afraid (Matt. 25:25), believing his master to be unfair and severe.[83] Jesus' audience might have assumed that the third servant was, in fact, the hero of the story for refusing to collaborate with the master in exploiting the poor.[84]

However, Jesus surprised his audience by depicting the master as a generous man and the third servant as a "bad and lazy servant" (Matt. 25:22, 23, 26). In early Jewish parables, the character featured as the authority figure (such as a king, a master, or a father) typically represented God.[85] So, Matthew's readers would have understood that the wealthy master alluded to God.[86] In fact, Jewish stories often drew upon commercial metaphors to describe God as doing business with men.[87]

Additionally, according to the tripartite structure of typical rabbinic parables, the first two servants established the precedent by which the third servant would be judged.[88] They served as good examples of what all servants should do.[89] Because they invested the master's wealth and received a 100% return, they were rewarded by the master. In contrast, the third servant hid his master's wealth to protect himself from any accusation of loss.[90] The first

---

[82] Richard Rohrbaugh, "A Peasant Reading of the Parable of the Talents/Pounds: A Text of Terror?" *Biblical Theology Bulletin: Journal of Bible and Culture* 23 (1993), p. 34, quoted in John Dominic Crossan, "The Parables of Jesus," *Interpretation* 56, no. 3 (2002), p. 252.

[83] Brisson, "Between Text and Sermon: Matthew 25:14-30," p. 309.

[84] Folarin, "The Parable of the Talents in the African Context," p. 102.

[85] Ben Chenoweth, "Identifying the Talents: Contextual Clues for the Interpretation of the Parable of the Talents (Matthew 25:14-30)," *Tyndale Bulletin* 56, no. 1 (2005), p. 62.

[86] Ibid.

[87] Derrett, "Law in the New Testament," p. 192.

[88] Brisson, "Between Text and Sermon: Matthew 25:14-30," p. 309.

[89] Ibid.

[90] Ibid.

two servants recognized their master's lavish generosity and invested his wealth to advance his happiness. The third servant, believing his master to be a hard man, prioritized his own justification and survival over the advancement of his master's happiness.[91]

Eschatology (The Master). Finally, we observe that the first two servants were rewarded and invited to share in their master's happiness (Matt. 25:21, 23) while the third servant was thrown outside "into the darkness, where people will cry and grind their teeth with pain" (Matt. 25:30). The overriding focus of the parable, however, is not the servants or the judgment they received. The focus is on the master. The servants all acted in accordance with the knowledge that they had about the master and his impending return.

The Parable of the Talents reveals that the economy of God's Kingdom is one of abundance, not of limited resources. The first two servants understood this secret knowledge of the Kingdom! The master trusted them with his extravagant wealth, and in return, they invested it all to make an increase for him. What bold confidence they had knowing they could take enormous risks with the master's resources! Because the master's economy was abundant and generous, they knew that any profit they earned would not be at the expense of others. So, they were faithful with what the master entrusted to them and, in the end, entered the happiness of their master. Brisson notes that, in Matthew, the verb "enter" and the noun "happiness" both carry eschatological meaning:

> The verb is regularly used in the sense of being invited into the reign of God (5:20; 7:13, 21; 19:23). The noun is the Greek equivalent of the Hebrew word for joy, *simhâ*, which reaches its most significant use in the Hebrew canon in reference to the festive ethos of God's final and fully effective presence with Israel and the gathered nations (Ps. 14:7; Isa. 9:3; Zech. 2:10-11).[92]

For the first two servants, the master's return was good news because they were prepared. They knew he would reward them for their faithfulness and invite them into his celebration of joy.

The third servant, on the other hand, believed the master to be hard and unfair (Matt. 25:24-25).[93] He believed the master's economy to be one of limited goods, and so he buried the wealth of the master to protect himself

---

[91] Ibid.
[92] Ibid. p. 308.
[93] Ibid. p. 309.

from loss.[94] What is interesting is that, upon his return, the master did not try to correct the servant's misperception about him.[95] Instead, he reprimanded him for not acting according to what knowledge he did have, however faulty, and deposit the money in the bank to show some return.[96] While the servant may have believed he was taking the safe, conservative route by protecting the resources the master entrusted to him, he was confronted by the master for being a bad, lazy, and useless servant.[97] In the end, the third servant is excluded from the happiness of the master and is thrown out into darkness, a place of extreme despair and regret.[98]

Matthew recounted Jesus' Parable of the Talents to illustrate true faithfulness in God's Kingdom. He pictured it as servantship that prepares for the return of our Master by investing everything entrusted to us to make the secret knowledge of his Kingdom real in this formless and empty world. He sets this against those who hide the treasure of the Kingdom away, out of reach to those who may "pollute" it. The parable illustrates for us that the Kingdom of God is one of extravagant abundance. And so, our King expects us, his servants, to invest our talents with the same extravagance.

Servantship as the Kingdom ethic of our leadership-in-community extends beyond simply doing nice things for others. It is, rather, the hopeful, generous, and costly spending of ourselves for the sake of others so that they may taste the goodness of our King Jesus and his eternal Kingdom. We serve with the joyous expectation that our Master will one day return. We desire to present to him the increase that our investment produces. We serve in the hope to be welcomed into his happiness.

Movement 3: *Meditatio*

As we contemplate the leadership ethic of servantship, let us reflect on the example of Jesus praised in the Philippian 2 hymn:

In your life together, think the way Christ Jesus thought.
He was like God in every way,

---

[94] Ibid.
[95] David C. Steinmetz, "Matthew 25:14-30," *Interpretation* 34, no. 2 (1980), p. 174.
[96] Ibid.
[97] Ibid.
[98] Tanner, "The 'Outer Darkness' in Matthew's Gospel," p. 449.

but he did not think that his being equal with God was something to use for his own benefit.
Instead, he gave up everything, even his place with God.
He accepted the role of a servant, appearing in human form.
During his life as a man,
he humbled himself by being fully obedient to God,
even when that caused his death—death on a cross.
So God raised him up to the most important place
and gave him the name that is greater than any other name.
God did this so that every person will bow down to honor the name of Jesus.
Everyone in heaven, on earth, and under the earth will bow.
They will all confess, "Jesus Christ is Lord,"
and this will bring glory to God the Father. (Phil. 2:5-11)

We learned from the Parable of the Talents that servantship is rooted in entrustment, empowerment, enactment, and eschatology. Whereas worldly leadership seeks to acquire power, Kingdom leadership spends power for the sake of God and others. Graham Hill agrees:

> Jesus re-conceives status in the kingdom of God as bonded service. Such service is accompanied by the forfeiture of social status and personal freedom and characterized by utter reliance on the one to whom bonded service is being rendered. Christian servanthood reflects the Spirit of Jesus Christ when it is saturated in the characteristics of servanthood in Philippians 2:1-22....[99]

Hill defines servantship as the "cultivation of self-emptying or downward missional leadership."[100] Servantship does not dismiss the notion of servant leadership, but rather places its focus on serving over self-interest.[101] It is leadership that seeks the glory of another even to the point of our own costly self-sacrifice. We serve in the hopeful expectation that God will use it to bring glory to Jesus as Lord and to advance his good reign throughout the cosmos.

In chapter 2, we explored how the *imago Dei* is a priestly vocation. We have been entrusted with the good care of God's creation and, in the context

---

[99] Graham Hill, "The Theology and Practices of Self-Emptying, Missional Servantship," in *Servantship: Sixteen Servants on the Four Movements of Radical Servantship*, Ed. Graham Hill (Eugene: Wipf & Stock Publishers, 2013), p. 4.
[100] Ibid.
[101] Hill, *GlobalChurch*, p. 353-354.

of fruitful and diverse relationships, the expansion of its horizons of possibility through culture-making. Servantship is rooted in the belief that God's Kingdom is an economy of abundance. As we invest all the resources God has entrusted to us, we believe such abundance will produce a fruitful return that increases his glory in the formless and empty places he sends us. While sin and death threaten to make our investments futile and barren, we are confident that Jesus has defeated these forces so that our servantship is never in vain. Reflect carefully on Paul's words to the Corinthians:

So this body that ruins will clothe itself with that which never ruins. And this body that dies will clothe itself with that which never dies. When this happens, the Scriptures will be made true:

"Death is swallowed in victory." *Isaiah 25:8*

"O death, where is your victory?
Where is your power to hurt?" *Hosea 13:14*

Death's power to hurt is sin, and the power of sin is the law. But we thank God who gives us the victory through our Lord Jesus Christ!

So, my dear brothers and sisters, stand strong. Don't let anything change you. Always give yourselves fully to the work of the Lord. You know that your work in the Lord is never wasted. (1 Cor. 15:54-38)

So, with this vision in our hearts, we have confidence to embrace a leadership-in-community ethic of servantship.

Ethics Themes

The Parable of the Talents highlights three themes of servantship as a leadership ethic that will shape our leadership-in-community: humility, investment, and power.

Humility. Virtue philosopher Kent Dunnington describes the traditional account of Christian humility as low self-estimate.[102] This rather negative perspective of humility follows from appraisals of human value as small, despicable, or incapable.[103] But the Philippians 2 hymn locates the

---

[102] Kent Dunnington, *Humility, Pride, and Christian Virtue Theory* (Oxford: Oxford University Press, 2019), p. 19.
[103] Ibid. p. 20-21.

source of Christian humility, not in human self-estimation, but in Jesus' willing sacrifice.[104] In other words, appropriate Christian humility imitates Jesus whose humility was expressed "most fully in his willingness to die on the cross."[105] Dunnington refers to this as the "No Concern" paradigm of humility and defines it as "the disposition to have no concern to develop, clarify, attain, maintain, or safeguard an ego ideal, because of a trust that one's well-being is entirely secured by the care of God."[106]

Contemporary and secular notions of humility are linked to strength: "*Because* I am strong, secure, and sufficient, I may serve you without any loss to myself."[107] Serving from out of our excess and self-sufficiency may seem like a common-sense approach: By securing my own needs and future first, I can give from a position of power.[108] But the humility of Christian servantship is characterized by the cross and the resurrection.[109] Dunnington expresses this poignantly:

> Jesus did what was preposterous in the light of this classical wisdom about flourishing. He abandoned the quest for self-sufficiency and set out to expend himself to death. He died young, destitute, friendless, and dishonored. He forfeited his life, his access to material goods, his network of relationships....in unrestrained love and service to his neighbor.[110]

But his resurrection reversed what, by nature, should be the outcome of such rich expenditure of self. Death no longer holds power, nor does it define the inevitable result of self-emptying service.[111] Dunnington continues:

> Death is not the inevitable outcome of dying, because death is not the inevitable outcome of self-expenditure and loss. Death is swallowed up in resurrection, which is to say that death is revealed to be an imposter, not the true outcome of a life of self-sacrifice. The sting of death is removed, which is to say that we can live as unto death without fear.[112]

---

[104] Ibid. p. 95.
[105] Ibid.
[106] Ibid. p. 88.
[107] Ibid. p. 98.
[108] Ibid.
[109] Ibid. p. 99.
[110] Ibid. p. 101.
[111] Ibid. p. 106.
[112] Ibid. p. 107.

Humble servantship, based on Jesus' death and resurrection, does not draw from our own internal strengths, but rather from the unreserved love of God in whom we rest in complete dependence.[113]

Greatness in the abundance economy of God's Kingdom is not measured in strength but in humble servantship (Matt. 20:25-28). Missiologist Darrell Jackson puts it this way:

> Quite simply, there can be no biblically authentic definition or expression of greatness and status that move beyond the twin domains of "service" and "humility." To put it another way, all there is to be said about Christian leadership can be said with reference to just these two words. Humility and sacrificial service are not steps to greatness; they *are* greatness that is the hallmark of the kingdom of God, of Jesus' messianic rule.[114]

And they are the hallmark of our leadership-in-community. Leadership-in-community prizes collaboration in which distributed leadership fosters creative connections with others, pouring into one another the resources God has entrusted to us.[115] This dynamic multiplies the social capital that the community can invest to expand the good reign of God's abundant Kingdom.[116] Humility fuels collaboration as each member approaches interpersonal interactions with a strong motive for learning that welcomes and appreciates the contributions of others.[117]

Investment. Servantship begins with the mindset that God's Kingdom economy is one of abundance and generosity (the *mercy* paradigm), not of limited goods that must be protected against others (the *purity* paradigm). Therefore, servantship imitates Jesus Christ whose example of humility and servantship are praised in the Philippians 2 hymn.[118] Leadership in the "limited goods" sense is hierarchical, controlling, and domineering.[119] It points away from Christ and corrupts the community, degrading its worship,

---

[113] Ibid. p. 114.

[114] Darrell Jackson, "For the Son of Man Did Not Come to Lead, but to Be Led: Matthew 20:20-28 and Royal Service," in *Servantship: Sixteen Servants on the Four Movements of Radical Servantship*, Ed. Graham Hill (Eugene: Wipf & Stock Publishers, 2013), p. 27.

[115] Lachlan R. Whatley, Adrian B. Popa, & Heidrum Kliewer, "Community and Leadership: The Role of Humility, Rhythm, and Experiential Learning," *Journal of Leadership, Accountability and Ethics* 9, no. 4 (2012), p. 118.

[116] Ibid.

[117] Owens, Johnson, & Mitchell, "Expressed Humility in Organizations," p. 1518-1519.

[118] Hill, *GlobalChurch*, p. 353.

[119] Ibid.

work, and witness.[120] But servantship, grounded in Christ's abundance economy, is practiced through love that reflects the incarnation and cross of Jesus.[121] It spends itself in order to be reproduced in others. It is collaborative and truly culture-making.

In his reflection on the Philippians 2 hymn, missional leadership expert Roger Helland proposes that servantship is "nothing leadership."[122] He states:

> If my mental model is a servant/love leader, I'll spend energy cultivating shared ownership of mission, and help others succeed as I direct them to the reign of God and the indwelling Spirit, for the sake of others. Our mission is to establish and empower missional, disciple-making leaders and churches. The result of effective missional servantship is *trust*, the basis of all relationships, forged by love.[123]

Investing in others is the heartbeat of servantship. Servantship empowers others to recognize and utilize the resources God has entrusted to them for the sake of his Kingdom. In doing so, servantship remakes the leader-follower relationships into a missional partnership that cultivates *shared* vision and goals that they will achieve together.[124]

Irving and Strauss propose a model of empowering leadership called The Leadership Square (Figure 5) based on a simple formula: *Equipping + Empowerment = Effectiveness*.[125] The model emphasizes that the leadership development of our people must include both equipping and empowerment so that their leadership investments in the Kingdom will indeed flourish.[126] Empowering without equipping leads to follower failure, and equipping without empowering leads to follower frustration.[127] The Leadership Square is a "developmental journey in the leader-follower relationship" that, as it cycles, replicates the formula in ongoing investments in others.[128]

---

[120] Ibid.

[121] Ibid. 354.

[122] Roger Helland, "Nothing Leadership: The Locus of Missional Servantship," in *Servantship: Sixteen Servants on the Four Movements of Radical Servantship*, Ed. Graham Hill (Eugene: Wipf & Stock Publishers, 2013), p. 32-33.

[123] Ibid. p. 37.

[124] Irving & Strauss, *Leadership in Christian Perspective*, p. 1-2.

[125] Ibid. p. 25.

[126] Ibid.

[127] Ibid.

[128] Ibid.

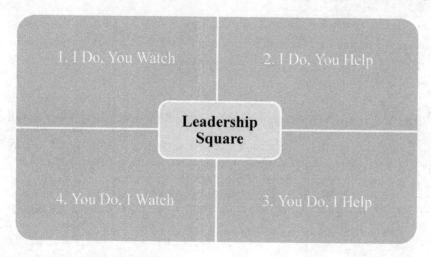

Figure 5: The Leadership Square[129]

The Leadership Square demonstrates that leadership development is an ongoing relational investment process rather than an event.[130] Servantship models to developing leaders what is important and provides them a pathway to prepare them for their own calling through experiential learning.[131] Irving and Strauss articulate:

> Under empowering models such as transformational leadership, the desired transformation is not simply about accomplishing organizational goals. The change is about people as well. The change is about moving followers from a place of compliance through extrinsic motivation to a place of mutual commitment through intrinsic motivation. As followers engage in this journey of personal transformation, leadership capacity and skills are developed.[132]

Essentially, servantship is transformational leadership that transforms followers into leaders who then invest in the development of other leaders.[133]

A good example of empowering leadership is Mavuno Church in Nairobi, Kenya. Wanjiru Gitau, author of *Megachurch Christianity Reconsidered*, traces the incredible growth of Mavuno Church since its genesis as a church

---

[129] Ibid.
[130] Ibid. p. 24.
[131] Ibid.
[132] Ibid. p. 28.
[133] Ibid. p. 27.

plant of megachurch Nairobi Chapel in 2005.[134] Pastor Muriithi Wanjau was mentored in Nairobi Chapel by pastor Oscar Muriu whose vision for leadership in Kenya was catalyzed by what Gitau describes as "the leadership malaise of the 1990s."[135] As she describes this malaise:

> One issue was the prevailing attitude toward leadership, that holding a public office was a source of privilege, an opportunity to cruise, exert power over others, and receive the perks of office, such as a good salary, cars, holidays, and international travels. Second, a latent assumption was that solutions to intractable problems could come from the outside. Dependence was far more insidiously expressed in the political leadership that looked to the West for financial aid instead of building local economies and nurturing talent. However, the churches were not in a much better position, largely because they did not know how to train new leaders and were relying on institution-based theological education and ordination to raise new clergy (which limited women). Muriu said that theological school was too expensive and took a good two to four years to produce a theologically astute minister. Yet when these came in as clergy, they would often be out of touch with the real needs in the church because they were sheltered in school.[136]

Under Muriu's mentorship, Muriithi began to understand that effective leadership is creative and draws upon internal resources to generate new ideas and solve problems.[137] When Muriithi and his colleagues planted Mavuno Church, they realized quickly that they needed to build a "leadership pipeline" that raised up diversely gifted people as leaders.[138] The church needed leaders capable of learning and leading change within the dynamics of a complex urban environment.[139]

Mavuno's leadership pipeline aligns with its ministry strategy, appropriately labeled the "Mavuno Marathon" in homage to Kenya's famed marathon runners.[140] The Mavuno Marathon is a discipleship tool based on the idea that conversion and discipleship are not sprints but

---

[134] Wanjiru M. Gitau, *Megachurch Christianity Reconsidered: Millennials and Social Change in African Perspective* (Downers Grove: IVP Academic, 2018), p. 91.

[135] Ibid. p. 98.

[136] Ibid. p. 98-99.

[137] Ibid. p. 94-100.

[138] Ibid. p. 103.

[139] Ibid.

[140] Ibid. p. 66

are life-long processes (a marathon) closely linked together.[141] The Mavuno Marathon is a journey of spiritual formation that grows disciples through five stages, displayed in Figure 6:

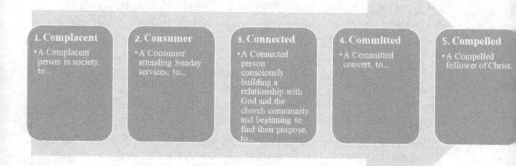

Figure 6: The Mavuno Marathon[142]

Mavuno's leadership then structured its leadership pipeline parallel to these five stages of the Mavuno Marathon. First, they organized staff into teams responsible for each stage of the marathon.[143] In this way, the church clarified the essential roles of each stage so that the different gifts of pastors and volunteers would be appropriately distributed to the places where they can best serve and grow.[144]

Second, they designed a growth path for leadership development within each step, formalized and coordinated through strong human resources systems and thinking.[145] Entry into the staff team begins with an internship whereby candidates undergo a rigorous selection process that

---

[141] Ibid. p. 69.

[142] Ibid. p. 69-70.

[143] Ibid. p. 103.

[144] Ibid. p. 104.

[145] Ibid.

confirms their relationship with God, sense of calling, and education.[146] During the one-year internship, the intern learns "how to lead and manage oneself, focusing on basics of time, relationships, personal values, administrative tasks, and spiritual disciplines" under the guidance of the supervisor responsible for that marathon stage.[147]

After the internship, the individual can move onto a two-year pastoral training stage where they are "expected to continue leading themselves and others by mobilizing volunteer teams, designing and delegating meaningful tasks, and facilitating team problem solving."[148] Individuals may choose to continue on as team managers and senior management staff who lead the teams within the church that make decisions about the church's daily, weekly, and annual calendar and events.[149] Finally, they can move into executive leadership that gives overall strategic direction to the church.[150] The Mavuno leadership pipeline is designed to invest into emerging generations of leaders who will be equipped and empowered to carry on the mission of the church into its complex and changing future.

Power. Power is a subject that many involved in Christian missions would rather not talk about! However, even in Christian leadership, power is a very real phenomenon that must be considered and wisely stewarded. Unfortunately, power is often negatively associated with control, domination, manipulation, or suppression. But power is actually the ability to influence and manage elements in the environment around us, including people, in order to get things done.[151] Power can be exercised positively or negatively, but power is the inevitable reality and necessity for teams and organizations trying to accomplish a mission.

Nineteenth-century German philosopher Friedrich Nietzsche, in his attempt to unmask what he perceived scornfully as the "slave morality" of Christianity, wrote this about power:

> My idea is that every specific body strives to become master over all space and to extend its force (its will to power) and to thrust back all that resists its extension. But it continually encounters similar efforts on the part of other bodies and ends by coming to an arrangement

---

[146] Ibid. p. 104.
[147] Ibid.
[148] Ibid.
[149] Ibid.
[150] Ibid. p. 105.
[151] Lingenfelter, *Leading Cross-Culturally*, p. 107-108.

("union") with those of them that are sufficiently related to it: thus they then conspire together for power. And the process goes on.[152]

This is power from the "limited goods" perspective – power that must be won through competition or conspiracy. Once individuals or teams have acquired this power, they use it to exercise control over others to obtain compliance or conformity to their will.[153] Evil emerges from the abuse of such power. Sherwood Lingenfelter explains:

> Perversion of the structures of relationship most often comes from our obsession to achieve a particular good, such as a biblically sound church. In view of that good, we may construct false paths (keeping control in our hands) to achieve the desired end and make our way the absolute and only way to that end. …when we accept the deception of sin and pursue a good in the wrong way, the end is misery both for us and for the people we seek to serve. The disruptions of will flow from our choices of lesser goods (e.g., my vision for ministry instead of obedience to God), rigid adherence to our worldview, and blindness to and rejection of others.[154]

These distortions of power expose the individual's or team's underlying belief that their power must be protected and defended against others who attempt to usurp it and frustrate, or even destroy, what they will to achieve. Essentially, the abuse of power is, in the words of theologian Marguerite Shuster, the "Devil spoiling what God has made."[155] And it leads to destructive patterns of behaviors and relationships that kill culture rather than make it.[156]

Because power is a reality in all social relationships, our leadership-in-community must redeem power as a God-given gift intended for the flourishing of our people, our cultures, and our missions. In fact, distributing power within an organization is the primary responsibility of leadership.[157]

---

[152] Friedrich Nietzsche, *The Will to Power* trans. Walter Kaufmann & R. J. Hollingdale (New York: Vintage, 1968), p. 636., quoted in Crouch, *Playing God*, p. 46.

[153] Lingenfelter, *Leading Cross-Culturally*, p. 109.

[154] Ibid. p. 110.

[155] Marguerite Shuster, *Power, Pathology, Paradox: The Dynamics of Evil and Good* (Grand Rapids: Zondervan, 1987), p. 140.

[156] Lingenfelter, *Leading Cross-Culturally*, p. 111.

[157] Anita Koeshall, "Navigating Power: Liquid Power Structures for Molten Times," in *Devoted to Christ: Missiological Reflections in Honor of Sherwood G. Lingenfelter*, Ed. Christopher L. Flanders (Eugene: Pickwick Publications, 2019), p. 66.

Because the distribution of power shapes the interactions and relationships throughout the organization, leaders must ensure that power is distributed in a way that catalyzes healthy participation of all members in the common mission.[158] Andy Crouch defines redeemed power as simply "the ability to make something of the world."[159] In other words, power is essential to creation. He states, "Remove power and you cut off life, the possibility of creating something new and better in this rich and recalcitrant world. Life is power. Power is life. And flourishing power leads to flourishing life."[160] In the same way, if you cut off the power of your people, you cut off the capacity of the entire organization to truly make a thriving culture that extends the good reign of God in the formless and empty places of this world.

Leadership-in-community is power-giving leadership.[161] It spends its power to build relationships because it recognizes that people are more important than structural authority and control.[162] It recognizes the gifts and latent potential of people and gives them the space to learn, try, and even fail so that they may grow into maturity as enthusiastic and empowered participants in the organization's mission.[163] Dr. Anita Koeshall, who spent much of her career training new missionaries, agrees:

> A leader's task is to guide the flow of relational power within the community of faith through turbulent social, generational, and demographic shifts in its outer environment and the dynamics of change internally. More than simply creating job descriptions and assigning roles, leadership involves the process of bringing people to maturity; that is, *enabling members to be reflexive agents who think biblically, exegete their culture, and envision the mission that God has for them.*[164]

Such power-giving leadership reflects the character of Jesus within the community. Hierarchical power structures, according to Koeshall, tend to "monopolize positions of prominence, control privilege, and perpetuate the dominant ideology through insulation and centralization."[165] Power-giving leadership, on the other hand, "images" God who, in the creation, delegated

---

158 Ibid.
159 Crouch, *Playing God*, p. 17.
160 Ibid. p. 24-25.
161 Lingenfelter, *Leading Cross-Culturally*, p. 111.
162 Ibid.
163 Koeshall, "Navigating Power," p. 66.
164 Ibid., italics added.
165 Ibid. p. 66.

power to his human regents and entrusted them to use that power to make a thriving world.[166]

Jesus said, "Whoever wants to be first must serve the rest of you like a slave. Do as I did: The Son of Man did not come for people to serve him. He came to serve others and to give his life to save many people" (Matt. 20:25-28). Crouch presents the following Kingdom vision for power as a direct counter in parallel to Nietzsche's dystopian viewpoint. Power in God's Kingdom of abundance is culture-creating:

> All true being strives to create room for more being and to expend its power in the creation of flourishing environments for variety and life, and to thrust back the chaos that limits true being. In doing so it creates other bodies and invites them into mutual creation and tending of the world, building relationships where there had been none: thus they then cooperate together in creating more power for more creation. And the process goes on.[167]

Kingdom power draws its source, not from competition, but from Jesus. In our leadership-in-community, he is enthroned in the highest place of power so that we draw from him, like living water, the power to bring healing, restoration, and 270halom in the world where he sends us.[168] He is the source of resurrection power that pours itself into others so that their gifts are called to life and they are empowered to invest their talents for the advance of God's Kingdom.[169] It is power inseparably infused to the love of Jesus that restores others to their full humanity, the *imago Dei*.[170] Love-driven power that, when spent, actually leads to more power for culture-creation. As Crouch says, "Love transfigures power. Absolute love transfigures absolute power. And power transfigured by love is the power that made and saves the world."[171]

Movement 4: *Oratio*

Heavenly Father,
You have said that the meek are blessed, that those who choose
to serve others for no personal gain will inherit the earth.

---

[166] Crouch, *Playing God*, p. 70.
[167] Ibid. p. 51.
[168] Shuster, *Power, Pathology, and Paradox*, p. 111.
[169] Koeshall, "Navigating Power," p. 75.
[170] Crouch, *Playing God*, p. 25.
[171] Ibid. p. 45.

But how can this be, Lord? Please show us how. In our world, the meek get ignored. The humble end up trampled and left for dead.

Yet meekness is what you modeled. You gave up all privilege in order to become weak. You had divine power and prestige at your disposal, yet you chose to disguise God as a servant – even when that choice brought you suffering and death.

Show us today how to live with faith and confidence in your upside-down kingdom. Change our imagination, rearrange our priorities, re-create our very way of seeing. Otherwise, pride and power and winning make so much more sense.

Show us the giant promise of your "little" ways. Help us to desire humility, honor it in others, and choose it for ourselves, that we may do your true work and reveal your beauty in this world.[172]

In Jesus' name, Amen.

Movement 5: *Imitatio*

+ Individual Reflection

  o Journal your responses to the following questions:

    ▪ What key points is God leading you to embrace and grow into?

    ▪ How can you live this out in your life and leadership?

    ▪ How can your missional leadership group pray for you in living this out?

+ Group Reflection

  o In your missional leadership group, share your individual reflections with each other.

  o Pray for one another.

---

[172] Prayer adapted from the ancient spiritual practice of the Prayer Wheel. Dodd, Riess, & Van Biema, *The Prayer Wheel*, p. 105.

Movement 6: *Missio*

- Experiencing Mission
  - o Level 1 *Awareness*
    - Pray each day that the Lord sends you into his mission that day.
    - At the end of each day, reflect on or journal about one experience you had that day where you witnessed the *missio Dei* personally. Describe what happened. What was significant about that experience for you?

  - o Level 2 *Personal Commitment*
    - Ask the Lord where he may be sending you to be his witness on a regular basis.
    - Make a commitment to serve in that way.

Movement 7: *Communio*

- Experiencing Mission
  - o Level 3 *Group Experience*
    - If possible, the small group may consider performing a mission or service project together to experience mission as a community.

- Group Reflection
  - o Where did you see the *missio Dei* in action this past week?
  - o What was the most significant or surprising observations you made about your experience?
  - o What did you learn about God from that experience? What did you learn about yourself from that experience?
  - o What difference does that make in your leadership? How will you apply what you have learned?

Movement 8: *Contemplatio*

Each week in your small group, spend time reflecting and celebrating the ways that you have seen "God on the move" in the past week.

- Spend some time in prayer or singing in thanksgiving and praise to our missionary God.

Chapter 9

Peacemaking

As we come to the end of our exploration of leadership-in-community, we must grapple with the inevitability of conflict. We can be sure that whenever two or more people live and work together in community, eventually they will disagree! Unfortunately, conflict often evokes negative connotations for us, carried on the back of painful memories, broken relationships, or tense environments. Because we think of conflict negatively, we spend incredible amounts of our resources – time, money, emotions, and mental energies – to "manage" our conflicts. We avoid it or pretend everything is fine. We leverage power, either our own or that of other higher-ups, to get what we want. We raise our voices and use intimidation. Or we "take one for the team" and safely keep our thoughts and feelings to ourselves even though they may be burning contempt and anger inside our hearts. These strategies expose what we really believe about conflict. We consider it an unnecessary complication – something we don't need – that we just need to "deal with" so we can get on with our work or our lives.

In her poem *Power failure*, poet Luci Shaw expresses that such strategies of conflict management are the antithesis of the *missio Dei*. Read through her poem several times and reflect on its imagery and language:

Power failure

By what
anti-miracle have we
lamed the man
who leaped for joy,
lost ninety-nine
sheep, clutched
the lunch fish
until they
not in our hands,
turned bread
back to stone
and wine
to water?[1]

---

[1] Luci Shaw, "Power failure," in *Polishing the Petoskey Stone: Selected Poems* (Vancouver: Regent College Publishing, 1990), p. 147.

What words or ideas here strike you? What conflicts or arguments does it call to your mind? What thoughts or feelings do those conflicts or arguments evoke for you? What would it take for God to transform them from "anti-miracles" to "miracles" in your life or community?

The *276halom276 Dei* casts a higher vision for conflict, one that is positive, creative, and expansive for our leadership-in-community. It reframes conflict as *peacemaking*. As image-bearers of our triune God, we are called to a higher ethic than merely resolving conflict. We are called to make peace, *276halom*, that extends the good reign of our merciful and compassionate God to the cosmos. Every conflict we face, no matter how large or small, is an opportunity to stem the power of the formless and empty within our communities and, by Christ's resurrection power, generate the "miracle" of a new creation. We must fervently embrace a vision of peacemaking for our leadership-in-community.

In the last chapter, we looked at one of Jesus' parables from the Olivet Discourse of Matthew's Gospel. In this chapter, we will look at a parable from his fourth discourse often referred to as the "Community Discourse."[2] This is the Parable of the Unmerciful Servant.

Movement 1: *Adspecto*

Prayer

✝ Pray for the Holy Spirit to speak to you through the Scripture. Use the following words of Psalm 133 as a prayer:

A song of David for going up to the Temple.

[1]Oh, how wonderful, how pleasing it is
when God's people all come together as one!

[2]It is like the sweet-smelling oil that is poured over the high priest's head,
that runs down his beard flowing over his robes.

[3]It is like a gentle rain from Mount Hermon falling on Mount Zion.
It is there that the LORD has promised his blessing of eternal life.

---

[2] Donald Senior, "Matthew 18:21-35," *Interpretation* 41, no. 4 (1987), p. 403.

Scripture Reading

✦ **Read Matthew 18:21-35.** Listen for words or phrases from the passage that stand out to you.

A Story About Forgiveness

21Then Peter came to Jesus and asked, "Lord, when someone won't stop doing wrong to me, how many times must I forgive them? Seven times?"

22Jesus answered, "I tell you, you must forgive them more than seven times. You must continue to forgive them even if they do wrong to you seventy-seven times.

23"So God's kingdom is like a king who decided to collect the money his servants owed him. 24The king began to collect his money. One servant owed him several thousand pounds of silver. 25He was not able to pay the money to his master, the king. So the master ordered that he and everything he owned be sold, even his wife and children. The money would be used to pay the king what the servant owed.

26"But the servant fell on his knees and begged, 'Be patient with me. I will pay you everything I owe.' 27The master felt sorry for him. So he told the servant he did not have to pay. He let him go free.

28"Later, that same servant found another servant who owed him a hundred silver coins. He grabbed him around the neck and said, 'Pay me the money you owe me!'

29"The other servant fell on his knees and begged him, 'Be patient with me. I will pay you everything I owe.'

30"But the first servant refused to be patient. He told the judge that the other servant owed him money, and that servant was put in jail until he could pay everything he owed. 31All the other servants saw what happened. They felt very sorry for the man. So they went and told their master everything that happened.

32"Then the master called his servant in and said, 'You evil servant. You begged me to forgive your debt, and I said you did not have to pay anything! 33So you should have given that other man who serves with you the

277

same mercy I gave you.' [34]The master was very angry, so he put the servant in jail to be punished. And he had to stay in jail until he could pay everything he owed.

[35]"This king did the same as my heavenly Father will do to you. You must forgive your brother or sister with all your heart, or my heavenly Father will not forgive you."

Reflection

✦ When you have finished reading, remain silent for one or two minutes.

✦ Read the entire passage again. If you have an audio Bible, listen through the passage.

✦ Journal your thoughts on the following questions:

   o What words or phrases from the passage stand out to you?

   o How do these words or phrases connect with your life right now?

   o How might God be inviting you to respond to this passage?

Movement 2: *Lectio*

Scripture Study

✦ Read or listen to **Matthew 18:21-35**.

✦ Answer the following study questions:

1. What does Peter ask Jesus (vs. 21)?

2. What do you sense is motivating Peter's question?

3. How does Jesus respond to Peter's question (vs. 22)?

4. What do you think Jesus' response means?

5. Jesus tells a story to describe God's Kingdom. How does the story begin (vs. 23)?

6. How much does the servant owe the king (vs. 24)?

7. The servant is not able to repay what he owes. How does the king deal with the servant because he cannot repay (vs. 25)?

8. How does the king's response to the servant's inability to pay impact you?

9. What does the servant do (vs. 26)?

10. How does the king treat the servant in response (vs. 27)?

11. How does the king's response to the servant impact you?

12. After he leaves the king, the servant found a fellow servant who owed him money. How much did the fellow servant owe him (vs. 28)?

13. How does the first servant respond to his fellow servant's inability to pay (vs. 28)?

14. What does the fellow servant do (vs. 29)?

15. How does the first servant treat the fellow servant in response (vs. 30)?

16. How does the first servant's response to his fellow servant impact you?

17. Who witnessed the event and what do they do (vs. 31)?

18. What does the master say to the first servant? What does he do to him (vs. 32-34)?

19. How does the master's words and actions toward the first servant impact you?

20. What does Jesus say is the application of this story (vs. 35)?

21. What do you think it means to forgive "with all your heart" (vs. 35)?

22. How do you react to Jesus' words: "This king did the same as my heavenly Father will do to you" (vs. 35)?

23. What does this parable teach you about forgiveness in the Kingdom of God? Why does forgiveness matter?

24. What does this story mean to you? When you consider conflict and forgiveness in your own experience, how does this parable and Jesus' application impact you?

25. Do you see any action steps regarding forgiveness to which God may be calling you?

Reading

The Context of Jesus' Community Rule

Matthew's Community Discourse was prompted by the disciples' question to Jesus: "Who is the greatest in God's kingdom?" (Matt. 18:1). The Kingdom of God is an upside-down Kingdom, one which draws its values and ethics from a completely different source than the world. The kingdoms of this world trade in pecking orders, control, strength, and the prestige of positions.[3] But in God's Kingdom, the greatest is the one who is humble like a little child (Matt. 18:3-5). The "little children" are favored by God. They have "angels in heaven" who Jesus said are "always with my Father in heaven" (Matt. 18:10). Jesus used exaggerated, hyperbolic language to stress how important "little children" are in the Kingdom. Causing one to sin invites the fire of hell (Matt 18:6-9) and losing one compels the shepherd to leave the rest of the sheep to find him or her (Matt. 18:12-14). With these rich sentiments, Jesus set the stage for what peacemaking means for the community of his people.

Considering that Matthew wrote to Jesus communities facing increasing hostility from their former Jewish kinship, Matthew possibly considered them to be like the "little children" of whom he wrote.[4] They were a vulnerable group of people that depended on a nurturing community for their faith to survive and grow in such inhospitable environments.[5] He presented Jesus' teaching on peacemaking as central to the identity and ethics of the Messiah's people.[6] This is a community forged by the amazing grace of the triune God![7] God is building this people into a temple that resounds throughout the world with their witness of his mercy (1 Pet. 2:5, 9-10). Reconciliation in the Jesus community gets right to the heart of the good news of the Kingdom.[8] Forgiveness is participation in the good reign of God. By forgiving others, we acknowledge the grace God has given to us and affirm

---

[3] DeSilva, *An Introduction to the New Testament*, p. 277.

[4] Bridget Illian, "Church Discipline and Forgiveness in Matthew 18:15-35," *Currents in Theology and Mission* 37, no. 6 (2010), p. 445.

[5] DeSilva, *An Introduction to the New Testament*, p. 277.

[6] Michael Patrick Barber, "Forgiving the Sinner: The Church as a Christ-like People in Matthew 18," *The Bible Today* 58, no. 1 (2020), p. 15.

[7] Eduard Schweizer, *The Good News According to Matthew* (Atlanta: John Knox Press, 1975), p. 379, quoted in Daniel Patte, "Bringing Out the Gospel-Treasure What Is New and What is Old: Two Parables in Matthew 18-23," *Quarterly Review* 10, no. 3 (1990), p. 82.

[8] Patte, "Bringing Out the Gospel-Treasure," p. 93.

our calling to be agents of his grace to others.[9] Jesus, our Savior, expects us to zealously guard the community against sin, bitterness, resentment, division, and other forces that would break us apart.

The Community Rule

With the advent of Jesus, the Messiah, a new order has broken into this world. And so, Jesus presented his community rule of reconciliation fitting for that new order (Matt. 18:15-17). This rule was similar to customs common for first-century Jewish communities, such as the Pharisees and the Essenes.[10] Their community rules drew from Leviticus:

> Don't secretly hate any of your neighbors. But tell them openly what they have done wrong so that you will not be just as guilty of sin as they are. Forget about the wrong things people do to you. Don't try to get even. Love your neighbor as yourself. I am the LORD. (Lev. 19:17-18)

They instituted regulations for resolving disputes that required witnesses to an accusation, the open rebuke of wrongdoing, and a series of disciplinary procedures that culminated in expulsion from the community.[11] Jesus was familiar with these practices. But in his Community Discourse, he repurposed them for the goals of his own Messianic community.[12]

Jesus framed his community rule with a story of a shepherd who left 99 sheep to look for the one lost sheep (Matt. 18:12-14). No reasonable shepherd would do such a thing for one lost sheep! But the implication is clear: in Jesus' Kingdom order, the goal of the community rule is not to exclude sinners but to reintegrate them back into the community.[13] While other Jewish communities may have been reluctant to welcome back a sinner who had been expelled, the overriding concern of the Jesus community was to help the offender become a "brother or sister again" (Matt. 18:15). Certainly, the process took sin seriously. But the community ethic prioritized mercy over purity. Even when it became necessary to treat the offender as "someone who does not know God or who is tax collector" (Matt. 18:17), Jesus does not let his community write them off as beyond the mercy of

---

[9] Susan E. Hylen, "Forgiveness and Life in Community," *Interpretation* 54, no. 2 (2000), p. 157.

[10] Illian, "Church Discipline," p. 446.

[11] Ibid.

[12] Ibid. p. 447-448.

[13] Patte, "Bringing Out the Gospel-Treasure," p. 90.

God.[14] In fact, he responded to those who criticized him for associating with tax collectors (such as Matthew himself!) and other sinners by saying:

> It is the sick people who need a doctor, not those who are healthy. You need to go and learn what this Scripture means: "I don't want animal sacrifices; I want you to show kindness to people.' I did not come to invite good people. I came to invite sinners. (Matt. 9:12-13)

While Jesus conferred on the community the authority to regulate the kinds of behaviors that promoted its flourishing (Matt. 18:18-20), he stressed that we must be a people of reconciliation.[15] That must always be our guiding attitude and vision. Why? Because it reflects the heart of our Father in heaven who "does not want any of these little children to be lost" (Matt. 18:14).

The Parable of the Unmerciful Servant

We can almost see Peter's head spin as he considered the implication of Jesus' community rule: "Lord, when someone won't stop doing wrong to me, how many times must I forgive them? Seven times?" (Matt. 18:21). Peter expressed the question that often nags at the back of our own minds. When is the point where we can legitimately give up on someone who hurts or offends us and still consider ourselves faithful to the Lord? Peter may have thought his suggestion of seven times was quite generous in comparison to the Pharisees' standard limits of three times.[16] But Jesus' surprising response to Peter expanded the limits of forgiveness beyond any horizon:[17]

> Jesus answered, "I tell you, you must forgive them more than seven times. You must continue to forgive them even if they do wrong to you seventy-seven times." (Matt. 18:22)

Jesus' use of "seventy-seven times" alluded to an Old Testament tale of blood vengeance. Lamech, a descendant of Cain, swore an oath of revenge against a man who hurt him: "I have killed a man for wounding me, a young man for injuring me. If Cain is avenged seven times, then Lamech seventy-seven times" (Gen. 4:23-24, NIV).[18] But the Messiah's new order overcame the law

---

[14] Barber, "Forgiving the Sinner," p. 19.
[15] Ibid. p. 18.
[16] Patte, "Bringing Out of the Gospel-Treasure," p. 82.
[17] Ibid. p. 404.
[18] Robert W. Heimburger, Christopher M. Hays, & Guillermo Mejía-Castillo, "Forgiveness and Politics: Reading Matthew 18:21-35 with Survivors of Armed Conflict in Colombia,"

of retaliation inscribed in the Levitical code (Matt. 5:38-42; cf. Lev. 24:19-21). It is greater and deeper than the logic of "an eye for an eye" out of which the world operates.

In this sense, Peter's question revealed that he completely missed the point of Jesus' community rule! He wanted to know how many times the community must go through this process with someone who continually offends. But Jesus' answer of "seventy-seven times" implied that keeping a ledger of offenses is old-world thinking. It is simply out-of-sync with his new Kingdom order. It denies the allegiance the community owes to its Messiah who has irretrievably captured it like a shepherd who left 99 sheep to go after one lost sheep. This community is now branded by the forgiveness and reconciliation that it has received by the generous grace of God. Christian action flows from the experience of God's extravagant mercy.[19]

Jesus illustrated this point by telling the Parable of the Unmerciful Servant. What is interesting is that the parable does not directly answer Peter's question. Peter asked about the limits of forgiveness. At first glance, Jesus' answer of seventy-seven times seems to indicate that forgiveness must be unlimited in God's Kingdom.[20] But then, Jesus told a story about a king who initially forgives and then later withdraws that forgiveness!

But as we consider the wider context of Matthew 18, we find that Peter's question actually interrupted the line of Jesus' teaching. We must remember that the heart of Jesus' community rule (Matt. 18:15-20) was his overriding concern for regaining a brother or sister, the "little children" who are so important to God (Matt. 18:6-14). So, Jesus' "seventy-times seven" was not about the ledger of offenses. It was about an overall mindset that was to precede and guide the life of the Messianic community. The story Jesus was about to tell illustrated this for Peter and the disciples.[21] New Testament professor Donald Senior explains:

> A fundamental message of this parable is that the Christian must act on the basis of God's incalculable graciousness. Reconciliation, from the Gospel's standpoint, is not strategy to win friends nor is it simply a sign of good breeding and natural virtue. Forgiveness is urgent because we are a forgiven people. What the servant first experienced

---

HTS Teologiese Studies/Theological Studies 75, no. 4 (2019), p. 4. Also, Senior, "Matthew 18:21-35," p. 404.

[19] Senior, "Matthew 18:21-35," p. 406.

[20] Patte, "Bringing Out the Gospel-Treasure," p. 83-84.

[21] Hylen, "Forgiveness and Life in Community," p. 153.

from the king – gratuitous, unconditional compassion – is the primal reality out of which he was expected to act. His own lack of compassion revealed a total disregard for the basic truth of his own existence.[22]

The king's compassion for the servant expressed in extravagant forgiveness created a new reality (a "new order") for the servant out of which he was now expected to live. Let's unpack the parable by considering the money, the servants, and the expectation of reciprocity.

The Money. As we saw in the last chapter, a talent was a significant measure of value in the first-century world. The talent was the largest monetary denomination, and the number 10,000 was the highest figure in which arithmetic was calculated.[23] Ten-thousand talents was the largest figure one could think of![24] It was something akin to the national debt and may have reminded Jesus' audience of the 10,000 talents that the Roman general Pompey levied upon Judea when he subjugated the area around 60 BCE.[25] So, when Jesus explained that the servant owed the king 10,000 talents, he was again using hyperbolic language to express a staggering sum of money impossible for the servant to pay back.[26] Such an extraordinary debt highlighted the depth of the king's mercy in forgiveness.[27]

The denarius, on the other hand, was the smallest form of currency.[28] The average daily wage for a laborer was one denarius.[29] So, the debt of the second servant of 100 denarii, while still a sizeable amount, was a much more realistic figure of debt.[30] Jesus' comparison between the 10,000-talent debt of the first servant and the 100-denarii debt of the second would have made the hypocrisy of the first servant's refusal to forgive quite astounding to Jesus' audience. Instead of extending the overwhelming kindness the servant had

---

[22] Ibid.

[23] Senior, "Matthew 18:21-35," p. 405.

[24] Patte, "Bringing Out the Gospel-Treasure," p. 82.

[25] Warren Carter, "Resisting and Imitating the Empire: Imperial Paradigms in Two Matthean Parables," *Interpretation* 56, no. 3 (2002), p. 266.

[26] Senior, "Matthew 18:21-35," p. 405.

[27] Martinus C. De Boer, "Ten Thousand Talents? Matthew's Interpretation and Redaction of the Parable of the Unforgiving Servant (Matt 18:23-35)," *The Catholic Biblical Quarterly* 50, no. 2 (1988), p. 228.

[28] Senior, "Matthew 18:21-35," p. 405.

[29] Ibid.

[30] Ronald F. Hock, "Romancing the Parables of Jesus," *Perspectives in Religious Studies* 29, no. 1 (2002), p. 26.

just experienced, he dealt cruelly with the second servant who owed a significantly lesser debt.[31]

The Servants. In the parable, we read of three servants: the first servant (Matt. 18:24-27), the second "fellow" servant (Matt. 18:28-30, NIV), and the other servants (Matt. 18:31). The first servant who owed the king 10,000 talents appeared to be a man who had some agency to handle the king's resources.[32] Often, in the first-century Roman political world, a certain class of servants had highly developed administrative, economic, and legal skills they used to carry out the king's policies.[33] These were individuals who could exercise incredible power. Some scholars suggest that the first servant was a tax collector because Jesus' audience may have associated the size of his debt with the high finances of the empire.[34] But, in any case, he represented the interests of the king. Yet, in his management of the king's finances, he failed to advance his king's interests.[35]

When threatened with punishment for this failure, the first servant "fell on his knees and begged, 'Be patient with me. I will pay you everything I owe.'" (Matt. 18:26). The Greek word Matthew used here for "begged" (*prosekynei*) was usually used in the sense of worship to God or gods.[36] The first servant fell on his knees and worshipped the king, pleading for his life! The enormity of this man's debt rendered his cries and his promise to repay ridiculous. Indeed, he had become a desperate man overwhelmed by an impossible financial burden, and his family and property were about to be taken from him.[37] But the king, out of a compassion unheard of by ancient monarchs, forgave him with no strings attached. According to Senior, the Greek word used to express the king's compassion (*splagnistheis*) "implies deep emotion, literally a 'stirring of the intestines,' and is used by Matthew to describe Jesus' own reaction of compassion toward the helpless crowds in 9:36; 14:14; and 15:34 and for the two blind men in 20:34."[38] Out of such deep pity, the king liberates the servant from the debt and gives him a new lease on life.

---

[31] Senior, "Matthew 18:21-35," p. 405.
[32] Carter, "Resisting and Imitating the Empire," p. 265.
[33] Ibid.
[34] Patte, "Brining Out of the Gospel-Treasure," p. 84.
[35] Carter, "Resisting and Imitating the Empire," p. 266.
[36] Eta Linnemann, *Parables of Jesus: Introduction and Exposition* (London: SPCK, 1966), p. 109, quoted in De Boer, "Ten Thousand Talents?" p. 222.
[37] Senior, "Matthew 18:21-35," p. 405.
[38] Ibid.

The second "fellow" servant may have also been a tax collector of a lower status as indicated by the significantly smaller size of his debt.[39] If so, he had a more reasonable case for repaying his debt if given more time.[40] Faced with certain calamity, he also, like the first servant, "fell on his knees and begged him, 'Be patient with me. I will pay you everything I owe.'" (Matt. 18:29). In this case, Matthew used the Greek word *parakaleō* for "begged," implying that the fellow servant merely beseeched or implored, rather than worshipped, the first servant.[41] This exacerbates the first servant's hypocrisy in the story. He was not on the same level as the king, yet his actions toward his fellow servant suggest that he believed he was worthy of more honor than the king. Technically, he was entirely within his rights to demand full repayment from his fellow servant.[42] But what makes his actions so abhorrent was his failure to extend mercy to his fellow servant, especially for a smaller debt, when he had just received such great mercy by the king he worshipped for his enormous debt. Martinus De Boer expresses well how out of place the first servant's actions were:

> [H]is action…is shown to be reprehensible by dramatic contrast with the new and unfamiliar world of mercy and forgiveness, a world that grants to another what he or she has no legal right to demand or expect… This world has broken in upon the familiar world of legal rights and claims, unmasking the brutality that lies underneath attempts to secure legitimate rights and claims over against another….[43]

The first servant found himself in a new order created by the king's forgiveness. But he failed to honor the "community rule" of that new order.

The other servants are important to the story as witnesses to the first servant's actions. The text reveals that they were "greatly distressed" (Matt. 18:31, NIV) over the lack of compassion they witnessed in the first servant's behavior. Daniel Patte, Professor Emeritus of Religious Studies at Vanderbilt University, notes that Matthew used the same phrase to describe the disciples' distress upon Christ's prediction of his death earlier (Matt. 18:23).[44] He believes that Matthew contrasted the two instances to stress that the disciples should not be distressed by Jesus' death; rather, they should be distressed

---

[39] De Boer, "Ten Thousand Talents?" p. 216.
[40] Senior, "Matthew 18:21-35," p. 405.
[41] De Boer, "Ten Thousand Talents?" p. 222.
[42] Ibid. p. 231.
[43] Ibid.
[44] Patte, "Bringing Out of the Gospel-Treasure," p. 89.

when "they see someone refusing to forgive and mistreating a brother or sister, as the fellow servants are in 18:31…"[45] Witnesses to an offense, as Jesus instructed in his community rule (Matt. 18:16), established the veracity of the offense for two communal purposes: first, so that the *offender* could be called to repentance; and second, so that the *offended* could not exaggerate the claim in a way that shamed the offender.[46] The witnesses were vital for the maintenance of the community during a conflict.

Reciprocity. What is really at stake in the story is the honor of the king! He had shown extravagant mercy upon the first servant, yet this servant failed to extend such mercy to his fellow servant. In first-century societies, the convention of reciprocity governed relationships between people.[47] Reciprocity involved the "moral obligation to reciprocate an act of mercy or benefaction with a roughly comparable act in return."[48] The principle of reciprocity established a social contract that bonded people together in mutual support.[49] In the case of socially unequal persons, if the person of higher status conferred a benefit upon another, the person of lower status was still expected to honor the rules of reciprocity.[50] But because this person could not possibly reciprocate with the person of higher status, he or she would be obligated to "pay it forward" by conferring a benefit upon someone else of lower status.[51]

Essentially, when the king forgave the enormous debt of the first servant, he actually further indebted the servant to extend the same mercy to others that he had received.[52] The king's mercy, in one sense, liberated the servant to a new life. But, in another sense, the king obligated the servant to reflect the honor of the king in his subsequent dealings with others. By refusing to forgive his fellow servant, the first servant dishonored the king in the vilest manner and threatened to break the harmony of the community. The severity of the king's response to the first servant reveals how serious was the servant's dishonoring behavior.

---

[45] Ibid.
[46] Illian, "Church Discipline and Forgiveness," p. 448.
[47] Hock, "Romancing the Parables of Jesus," p. 28.
[48] Ibid.
[49] Malina, *The New Testament World*, p. 94.
[50] Ibid. p. 29-30.
[51] Ibid.
[52] Carter, "Resisting and Imitating the Empire," p. 267.

The Gospel is Peacemaking

Jesus stated plainly the point of the parable: "This king did the same as my heavenly Father will do to you. You must forgive your brother or sister with all your heart, or my heavenly Father will not forgive you" (Matt: 18:35). Our heavenly Father extended extravagant mercy to us through the life, death, and resurrection of Jesus Christ, our Messiah. We now live under his reign in a new order, one in which we are "indebted" to Jesus by reflecting the same mercy and forgiveness to one another. This is a mercy that leaves the 99 sheep to go after the lost one (Matt. 18:12). It takes sin seriously and is concerned with justice, not with the spirit of vengeance or expelling the sinner, but in the spirit and hope of regaining a brother or sister. Peacemaking is the real-life proclamation of the Gospel story in the community of God's people.

As we conclude this lectio on peacemaking, spend a few moments to meditate on these words from Paul's letter to the Corinthians. Pay special attention to the italicized portions:

The love of Christ controls us, because we know that one person died for everyone. So all have died. He died for all so that those who live would not continue to live for themselves. *He died for them and was raised from death so that they would live for him.*

From this time on we don't think of anyone as the world thinks of people. It is true that in the past we thought of Christ as the world thinks. But we don't think that way now. *When anyone is in Christ, it is a whole new world. The old things are gone; suddenly, everything is new! All this is from God. Through Christ, God made peace between himself and us. And God gave us the work of bringing people into peace with him. I mean that God was in Christ, making peace between the world and himself. In Christ, God did not hold people guilty for their sins. And he gave us this message of peace to tell people.* So we have been sent to speak for Christ. It is like God is calling to people through us. We speak for Christ when we beg you to be at peace with God. Christ had no sin, but God made him become sin so that in Christ we could be right with God. (2 Cor. 5:14-21, italics added)

Movement 3: *Meditatio*

Jesus taught us, "Great blessings belong to those who work to bring peace. God will call them his sons and daughters" (Matt. 5:9). Our peacemaking images the family name we bear: We are the children of God who made peace with us, even when we were his enemies, through his Son's death (Rom. 5:10). Dr. Brenda Salter McNeil, author, speaker, and advocate for racial reconciliation, defines peacemaking in the context and spirit of the *missio Dei*: "Reconciliation is an ongoing spiritual process involving forgiveness, repentance and justice that restores broken relationships and systems to reflect God's original intention for all creation to flourish."[53] Peacemaking is an ethic of our leadership-in-community because it expands the horizons of what is possible and extends the good reign of God over the cosmos.

Poet David Whyte wrote a beautiful piece that evokes the power of forgiveness in spite of the flippant way the word is used in everyday parlance. Listen carefully to his prose:

Forgiveness

Forgiveness is a heartache and difficult to achieve because strangely, it not only refuses to eliminate the original wound, but actually draws us closer to its source. To approach forgiveness is to close in on the nature of the hurt itself, the only remedy being, as we approach its raw center, to reimagine our relation to it.

It may be that the part of us that was struck and hurt can never forgive, and that strangely, forgiveness never arises from the part of us that was actually wounded. The wounded self may be the part of us incapable of forgetting, and perhaps, not actually meant to forget, as if, like the foundational dynamics of the physiological immune system our psychological defenses must remember and organize against any future attacks – after all, the identity of the one who must forgive is actually founded on the very fact of having been wounded.

Stranger still, it is that wounded, branded, un-forgetting part of us that eventually makes forgiveness an act of compassion rather than one of simple forgetting. To forgive is to assume a larger identity than the person who was first hurt, to mature and bring to fruition an identity that can put its arm, not only around the afflicted one within but also around the memories seared within us by the original blow and

---

53 Brenda Salter McNeil, *Roadmap to Reconciliation: Moving Communities to Unity, Wholeness and Justice* (Downers Grove: InterVarsity Press, 2015), p. 22.

through a kind of psychological virtuosity, extend our understanding to one who first delivered it.

Forgiveness is a skill, a way of preserving clarity, sanity and generosity in an individual life, a beautiful way of shaping the mind to a future we want for ourselves; an admittance that if forgiveness comes through understanding, and if understanding is just a matter of time and application then we might as well begin forgiving right at the beginning of any drama rather than put ourselves through the full cycle of festering, incapacitation, reluctant healing and eventual blessing.

To forgive is to put oneself in a larger gravitational field of experience than the one that first seemed to hurt us. We reimagine ourselves in the light of our maturity and we reimagine the past in the light of our new identity, we allow ourselves to be gifted by a story larger than the story that first hurt us and left us bereft.

At the end of life, the wish to be forgiven is ultimately the chief desire of almost every human being. In refusing to wait; in extending forgiveness to others now, we begin the long journey of becoming the person who will be large enough, able enough and generous enough to receive, at the very end, that absolution ourselves.[54]

Peacemaking is not merely resolving conflict. Rather, as Whyte articulates, peacemaking is embracing a new identity, for ourselves and our community, gifted to us by a "story larger than the story that first hurt us and left us bereft." That larger story is the Gospel!

Ethics Themes

In this final *Meditatio*, we will consider how we can imbue our culture with peacemaking as an ethic of our leadership-in-community. The Parable of the Unmerciful Servant highlights three ethics themes that will shape our leadership-in-community: forming a goodness culture, fostering a peacemaking vision, and developing peacemaking competencies.

Forming a Goodness Culture. Peacemaking and reconciliation are ultimately about restoring God's original intention for his creation – that which he made "very good" (Gen. 1:31). Therefore, leadership-in-community

---

[54] David Whyte, "Forgiveness," *Consolations: The Solace, Nourishment and Underlying Meaning of Everyday Words* (Langley: Many Rivers Press, 2015), p. 67-69.

desires to form cultures of goodness. Cultures of goodness involve relationships and systems that reflect the goodness of God – not only his good character, but also the goodness that he *does* when his "goodness and love" follow us all the days of our lives (Psalm 23:6).[55] The marks of a goodness culture include empathy and compassion, grace and graciousness, putting people first, truth-telling, justice, service, and Christlikeness.[56] In the community filled with these attributes, conflict actually presents tremendous opportunities for growth, creativity, relationship, and hospitality that advance God's Kingdom in the formless and empty spaces. Goodness cultures are, in fact, the spaces where what God wants "will be done here on earth, the same as in heaven" (Matt. 6:10). Leadership-in-community intentionally and strategically nurtures a goodness culture.

Fostering a Peacemaking Vision. Forming a goodness culture begins when leadership-in-community fosters a vision for healthy conflict as mission opportunity. People tend to approach conflict fearfully as an unpleasant or unnecessary experience. They fear losing something important to them through the conflict. Consequently, their conflict strategies focus on defending and preserving what they fear to lose. Leadership-in-community courageously and openly steps into conflict and frames it positively for the sake of their community and their mission. Peacemaking author Ken Sande states that a culture of peace develops when a community is "eager to bring glory to God by demonstrating the reconciling love and forgiveness of Jesus Christ, and therefore sees peacemaking as an essential part of the Christian life."[57] Leaders must tenaciously cast vision in their communities for healthy conflict. Otherwise, the "formless and empty" insidiously creeps back into the heart of their community when it faces conflict.

Developing Peacemaking Competencies. Leadership-in-community advances this vision through human resource strategies that develop peacemaking competencies. Human resource consultants, Enyonam Kudonoo, Kathy Schroeder, and Sheila Boysen-Rotelli, define five focus areas for human resource strategies that promote healthy community conflict:[58]

---

[55] McKnight & Barringer, *A Church Called TOV*, p. 87.
[56] Ibid. p. 96.
[57] Ken Sande, *The Peacemaker: A Biblical Guide to Resolving Personal Conflict* Revised and Updated (Grand Rapids: BakerBooks, 2004), p. 198.
[58] Enyonam Kudonoo, Kathy Schroeder, & Sheila Boysen-Rotelli, "An Olympic Transformation: Creating an Organizational Culture that Promotes Healthy Conflict," *Organizational Development Journal* 30, no. 2 (2012), p. 56.

1. Building Individual Competencies in Conflict

Building individual competencies in conflict begins with the recruitment and onboarding of new employees or team members.[59] New member onboarding is a socialization process in which the organization conveys to new members the expectations of the community as they are communicated through their core values, philosophies, codes of conduct, and policies.[60] This is an important moment for new members to learn the community's vision for conflict as well as how conflict is handled in the community.

Entry Posture. Figure 7 presents the Dealing with Differences Model. This model provides a useful conversation and training tool for new team members (as well as a refresher for seasoned team members) about how to enter well into teamwork with others. Inevitably, we will encounter differences with other people in our teamwork. Everyone on the team will approach the task from vastly different perspectives, worldviews, and ideas for how to proceed. These differences are a valuable and indispensable aspect of true teamwork. They help us think expansively and find creative solutions we may not come up with individually. However, they can also be the source of conflict when team members do not receive those differences hospitably.

A healthy entry posture ensures that when conflicts arise, the team can work through them with a readiness to learn from one another. As the model illustrates, if team members enter teamwork with openness, trust, acceptance, and adaptability, they will be more likely to navigate through dissonance with successful coping skills. They will observe, listen, inquire, and initiate in the effort to build understanding and empathy on the team. However, if team members enter teamwork with suspicion, attitudes of superiority, fear, and prejudice, they will most like adopt negative coping skills when they encounter differences. They will criticize, rationalize, and isolate themselves from others. Even worse, they will categorize people into in-groups and out-groups.[61] When this happens, tragically, they begin to stereotype members of the out-group so that they may dismiss or silence their voices.[62] This leads to alienation and withdrawal between team members. Ultimately, it fosters

---

[59] Ibid. p. 56.
[60] Ibid.
[61] Esler, "Jesus and the Reduction of Intergroup Conflict," p. 327-328.
[62] Ibid.

broken relationships that destroy a goodness culture that reflects the good reign of God.

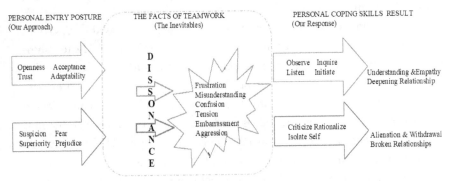

Figure 7: Dealing with Differences[63]

Ongoing Skill Development. Furthermore, the community must consider how it will continually strengthen the peacemaking skills of all members. Ongoing training should be informed by a regular needs identification and analysis related to the community's capacity in both relationship conflict and task conflict.[64] *Relationship conflict* includes the interpersonal incompatibilities that exist between people, including tension, animosity, and annoyance.[65] *Task conflict* includes the disagreements about the content of the task and how the task should be conducted.[66] Each type of conflict requires different skills for resolving and promoting peace. Needs assessment at the individual, team, and organizational levels is necessary to develop training and communication targeted for the community's specific needs.

2. Supporting Practice and Feedback on Conflict Skills

The attitudes and behaviors of team or organizational leaders impact their community's commitment to healthy conflict. Leaders who both model healthy conflict and provide feedback to their team members regarding conflict behaviors reinforce a culture of goodness. Leaders encourage the healthy expression of conflict by providing feedback. The Peacemaker's Pledge, issued by Peacemaker Ministries, is an excellent framework by which

---

[63] Adopted from "Dealing with Differences." Workshop, InterVarsity Christian Fellowship Kenya Global Project, Nairobi, June 2001.
[64] Kudonoo, Schroeder, & Boysen-Rotelli, "An Olympic Transformation," p. 57.
[65] Ibid. p. 53.
[66] Ibid. p. 53.

teams and organizations can discuss and commit to peacemaking competencies within their community. The Peacemaker's Pledge is included in the addendum at the end of this chapter.

According to organizational development experts, David Cooperrider and Diana Whitney, "words create worlds in unintended ways."[67] Leadership-in-community strives to create an atmosphere where conflict is given healthy, explicit expression so that it can be dealt with in a way that creates new meanings and possibilities for the team and their mission.[68] Unexpressed conflict that remains in the heads and hearts of members festers into resentments and brittle relationships into the future. These unspoken conflicts damage the culture of goodness of the community.

The GHOST Protocol. A helpful protocol that guides healthy expressions of conflict is the GHOST Protocol. This framework helps team members proceed through conflict conversations successfully.

- **G – Gentle**. Agree to speak gently with each other.

- **H – Honest.** Speak honestly with each other about the issues involved in the conflict as well as each other's experiences of the conflict.

- **O – Open.** Be open to hearing and receiving new information from the other person that may influence how you perceive the conflict.

- **S – Specific.** Clarify the meaning of your words by using specific explanations and examples. Because words create worlds, each member may use the same word to describe different experiences.

- **T – Talk!** Do not avoid expressing conflict but take the necessary risks to talk about the conflict in a manner that helps the other person keep listening.[69]

The GHOST Protocol also provides leadership-in-community a framework for training, coaching, and providing feedback to their team members. Feedback on peacemaking skills is useful for team members to "test the reality

[67] David L. Cooperrider & Diana Whitney, "A Positive Revolution in Change: Appreciative Inquiry," in *Appreciative Inquiry: Foundations in Positive Organization Development*, Eds. D. Cooperrider, P. Sorensen, T. Yaeger, & D. Whitney (Champaign: Stipes Publishing L.L.C., 2005) p. 30.
[68] Kudonoo, Schroeder, & Boysen-Rotelli, "An Olympic Transformation," p. 58.
[69] ADR Daily, "GHOST Principle: Protocol for Conflict Resolution," ADR Daily (blog), June 6, 2017, https://adrdaily.com/ghost-principle-protocol-conflict-resolution/

of [their] perceptions, reactions, observations or intentions; share feelings; influence a person to start, stop or modify a behavior; and help the recipient increase personal and interpersonal effectiveness."[70]

3. Developing Team Effectiveness in Addressing Conflict

In this area of focus, leadership-in-community expands the scope of peacemaking skills from individuals to the whole team.[71] The goal is to build trust through conflict so that the members experience increasingly strong team relationships. What may surprise some is that conflict is necessary for strong relationships! The differences between people force the team into expansive thinking that helps each member get to know the others better and spark creative solutions to the issues.[72] The problems in conflict occur when we turn off the GHOST Protocol, make fatal assumptions about the other, and fail to appreciate and value their differences.

Path to Action. Leadership-in-community encourages its members to master the story of conflict. Implicit in any conflict are the narratives that we construct tacitly in our minds about both the conflict and the others with whom we are in conflict.[73] In fact, we do not react to the conflict itself; we react to the story we tell ourselves about the conflict.[74] In any conflict we face, we must first master the story we tell ourselves so that we can enter into the conflict with a peacemaker's mindset.

The Path to Action, presented in Figure 7, explains how our emotions, thoughts, and experiences lead to our actions. When we are unaware of the functional narratives that we tell ourselves during a conflict, we give those stories power to control us and our responses to others.[75]

---

[70] Kudonoo, Schroeder, & Boysen-Rotelli, "An Olympic Transformation," p. 59.

[71] Ibid. p. 60.

[72] Brown & Sandage, "Relational Integration, Part II," p. 183.

[73] Kerry Patterson, Joseph Grenny, Ron McMillan, & Al Switzler, *Crucial Conversations: Tools for Talking When Stakes are High* (New York: McGraw-Hill, 2002), p. 98-101.

[74] Ibid.

[75] Ibid. p. 101.

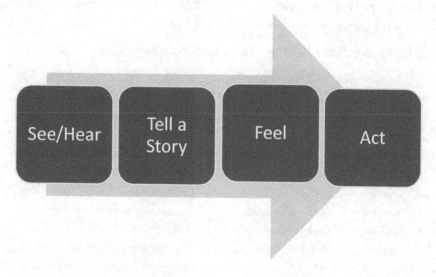

Figure 8: The Path to Action[76]

Mastering the story requires a level of emotional intelligence to manage our emotions during conflict so that we can step back and explore the stories operating in our minds and hearts.[77] When we have taken the time to articulate that story for ourselves, we can then enter into a GHOST dialogue with the other in order to test our assumptions, listen to the others' perspectives, and understand their stories. Healthy dialogue creates a pool of shared meaning from which every party to the conflict can draw new understandings with more complete and accurate information.[78]

The SBI Feedback Method. A helpful tool for mastering the story through dialogue is the SBI Feedback Method. The SBI Feedback method helps us communicate to others so that they can hear what we are saying as we invite them to dialogue with us.[79] The steps of the SBI Feedback Method are:

- **S – Capture the Situation**

---

[76] Ibid. p. 99.
[77] Kudonoo, Schroeder, & Boysen-Rotelli, "An Olympic Transformation," p. 59.
[78] Patterson et al., *Crucial Conversations*, p. 21.
[79] Center for Creative Leadership, "The SBI Feedback Method," in *Feedback that Works: How to Build and Deliver Your Message* 2nd ed. (Greensboro: CCL Press, 2019).

In this stage, we anchor our feedback in the specific situation in which the other person's behavior occurred.[80] Describing the location and events specifically provides context for the other person so that he or she can remember the circumstances and what he or she was thinking at the time.[81]

- **B – Describe the Behavior**

Next, we describe the specific behaviors of the other person. The biggest mistake commonly made in this step is to communicate judgment of the other person's behavior using adjectives.[82] For example, a statement such as "you were rude during that meeting" is a judgment about a perceived behavior. Rather, in this step, we describe the behaviors specifically to give the other person information about them.[83] For example, a statement such as "you spoke at the same time I was trying to speak" describes the specific behavior.

- **I – Explain the Impact**

Finally, we explain the impact of the other person's behavior on ourselves or others.[84] We should avoid explaining the impact the other person's behavior *might have* on the organization, coworkers, clients, or others.[85] Rather, we focus on the impact that we and others experienced as a result of their behavior. The following format can be used in explaining impact: "When you said/did _____, I felt/was _____."[86]

Once we have explained the impact, we can invite the other to respond and share information with us about why they behaved the way they did. Following the GHOST Protocol during this dialogue allows the conversation to construct meaning and trust in the relationship, rather than build barriers to trust.

Listening for Interests. An important skill in conflict dialogue is to listen for interests. Often, conflict gets stuck at the point of a person or group's position. A position is a "desired outcome or definable perspective on an issue."[87] Interests, on the other hand, are the underlying concerns, desires, needs, limitations, or values that motivate a person's or group's positions.[88] If parties to a conflict stay on the level of positions, they may never find

---

[80] Ibid.
[81] Ibid.
[82] Ibid.
[83] Ibid.
[84] Ibid.
[85] Ibid.
[86] Ibid.
[87] Sande, *The Peacemaker*, p. 234.
[88] Ibid.

positive solutions and create peace. However, if they can share their own interests and listen for the interests of others, they may be able to find new and creative solutions that satisfy everyone. The key in the dialogue is to keep asking one another "Why?" and "Why not?" at the appropriate times.[89]

4. Encouraging Social Relations in Organizations

While it may seem like a very simple idea, this area of focus encourages team members to become friends. Strong social relationships between team members can, indeed, lead to higher levels of comfort in working through conflicts with one another.[90] Friendships allow team members to view others as human beings, with their own histories, experiences, hopes, desires, and problems. Consequently, friendships build empathy that fosters respect, consideration, and appreciation for one another. They break apart the categorizations and stereotypes of "in-group/out-group" mentalities that impede real listening and learning from one another.

5. Promoting an Open Environment for Transparency of Conflict

The final area of focus for skill development in peacemaking is to promote an open environment for healthy conflict. Unfortunately, many organizations and leaders are uncomfortable with conflict, choosing to attack it, avoid it, or sweep it under the rug. However, when unexpressed conflict happens, and people are not given an opportunity to express and safely work through it, the conflict tends to fester and grow. It leads to resentments, stereotypes, bad will, and simmering anger between people. Eventually, these unresolved conflicts tend to find the "cracks" through which they can come out, albeit in toxic and destructive ways. They leak out through gossip, sarcasm, or contempt. Or they burst out in eruptions of anger or even violence. Creating a transparent environment enables people and teams to manage their conflicts so that they lead to peace.

The Triphonic Levels of Communication. When thinking about conflict, it is helpful to consider three levels in which all communication occurs. When we communicate at only one or two of these levels, we miss very important data that leads to understanding, empathy, and true resolution of issues.[91] Cultural engagement expert Darrell Bock describes these three triphonic levels as follows:

---

[89] Ibid. p. 237.
[90] Kudonoo, Schroeder, & Boysen-Rotelli, "An Olympic Transformation," p. 59.
[91] Bock, *Cultural Intelligence*, p. 54.

- *Triphonics Level 1: Facts*

At this level of communication, we are dealing only with the substantive issues at hand.[92] Here, we concentrate on what we observe in order to make assertions, build evidence, and persuade others to our point of view.[93] While this is a necessary level of communication, the misunderstandings in conflict occur when we stay on this level. It sets up the communication as a debate rather than a conversation.[94] It denies the relational dynamics occurring underneath the surface.

- *Triphonics Level 2: Filters*

The second level of communication is the combination of emotions, perceptions, and judgments we make about the facts of the first level.[95] Here, we recognize that people can look at the same set of facts and yet read them in vastly different ways.[96] When teams recognize that these filters are in play during conversations, they realize that the communication must drive toward some degree of mutual understanding before the team can progress.[97] At this stage, the GHOST Protocol and the SBI Feedback Method are very useful in building shared meaning. The goal at this level is respectful dialogue.

- *Triphonics Level 3: Identity*

Level 3 is the most overlooked level of communication. At this level, we recognize that how members see themselves is also at stake in any conversation and conflict.[98] The question that parties to the conflict are asking is how their identity and self-understanding will be impacted by what they are discussing.[99] Bock articulates the following questions that the parties may ask: *What is at stake for me in this conversation, and how am I seen as a result? How am I impacted in my soul by what is happening? How is this playing out? Am I looking good or bad?*[100] The identity dynamics that happen at level 3 fuel how a person responds in the other two levels.

The triphonic levels of communication reveal that conflicts involve both task and relational dynamics. But it is the relational dynamics that are most likely to add the heat to conflict situations. At the relational level of

---

[92] Ibid.
[93] Ibid.
[94] Ibid. p. 55.
[95] Ibid.
[96] Ibid.
[97] Ibid. p. 56.
[98] Ibid. p. 58.
[99] Ibid.
[100] Ibid.

conflict, the identities of each party are at stake. Leadership-in-community must create an environment where those relational and identity dynamics can be expressed, without shame, in order to build understanding and strong relationships.

Establishing a Relationship Restoration Ritual. A vital component of creating a goodness culture is to establish a restoration ritual. Once established, organizations and teams can communicate this ritual, stress the community's commitment to the ritual, and build the accountability structures that empower people to express and manage their conflicts effectively.

Figure 9 presents the Restoration Process for Relationship Conflict Model. This model guides organizations and teams in developing a restoration process that fits their specific organizational contexts. The model begins with the violation. A violation occurs when one party perceives a disequilibrium in their relationship with another person or with their team.[101] Violations disrupt the social order of the team and jeopardize core needs of the one who has been offended.[102] Because healthy relationships are the lifeblood of organizations, these violations will impede individual, group, and organizational performance.[103]

In a transparent environment, the violation triggers a four-stage process for righting the wrong and restoring relationships:

- **Stage 1: Challenge** – The offended party calls attention to his or her perceived grievance by naming it, attributing responsibility for the harm, and voicing his or her complaint explicitly.[104] The SBI Feedback Model is a helpful tool during the challenge stage.

- **Stage 2: Offering** – Upon receiving the challenge, the offender makes an offering that conveys his or her knowledge of the offense and its consequences for the person offended. The offender can apologize, offer an explanation, provide recompense, or any other type of offering appropriate for the situation. Above all, the offender must

---

[101] Hong Ren & Barbara Gray, "Repairing Relationship Conflict: How Violation Types and Culture Influence the Effectiveness of Restoration Rituals," *The Academy of Management Review* 34, no. 1 (2009), p. 106.
[102] Ibid.
[103] Ibid. p. 105.
[104] Ibid. p. 107-108.

display a sincere desire to restore what has been jeopardized for the offended person.[105]

- **Stage 3: Acceptance** – The offended person can accept or reject the offering, extend forgiveness, and revise his or her assessments of the offender. In the offering stage, the offended person may even discover that his or her own behaviors contributed to the conflict.[106] Therefore, in the acceptance stage, he or she may "get the log out" of his or her eye (Matt. 7:5, ESV) by acknowledging and confessing his or her contribution.[107]

- **Stage 4: Thanks** – Finally, the relationship is restored by an expression of gratitude.[108] In this stage, both parties forgive one another and commit once again to the relationship.[109]

---

[105] Ibid. p. 108.
[106] Ibid.
[107] Sande, *The Peacemaker*, p. 117-135.
[108] Ren & Gray, "Repairing Relationship Conflict," p. 108.
[109] Sande, *The Peacemaker*, p. 207-210.

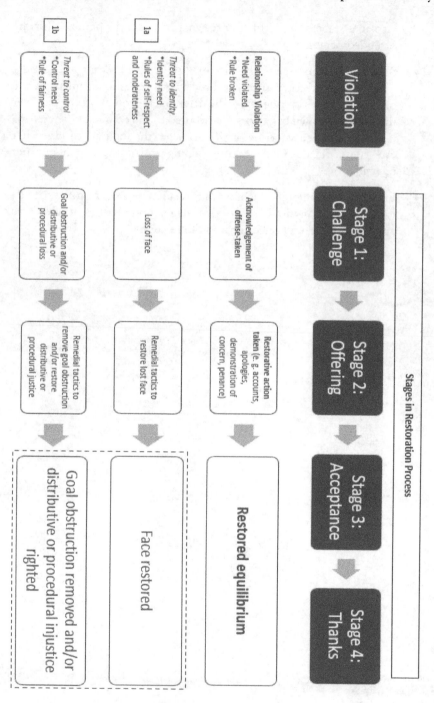

Figure 9: Restoration Process for Relationship Conflict[110]

The model illustrates that relationship violations include two threats: threats to *identity* and threats to *control*. An effective restoration ritual that builds a transparent environment must address both identity and control losses for the offended person. Identity violations occur when the offender crosses boundaries that preserve the identity of the offended, whether knowingly or not, during an interaction.[111] In other words, the offended person "loses face" in terms of both his or her own self-respect and the consideration others in the group show him or her.[112] Sociologist Erving Goffman explained "face" this way:

> A person may be said to *have*, or *be in*, or *maintain* face when the line he effectively takes presents an image of him that is internally consistent, that is supported by judgments and evidence conveyed by other participants, and that is confirmed by evidence conveyed through impersonal agencies in the situation.[113]

Identities are continually socially negotiated.[114] Therefore, when an offender responds to an offended person in a manner that is inconsistent with the offended person's sense of identity, the offender has caused the offended person to lose face. The ultimate goal of restoration regarding loss of identity is to restore face for the offended person.

Control violations occur when an offender blocks an individual's goals or impedes his or her access to the resources necessary to achieve those goals.[115] Control violations are issues of distributive and procedural justice.[116] The ultimate goal for restoration of control violations is to remove the obstacles to the offended person's achievement of his or her goals, including access to the resources he or she needs to achieve those goals.

While establishing a Restoration Ritual in a community, leaders must address both identity and control issues. When both are satisfied, the relationships between people and the equilibrium of the social order are restored into a flourishing, goodness culture where the team may continue to expand the horizons of their mission.

---

[111] Ibid. p. 111.

[112] Ibid.

[113] Erving Goffman, *Interaction Ritual: Essays on Face-to-Face Behavior* (Garden City: Anchor Books, 1967), p. 7.

[114] Ren & Gray, "Repairing Relationship Conflict," p. 111.

[115] Ibid. p. 112.

[116] Ibid.

Movement 4: *Oratio*

Heavenly Father,

You said, *Blessed are the peacemakers.*

Help us to become peacemakers. Show us how.

Where can we show up?
Where can we be present where there is no peace?
What conflict do we need to go toward, not run from?
Where do we need to speak up for reconciliation?
To whom do we need to listen?
Where is our opportunity to make peace?

Thank you for those who defend the poor and powerless all over the world today. Thank you for those who devote their lives to the cause of nonviolence, restoration, and healing. May they know the blessing of your comfort and refreshment.

Help us all to notice in our own lives where we can invite and create peace – and nudge us to act.[117]

In Jesus' name, Amen.

Movement 5: *Imitatio*

🔸 Individual Reflection

    o Journal your responses to the following questions:

        ▪ What key points is God leading you to embrace and grow into?

        ▪ How can you live this out in your life and leadership?

        ▪ How can your missional leadership group pray for you in living this out?

🔸 Group Reflection

    o In your missional leadership group, share your individual reflections with each other.

    o Pray for one another.

---

[117] Prayer adapted from the ancient spiritual practice of the Prayer Wheel. Dodd, Riess, & Van Biema, *The Prayer Wheel*, p. 25.

Movement 6: *Missio*

- Experiencing Mission
  - Level 1 *Awareness*
    - Pray each day that the Lord sends you into his mission that day.
    - At the end of each day, reflect on or journal about one experience you had that day where you witnessed the *missio Dei* personally. Describe what happened. What was significant about that experience for you?
  - Level 2 *Personal Commitment*
    - Ask the Lord where he may be sending you to be his witness on a regular basis.
    - Make a commitment to serve in that way.

Movement 7: *Communio*

- Experiencing Mission
  - Level 3 *Group Experience*
    - If possible, the small group may consider performing a mission or service project together to experience mission as a community.

- Group Reflection
  - Where did you see the *missio Dei* in action this past week?
  - What was the most significant or surprising observations you made about your experience?
  - What did you learn about God from that experience? What did you learn about yourself from that experience?
  - What difference does that make in your leadership? How will you apply what you have learned?

Movement 8: *Contemplatio*

Each week in your small group, spend time reflecting and celebrating the ways that you have seen "God on the move" in the past week.

✦ Spend some time in prayer or singing in thanksgiving and praise to our missionary God.

Addendum: The Peacemaker's Pledge[118]

As people reconciled to God by the death and resurrection of Jesus Christ, we believe that we are called to respond to conflict in a way that is remarkably different from the way the world deals with conflict.[1]

We also believe that conflict provides opportunities to glorify God, serve other people, and grow to be like Christ.[2]

Therefore, in response to God's love and in reliance on his grace, we commit ourselves to respond to conflict according to the following principles:

Glorify God — Instead of focusing on our own desires or dwelling on what others may do, we will rejoice in the Lord and bring him praise by depending on his forgiveness, wisdom, power, and love, as we seek to faithfully obey his commands and maintain a loving, merciful, and forgiving attitude.[3]

Get the Log out of Your Eye — Instead of blaming others for a conflict or resisting correction, we will trust in God's mercy and take responsibility for our own contribution to conflicts—confessing our sins to those we have wronged, asking God to help us change any attitudes and habits that lead to conflict, and seeking to repair any harm we have caused.[4]

Gently Restore — Instead of pretending that conflict doesn't exist or talking about others behind their backs, we will overlook minor offenses or we will talk personally and graciously with those whose offenses seem too serious to overlook, seeking to restore them rather than condemn them. When a conflict with a Christian brother or sister cannot be resolved in private, we will ask others in the body of Christ to help us settle the matter in a biblical manner.[5]

Go and be reconciled — Instead of accepting premature compromise or allowing relationships to wither, we will actively pursue genuine peace and reconciliation—forgiving others as God, for Christ's sake, has forgiven us, and seeking just and mutually beneficial solutions to our differences.[6]

By God's grace, we will apply these principles as a matter of stewardship, realizing that conflict is an assignment, not an accident. We will remember that success in

---

[118] Sande, *The Peacemaker*, p. 259-261

God's eyes is not a matter of specific results, but of faithful, dependent obedience. And we will pray that our service as peacemakers will bring praise to our Lord and lead others to know His infinite love.[7]

---

[1] Matt. 5:9; Luke 6:27-36; Gal. 5:19-26.

[2] Rom. 8:28-29; 1 Cor. 10:31-11:1; James 1:2-4.

[3] Ps. 37:1-6; Mark 11:25; John 14:15; Rom. 12:17-21; 1 Cor. 10:31; Phil. 4:2-9; Col. 3:1-4; James 3:17-18; 4:1-3; 1 Peter 2:12.

[4] Prov. 28:13; Matt. 7:3-5; Luke 19:8; Col. 3:5-14; 1 John 1:8-9.

[5] Prov. 19:11; Matt. 18:15-20; 1 Cor. 6:1-8; Gal. 6:1-2; Eph. 4:29; 2 Tim. 2:24-26; James 5:9.

[6] Matt. 5:23-24; 6:12; 7:12; Eph. 4:1-3, 32; Phil. 2:3-4.

[7] Matt. 25:14-21; John 13:34-35; Rom. 12:18; 1 Peter 2:19; 4:19.

Conclusion:

The Rest of God

In the 2019 film *Godzilla: King of Monsters*, directed by Michael Dougherty, Dr. Emma Russell, a paleobiologist, uses a device called the Orca to emit bioacoustic frequencies to control the behavior of giant monsters, called Titans, that have been discovered lying asleep and hidden all over the planet. Emma works for Monarch, the organization that discovered the creatures and has been monitoring them for the past five years since two had awakened and left a trail of devastation. In those tragic events, Emma and her now estranged husband, Dr. Mark Russell, an animal behavior specialist who co-created the Orca with Emma, lost their son, Andrew. That event pushed the couple apart. Mark retreated to an isolated life of wildlife photography. Emma immersed herself in her work with Monarch to save the world from future havoc wrought by the Titans.

Emma and her daughter Madison are kidnapped by a group of ecoterrorists, led by former British Army Colonel Alan Jonah, a mercenary who has become disillusioned with humanity. Jonah's anarchist group traffics Titan DNA and intends to awaken them to restore the natural balance of the Earth. He believes that Emma and the Orca are the key to his plans. However, as the story progresses, we discover that Emma colluded with Jonah to stage the kidnapping. She is in league with Jonah and falls in with his plan to awaken the Titans. After the terrorists sabotage a Monarch facility in Antarctica and, with Emma's help, awaken the three-headed monster, Ghidorah, Monarch and Mark discover the shocking truth about Emma's intentions. In a scene where Emma contacts Monarch to explain, she divulges the motivation for her betrayal:

> **Colonel Diane Foster** (leader of the Monarch's special military force): Trust is a little hard to come by, Dr. Russell. Especially after what you pulled.
>
> **Dr. Emma Russell**: I know. And, uh, I can only imagine what you're all thinking. But if there were any other way to do this, I would.
>
> **Dr. Mark Russell**: Do what, Emma?
>
> **Emma:** I'm saving the world.
>
> **Mark:** By releasing those things? That doesn't make sense.
>
> **Emma:** As impossible as it seems, it does. Hear me out, Mark. After we lost Andrew, I swore his death would not be in vain. That I would find an answer. A solution to why the Titans were rising. But as I dug deeper, I realized that they were here for a reason. And that despite all

the years that we spent trying to stop them, we never dared to confront the truth.

Mark: Which truth?

Emma: Humans have been the dominant species for thousands of years and look what's happened. Overpopulation. Pollution. War. The mass extinction we feared has already begun. *And we are the cause. We are the infection.* But like all living organisms, the Earth unleashed a fever to fight this infection, its original and rightful rulers, the Titans. They are part of the Earth's natural defense system. A way to protect the planet, to maintain its balance. But if governments are allowed to contain them, destroy them, or use them for war, the human infection will only continue to spread. And within our lifetime, our planet will perish, and so will we. Unless we restore balance.

Dr. Rick Stanton (Monarch's crypto-sonographer): And what's gonna be left if you do this? A dead, charred world overrun by monsters?

Emma: No, Dr. Stanton, the exact opposite. Just like how a forest fire replenishes the soil, or how a volcano creates new land, we have seen signs that these creatures will do the same. San Francisco, Las Vegas, wherever the Titans go, life follows, triggered by their radiation. They are the only thing that can reverse the destruction that we started. They are the only guarantee that life will carry on. But for that to happen, we must set them free.

Dr. Ilene Chen (a Monarch operative and mythologist): You are murdering the world.

Emma: No. Because as difficult as this will be, I promise, humanity will not go extinct. Using the Orca, we will return to a natural order. A forgotten order where we coexisted in balance with the Titans, the first gods.[1]

What is the message conveyed by this film? The narrative depicts a world in which humankind is the problem – an infection, an invasive species that, through its dominance, destroys the earth. The only hope for this earth is to awaken the "the first gods," the warring Titans, some benevolent toward humans and some not. These gods may return the earth to its primordial, uncultivated "balance" through their domination and conflict. So much of

---

[1] *Godzilla: King of Monsters.* Directed by Michael Dougherty. Screenplay by Michael Dougherty & Zach Shields. Story by Max Borenstein, Michael Dougherty, & Zach Shields. Burbank: Legendary Pictures Productions LLC, 2019.

our current non-Christian or post-Christian environments propagate the same belief that humans are merely helpless pawns amidst the random, meaningless forces that act upon this world. The spiritual, environmental, political, economic, or cultural "Titans" around us often make us feel small, fearful, and without hope.

But in contrast to *Godzilla's* pessimistic vision of creation's purpose and human agency, Scripture presents a beautiful picture of a world, lovingly and purposefully ordered by our creative God. In this garden, he places his image – the humans. Humans are not an infection! We are regents of God who he has commissioned to continue his creative work. We have a wonderful purpose to cultivate this garden and give it meaning as we extend the good reign of God, who we image, to the ends of the earth. And we do that through relationships of peace with God and with others.

The Scripture's alternative vision to *Godzilla's* nihilistic narrative is one in which human flourishing, under the redemptive reign of King Jesus, the ultimate *imago Dei*, is the hope of the entire cosmos. Luci Shaw's poem, *seventh day*, captures this vision poignantly:

Seventh day

  Come Adam, son, mirror of myself,
   walk with me, talk, tell me
    do you see over there (your heart stirring)
  the grey down-dappled foals, ungainly,
    galloping down the brow of the world
  (fresh cooled with milky light, and
    frosted with sharp first foliage below)?
  How startled the bird is
   at their hoofs' unheard-of thunder!
  She springs unthinking
    into her first fine tentative lonely flight
   splitting the unwinged space
    beyond this perfect hill.

  And Eve, as the clean mist unveils
    the unscarred grassy slope,
     distills, drips fragrant from the twigs
  to water the primeval greenery,
   do you smell now, on the warm-breathing breeze
   the fertile flavors of my undepleted earth?

damp subtle essences of unploughed plains?

Listen, you two, gathering bunches from my heavy vines
 (purple and green and swung from tender stems
 with fragile bloom unrubbed)
   do you hear ground-hogs rooting happily
   in the rich undergrowth?

Below you, down a dustless avenue of oaks
 greenwashed as this first spring
 cool runs the river. Does it delight you both
 poured from my palm into my finger's furrow?
Up through the water shines the unmined gold
 and the thin silver slivers of the fish.

But here and now on your mid-morning hilltop,
  innocents, touch each other's hands, hold, yield yourselves together
  and fulfill the ardent rhythm of the sun.
Bathe in the blue aisles of light over you
and in them feel the farthest reaches of my love
 and urgent joy, in you,
Laugh with me! Join in my delight!

Now restunder my hand, which also rests today.
 For your strong answering pleasure in my toil, my
 touch, is my contentedness.[2]

The rest of God is the hope of our leadership-in-community (Gen. 2;
Heb. 4). It is *shalôm* – the consummation of God's kingdom where the
formless and empty has finally been filled with life and the whole cosmos is
the sanctuary of God's presence and good reign. To be properly oriented
toward the Kingdom of God, the leadership-in-community that we have
explored throughout this study must be guided by this ultimate vision of the
rest of God. Scot McKnight explains:

> Peace was at the core of what Jesus meant by kingdom.
> Kingdom means love, justice, and peace.
> Kingdom means love, justice, and peace in a society.
> Kingdom means love, justice, and peace in a society on earth.

---

[2] Luci Shaw, "seventh day," in *Polishing the Petoskey Stone*, p. 70-71.

As in heaven.

Jesus prayed for this very thing.

We are to pray for love, justice, and peace in society every day.[3]

Our leadership-in-community is our priestly role as God's image-bearers in this world as we pray for his Kingdom to come. And so, as we depart from this study, may the vision of the apostle John burn in our hearts and orient our missional leadership:

Then I saw a new heaven and a new earth. The first heaven and the first earth had disappeared. Now there was no sea. And I saw the holy city, the new Jerusalem, coming down out of heaven from God. It was prepared like a bride dressed for her husband.

I heard a loud voice from the throne. It said, "Now God's home is with people. He will live with them. They will be his people. God himself will be with them and will be their God. He will wipe away every tear from their eyes. There will be no more death, sadness, crying, or pain. All the old ways are gone."

The one who was sitting on the throne said, "Look, I am making everything new!" Then he said, "write this, because these words are true and can be trusted."

The one on the throne said to me, "It is finished! I am the Alpha and the Omega, the Beginning and the End. I will give free water from the spring of the water of life to anyone who is thirsty. All those who win the victory will receive all this. And I will be their God, and they will be my children. But those who are cowards, those who refuse to believe, those who do terrible things, those who kill, those who sin sexually, those who do evil magic, those who worship idols, and those who tell lies – they will all have a place in the lake of burning sulfur. This is the second death."

...I did not see a temple in the city. The Lord God All-Powerful and the Lamb were the city's temple. The city did not need the sun or the moon to shine on it. The glory of God gave the city light. The Lamb was the city's lamp.

The people of the world will walk by the light given by the Lamb. The rulers of the earth will bring their glory into the city. The city's gates will never close on any day, because there is no night there. The

---

[3] Scot McKnight, *One.Life: Jesus Calls, We Follow* (Grand Rapids: Zondervan, 2010), p. 77.

greatness and honor of the nations will be brought into the city. Nothing unclean will ever enter the city. No one who does shameful things or tells lies will ever enter the city. Only those whose names are written in the Lamb's book of life will enter the city. (Rev. 21:1-8; 22-27)

Leadership Declaration

Appendix A is a template for a Leadership Declaration. As you complete the journey through this study on leadership-in-community, now is an excellent time to reflect on your experience and consider the Lord's calling upon you in his great mission. The Leadership Declaration is designed to guide you through a process to reflect on the leadership themes in this curriculum, as well as your own leadership history, and draft a commitment to grow into leadership-in-community.

Once drafted, your Leadership Declaration will exist to challenge and prompt you toward continual growth into your desired leadership. It contains four sections:

1. **Leadership Philosophy**: Your leadership philosophy is a brief paragraph that presents how you think about leadership – how you define leadership and how leadership functions in the mission of God. This philosophy will emerge through your reflections on your experience through this spiritual formation curriculum, the significant moments in your life that have shaped you, and what legacy you wish for your leadership to leave behind.

2. **Leadership Declaration**: Your leadership declaration is a one- or two-sentence expression of the vision and purpose of your leadership. Here, you are declaring something to be true about your leadership that orients you toward that vision throughout your life.

3. **Leadership Guiding Principles**: Your guiding principles are a bullet point list of the values and priorities that will guide your leadership toward your leadership vision. These principles may come from significant Scriptures or leadership themes that you encountered during this curriculum.

4. **Leadership Commitment**: Your leadership commitment is the specific action steps that you will take to grow into your vision for your leadership. This section may also be a bullet point list of commitments that begin with the phrase, "I commit to…"

Once you have drafted your Leadership Declaration, share it with your community group and seek their feedback and prayer for you. Finally, get into a regular habit of reflecting on your Leadership Declaration in prayer. As the Lord continues to guide and grow you, this reflection may be an occasion for celebration, for recommitment, or for change.

Closing Blessing

May the words of this prayer of blessing encourage and cover you as you grow into the vision of your leadership that God has given you through this study:

> *May the Father of Life pour out His grace on you;*
> *may you feel His hand in everything you do*
> *and be strengthened by the things He brings you through:*
> *this is my prayer for you.*
>
> *May the Son of God be Lord in all your ways;*
> *may He shepherd you the length of all your days,*
> *and in your heart may He receive the praise:*
> *this is my prayer for you.*
>
> *And despite how simple it may sound,*
> *I pray that His grace will abound*
> *and motivate everything you do;*
> *and may the fullness of His love be shared through you.*
>
> *May His Spirit comfort you, and make you strong,*
> *may He discipline you gently when you're wrong,*
> *and in your heart may He give you a song:*
> *this is my prayer for you.*
>
> *May Jesus be Lord in all your ways,*
> *may He shepherd you the length of all your days,*
> *and in your heart may He receive the praise:*
> *this is my prayer for you, my prayer for you.*[4]

---

[4] The Northumbria Community, *Celtic Daily Prayer*, p. 292-293.

Appendix A:

Leadership Declaration Template

Leadership Declaration

[Name]
[Organization]

[Date]

I. Leadership Philosophy

[Text]

Instruction: Write a brief 2 or 3 paragraph reflection on how you think about leadership now that you have completed the curriculum. The following questions will guide your reflection and help you draft your leadership philosophy:

- What Scriptures have influenced how you think about leadership?

- What is your vision of leadership?

- What do you sense God has spoken into your leadership through this spiritual formation curriculum?

- What fuels your sense of passion and meaning in leadership?

- What legacy of leadership do you want to leave behind?

- When you think over your life, what significant moments stand out to you that God has used to shape you as a leader?

- How do you want people to be impacted by your leadership during and after your interaction with them?

II. Leadership Declaration

[Text]

Instruction: Write in 1 or 2 sentences a statement of declaration that expresses succinctly the vision and purpose of your leadership. Make this statement broad enough that it will apply in any situation where you lead.

III. Leadership Guiding Principles

- [Leadership Principle]
- [Leadership Principle]

Instruction: Write out a set of guiding principles that will guide you to live out your leadership declaration. Write these principles out as bullet points in brief sentences that will be easy for you to remember. You may consider looking back through the curriculum to guide your thinking.

Recommendation: You may consider including a key Bible verse that speaks to each of your leadership principles. You may memorize these Bible verses so that you may meditate on them and allow the Holy Spirit to continue to speak into your leadership.

IV. Leadership Commitment

[Text]

Instruction: Write how you intend to make your leadership declaration a reality in your life. This can be either in paragraph or bullet point form. What specific actions will you take so that your leadership declaration grows in your heart, mind, and actions? If you choose a bullet point approach, you may begin each point with the phrase "I commit to…"

Bibliography

ADR Daily. "GHOST Principle: Protocol for Conflict Resolution." ADR Daily (blog), June 6, 2017, https://adrdaily.com/ghost-principle-protocol-conflict-resolution/

Ambrose, Colin M. "Desiring to Be Justified: An Examination of the Parable of the Good Samaritan in Luke 10:25-37." *Sewanee Theological Review* 54, no. 1 (2010): 17-28.

Argandoña, Antonio. "Fostering Values in Organizations." *Journal of Business Ethics* 45, no.1/2 (2003): 15-28.

St. Augustine. *Confessions of a Sinner* (translated by R. S. Pine-Coffin). London: Penguin Group, 2004.

Avolio, Bruce J. "Promoting More Integrative Strategies for Leadership Theory-Building." *American Psychologist* 62, no. 1 (2007): 25-33.

Barber, Michael Patrick. "Forgiving the Sinner: The Church as a Christ-like People in Matthew 18." *The Bible Today* 58, no. 1 (2020): 14-21.

Barna Group. *The Future of Missions: 10 Questions About Global Ministry the Church Must Answer with the Next Generation.* Ventura: Barna, 2020.

Beck, Richard. *Unclean: Meditations on Purity, Holiness, and Mortality.* Eugene: Cascade Books, 2011.

Bennema, Cornelius. "The Ethnic Conflict in Early Christianity: An Appraisal of Bauckham's Proposal on the Antioch Crisis and the Jerusalem Council." *Journal of the Evangelical Theological Society* 56, no. 4 (2013): 753-763.

Bible Odyssey, "The Good Samaritan," accessed December 7, 2020, https://bibleodyssey.org/tools/image-gallery/g/good-samaritan-van-gogh.

Blackwell, Ben C. "You Are Filled in Him: Theosis and Colossians 2-3." *Journal of Theological Interpretation* 8, no. 1 (2014): 103-123.

Bock, Darrell L. *Cultural Intelligence: Living for God in a Diverse, Pluralistic World.* Nashville: B&H Academic, 2020.

Boersma, Hans. *Violence, Hospitality, and the Cross: Reappropriating the Atonement Tradition.* Grand Rapids: Baker Academic, 2004.

Boice, James Montgomery. *Foundations of the Christian Faith: A Comprehensive & Readable Theology.* Downers Grove: InterVarsity Press, 1986.

Branson, Christopher M. "Achieving Organisational Change through Values Alignment." *Journal of Educational Administration* 46, no. 3 (2008): 376-395.

Brisson, E. Carson. "Between Text and Sermon: Matthew 25:14-30." *Interpretation* 56, no. 3 (2002): 307-310.

Bronnenmayer, Matias, Bernd W. Wirtz, & Vincent Göttel. "Determinants of Perceived Success in Management Consulting: An Empirical Investigation from the Consultant Perspective." *Management Research Review* 39, no. 6 (2016): 706-738.

Brown, Jeannine K. & Steven J. Sandage. "Relational Integration, Part II: Relational Integration as Developmental and Intercultural." *Journal of Psychology & Theology* 43, no. 3 (2015): 179-191.

Brown, Sherri. "Water Imagery and the Power and Presence of God in the Gospel of John." *Theology Today* 72, no. 3 (2015): 289-298.

Brown, Tim. *Change by Design: How Design Thinking Transforms Organizations and Inspires Innovation.* New York: HarperCollins, 2019.

Bruce, F. F. *The Book of Acts: New International Commentary on the New Testament.* Grand Rapids: William B. Eerdmans Publishing Co., n. d. Quoted in Kenneth R.Cooper, "The Tabernacle of David in Biblical Prophecy," *Bibliotheca Sacra* 168 (2011): 402-412.

Burris, Ronald. "Another Look at the Good Samaritan: Luke 10:25-37." *Review and Expositor* 114, no. 3 (2017): 457-461.

Carbery, Ronan. "Organizational Learning," in *Human Resource Development: A Concise Introduction,* Eds. Ronan Carbery & Christine Cross. London, UK: Palgrave, 2015, 84-102.

Carlson, Richard P. "Between Text and Sermon: Matthew 25:13-46." *Interpretation: A Journal of Bible and Theology* 69, no. 3 (2015): 344-346.

Carpenter, John B. "The Parable of the Talents in Missionary Perspective: A Call for an Economic Spirituality." *Missiology: An International Review* 25, no. 2 (1997): 165-181.

Carter, Terrell. "Love is the Appropriate Response: Colossians 3:12-17." *Review and Expositor* 116, no. 4 (2019): 475-478.

Carter, Warren. "Resisting and Imitating the Empire: Imperial Paradigms in Two Matthean Parables." *Interpretation* 56, no. 3 (2002): 260-272.

Center for Creative Leadership, "The Active Listening Skill Set" in *Active Listening: Improve Your Ability to Listen and Lead* 2nd ed. Greensboro: CCL Press, 2019.

Center for Creative Leadership. "The SBI Feedback Method," in *Feedback that Works: How to Build and Deliver Your Message* 2nd ed. Greensboro: CCL Press, 2019.

Charry, Ellen T. *God and the Art of Happiness*. Grand Rapids: William B. Eerdmans Publishing Company, 2010.

Chatterjee, Debashis. "Wise Ways: Leadership as Relationship." *Journal of Human Values* 12 (2006): 153-160.

Chenoweth, Ben. "Identifying the Talents: Contextual Clues for the Interpretation of the Parable of the Talents (Matthew 25:14-30)," *Tyndale Bulletin* 56, no. 1 (2005): 61-72.

Choi, Thomas Y., Kevin J. Dooley, & Manus Rungtusanatham. "Supply Networks and Complex Adaptive Systems: Control Versus Emergence." *Journal of Operations Management* 19 (2001): 351-366.

Collins, Jim. *Good to Great: Why Some Companies Make the Leap…and Others Don't*. New York: Harper Business, 2001.

Cooperrider, David L. & Diana Whitney. "A Positive Revolution in Change: Appreciative Inquiry," in *Appreciative Inquiry: Foundations in Positive Organization Development*, Eds. D. Cooperrider, P. Sorensen, T. Yaeger, & D. Whitney. Champaign: Stipes Publishing L.L.C., 2005: 9-34.

Cooperrider, David L., Diana Whitney, & Jacqueline M. Stavros. *Appreciative Inquiry Handbook: For Leaders of Change* 2nd ed. Brunswick: Crown Custom Publishing, Inc., 2008.

Costas, Orlando. *Christ Outside the Gate: Mission Beyond Christendom*. Eugene: Wipf & Stock Publishers, 1982.

Costas, Orlando E. *Liberating News: A Theology of Contextual Evangelization*. Eugene: Wipf and Stock Publishers, 1989.

Cox, Jr., Taylor. "The Multicultural Organization," *Academy of Management Executive* 5, no. 2 (1991): 34-47.

Cremer, Hermann. *Biblisch-theologisches Worterbuch*, 7th ed. Gotha: F. A. Perthes, 1893.

Crossan, John Dominic. "The Parables of Jesus." *Interpretation* 56, no. 3 (2002): 247-259.

Crouch, Andy. *Culture Making: Recovering Our Creative Calling.* Downers Grove: InterVarsity Press, 2009.

Crouch, Andy. *Playing God: Redeeming the Gift of Power.* Downers Grove: InterVarsity Press, 2013.

"Dealing with Differences." Adopted from Workshop, InterVarsity Christian Fellowship Kenya Global Project, Nairobi, June 2001.

De Boer, Martinus C. "Ten Thousand Talents? Matthew's Interpretation and Redaction of the Parable of the Unforgiving Servant (Matt 18:23-35)." *The Catholic Biblical Quarterly* 50, no. 2 (1988): 214-232.

Deffinbaugh, Robert. "The Work of the Ministry: The Meaning of New Testament Ministry." Bible.org, October 7, 1979: 1-10.

Deneen, Patrick J. *Why Liberalism Failed.* New Haven: Yale University Press, 2018.

Derrett, J. Duncan M. "Law in the New Testament: The Parable of the Talents and Two Logia." *Zeitschrift für die neutestamentliche Wissenschaft und die Kunde der älteren Kirche* 56, no. 3-4 (1965): 184-195.

DeSilva, David A. *An Introduction to the New Testament: Contexts, Methods & Ministry Formation.* Downers Grove: InterVarsity Press, 2004.

Dickson, John. *The Best Kept Secret of Christian Mission: Promoting the Gospel with More than Our Lips.* Grand Rapids: Zondervan, 2010.

Dinkler, Michal Beth. "New Testament Rhetorical Narratology: An Invitation Toward Integration." *Biblical Interpretation* 24 (2016): 203-228.

Dodd, Patton, Jana Riess & David Van Biema. *The Prayer Wheel: A Daily Guide to Renewing Your Faith with a Rediscovered Spiritual Practice.* New York: Convergent Books. 2018.

Douglas, J. D., F. F. Bruce, J. I. Packer, N. Hillyer, D. Guthrie, A. R. Millard, & D. J. Wiseman (Eds.). *New Bible Dictionary* 2nd ed. Downers Grove, InterVarsity Press, 1962.

Drath, Wilfred H. *The Deep Blue Sea: Rethinking the Source of Leadership.* San Francisco: Jossey-Bass, 2001. Kindle.

Drath, Wilfred H., Cynthia D. McCauley, Charles J. Palus, Ellen Van Velsor, Patricia M. G. O'Connor, & John B. McGuire. "Direction, Alignment,

Commitment: Toward a More Integrative Ontology of Leadership." *The Leadership Quarterly* 19 (2008): 635-653.

Dunnington, Kent. *Humility, Pride, and Christian Virtue Theory.* Oxford: Oxford University Press, 2019.

Dyck, Bruno & Kenman Wong. "Corporate Spiritual Disciplines and the Quest for Organizational Virtue." *Journal of Management, Spirituality & Religion* 7, no. 1 (2010): 7-29.

Eriksson, Per Erik, Pankaj C. Patel, David Rönnberg Sjödin, Johan Frishammar, & Vinit Parida. "Managing Interorganizational Innovation Projects: Mitigating the Negative Effects of Equivocality Through Knowledge Search Strategies." *Long Range Planning* 49 (2016): 691-705.

Escobar, Samuel. *The New Global Mission: The Gospel from Everywhere to Everyone.* Downers Grove: InterVarsity Press, 2003.

Esler, Philip E. "Jesus and the Reduction of Intergroup Conflict: The Parable of the Good Samaritan in Light of Social Identity Theory." *Biblical Interpretation* 8 (2000): 325-357.

ESV Study Bible. "Introduction to Leviticus." Wheaton: Crossway Bibles, 2008: 211-213.

Fichtner, Johannes. "πλησίον in the LXX and the Neighbour in the Old Testament," in *Theological Dictionary of the New Testament*, Ed. Gerhard Kittel & Gerhard Friedrich. Grand Rapids: William B. Eerdmans Publishing Company, 1977: 6.

Folarin, George O. "The Parable of the Talents in the African Context: An Intercultural Hermeneutics Approach." *Asia Journal of Theology* 22, no. 1 (2008): 94-106.

Franklin, Kirk. *Towards Global Missional Leadership: A Journey Through Leadership Paradigm Shift in the Mission of God.* Oxford: Regnum, 2017.

Georges, Jayson & Mark D. Baker. *Ministering in Honor-Shame Cultures: Biblical Foundations and Practical Essentials.* Downers Grove: IVP Academic, 2016.

Gervais, Timothy. "Acts 15 and Luke's Rejection of Pro-Circumcision Christianity." *Journal of Theta Alpha Kappa* 41, no. 2 (2017): 7-20.

Gitau, Wanjiru M. *Megachurch Christianity Reconsidered: Millennials and Social Change in African Perspective.* Downers Grove: IVP Academic, 2018.

Glenny, W. Edward. "The Septuagint and Apostolic Hermeneutics: Amos 9 in Acts 15." *Bulletin for Biblical Research* 22, no. 1 (2012): 1-26.

Godzilla: King of Monsters. Directed by Michael Dougherty. Screenplay by Michael Dougherty & Zach Shields. Story by Max Borenstein, Michael Dougherty, & Zach Shields.Burbank: Legendary Pictures Productions LLC, 2019.

Goffman, Erving. *Interaction Ritual: Essays on Face-to-Face Behavior.* Garden City: Anchor Books, 1967.

Goldingay, John. *Old Testament Ethics: A Guided Tour.* Downers Grove: IVP Academic, 2019.

Goroncy, Jason. "Ethnicity, Social Identity, and the Transposable Body of Christ." *Mission Studies* 34 (2017): 220-245.

Gould, Paul M. *Cultural Apologetics: Renewing the Christian Voice, Conscience, and Imagination in a Disenchanted World.* Grand Rapids: Zondervan, 2019.

Gow, Murray D. "Jesus and the Samaritan Woman." *Stimulus* 6, no. 1 (February 1998): 26-30.

Grandy, Gina & Martyna Sliwa. "Contemplative Leadership: The Possibilities for the Ethics of Leadership Theory and Practice." *Journal of Business Ethics* 143 (2017): 423-440.

Greenberg, Jan & Sandra Jordan. *Vincent van Gogh: Portrait of an Artist.* New York: Dell Yearling, 2001. Kindle.

Harrington, S. J., Daniel J. "Polemical Parables in Matthew 24-25." *Union Seminary Quarterly Review* 44 (1991): 287-298.

Harrison, Ircel. "A Word About…Equipping Leaders for Twenty-First Century Ministry." *Review and Expositor* 116, no. 4 (2019): 391-393.

Hauser, Alan Jon. "Jonah: In Pursuit of the Dove." *Journal of Biblical Literature* 104, no. 1 (1985): 21-37.

Hawthorne, Steven C. "The Honor and Glory of Jesus Christ: Heart of the Gospel and the Mission of God," in *Honor, Shame, and the Gospel: Reframing Our Message and Ministry,* Eds. Christopher Flanders & Werner Mischke. Littleton: William Carey Publishing, 2020.

Heimburger, Robert W., Christopher M. Hays, & Guillermo Mejía-Castillo. "Forgiveness and Politics: Reading Matthew 18:21-35 with Survivors of Armed Conflict in Colombia." *HTS Teologiese Studies/Theological Studies* 75, no. 4 (2019): 1-9.

Helland, Roger. "Nothing Leadership: The Locus of Missional Servantship," in *Servantship: Sixteen Servants on the Four Movements of Radical Servantship,* Ed. Graham Hill. Eugene: Wipf & Stock Publishers, 2013.

Hertig, Paul. "The Powerful and Vulnerable Intercultural Encounters with Jesus." *Mission Studies* 32 (2015): 292-314.

Hiebert, Paul G. *The Gospel in Human Contexts: Anthropological Explorations for Contemporary Missions.* Grand Rapids: Baker Academic, 2009.

Hill, Graham. "The Theology and Practices of Self-Emptying, Missional Servantship," in *Servantship: Sixteen Servants on the Four Movements of Radical Servantship*, Ed. Graham Hill. Eugene: Wipf & Stock Publishers, 2013.

Hill, Graham. *GlobalChurch: Reshaping Our Conversations, Renewing Our Mission, Revitalizing Our Churches.* Downers Grove: InterVarsity Press, 2016.

Hill, Graham. *Salt, Light, and a City: Ecclesiology for the Global Missional Community, Volume 1: Western Voices* 2nd ed. Eugene: Cascade Books, 2017.

Hill, Graham. *Salt, Light, and a City: Conformation – Ecclesiology for the Global Missional Community, Volume 2: Majority World Voices* 2nd ed. Eugene: Cascade Books, 2020.

Hobbie, Peter H. "1 Peter 2:2-10." *Interpretation* 47, no. 2 (1993): 170-173.

Hock, Ronald F. "Romancing the Parables of Jesus." *Perspectives in Religious Studies* 29, no. 1 (2002): 11-37.

"Honor and Shame as (New) Covenant Language." HonorShame (blog). Honorshame.com, June 3, 2020, http://honorshame.com/honor-and-shame-as-new-covenant-language/.

Hugo, Victor (Translated by Isabel F. Hapgood). *Les Misérables.* San Diego: Canterbury Classics, 2015.

Hylen, Susan E. "Forgiveness and Life in Community." *Interpretation* 54, no. 2 (2000): 146-157.

Illian, Bridget. "Church Discipline and Forgiveness in Matthew 18:15-35." *Currents in Theology and Mission* 37, no. 6 (2010): 444-450.

Innes, James E. & David E. Booher. "Consensus Building and Complex Adaptive Systems: A Framework for Evaluating Collaborative Planning." *Journal of the American Planning Association* 65, no. 4 (1999): 412-423.

Irving, Justin A. & Mark L. Strauss. *Leadership in Christian Perspective: Biblical Foundations and Contemporary Practices for Servant Leaders.* Grand Rapids: BakerAcademic, 2019.

Jackson, Darrell. "For the Son of Man Did Not Come to Lead, but to Be Led: Matthew 20:20-28 and Royal Service," in *Servantship: Sixteen Servants on the Four Movements of Radical Servantship*, Ed. Graham Hill. Eugene: Wipf & Stock Publishers, 2013.

Jansen, Leo, Hans Luijten, & Nienke Bakker (Eds.). "Report drawn up by Joseph d'Ornano, Chief of Police, in response to the petition from local residents, Arles, 27 February 1889," *Vincent van Gogh – The Letters* (Amsterdam: Van Gogh Museum & Huygens ING., 2009), Accessed January 18, 2021, http://vangoghletters.org/vg/documentation.html

Jansen, Leo, Hans Luijten, & Nienke Bakker (Eds.). "898: To Theo van Gogh and Jo van Gogh-Bonger. Auvers-sur-Oise, on or about Thursday, 10 July 1890." *Vincent van Gogh – The Letters* (Amsterdam: Van Gogh Museum & Huygens ING., 2009), accessed December 7, 2020, http://vangoghletters.org/vg/letters/let898/letter.html.

Jenkins, Philip. *The Next Christendom: The Coming of Global Christians*, 3rd ed. Oxford: Oxford University Press, 2011.

Jipp, Joshua W. *Saved by Faith and Hospitality*. Grand Rapids: William B. Eerdmans Publishing Company, 2017.

Jobes, Karen H. & Moisés Silva. *Invitation to the Septuagint*. Grand Rapids: Baker, 2000.

Johnson, David H. "The Image of God in Colossians." *Didaskalia (Otterburne, Man.)* 3, no. 2 (1992): 9-15.

Johnston, Andrew. *Fired Up: Kindling and Keeping the Spark in Creative Teams*. Nashville: SALT Conferences, 2017.

Joustra, Jessica. "An Embodied *Imago Dei*." *Journal of Reformed Theology* 11 (2017): 9-23.

Keathley III, J. Hampton. "What is the Gospel?" Bible.org (blog), May 18, 2004, https://bible.org/article/what-gospel.

Keener, Craig S. *Spirit Hermeneutics: Reading Scripture in Light of Pentecost*. Grand Rapids: William B. Eerdmans Publishing Company, 2016.

Khan, Pinchas. "The Epilogue to Jonah." *Jewish Bible Quarterly* 28, no. 3 (2000): 146-155.

Kidner, Derek. *Genesis: An Introduction and Commentary*. Downers Grove: IVP Academic, 1967. Kindle.

Kim, David, Dan Fisher, & David McCalman. "Modernism, Christianity, and Business Ethics: A Worldview Perspective." *Journal of Business Ethics* 90 (2009): 115-121.

Koeshall, Anita. "Navigating Power: Liquid Power Structures for Molten Times," in *Devoted to Christ: Missiological Reflections in Honor of Sherwood G. Lingenfelter*, Ed. Christopher L. Flanders. Eugene: Pickwick Publications, 2019.

Kok, Jacobus. "Why (Suffering) Women Matter for the Heart of Transformative Missional Theology Perspectives on Empowered Women and Mission in the New Testament and Early Christianity." *HTS Teologiese Studies/Theological Studies* 72, no. 4 (2016), http://dx.doi.org/10.4102/hts.v72i4.3519.

Kolb, David A. *Experiential Learning: Experience as the Source of Learning and Development*. Englewood Cliffs: Prentice-Hall, 1984.

Kudonoo, Enyonam, Kathy Schroeder, & Sheila Boysen-Rotelli. "An Olympic Transformation: Creating an Organizational Culture that Promotes Healthy Conflict." *Organizational Development Journal* 30, no. 2 (2012): 51-65.

Kuhn, Thomas S. *The Structure of Scientific Revolutions: 50th Anniversary Edition*. Chicago: The University of Chicago Press, 2012.

Kumar, Vijay. *101 Design Methods: A Structured Approach for Driving Innovation in Your Organization*. Hoboken: John Wiley & Sons, Inc., 2013.

Kuyper, Abraham. *Wisdom & Wonder: Common Grace in Science & Art*. Grand Rapids: Christian's Library Press, 2011.

Lally, Phillippa & Benjamin Gardner. "Promoting Habit Formation." *Health Psychology Review* 7, no. 1 (2013): 137-158.

Lane, Patty. *A Beginner's Guide to Crossing Cultures: Making Friends in a Multicultural World*. Downers Grove: InterVarsity Press, 2002.

Leslie, Andrew. "How Stories Argue: The Deep Roots of Storytelling in Political Rhetoric." *Storytelling, Self, Society* 11, no. 1 (2015): 66-84.

Lewis, C. S. *The Lion, the Witch and the Wardrobe*. New York: HarperTrophy, 1950.

Liedtka, Jeanne & Tim Ogilvie, *Designing for Growth: A Design Thinking Tool Kit for Managers*. New York: Columbia Business School Publishing, 2011.

Lingenfelter, Sherwood G. *Leading Cross-Culturally: Covenant Relationships for Effective Christian Leadership*. Grand Rapids: Baker Academic, 2008.

Linnemann, Eta. *Parables of Jesus: Introduction and Exposition*. London: SPCK, 1966.

Livermore, David. *Leading with Cultural Intelligence: The Real Secret to Success* 2nd ed. New York: AMACON, 2015.

Lowney, Chris. *Heroic Leadership: Best Practices from a 450-Year-Old Company that Changed the World*. Chicago: LoyolaPress, 2003.

MacIntyre, Alasdair. *After Virtue: A Study of Moral Theory* 2nd ed. Notre Dame: University of Notre Dame Press, 1984.

MacLeod, David J. "The Eternality and Deity of the Word: John 1:1-2." *Bibliotheca Sacra* 160, no. 637 (January-March 2003): 48-64.

Mahmood, Arshad, Mohd Anuar Arshad, Adeel Ahmed, Sohail Akhtar, & Shahid Khan. "Spiritual Intelligence Research within Human Resource Development: A Thematic Review." *Management Research Review* 41, no. 8 (2018): 987-1006.

Malina, Bruce J. *The New Testament World: Insights from Cultural Anthropology* 3rd ed. Louisville: Westminster John Knox Press, 2001.

Marquardt, Michael J. *Building the Learning Organization: Achieving Strategic Advantage Through a Commitment to Learning*. Boston: Nicholas Brealey Publishing, 2011.

Marsh, Nick, Mike McAllum, & Dominique Purcell. *Strategic Foresight: The Power of Standing in the Future*. Australia: Crown Content, 2002.

Martin, Roger. *The Design of Business: Why Design Thinking is the Next Competitive Advantage*. Boston: Harvard Business Press, 2009.

The Matrix. Written & Directed by The Wachowskis. Burbank: Warner Bros. Pictures, 1999.

McConnell, Douglas. *Cultural Insights for Christian Leaders: New Directions for Organizations Serving God's Mission*. Grand Rapids: Baker Academic, 2018.

McConnell, James R. "Colossians: Background and Contexts." *Review and Expositor* 116, no. 4 (2019): 397-410.

McKnight, Scot. *One.Life: Jesus Calls, We Follow*. Grand Rapids: Zondervan, 2010.

McKnight, Scot. *A Fellowship of Differents: Showing the World God's Design for Life Together*. Grand Rapids: Zondervan, 2014.

McKnight, Scot. *The King Jesus Gospel: The Original Good News Revisited*. Grand Rapids: Zondervan, 2016.

McKnight, Scot. *The Blue Parakeet* 2nd ed. Grand Rapids: Zondervan, 2018.

McKnight, Scot & Laura Barringer. *A Church Called Tov: Forming a Goodness Culture*. Carol Stream: Tyndale Momentum, 2020.

McNeil, Brenda Salter. *Roadmap to Reconciliation: Moving Communities to Unity, Wholeness and Justice*. Downers Grove: InterVarsity Press, 2015.

Medley, Mark S. "Subversive Song: Imagining Colossians 1:15-20 as a Social Protest Hymn in the Context of the Roman Empire." *Review and Expositor* 116, no. 4 (2019): 421-435.

Montello, Martha. "Narrative Ethics: The Role of Stories in Bioethics." *The Hastings Center Report* 44 (2014): S2-S6.

Moore, Mike. "Pentecost and the Plan of God." *The Reformed Theological Review* 72, no. 3 (December 2013): 172-184.

Najarian, Hovak. "The Good Samaritan: Art for Proper 10C," Hear What the Spirit is Saying (blog). St. Hugh's Episcopal Church, Idyllwild, CA. Accessed December 6, 2020, https://smecsundaymorningforum.org/tag/the-good-samaritan

Neely, Brent. "Kevin Vanhoozer's Theodramatic Improvisation and the Jerusalem Council of Acts 15." *Evangelical Review of Theology* 43, no. 1 (2019): 5-16.

New Bible Dictionary 2nd ed., J. D. Douglas, F. F. Bruce, J. I. Packer, N. Hillyer, D. Guthrie, A. R. Millard, & D. J. Wiseman (Eds.). Downers Grove: InterVarsity Press, 1982.

Newbigin, Lesslie. *The Gospel in a Pluralist Society*. Grand Rapids: William B. Eerdmans Publishing Company, 1989.

Newbigin, Lesslie. *The Open Secret: An Introduction to the Theology of Mission* Revised Edition. Grand Rapids: William B. Eerdmans Publishing Company, 1995.

Ng, Kok-Yee, Linn Van Dyne, & Soon Ang. "From Experience to Experiential Learning: Cultural Intelligence as a Learning Capability for Global Leader Development." *Academy of Management Learning & Education* 8, no. 4 (2009): 511-526.

Niebuhr, H. Richard. *Christ & Culture* 50th Anniversary Expanded Edition. New York: HarperOne, 1951, 2001.

Nietzsche, Friedrich. *The Will to Power* trans. Walter Kaufmann & R. J. Hollingdale. New York: Vintage, 1968.

Northouse, Peter G. *Leadership: Theory and Practice*, 7th ed. Thousand Oaks: SAGE Publications, Inc., 2016.

The Northumbria Community. *Celtic Daily Prayer: Prayers and Readings from the Northumbria Community.* New York: HarperCollins, 2002.

O'Day, Gail R. *The Word Disclosed: Preaching the Gospel of John.* St. Louis: Chalice Press, 2002.

Olson, Edwin E. & Glenda H. Eoyang. *Facilitating Organization Change: Lessons from Complexity Science.* San Francisco: Jossey-Bass/Pfeiffer, 2001. Kindle.

Ott, Craig & Gene Wilson. *Global Church Planting: Biblical Principles and Best Practices for Multiplication.* Grand Rapids: Baker Academic, 2011.

Owens, Bradley P. Michael D. Johnson, & Terence R. Mitchell. "Expressed Humility in Organizations: Implications for Performance, Teams, and Leadership." *Organization Science* 24, no. 5 (2013): 1517-1538.

Oxley, Simon. "Certainties Transformed: Jonah and Acts 10:9-35." *The Ecumenical Review* 56, no. 3 (2004): 322-326.

Packer, J. I. *Keep in Step with the Spirit: Finding Fullness in Our Walk with God* 2nd ed. Grand Rapids: Baker Books, 2005.

Padilla, C. René. "What is Integral Mission?" *Del Camino Network for Integral Mission in Latin America* (n. d.). Retrieved from http://www.dmr.org/images/pdf%20dokumenter/C._Ren%C3%A9_Padilla_-_What_is_integral_mission.pdf.

Padilla DeBorst, Ruth. "'Unexpected' Guests at God's Banquet Table: Gospel in Mission and Culture." *Evangelical Review of Theology* 33 (2009): 62-76.

Park, Hyung Dae. "Drawing Ethical Principles from the Process of the Jerusalem Council: A New Approach to Acts 15:4-29." *Tyndale Bulletin* 61, no. 2 (2010): 271-291.

Patte, Daniel. "Bringing Out the Gospel-Treasure What Is New and What is Old: Two Parables in Matthew 18-23." *Quarterly Review* 10, no. 3 (1990): 79-108.

Patterson, Kerry, Joseph Grenny, Ron McMillan, & Al Switzler. *Crucial Conversations: Tools for Talking When Stakes are High.* New York: McGraw-Hill, 2002.

Pew Research Center. "Global Christianity – A Report on the Size and Distribution of the World's Christian Population." *Pew Research Center* (2011, December 19). Retrieved from https://www.pewforum.org/2011/12/19/global-christianity-exec/.

Phan, Peter C. "An Interfaith Encounter at Jacob's Well: A Missiological Interpretation of John 4:4-42." *Mission Studies* 27 (2010): 160-175.

Plantinga, Cornelius. *Not the Way It's Supposed to Be: A Breviary of Sin.* Grand Rapids: William B. Eerdmans Publishing Company, 1996.

Preiser, Rika, Reinette Biggs, Alta De Vos, & Carl Folke. "Social-Ecological Systems as Complex Adaptive Systems: Organizing Principles for Advancing Research Methods and Approaches." *Ecology and Society* 23, no. 4 (2018): 46-60.

Proctor, Mark A. "'Who Is My Neighbor?' Recontextualizing Luke's Good Samaritan (Luke 10:25-37)," *Journal of Biblical Literature* 138, no. 1 (2019): 203-219.

Ramachandra, Vinoth. *The Recovery of Mission: Beyond the Pluralist Paradigm.* Grand Rapids: William B. Eerdmans Publishing Company, 1996.

Rawson, Katie J. "A Gospel That Reconciles: Teaching about Honor-Shame to Advance Racial and Ethnic Reconciliation," in *Honor, Shame, and the Gospel: Reframing Our Message and Ministry*, Eds. Christopher Flanders & Werner Mischke. Littleton: William Carey Publishing, 2020.

Ren, Hong & Barbara Gray. "Repairing Relationship Conflict: How Violation Types and Culture Influence the Effectiveness of Restoration Rituals." *The Academy of Management Review* 34, no. 1 (2009): 105-126.

Richards, Luke. "Deep Community and Beautiful Hospitality (Sermon)." Pocono Lake Wesleyan Church, accessed December 8, 2020, https://poconolakewesleyan.org/uploads/1/5/3/9/15395128/5_deep_community_and_beautiful_ hospitality_2.pdf.

Richardson, Rick. *Evangelism Outside the Box: New Ways to Help People Experience the Good News.* Downers Grove: InterVarsity Press, 2000.

Richardson, Rick. *Reimagining Evangelism: Inviting Friends on a Spiritual Journey.* Downers Grove: InterVarsity Press, 2006.

Roberts, Robert. "Narrative Ethics." *Philosophy Compass* 7, no. 3 (2012): 174-182.

Robertson, C. K. "Proto-Conciliarism in Acts 15." *Sewanee Theological Review* 61, no. 2 (2018): 417-423.

Rohrbaugh, Richard. "A Peasant Reading of the Parable of the Talents/Pounds: A Text of Terror?" *Biblical Theology Bulletin: Journal of Bible and Culture* 23 (1993): 32-39.

Rosenzweig, Franz. *The Star of Redemption* translated by William W. Hallo. New York: Holt, Rinehart, Winston, 1971.

Routledge, Robin. "Did God Create Chaos? Unresolved Tension in Genesis 1:1-2," *Tyndale Bulletin* 61, no. 1 (2010): 69-88.

Rule, Peter N. "The Pedagogy of Jesus in the Parable of the Good Samaritan: A Diacognitive Analysis." *HTS Teologiese Studies/Theological Studies* 73, no. 3 (2017): 1-8.

Ryu, Chesung Justin. "Silence as Resistance: A Postcolonial Reading of the Silence of Jonah in Jonah 4:1-11." *Journal for the Study of the Old Testament* 34, no. 2 (2009): 195-218.

Sadiq, Yousaf. "Jesus' Encounter with a Woman at the Well: A South Asian Perspective." *Missiology: An International Review* 46, no. 4 (2018): 363-373.

Sande, Ken. *The Peacemaker: A Biblical Guide to Resolving Personal Conflict* Revised and Updated. Grand Rapids: BakerBooks, 2004.

Sanders, John. *Theology in the Flesh: How Embodiment and Culture Shape the Way We Think about Truth, Morality, and God.* Minneapolis: Fortress Press, 2017.

Sanneh, Lamin. "The Gospel, Language and Culture: The Theological Method in Cultural Analysis." *International Review of Mission* 84, no. 332/333 (1995): 47-60.

Sanneh, Lamin. *Whose Religion is Christianity? The Gospel Beyond the West.* Grand Rapids: William B. Eerdmans Publishing Co., 2003.

Sanneh, Lamin. *Translating the Message: The Missionary Impact on Culture* Revised and Expanded. Maryknoll: Orbis Books, 2009.

Schein, Edgar H. with Peter Schein, *Organizational Culture and Leadership* 5th ed. Hoboken: John Wiley & Sons, Inc., 2017.

Schiffman, Lawrence H. "The Samaritan Schism." Biblical Archaeological Society, last modified August 11, 2014, https://www.biblicalarchaeology.org/daily/ancient-cultures/daily-life-and-practice/the-samaritan-schism/

Schneider, Anselm, Christopher Wickert, & Emilio Marti. "Reducing Complexity by Creating Complexity: A Systems Theory Perspective on How Organizations Respond to Their Environments." *Journal of Management Studies* 54, no. 2 (March 2017): 182-208.

Schuele, Andreas. "Uniquely Human: The Ethics of the *Imago Dei* in Genesis 1-11." *Toronto Journal of Theology* 27, no 1. (2011): 5-16.

Schweizer, Eduard. *The Good News According to Matthew*. Atlanta: John Knox Press, 1975.

Senge, Peter M. *The Fifth Discipline: The Art & Practice of the Learning Organization*. New York: Currency, 2006.

Senior, Donald. "Matthew 18:21-35." *Interpretation* 41, no. 4 (1987): 403-407.

Shaw, Luci. *Polishing the Petoskey Stone: Selected Poems*. Vancouver: Regent College Publishing, 1990: 147.

Shepherd, Hana. "Culture and Cognition: A Process Account of Culture," *Sociological Forum* 29, no. 4 (2014): 1007-1011.

Shuster, Marguerite. *Power, Pathology, Paradox: They Dynamics of Evil and Good*. Grand Rapids: Zondervan, 1987.

Sigmon, Casey Thornburgh. "Homiletical Possibilities and Challenges in Colossians," *Review and Expositor* 116, no. 4 (2019): 458-465.

Smith, Gordon T. *Institutional Intelligence: How to Build an Effective Organization*. Downers Grove: InterVarsity Press, 2017.

Smith, James K. A. *Desiring the Kingdom: Worship, Worldview and Cultural Formation*. Grand Rapids: Baker Academic, 2009. Kindle.

Smith, James K. A. *You Are What You Love: The Spiritual Power of Habit*. Grand Rapids: Brazos Press, 2016.

Smith, James K. A. *On the Road with Saint Augustine: A Real-World Spirituality for Restless Hearts*. Grand Rapids: BrazosPress, 2019.

Snyder, Nancy Tennant & Deborah L. Duarte. *Unleashing Innovation: How Whirlpool Transformed an Industry*. San Francisco: Jossey-Bass, 2008.

Sonnenschein, William. *The Diversity Toolkit: How You Can Build and Benefit from a Diverse Workforce*. Lincolnwood: Contemporary Books, 1997.

Stählin, Gustav. "φίλος, φίλη, φιλια," in *Theological Dictionary of the New Testament*, Eds. Gerhard Kittel & Gerhard Friedrich. Grand Rapids: William B. Eerdmans Publishing Company, 1977: 9.

Steinmetz, David C. "Matthew 25:14-30." *Interpretation* 34, no. 2 (1980): 172-176.

Steuernagal, Valdir R. "An Exiled Community as a Missionary Community: A Study Based on 1 Peter 2:9, 10." *Evangelical Review of Theology* 40, no. 3 (2016): 196-204.

Strahan, Joshua Marshall. "Jesus Teaches Theological Interpretation of the Law: Reading the Good Samaritan in Its Literary Context." *Journal of Theological Interpretation* 10, no. 1 (2016): 71-86.

Sueldo, Mariana & Dalia Streimikiene. "Organizational Rituals as Tools of Organizational Culture Creation and Transformation: A Communicative Approach," *Transformations In Business & Economics* 15, no. 2 (2016): 89-110.

Sunquist, Scott W. *Understanding Christian Mission: Participation in Suffering and Glory.* Grand Rapids: Baker Academic, 2013.

Swart, Gerhard. "Eschatological Vision or Exhortation to Visible Christian Conduct? Notes on the Interpretation of Colossians 3:4." *Newtestamentica* 33, no. 1 (1999): 169-177.

Tanner, J. Paul. "James's Quotation of Amos 9 to Settle the Jerusalem Council Debate in Acts 15." *Journal of the Evangelical Theological Society* 55, no. 1 (2012): 65-85.

Tanner, J. Paul. "The 'Outer Darkness' in Matthew's Gospel: Shedding Light on an Ominous Warning." *Bibliotheca Sacra* 174 (2017): 445-459.

Tasker, R. V. G., *Matthew.* London: The Tyndale Press, 1961.

Thompson, Marianne Meye. *Colossians & Philemon.* Grand Rapids: William B. Eerdmans Publishing Company, 2005.

Tibbs, Hardin. "Making the Future Visible: Psychology, Scenarios, and Strategy." Paper presented to the Australian Public Service Futures Group, Canberra (1999): 1-7.

Timmer, Daniel C. *A Gracious and Compassionate God: Mission, Salvation and Spirituality in the Book of Jonah.* Downers Grove: IVP Academic, 2011. Kindle.

Trice, Harrison M. & Janice M. Beyer. "Cultural Leadership in Organizations." *Organization Science* 2, no. 2 (1991): 149-169.

Turner, Mary Donovan. "Jonah 3:10-4:11." *Interpretation* 51, no. 4 (1998): 411-414.

Uhl-Bien, Mary, Russ Marion, & Bill McDelvey. "Complexity Leadership Theory: Shifting Leadership from the Industrial Age to the Knowledge Era." *The Leadership Quarterly* 18 (2007): 298-318.

The University of Notre Dame Alumni Association, "The Good Samaritan – Van Gogh," Faith ND, accessed December 7, 2020, http://faith.nd.edu/s/1210/faith/interior.aspx?

sid=1210&gid=609&pgid=44542&cid= 85960&ecid=85960&crid=0&calpgid= 44241&calcid=85766.

Van Den Toren, Benno. "God's Purpose for Creation as the Key to Understanding the Universality and Cultural Variety of Christian Ethics." *Missiology: An International Review* 30, no. 2 (2002): 215-233.

Van Eck, Ernest. "A Samaritan Merchant and His Friend, And Their Friends: Practicing Life-Giving Theology." *HTS Teologiese Studies/Theological Studies* 75, no. 1 (2019): 1-8.

Van Gelder, Craig. *The Essence of the Church: A Community Created by the Spirit.* Grand Rapids: Baker, 2000.

Van Gogh, Vincent. "The Good Samaritan (after Delacroix)." Oil on Canvas Painting, 1890, Kröller-Müller Museum, Otterlo, The Netherlands.

Vanhoozer, Kevin J. "'Rule to Rule Them All?' Theological method in an Era of World Christianity," in Craig Ott and Harold A. Netland Eds., *Globalizing Theology: Belief and Practice in an Era of World Christianity.* Grand Rapids: Baker Academic, 2006.

Volf, Miroslav. *Exclusion & Embrace: A Theological Exploration of Identity, Otherness, and Reconciliation.* Nashville: Abingdon Press, 1996.

Volf, Miroslav & Matthew Croasmun. *For the Life of the World: Theology That Makes a Difference.* Grand Rapids: Brazos Press, 2019.

Von Rad, Gerhard. *Old Testament Theology,* trans. D. M. G. Stalker, vol.1. San Francisco: Harper, 1965.

Wall, Robert. "Israel and the Gentile Mission in Acts and Paul: A Canonical Approach," in *Witness to the Gospel: The Theology of Acts*, Eds. I. Howard Marshall & David Peterson. Grand Rapids: William B. Eerdmans Publishing Company, 1998: 437-458.

Walls, Andrew F. "Culture and Coherence in Christian History." *Evangelical Review of Theology* 9, no. 3 (1985): 214-255.

Walls, Andrew F. *The Missionary Movement in Christian History: Studies in the Transmission of Faith.* Maryknoll: Orbis Books, 1996.

Walsh, Brian J. & Sylvia C. Keesmaat. *Colossians Remixed: Subverting the Empire.* Downers Grove: IVP Academic, 2004.

Walton, John H. "The Object Lesson of Jonah 4:5-7 and the Purpose of the Book of Jonah." *Bulletin for Biblical Research* 2 (1992): 47-57.

Walvoord, John F. "Christ's Olivet Discourse on the End of the Age." *Bibliotheca Sacra* 129, no. 515 (1972): 206-210.

Ward, Pete. *Liquid Church.* Peabody: Hendrickson, 2002.

Warren, Liz & Stephanie Luz Cordel, "Storytelling as a Catalyst for Systems Change," Vitalyst Health Foundation, August 2018. https://vitalysthealth.org/wp-content/uploads/2018/08/Storytelling-Brief.pdf.

Weaver, Alan. "Activating Kingdom Agents: Toward a Model of Awakening and Releasing God's People For Ministry and Leadership." In *Devoted to Christ: Missiological Reflections in Honor of Sherwood G. Lingenfelter*, Ed. Christopher L. Flanders. Eugene: Pickwick Publications, 2019.

Webster, John B. *Confessing God: Essays in Christian Dogmatics II.* London: T. & T. Clark, 2005.

Wells, Sam & Josie McLean. "*One Way Forward* to Beat the Newtonian Habit with a Complexity Perspective on Organisational Change." *Systems* 1 (2013): 66-84.

Whatley, Lachlan R., Adrian B. Popa, & Heidrum Kliewer. "Community and Leadership: The Role of Humility, Rhythm, and Experiential Learning." *Journal of Leadership, Accountability and Ethics* 9, no. 4 (2012): 113-143.

Wheeler, Nathan. "For a Holy Priesthood:" A Petrine Model for Evangelical Cultural Engagement." *Journal of Evangelical Theological Society* 59, no. 3 (2016): 523-539.

Whyte, David. "Forgiveness." *Consolations: The Solace, Nourishment and Underlying Meaning of Everyday Words.* Langley: Many Rivers Press, 2015: 67-69.

Willard, Dallas. *The Divine Conspiracy: Rediscovering Our Hidden Life in God.* London: William Collins, 1998.

Witherington III, Ben. *Work: A Kingdom Perspective of Labor.* Grand Rapids: William B. Eerdmans Publishing Company, 2011.

Wolff, Hans Walter. *Obadiah and Jonah: A Commentary*, trans. By Margaret Kohl. Minneapolis: Augsburg, 1986.

Wright, Jr., Arthur M. "Disarming the Rulers and Authorities: Reading Colossians in its Roman Imperial Context." *Review and Expositor* 116, no. 4 (2019): 446-457.

Wright, N. T. *What Saint Paul Really Said: Was Paul of Tarsus the Real Founder of Christianity?* Grand Rapids: Eerdmans, 1997.

Wright, N. T. *Paul for Everyone: The Prison Letters*. Louisville: Westminster John Knox Press, 2004.

Wright, N. T. *Simply Christian: Why Christianity Makes Sense*. New York: HarperCollins, 2006.

Wright, N. T. *After You Believe: Why Christian Character Matters*. New York: HarperCollins Publishers, 2010.

Wright, N. T. & Michael F. Bird. *The New Testament in its World: An Introduction to the History, Literature, and Theology of the First Christians*. Grand Rapids: Zondervan Academic, 2019.

ABOUT
KHARIS PUBLISHING

KHARIS PUBLISHING is an independent, traditional publishing house with a core mission to publish impactful books, and channel proceeds into establishing mini-libraries or resource centers for orphanages in developing countries, so these kids will learn to read, dream, and grow. Every time you purchase a book from Kharis Publishing or partner as an author, you are helping give these kids an amazing opportunity to read, dream, and grow. Kharis Publishing is an imprint of Kharis Media LLC. Learn more at https://www.kharispublishing.com.

CPSIA information can be obtained
at www.ICGtesting.com
Printed in the USA
LVHW050834231121
704194LV00004B/10

9 781637 460825